MW01096903

Transforming & Understanding

.

Exploration
Vygotskij: oeuvres et études

La pluralité des disciplines et des perspectives en sciences de l'éducation définit la vocation de la collection Exploration, celle de carrefour des multiples dimensions de la recherche et de l'action éducative. Sans exclure l'essai, Exploration privilégie les travaux investissant des terrains nouveaux ou développant des méthodologies et des problématiques prometteuses.

Collection de la Société Suisse pour la Recherche en Education, publiée sous la direction de Rita Hofstetter, Gaëlle Molinari, Zoé Moody et Bernard Schneuwly.

Secrétariat scientifique: Viviane Rouiller.

Yannick Lémonie

Transforming & Understanding

An Introduction to Cultural-Historical Activity Theory

PETER LANG

Bruxelles - Berlin - Chennai - Lausanne - New York - Oxford

Library of Congress Cataloging-in-Publication Data
A CIP catalog record for this book has been applied for at the
Library of Congress.

Bibliographic information published by the Deutsche Nationalbibliothek. The
German National Library lists this publication in the German National Bibliography;
detailed bibliographic data is available on the Internet at http://dnb.d-nb.de.

This book was funded by the ANR as part of the ANR PRCI
ITAPAR project (ANR 19-CE-26-0021).

ISSN 0721-3700
ISBN 978-3-0343-5147-8
ISBN 978-3-0343-5148-5 eBook
ISBN 978-3-0343-5149-2 ePUB
D/2024/5678/54
DOI 10.3726/b22324
D/2024/5678/56

Peter Lang Éditions Scientifiques Internationales –

P.I.E., Bruxelles, Belgique

info@peterlang.com - www.peterlang.com

To my sons, Lucas and Tom.

To the troika, who I hope will recognize themselves in it.

To the actors of human emancipation.

Table of Contents

Part 2 Four Central Concepts for Analyzing Activity

Part 3 The Interventionist Dimension of Chat: Formative Intervention and Change Laboratory

Postface
The where-to of 4th generation culturalhistorical activity theory

Foreword
The Future of Activity Theory Is Happening

– By Yrjö Engeström –

Fifteen years ago I published a paper titled '*The future of activity theory: A rough draft*' (Engeström, 2009b). I examined several emerging issues as indicators or signposts of the future development of cultural-historical activity theory. These included the growing importance of '*runaway objects*'; the need for a fourth generation of activity theory; the significance of new forms of mediation and digital media; the necessity to understand key mechanisms of development of activities; the challenge of grasping authority and agency in activity theory; and the centrality of formative interventions in activity-theoretical research.

What I did not foresee in that paper was the globally distributed emergence of flesh-and-blood people, individuals and collectives, who take initiatives, make long-term commitments and produce durable contributions to actually push and pull activity theory forward, both in academic research and in practical efforts to transform activity systems in various fields. Such living movement of human actors has emerged in the past few years, distributed in various parts of the world. The book of Yannick Lémonie is a powerful testimony of that. The future of activity theory is happening as a result of the actions of people like Yannick.

This book is special in several ways. It is a full-scale introduction to cultural-historical activity theory—a rare accomplishment in itself. But it is not just a book *about* a theory. It is a book that interprets and develops further the theory for the purposes of intervention and transformation. The book presents activity theory as '*an instrument for empowering operators and enabling them to take back control of their own work, an instrument for transforming and developing collective agency, and an instrument for cultural production*' (p. 45). This is exactly the spirit of the living movement that today carries forward the application and development of activity theory.

The issues I proposed as markers of the future in 2009 are integral components of the present book. The future is happening in this text, not anymore as a projection but as a working conceptual and methodological instrumentality. Lémonie's discussion of *'runaway objects'* is a good example. He starts by defining the concept of runaway object, using the COVID-19 pandemic as an illuminating example. He points out that runaway objects are not simply negative or threatening; they have great transformative potential, *'articulating levels of analysis ranging from the local to the global'* (p. 167).

The author then expands the concept by invoking Eric Olin Wright's idea of real utopias and Annalisa Sannino's concept of enacted utopias. The latter is presented by examining Sannino's formative Change Laboratory interventions in support of the eradication of homelessness in Finland—a research program emblematic to the fourth generation of cultural-historical activity theory. Thus, in this segment of the book, the concepts of runaway object, fourth generation activity theory, and formative interventions are organically interconnected. They have become integrated into an instrumentality that is put to work on a daily basis.

This book also opens up and elaborates on themes that are only now becoming focal for activity theorists around the world. Here I want to highlight but two such themes. The first one is power and politics. Some critics argue that activity theory has been too narrowly focused on local transformations, thus neglecting broader political forces and power relations. Lémonie points out that these criticisms were formulated *'prior to the emergence of what Engeström describes as the fourth generation of CHAT. However, in order to transcend the limitations of localism within a single interacting activity system, it is necessary to implement interventions that can effectively address the societal scale. This is the objective of the fourth generation of CHAT'* (p. 238).

Steps toward incorporating politics into the conceptual framework of CHAT are indeed being taken, primarily by examining and redefining the concept of power. Examples of this work come from different domains, from classroom studies (Choudry, 2023) to studies on the eradication of homelessness (Sannino, 2023b) and research on information systems (Simeonova, Kelly, Karanasios, & Galliers, 2024). Common to these studies is that power is seen as *'present-in-actions'* rather than as static structures. This leads to the realization that *'power can be put in motion [...] as demonstrated by the influence of agentive use of specific instruments offered by the professionals to their colleagues, as well as by the Change Laboratory researchers to the participants of the interventions'* (Sannino, 2023b, p. 51).

The second theme is that of dialectics. Dialectics is the epistemological and methodological foundation of activity theory. However, especially in empirical and interventionist research, it is often difficult to make explicit how dialectics is actually informing and guiding the research – there is a gap between concrete studies and their underlying philosophy. Lémonie tackles and bridges this gap, especially in Chapter 7, devoted to the concept of contradiction, and in Chapter 10, focused on Change Laboratories and the processes of ascending from the abstract to the concrete in these interventions. The dialectical concept of contradiction is powerfully explained by means of three empirical examples, namely studies of food production in the United States, on preventing accidents at work and occupational illnesses in France, and on the development of different models of co-working.

In Chapter 10, Lémonie addresses the difficult issue of specifying steps in the dialectical method. *'While the method of ascending from the abstract to the concrete is not reduced to a set of rules and procedures, it makes progress through stages that can be described. It can thus be seen as a 'dance with time', as Ollman (2008) puts it, with four stages that proceed from the present to the past to the future, and then back to the present. The typical ideal cycle of expansive learning and the seven expansive learning actions represent this dance over time'* (p. 316). The author again examines powerful empirical examples, showing that the dialectical method is actually something extremely practical and consequential in formative intervention research.

The appearance of a book like this makes it clear that the future of cultural-historical activity theory is happening here and now.

Chapter 1

Introduction
Unity and Diversity of Cultural-Historical Activity Theory

I regard Activity Theory, in this sense, as a family of practices sharing grandparents but which over the years, like any family, has diverged in interests and characteristics (Blunden, 2023, p. ix).

Separated from practice, theory is imperious verbalization; unbound from theory, practice is blind activism (Freire, 1975, p. 11).

Some thirty years ago, Engeström suggested that Cultural-Historical Activity Theory (CHAT) was a *'best-kept secret in academia'* (Engeström, 1993, p. 64). Since this statement was made, there has been a growing interest in the theory, which has led to the diversification of fields of study and interventions, as well as an exponential increase in references to the original work of Vygotsky and Leontiev, or to the more recent work of what can be called the Scandinavian school of CHAT (Daniellou & Rabardel, 2005), referring to the work of Engeström and his colleagues.

Today, some thirty years later, the secret seems, to say the least, out in the open, internationally widespread, despite the difficulty of circumscribing, appropriating, and mobilizing CHAT in dialectical thinking (Langemeyer & Roth, 2006).

[…] When a Western researcher begins to realize the impressive dimensions of the theorizing behind the activity approach, he or she may well ask: Is it worth the trouble? Can it be used to produce anything interesting? How do you do concrete research based on activity theory? (Engeström, 1993, pp. 64–65).

We believe deeply, as Paolo Freire suggests in the quotation that opens this chapter, in the profound connections between theory and practice. In this sense, Activity Theory[1] is not speculative. Nor is it blind activism.

---

[1] The acronym CHAT is often used synonymously with Activity Theory in the literature.

It is a profoundly *'practical'* theory, oriented towards the transformation of human productive activity. It is activist and transformative, placing the question of intervention at the heart of its methodology (Sannino & Sutter, 2011). But it's a challenging theory. That's what this book is about. Its aim is to present CHAT, its origins, its past and emerging developments, and its interventionist orientation.

What Is Cultural-Historical Activity Theory?

CHAT is a *'theory'* in the sense that it provides a coherent set of concepts, principles, and ideas for the study of human activity (Allen, Karanasios, & Slavova, 2011; Engeström, 1993, 2000a): *'It provides tools for understanding activity, empirically studying its individual and collective components, and supporting its development'* (Eyme, 2017, p. 497). If we follow these initial definitions, then CHAT would be better placed in the category of theories of analysis, description or explanation (as a theory for describing or understanding how and why things happened) rather than in that of *'predictive theories'* (see Gregor, 2006).

However, it would be a profound mistake to categorize CHAT too quickly as an analytical or descriptive theory. CHAT is first and foremost a theory aimed at transforming human practices, mobilizing a dialectical framework of thought based on the values of social justice and emancipation (Stetsenko, 2015). It is a predictive theory in that it mobilizes dialectical thinking to project and implement a desirable future. It is also a descriptive theory in that it provides a framework for explaining human activity and its development. As Blunden (2023, p. ix) notes, *'Activity theory is a powerful theory for the transformation of human life toward social justice and emancipation'*.

CHAT is thus part of a model of science that is neither neutral nor purely contemplative (Vianna & Stetsenko, 2014), but rather focused on the realization of a future (Engeström, Rantavuori, Ruutu, & Tapola-Haapala, 2023b), the overcoming of the status quo (Stetsenko, 2022), and the realization of real utopias (Sannino, 2020). CHAT transcends the traditional dichotomy between research and practice by refuting positivist and empiricist approaches.

However, CHAT's commitment to this transformative and emancipatory orientation is neither fully shared nor fully understood, judging by current scholarly publications. Most of these publications focus on qualitative analysis to understand and explain current practices (e.g. Nussbaumer, 2012; Yamagata-Lynch, 2010), without adopting and mobilizing interventionist methodologies capable of supporting desirable transformations in human activities. In this orientation, the question of the possible future of human activity remains in abeyance, diluting both the practical dimension and the dialectical anchoring of CHAT, which allows us to analyze the past, present and potentially future movement of phenomena (Langemeyer & Roth, 2006).

Nevertheless, the relevance of CHAT's main concepts seems to make it increasingly attractive to a generation of researchers who wish to ground their work in the reality of social practices, freeing themselves from disciplinary boundaries. In the field of educational research, Roth, Lee, and Hsu (2009) note an exponential increase in references to three major CHAT authors (Vygotsky, Leontiev, and Engeström, respectively) between 1987 and 2010. We did the same work with Vygotsky and Engeström respectively, over a 25-year period from 1995 to 2019. The result is the same: the increase in the number of citations continues after 2010. Figure 1 shows the significant increase in these citations over 25 years, based on data obtained via *Google Scholar*.

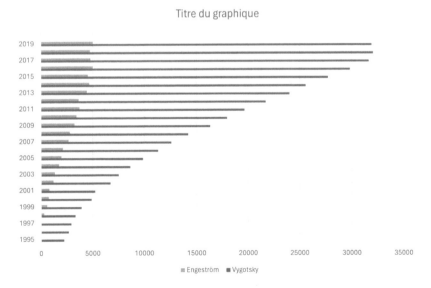

Figure 1: Increase in number of citations of two major activity theorists: Vygotsky and Engeström.

Although CHAT developed in the field of psychology from the initial work of Soviet psychologists, especially Vygotsky, its postulates on the sociocultural determination of the mind, as well as its roots in the ideas developed by Marx, make it a transdisciplinary theory of human life. CHAT is characterized by the great diversity of its fields of study and intervention. These include:

- Human-computer interaction (HCI) and the design of new technologies (e.g. Bertelsen & Bødker, 2003; Bødker, 1991; Bødker, Ehn, Sjögren, & Sundblad, 2000; Bødker & Klokmose, 2011; Clemmensen, Kaptelinin, & Nardi, 2016; Kaptelinin, 2003; Kaptelinin & Nardi, 2006, 2018).
- Work organization (e.g. Blackler, 2011; Blackler, Crump, & McDonald, 2000; Blackler & McDonald, 2000).
- Prevention of occupational risks and diseases (e.g. Boudra, Lémonie, Grosstephan, & Nascimento, 2023; Ferreira et al., 2023; Vilela et al., 2018; Vilela, Querol, Hurtado, & Lopes, 2020; Vilela, Querol, Lopes, & Virkkunen, 2014).
- Education and pedagogy (e.g. Hardman, 2008; Lémonie, Grosstephan, & Tomás, 2021; Stetsenko, 2017, 2019; Yamazumi, 2007, 2008, 2021).
- Adult education (e.g. Engeström & Keruoso, 2007; Frambach, Driessen, & vander Vleuten, 2014; Larsen, Nimmon, & Varpio, 2019; Lémonie, 2020; O'Keefe et al., 2014).
- Management and human resources (Ho, Victor Chen, & Ng, 2016; Lorino, 2017; Tkachenko & Ardichvili, 2017).
- Agriculture (e.g. Junior, Lesama, & Querol, 2023; Mukute, 2015; Mukute & Lotz-Sisitka, 2012; Mukute, Mudokwani, McAllister, & Nyikahadzoi, 2018; Świergiel, Pereira Querol, Rämert, Tasin, & Vänninen, 2018; van der Riet, 2017; Vänninen, Querol, & Engeström, 2015, 2021)
- Therapy (e.g. Holzman, 2006; Vasilyuk, 1991).

This list is by no means exhaustive. This brief overview reinforces the idea that CHAT provides a transdisciplinary framework conducive to interdisciplinary research and intervention projects. This is what Durand and Barbier (2003) emphasize when they share an observation in which they see as the concept of activity as a possible integrator for the social sciences:

Today, it seems that there's a general pressure to format the objects of the social sciences in terms of activity or in relation to activity. We are convinced that, even if this pressure runs up against the compartmentalized organization of scientific and social fields, activity constitutes a privileged entry point for the progressive construction of transversal tools of thought in several corresponding fields of research and practice (Durand & Barbier, 2003, p. 100).

Its transdisciplinary nature and the values embodied in its central concepts make CHAT a theory capable of responding to the issues identified by researchers in the field of labor studies. For example, in a recent book, Guérin et al. (2021) set out some of the challenges facing workplace interventions: to enable '*emancipation through work*', '*well beyond emancipation in work*', which implies, among other things, '*changing scale*'. For these authors, this change of scale implies, '*bringing together several disciplines: economics, management, anthropology, history, geography, political science, urban planning, engineering, public health, psychology, law, etc.*'. (Guérin et al., 2021, p. 375). These challenges are already being addressed by work rooted in CHAT, which emphasizes the emancipatory dimension of transformative agency and expansive learning processes. Meeting these challenges means revising the concept of activity and restoring its emancipatory nature: activity is not a process '*determined*' by socio-technical contexts. Rather, activity is the process by which people shape, construct, and develop these contexts.

The primary abstraction, the central concept of CHAT, conceived here as a transdisciplinary and emancipatory theory, is, of course, the concept of activity. Not behavior, not practice, not action. Vygotsky (1997c) gives an example of how a primary abstraction determines the content of a science, based on the difference in the observation of a solar eclipse between an astronomer and an ordinary onlooker. It is the concepts mobilized by the astronomer that transforms a natural phenomenon into an object of scientific knowledge. The astronomer will see something different in the eclipse than the simple onlooker, insofar as he mobilizes a conceptual ensemble in a project aimed at building new knowledge in astronomy.

In the context of CHAT, it is essentially the way in which the activity is conceptualized that makes it possible to transform a phenomenon – what subjects do – into a scientific fact and a methodology of an emancipatory nature. Here, it is undoubtedly necessary to break with the commonsense acceptance of the concept of activity (Chaiklin, 2019):

Another challenge in practical scientific work with the activity concept is the legitimate similarities and important differences in the everyday and scientific meanings of activity. It is important to recognize that it is possible to make a statement like '*a person develops through their activity*', [...] which can be read meaningfully with both scientific and everyday meanings of the term activity. Everyday meanings of activity focus on observable appearances, referring to '*states*' (e.g. being in motion), '*qualities*' (e.g. doing something), and '*things*' (e.g. a particular task; cf. Oxford English Dictionary). The scientific meaning focuses on the essential relations that underlie or motivate activity (in an everyday sense). In everyday speech, one can do an activity to make transformations where one's activity is the transforming action. It is not immediately apparent that the scientific meaning of activity in this case is referring to specific structural relations within the everyday meanings. At the same time, it is valid to say that activity, in its everyday meaning, is relevant to activity in the systematic meaning (even if it is not sufficient and is missing the most critical aspects); therefore it is all too easy for scientific speakers to sometimes shift into using an everyday meaning or for listeners to interpret a scientific meaning in an everyday way (Chaiklin, 2019, p. 11).

Chaiklin's distinction between appearances and underlying relationships is an important one. It lies at the heart of dialectical thinking, and we'll return to it regularly throughout the book.

The Difficulties Behind CHAT Appropriation

However, this increase in references to activity theorists, as well as the extension of CHAT to a variety of disciplines and fields of study, is not without its difficulties for those who wish to appropriate CHAT, as it tends to transform its initial conceptual content. In this sense, CHAT is a theory that 'travels' and is transformed as it travels. Thus, in a recent book chapter, Dafermos (2020) points out that the exponential growth of references to CHAT raises several epistemological, theoretical, and methodological questions. He sees the reception of CHAT in different research and intervention cultures as a challenge that is likely to transform the original project from which the theory emerged:

Scholars and practitioners tend to accept these sides, dimensions or ideas of the initial theory that make sense in their own intellectual and cultural milieu, from the perspective of the problems that arise within their social and intellectual space. At the same time, scholars and practitioners tend to ignore other sides, dimensions or ideas of the initial theory that have no direct connection or link with their context (Dafermos, 2020, p. 15).

The Journey of Cultural-Historical Activity Theory

Theories and their key concepts travel, cross borders, are mobilized in other research cultures, and inevitably transform themselves (Stengers, 1987). In this book, therefore, we do not intend to criticize other possible uses of the central concepts of activity theory (activity, development, contradiction, object, instruments, mediation, etc.), but to emphasize the need to understand the scientific and practical project from which these concepts derive their meanings and, from a usage point of view, of to use them.

But the difficulty of understanding the scientific project in which the CHAT concepts are embedded lies precisely in the geographical journey and the progressive internationalization of activity theory. For (Dafermos, 2018):

> One of the difficulties in understanding cultural-historical theory lies in the difference between the context of its emergence in the first decades of the 20th century in the USSR, and the multiple contexts of its reception and implementation in various parts of the world (Dafermos, 2018, p. 14).

Separating theories and their concepts from the environment in which they emerge inevitably leads to a dead end in understanding the broader project in which they emerge, and by the same token to a superficial understanding of the theory and the concepts themselves. The dominant trend in the history of scientific ideas, i.e. an understanding of the development of these ideas in terms of essentially endogenous factors, leads to an underestimation of the study of the social environment that affects scientific production. Thus, it is hardly possible to understand the work of Vygotsky or Leontiev without situating it in the social, cultural, and political context of the Soviet Union in the first half of the 20th century.

The same applies to other authors. We've also come to read Paulo Freire's work in a very different light, having become thoroughly familiar with the Brazilian political context of the 1960s and 1970s. But instead of looking at context as a set of factors, we need to consider that the essential authors of CHAT are actors engaged in these very particular social, cultural, and political contexts. Whether it's Freire or Vygotsky (whose similarities are remarkable even though their works do not overlap), or Leontiev, Engeström, or Sannino, to name a few. Stetsenko and

Arievitch (2014) think no differently when they critically point out that most historical accounts treat context as a set of factors external to the production of knowledge:

> That is, although this approach pays attention to sociocultural contexts in the production of knowledge, it does not (paralleling the discipline of psychology) raise above simply describing various aspects of these contexts, in often fortuitous combinations, and continues to view them as factors external to knowledge itself. Culture, history, politics, and other contexts remain to be thought of as external factors that somehow influence the process of knowledge construction but do not belong into it (Stetsenko & Arievitch, 2014, p. 64).

Thus, to understand a theory, it is necessary to consider not only the context of its emergence, but also the commitment of the theorists to transform the social practices of their time. As Kaptelinin and Nardi (2006) note, introducing CHAT without considering its historical context and development is not always very effective: '*The ideas underlying activity theory are difficult to grasp without understanding where these ideas came from*' (p. 30). Can we really understand Vygotsky or Leontiev without considering their commitment to the emergence of a post-revolutionary society? (Stetsenko & Arievitch, 2014) Can we really understand Engeström's work without resituating its birth in the student movements of the late '60s? (Sannino, Daniels, & Gutierrez, 2009a).

With a history spanning more than a century, CHAT inevitably evolves, changes, and develops. As a result, it is generally presented in the form of several generations of work (Engeström, 2001; Engeström & Sannino, 2020; Lompscher, 2006; Spinuzzi, 2020b) since its origins in Vygotsky's work of the 1920s and 1930s. As CHAT's scientific and interventionist project evolves, the concepts-the building blocks of this theory change in content and meaning. In short, CHAT is more than a static, finite, ready-to-use theory; it's an open scientific project for social transformation that is historically evolving. CHAT opens to new possibilities as social issues evolve and as it spreads internationally. For Engeström (1993), activity theory is a double-edged concept:

> On the one hand, it is necessary to emphasize the unique and self-consciously independent nature of the Soviet cultural-historical research tradition, which today is commonly called activity theory (see Leont'ev, 1978; Leontyev, 1981; Wertsch, 1981). On the other hand, this tradition is not a fixed and finished body of strictly defined statements—it is itself an internationally evolving, multivoiced activity system (Engeström, 1993, p. 64).

Several authors have called for a fourth generation of activity theory as further evidence of its vitality (Engeström, 2009b; Engeström & Sannino, 2020; Lompscher, 2006; Rückiem, 2009). The first three generations refer to the work of Vygotsky, Leontiev, and Engeström. In a way, appropriating the CHAT means understanding its history, its permanence, and its mutations in the light of transformative projects capable of meeting the challenges of each era.

Beyond the geographical journey, the journey of a theory and its concepts across disciplines is not without its problems (Stengers, 1987). For example, psychologists and social workers tend to mobilize the double stimulation method, educators, the Zone of Proximal Development (ZPD), and so on. This tendency leads to a fragmented reception of the work of Vygotsky and his followers, which is not without its problems. Indeed, fragments of a theory (i.e. concepts) can only be interpreted in relation to the whole or its totality. For example, the central concept of activity, to which we will return later, can only be understood in the context of a broader practical theoretical project from which it derives its meaning. Thus, to understand the genesis of CHAT, its function, and the questions it seeks to answer, we need a presentation that is more firmly rooted in the context of its emergence.

One or More Theories of Activity?

Having reached this stage of the presentation, it is necessary to consider whether, through this triple journey and the significant developments in CHAT, we are not dealing with three quite distinct theories of activity. Therefore, it would be more appropriate to speak of activity theories (in the plural) rather than activity theory (in the singular). The description provided by Spinuzzi (2018a) of CHAT's evolution suggests that, as objects and disciplinary orientations are contingent upon a specific context, we may have distinct theories rather than variations of a single theory.

> Just as Vygotsky's focus on the New Man was grounded in post-Revolution expectations, 3GAT's focus on mediators and its de-emphasis on individual human capabilities was grounded in contemporary Western perspectives. For Vygotsky's USSR of 1930, the nation was united in a march toward a shared, transcendent future; the transformation of individuals happened mainly in schools and rehabilitation settings, where the individuals had little said over their transformation. What was required was a psychology

[...] In contrast, for Engeström's Finland and Bødker's Denmark of 1987, no entity–neither State nor employer–had the authority to unilaterally direct individuals; their role was to empower those citizens to reach mutual goals in defined organizations. The individuals could change if they wanted to; but the researchers could work with individuals to codesign mediators. What was required was a sociology of organizations (Spinuzzi, 2018a, p. 153).

Despite their diversity, we feel that all these works retain a certain unity, a kind of 'germ cell'. In this context, it is essential to preserve, beyond the presentation of differences, what makes up the 'essence' of CHAT, i.e. a form of permanence in the succession of different generations of activity theory.

One of the central pillars of CHAT is the idea that human development is based on the active transformation of existing environments and the creation of new ones through collaborative processes of tool production and deployment. These collaborative processes represent a form of exchange with the world that is unique to humans–the social practice of human work, or human activity. In these exchanges with the world, humans are not just constantly transforming and creating their environment; they are constantly creating and transforming their very lives, thus fundamentally transforming themselves. Consequently, human activity is the basic form of human life. This practical, social, and voluntary activity (or human work), as the principal and primary form of human life, and the constraints associated with its development, are the very basis and foundation of all that is human in human beings.

Of course, this germ cell of CHAT has led to the development of an analytical framework that is not without controversy. Today, it is customary to emphasize the differences between Vygotsky's socio-historical framework and Leontiev's activity theory. It is also customary to make a distinction between a philosophical approach and an 'organizational' approach (Bakhurst, 2009). But despite the differences, despite the multiple orientations, we believe that activity theory retains a certain unity. The concept of activity has a generative character that allows for diversity and multiplicity of perspectives. Levant (2018) puts it this way:

I see activity theory as a broad tent, a theoretical tradition in the making. There are common origins and very different directions and developments from the perspective of which the origins appear to diverge as well (Levant, 2018, p. 107).

As Cole and Engeström (2007) point out, the term CHAT was coined precisely to overcome the difference between Leontiev's and Vygotsky's approaches. In this sense, for proponents of the CHAT approach, there is more continuity than rupture between the work of Vygotsky, Leontiev, and Engeström. In this book we will return to these elements of continuity: inclusion in transformative practices and methodologies, mobilization of dialectics, overcoming traditional dichotomies (subject-object; local-global; individual-society, etc.), orientation towards human emancipation and the future, etc.

The Antecedent of Cultural-Historical Activity Theory: The Theses on Feuerbach

When the concept of activity travels, it is integrated or assimilated into a pre-existing research culture. Cut off from its philosophical roots and the context of its emergence, the concept of activity becomes particularly difficult for researchers to pin down, since:

> The cross-disciplinary dimensions and philosophical foundations of this concept make it relatively difficult for western researchers often more comfortable with ideas can be used without much philosophical scrutiny and safely confined within a particular discipline (Lektorski, 1990, pp. ix–x).

The roots of the concept of activity can be found in classical German philosophy and in the writings of Marx, especially in his Theses on Feuerbach. This short text written by Marx in 1845 can be considered as the founding act of CHAT. Theses on Feuerbach *'is surely the founding document of Activity Theory, even though it remained unknown until after the author's death'* (Blunden, 2010, p. 94). These theses consist of eleven short philosophical notes. Let's begin with the first of these theses, which is as critical of Feuerbach's materialism as it is of idealism:

> [Thesis 1] The main defect in the materialism of all previous philosophers—including Feuerbach's—is that the object, reality, the sensible world, is grasped only as an object or intuition, but not as concrete human activity, as practice, in a non-subjective way. This explains why the active aspect was developed by idealism in opposition to materialism—but only abstractly, since idealism naturally does not know real, concrete activity as such. Feuerbach wants concrete objects, truly distinct from the objects of thought, but he does not consider human activity itself as objective activity.

This first thesis was written against the background of the importance of the natural sciences for social progress in the twentieth century. In their materialist reductionist orientation, the natural sciences study an object that is thought to be independent of the observer, according to its own laws. Idealism, on the other hand, rejects the idea of a world independent of human thought and activity and emphasizes experience and thought as the production of the subject's activity. But for Marx, what idealism ignores is concrete, real, objective activity, in the sense that in human activity subjects are both engaged and constrained by a world that exists independently of them. This opposition between idealism and materialism gives rise to the idea that the world can only be known through practice or activity, not through a contemplative stance. Activity, in this context, manifests the property of the object existing independently of a subject and is the objective, practical form of thought.

The idea of a *'contemplative'* approach is a form of illusion insofar as *'the sensible world [...] is a concrete practical activity of man'* [Thesis 5].

The question of whether human thought should be recognized as having objective truth is not a theoretical question, but a practical one. It is in practice that man must prove the truth, i.e. the reality and power of his thought, in this world and for our time. The discussion of the reality or unreality of a thought isolated from practice is purely scholastic.

In this sense, activity, or concrete practice, is the criterion of truth. But activity is not that of a subject independent of society. In his theses, Marx criticizes Feuerbach for failing to recognize that the abstract individual he analyzes belongs to a specific social form: *'The essence of man is not an abstraction inherent in the isolated individual. In its reality it is the totality of social relations'* [Thesis 6].

The concept of activity thus constitutes a *'theoretical bridge'* between the individual and society, between the constructive potential of the human subject and the social constraints and cultural means accumulated over the course of history that mediate everything the subject does. Thus, unlike biologically determined behavior in the animal world, activity in human society is partly determined by sociocultural structures developed over the course of history. It is the presence of these structures that allows us to speak of a transition from behavior aimed at maintaining biological existence within the limits of the *'genetically conditioned ecological niche'* to activity whose content consists in changing and transforming this world by developing the available forms of culture. As a logical conclusion to these theses, Marx states:

> [Thesis 2] Philosophers have only interpreted the world in different ways; what matters is to transform it.

In his most recent book, Theureau (2019), who seeks to treat political economy in terms of human activity, linking it to his program of cognitive anthropology of the '*course of action*', does not have the same reading as we do. His interpretation of these theses is cleverly replaced by '*theses on Marx*'. In particular, he formulates the idea that these theses '*introduce the notion of practice and subordinate epistemology to it*' (p. 53), while a little further on in a footnote he adds that the various interpretations of these theses on Feuerbach '*repeatedly show the ambiguity of the concept of practice and the impossibility of basing any kind of clear epistemology on it*' (p. 55).

For Marx and Engels (2012), it is precisely the productive activity (*Tätigkeit*) that distinguishes human beings from animals and is the source of their material life:

> Human beings can be distinguished from animals by conscience, by religion, by anything you like. They begin to distinguish themselves from animals as soon as they begin to produce their means of life, a step forward conditioned by their bodily organization. By producing their means of subsistence, human beings indirectly produce their own material life (Marx & Engels, 2012, p. 15).

If Feuerbach's theses are important for activity theory, it's because they subsequently orient the work of activity theorists by bringing the concept of activity ('*Tätigkeit*' and not practice)[2] into epistemology. This is undoubtedly a starting point for CHAT, as Leontiev suggests:

> By introducing the concept of activity into the theory of knowledge, Marx gave it a strictly materialist meaning. For Marx, activity in its initial and fundamental form is the sensible practical activity by which man comes into practical contact with the objects of the surrounding world, experiences their resistance and acts upon them in accordance with their objective properties. Herein lies the radical difference between Marxist theory of activity and idealist theory, which conceives of activity only in its abstract, speculative form. Marx's profound change in the theory of knowledge consists

---

[2] For a discussion see Sève (2014).

in seeing human activity as the basis of human knowledge, as the process in which cognitive tasks arise, in which perception and thought are born and develop, and which at the same time carries within itself the criterion of adequacy, the truth of knowledge: '*It is in practice,*' says Marx, '*that man must prove the truth, that is, the reality of the power of his thinking, the proof that it is of this world*' (Leontiev, 1975/2021, p. 23).

Let's return to the conclusion of these theses. In concrete terms, what does it mean to transform the world? To be human is not to adapt to a world that is already constituted, but to collaborate in its transformation. We need to distinguish between adaptation and transformation, change and transformation. Transformation means changing an object or activity from within. It is to be distinguished from forms of adaptation to what is predetermined. These are important distinctions that we will return to later in the book. The notion of adaptation, on the other hand, conveys a prejudicial form of conservatism. For Vianna and Stetsenko (2014), most of the theoretical frameworks and intervention approaches mobilized in education don't really take hold of this transformative orientation and align themselves with an adaptive dimension that preserves the status quo of social relations:

> For example, the premise that development and learning are rooted in experiential presence or experiential encounter with the world (Heron & Reason, 1997), central in participatory approaches, does not completely avoid connotations of adapting to the status quo. These – and related notions of interpretation, dialogue, and situativity of knowing – have been important in challenging traditional '*objectivist*' models and accounts. Yet these notions require further critical elaboration to more resolutely break away from the idea that individuals need to adapt to what is 'given' in the present in order to develop and learn. The notion of participation as the basis for development and learning (e.g. Lave & Wenger, 1991) only partly revokes this connotation because it is premised on similar dynamics of learners being situated in community practices as they exist in the present, rather than transforming and transcending them (Vianna & Stetsenko, 2014, pp. 578–579).

Activity as a Collective Process of Transformation

Thus conceived, the concept of activity is a theoretical bridge between the individual and society. For (Marx, 1968, p. 81), '*Just as society creates man as man, so it is created by him*'. Activity in this sense refers to the transformation of the social world, and not strictly to biological adaptation to an environment:

> This mode consists of the fact that man does not simply adapt to the world, but rather changes it in accordance with his needs and interests, that is, creates his own socially conditioned human world, including the world of his own relationships – i.e., social reality. Consequently, man here acts as a subject. And it is this subject characteristic of man that the principle of activity concentrates on. It is in this way that it is discovered that man also acts as the subject of his own development as a social being, and as a subject of history in the process of material, object-transforming interaction with nature. Or, in other words, in the way that the development of society as a natural historical process at the same time presents itself as a cultural-historical process (Zlobin, 1990, p. 57).

By transforming their world through activity, human beings transform themselves. The social world is thus both the product of human activity and the origin of its own development. But not all action, however spontaneous, is activity. Extending Feuerbach's theses, we can say that the philosophical meaning of activity is that human beings make history and history is the product of human activity that social reality does not exist outside of their activity, and that social relations and the laws of history exist and manifest themselves in various forms of activity. For Davydov (1990a):

> The most significant special feature of activity is its transforming and goal-setting nature, which enables the subject to go beyond the framework of any situation, to rise above the determination it sets and to place it in a broader context of being, thereby finding a means that goes beyond the possibilities of a given determination. [...] This reveals the inherent openness and universality of activity. Activity should be understood as a form of historical cultural creativity (Davydov, 1990a, p. 127).

In other words, to limit the analysis of activity to a form of situated determination is to make it nothing more than a determined product of history. Rather activity in this conception is, on the contrary, the process of human creation of history, a form of cultural creativity. This last point is fundamental to any analysis of activity. To analyze activity isn't simply to analyze what people do in a situation, this way of doing things being itself partly determined by '*determinants*'[3] external to the situation under study, it is to enable subjects to be actors in history, i.e. to be actors in

---

[3] The term determinant is frequently used in French-language research on work. In its use, it is not so obvious that its meaning is fundamentally different from that of variable or factor.

determining their own activity. Without this, the activity runs the risk
of becoming '*foreign*' to the subject. This feeling of being a stranger to
one's own activity brings us back to the concept of alienation, a concept
that, for (Quiniou, 2006):

> indicates the paradox or tragic contradiction of a situation of enslavement
> resulting from an activity that, on the contrary, by definition, should be the
> principle of concrete freedom, i.e., of self-mastery based on the mastery of
> the conditions of practice. Alienation is the becoming passivity of activity,
> the becoming impotence of power, and thus the becoming other of action
> because of the historical conditions (neither merely natural nor merely tech-
> nical) of that action. What is at stake, then, is a relation of activity to itself
> that, by virtue of the context of its concrete deployment, inverts its essence
> and makes it different from what it could be (Quiniou, 2006, pp. 73–74).

Borer, Yvon, and Durand (2015, pp. 11–12), citing De Montmollin's
analysis of Taylor's work (1991), note that '*activity analysis*' carries with
it the original crime of defining '*what to do*' by depriving operators of
their own work. The analysis of '*what operators do*' (a commonsense definition of activity) in a work situation thus easily runs the risk of slipping
into recommendations (just as external to them) that induce a form of
dispossession. Surely, this risk can only be overcome if operators take
responsibility for their own work and its organization. Repositioning
professionals as designers of their own work thus means truly unleash-
ing the emancipatory potential contained in the philosophical roots of
activity.

In this sense, activity analysis is an instrument for empowering professionals and enabling them to regain control over their own work,
an instrument for transforming and developing collective agency, and
finally an instrument for cultural production. But for this to happen,
it is necessary to go beyond immediate experience and develop a '*critical awareness*' that goes beyond the surface of phenomena and seeks to
account for their historicity and genesis. Understood in this way, activity analysis is a tool for conscientization in the sense attributed to it by
the famous Brazilian educator Paulo Freire (1975). In this sense, too,
the goal of activity analysis is not to have an external analyst design the
work, but to enable professionals to truly design their activity and the
object of their activity.

The Author's Position

It's undoubtedly necessary to position myself so that the reader can understand the point of view from which I approach the presentation of CHAT in this book. My background is multidisciplinary: trained in the sciences and techniques of physical and sports activities, Physical Education Teacher with a doctorate in educational sciences, I was recruited as an associate professor in an ergonomics team at the Conservatoire National des Arts et Métiers. I have recently joined the occupational psychology and clinical activities team at the same institution.

Given this background, readers will understand that I don't see the concept of activity as the property of any one discipline. As Leontiev points out, *'Nowhere was activity marked as to which science it belongs to'* *(1978, p. 88)*. I see the concept of activity as a tool for liberating ourselves from disciplines, and even for developing disciplines. Hence, a personal position that doesn't take refuge behind the disciplinary umbrella or defense but tries to develop or build frameworks that allow for disciplinary dialogue, sometimes beyond SHS (e.g. Lémonie, 2019). This seems to me to be a necessity for both scholarly work and intervention. As Latour (2006, p. 20) points out in his own way, and we agree with him on this point, *'Polemics between disciplines don't produce good concepts, only barricades built with the available debris.'*

This positioning means that the research examples included in the book come from a wide range of fields and disciplines: training, teaching, ergonomics, occupational psychology, and social work. This diversity may confuse the reader. We invite them to free themselves from disciplinary categories: whatever the field, it's all about work and human activity, whether in a school or a waste processing plant. I'll also sometimes use examples from everyday life rather than research to illustrate certain dimensions of a concept: shaving to talk about development, the doctor to talk about contradictions, and so on. These examples are used as images to illustrate a particular point. This type of example is often used in activity theory: the knot on a handkerchief to remember, primitive hunting, perceiving the elasticity of an object, the doctor settling in. These examples are not the result of research per se but are intended to facilitate the reader's understanding.

I became involved with CHAT after reading the work of Yrjö Engeström and his collaborators. It seemed to me that I had found some answers to the dissatisfaction I had felt both in reading scientific articles and in my own work. I found the transdisciplinary orientation as well as the interventionist dimension. So, it's both my entry point into CHAT and the framework from which I develop my own research. But understanding Yrjö's work requires a retrospective effort to grasp both its scope and direction. The mere presentation of the activity triangle (as is often the case) does not seem satisfactory to us.

Finally, the interventionist dimension is often overlooked in the presentation of CHAT. In this way, the work of theoretical elaboration is cut off from its roots. We felt it necessary to present this interventionist dimension in a separate section, through the formative interventions and methodology of the Change Laboratory. It seems to us that CHAT can become a real tool for transforming activities to meet the challenges of our time. May this book become a tool for researchers and professionals who wish to mobilize this theory to support expansive learning processes that transform human activities. This is its ambition.

Book Structure

The book is divided into three parts.

In the first part, we attempt to explain the genesis and development of activity theory over four generations. Chapter 2 deals with the progressive construction of CHAT in Vygotsky's work. Chapter 3 will present the theoretical development of Leontiev and the Kharkov School. Chapter 4 will present the work of Engeström. Finally, chapter 5 will deal with the emergence of a fourth generation of work based on the work of Sannino. Despite its successive developments and transformations, CHAT retains a kind of historical coherence. In the concluding chapter of this first part, we'll look at the continuities beyond the evolutions.

The second part will focus on four basic concepts and their use in empirical research. We will report on four main CHAT concepts and use research to illustrate their use in analyzing activity. The concepts of object of activity (Chapter 6), contradiction (Chapter 7), expansive learning (Chapter 8), and development (Chapter 9) will be discussed in turn.

The third part will allow us to branch out and change our frame of reference in relation to several approaches that mobilize CHAT in a qualitative analysis orientation. No longer analyzing activity (as a researcher) but enabling operators to analyze their activity to support expansive learning and the development of activity systems. Activity analysis is usually presented as the work of an analyst who diagnoses, makes recommendations, and accompanies transformations. The change laboratory method is presented as a particular form of developmental intervention rooted in CHAT (Chapter 10). Finally, the specific characteristics of this type of intervention are presented in relation to other approaches (Chapter 11). At the heart of activity analysis is dialectical thinking, the *'ascent from the abstract to the concrete'*.

This book invites you on a theoretical, methodological, and, we hope, expansive journey. At the end of this introduction, it remains for me to wish the reader a safe journey, in the hope that the structure of the book will serve as a compass on the path to the appropriation of this theory turned towards practice, the transformation of the world and the emergence of real utopias.

Part 1

FOUR GENERATIONS OF CULTURAL-HISTORICAL ACTIVITY THEORY

Introduction to Part 1

In this first part, the metaphor of the journey will guide our understanding of CHAT. It will be a journey through different generations of CHAT work. Through this journey through more than 150 years of history, the reader will perceive both the interventionist and activist continuity of this theory, which justifies the use of the term theory in the singular, and the qualitative developments inherent in each generation of work, which ventures into different issues while progressively emancipating itself from disciplinary boundaries.

An interest in CHAT as an open process that evolves and transforms itself thus implies a threefold geographical, disciplinary, and historical journey that undoubtedly deserves much more development than we can provide in this book. Some authors have presented this journey in geographical terms (e.g. Dafermos, Chronaki, & Kontopodis, 2020), in historical and philosophical terms (e.g. Blunden, 2010). We refer the reader to these authors for more developments than this book can offer. In line with the current literature, we have chosen to present the evolution of activity theory in four generations of work.

However, presenting the evolution of CHAT as a succession of generations of work, as we will do in this book, is not without its critics. On the one hand, this form of presentation tends to narrow the diversity of approaches to CHAT, making it very difficult to divide it into several geographical locations or several generations of work (Stetsenko, 2021). On the other hand, this form of presentation has many advantages in that it provides a readable and '*didactic*' account of CHAT that can be used to shape a form of tradition for research orientation (Bakhurst, 2009).

As Dafermos (2015) points out, this generational description of CHAT certainly suffers from an oversimplification that doesn't really allow us to understand the transition from one generation to the next. The emphasis on Vygotsky, Leontiev, and Engeström also overlooks the important role played by other activity theorists: Rubinstein, for example, who introduced the concept of activity into the field of Russian psychology (Mironenko, 2013), whose work was the subject of a French-language book (Nosulenko & Rabardel, 2007); Luria (Cole, Levitin, & Luria, 2006), but also Bernstein (Feigenberg, 2014; Kant, 2016; Meijer & Bruijn, 2007), who inspired the theory of nonlinear dynamical systems; Davydov (Davydov, 1990b, 2008), Galperine (Arievitch, 2017; Engeness & Lund, 2020; Galperine, Engeness, & Thomas, 2023), and many other eminent figures. Where appropriate, we will refer to these authors for each period.

The second weakness of this generational representation of CHAT is that each of the preceding generations is likely to be seen as superior to, or having overcome, the weaknesses of the previous generation. Thus, the multi-generational presentation could suggest that only the latest generation of the theory is the most advanced form, with the older generations somehow incorporated into this latest generation. As observed by Fenwick, Edwards, and Sawchuk (2015, p. 71), the CHAT tradition is presented as a trajectory of development in consecutive and successive generations. This assumption is based on the premise that the most recent generation has successfully built upon the tradition, effectively integrated it, and can represent it. We don't think that way. There's no such thing as superiority; there are developments, qualitative reorganizations that take place to adjust the theory of activity to the times. Hasse (2024) expresses this very clearly in a recent essay chapter:

> When the cultural-historical focus shifted from the historically continuously formed psychological processes tied to thinking and learning in a material and social world to the collective object-oriented activity system, Vygotsky's mediations no longer took center stage (Hasse, 2024, p. 223).

But despite qualitative reorganizations, there are still forms of permanence. Vygotsky's principles continue to inform the fourth generation of CHAT (Engeström & Sannino, 2020). However, the orientation differs significantly in terms of the unit of analysis and the issues targeted. In this context, Vygotsky is not forgotten; rather, his work is developed within a different framework. The evidence of this can be found in the numerous publications that revisit Vygotsky and pursue his initial work in the context of contemporary social transformation issues (Dafermos, 2018; Stetsenko, 2017; Tanzi Neto, Liberali, & Dafermos, 2020). We posit that it is the *generative character* of each generation that enables the emergence of a diversity of orientations. Each generation, while retaining the principles of the previous generation, transforms the unit of analysis regarding quite distinct projects. This transformation can be observed in the shift from mediated action to the articulation of multiple interacting activity systems, which represents a change in scale in intervention, as well as an expansion of the unit of analysis. Nevertheless, the principles of CHAT remain. We will return to this topic at the conclusion of this section.

Finally, it is important to note that each generation is not a monolithic block. CHAT is an open theory that is subject to debate, contestation, and fragmentation between different research orientations. This fragmentation is what gives CHAT its dynamic, evolving, and living character (Levant, 2018). We will be reporting on CHAT's multigenerational journey, but also on the debates and controversies that animate the community of activity theorists.

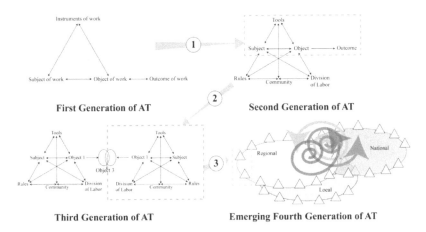

Figure 2: Four generations of Cultural-Historical Activity Theory unit of analysis.

Chapter 2

The First Generation of CHAT and the Vygotskian Revolution

It is no exaggeration to say that Vygotsky was a genius. Through more than five decades in science, I never again met a person who even approached his clearness of mind, his ability to lay bare the essential structure of complex problems, his breadth of knowledge in many fields, and his ability to foresee the future development of his science (Luria in Cole et al., 2006, p. 38).

This is why practice reforms the whole methodology of science (Vygotsky, 1997c, p. 306).

It is not possible to convey the full complexity of Vygotsky's work in just a few pages. This chapter will therefore provide an overview of the trajectory of Vygotsky's ideas, the stages of his intellectual development, and a few key ideas that will be useful for understanding the rest of the book.

Although Vygotsky's work spanned a short period of approximately ten years, it remains an important source of inspiration for researchers today. It is also undoubtedly an unfinished project, given the brevity of Vygotsky's life (he died of tuberculosis in 1934), but one that is both fruitful and topical for educational research (Stetsenko, 2017), for occupational psychology (Clot, 2006, 2009), for ergonomics (Rabardel, 1995), for management (de La Ville, Leca, & Magakian, 2011), for adult education (Prot & Schneuwly, 2013), or for collective action within social movements (Tanzi Neto et al., 2020).

This chapter is not intended to be exhaustive. Those seeking further details on Vygotsky's work are encouraged to consult the numerous books on intellectual biography, including Van der Veer and Valsiner (1991), Wertsch (1985), and Yasnitsky (2018, 2019). One may consult introductory books to his thought (Daniels, 2001; Daniels, Cole, & Wertsch, 2007), or books that explicitly seek to develop Vygotskian thought (Dafermos, 2018; Stetsenko, 2017). It is evident that Vygotsky's work can be accessed in both French and English. The French-language editions include, among others, the following titles: Vygotsky (Vygotski, 1927/1999, 1987, 1994, 2002, 2014, 2018)[4]. The English-language editions are grouped under the title Collected Papers (Vygotsky, 1987a, 1987b, 1993a, 1997a, 1998, 2012).

Vygotsky's work is immense, fertile, and generative, yet it is relatively short, spanning only ten years. Its multifaceted reception allows for the evocation of several Vygotsky (Ageyev, 2003). Translation issues also contribute to this situation (Cole, 2009; Van der Veer & Yasnitsky, 2016a).

The objective of this chapter is to delineate the genesis of ideas that are pivotal to the CHAT, contextualizing their emergence within the post-revolutionary Russia of the 1920s and 1930s. This historical backdrop is of paramount importance in comprehending the ideas that permeate Vygotskian scholarship, their subsequent erasure under Stalin, as well as their rediscovery and republication from the 1960s onwards.

In the post-revolutionary years, Vygotsky's objective of enabling psychology to master its own behavior proved crucial to the overall project of reforming Russian society. In a note in his notebooks, he states that '*it is impossible to master nature without mastering oneself*' (Zavershneva & Van der Veer, 2018, p. 117). For Vygotsky, the mastery of one's own behavior represents a central issue in the new society being developed in the wake of the 1917 Revolution:

> [...] in the new society our science will take a central place in life. '*The leap from the kingdom of necessity into the kingdom of freedom*' inevitably puts the question of the mastery of our own being, of its subjection to the self, on the agenda (Vygotsky, 1997c, p. 342).

The question must be asked why this book devotes so much attention to Vygotsky, when, as we have seen, the concept of activity (in the sense of Tätigkeit, see next chapter) is not a central concept for him. Indeed, for Veresov (2005, p. 41), '*It seems, therefore, that we do not have sufficient grounds for the assertion that the concept of activity (deyatelnost, Tätigkeit) played an essential role in his cultural-historical theory.*' Furthermore, Veresov (2005) notes that Vygotsky's use of the term '*activity*' was

---

[4]   In French, Vygotsky's name is usually write Vygotski.

consistent with the usage of physiologists and psychologists of his era. Contrary to popular belief, the concept of activity and its theoretical development cannot be definitively traced back to Vygotsky's early writings. Therefore, the theory of activity attributed to Leontiev represents a distinct theoretical framework from that of Vygotsky. However, as we shall see, it is its continuation. A continuation in a different form, probably less risky to follow when Vygotsky's writings were banned in the 1930s. Leontiev's theory of activity undoubtedly enabled Vygotsky's work to survive in the Soviet culture of orality (Bakhurst, 2023).

Vygotsky's work serves as the foundation for the cultural-historical school of psychology and the cultural-historical theory of activity. Consequently, it is often referred to as the inaugural work in CHAT (Engeström, 2001; Spinuzzi, 2020b). Leontiev's activity theory, which was developed during his collaboration with Vygotsky in Moscow, draws its roots from Vygotsky's historical-cultural psychological theory. Despite the challenging context of the 1930s, which included the banning of Vygotsky's work and the termination of pedology, the importance of Vygotsky and his theories cannot be overlooked. They continue to play an essential role in understanding the subsequent developments and the construction of the cultural-historical theory of activity. In this regard, Kozulin (1984) notes that:

> In 1940 Leontiev completed his Essays in the Development of Mind (published in 1947), which contained a sketch of Vygotsky's cultural-historical theory. Vygotsky, however, is not mentioned in the text. This fact might be attributed to Leontiev's desire to see his book published, which would have been impossible had there been clear references to his teacher. On the other hand, as later became clear, by the late 1930s Leontiev had already dissociated his 'theory of activity' from that of Vygotsky (Kozulin, 1984, pp. 110–111).

In presenting Vygotsky's career path, we will proceed to present the essential ideas that we have retained. These include mediation and the notion of the psychological instrument, the instrumental method and indirect methods, the double line of development, and finally, the notion of unity of analysis.

The Main Scientific Milestones in Vygotsky's Career

Lev Semenovich Vygotsky was born into a cultured Jewish family in Orcha in 1896. He subsequently relocated to Gomel in Byelorussia, where he spent his childhood and adolescence. He commenced his teaching career after studying medicine and law at Moscow Imperial University and history and philosophy at Chaniavski People's University (Yasnitsky, 2018).

The emergence of cultural-historical theory in Vygotsky's work cannot be understood without restoring it to overcome the dichotomy between theory and practice. Indeed, Vygotsky's work must be seen as an attempt to provide scientific answers to practical problems that arose in his work as an educator with disabled children. Elements of his biography attest to this. In 1924, for instance, he was appointed head of the Bureau for the Education of Physically and Mentally Handicapped Children. His sole excursion outside the USSR was to London in 1925 for a congress on the education of deaf children (van der Veer & Zavershneva, 2011). The question of practice pervades the entirety of his oeuvre. The cultural-historical theory he develops in psychology thus constitutes a project that can be described as activist and interventionist (Sannino, 2011). As Stetsenko (2015) points out:

> Rather than being confined to an '*ivory tower*' of purely academic pursuits, Vygotsky and his followers were directly engaged in practical endeavors, first and foremost in policies of reorganizing the national system of education and devising special programs for the homeless, poor, and children with special needs. This engagement situated Vygotsky and his colleagues directly at the epicenter of highly charged sociopolitical practices of the time, as immediate participants and actors (Stetsenko, 2015, p. 105).

The scientific background and development of Vygotsky's cultural-historical theory are a source of controversy and debate in current scientific literature. The analysis of the genealogy of the ideas he developed between 1924 and his death from tuberculosis in 1934 is further complicated by the fact that the publication date of his writing is often later than the date of writing, and sometimes posthumously (Van der Veer & Yasnitsky, 2016b). Figure 3 illustrates the various periodizations that have been proposed in the literature (Minick, 2005; Van der Veer & Valsiner, 1991; Veresov, 1999; Zavershneva & Van der Veer, 2018). Despite the differences between authors in the criteria used to establish this periodization, it is possible to perceive that Vygotsky's work in psychology can be analyzed as a developing process with continuity and rupture, rather than as an accumulation of knowledge (Dafermos, 2018).

In what follows, we will distinguish three periods. The first period is referred to as the reactologist period and corresponds to Vygotsky's entry into the Moscow Psychological Institute. The second period is intermediate and corresponds to Vygotsky's reflection on the crisis in psychology. Finally, the last period corresponds to the development of historical-cultural theory in psychology.

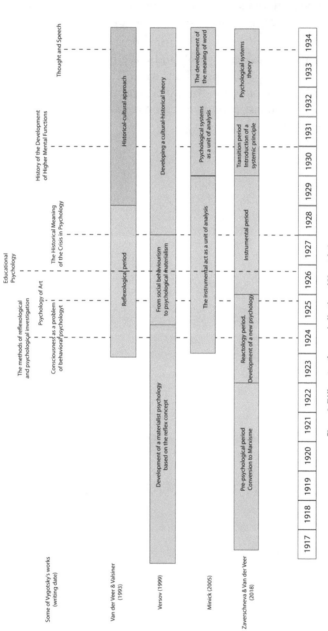

Figure 3: Different authors periodization of Vygotsky's career.

Figure 3: Different authors periodization of Vygotsky's career.

1924–1926: Entry into Psychology and the Reactologist Period

Vygotsky's initial period of research can be described as reactological. Despite initially distancing himself from the study of reflexes, which was pioneered by Pavlov and Beckterev, he adopted their vocabulary and mobilized the central concept of reflex and then of reaction. This was in line with the reactologist orientation of the Moscow Institute of Psychology.

Although biographically partially inaccurate, we will commence with Vygotsky's presentation at the Second Congress of Neuropsychology in Leningrad in 1924. As outlined by Friedrich (2010, p. 12), Vygotsky's contributions, particularly his lecture entitled *'Research Methods in Reflexology and Psychology,'* were not overlooked and significantly influenced the trajectory of his career. This lecture made a profound impression on Luria, who subsequently invited Kornilov, then Director of the Moscow Institute of Experimental Psychology, to recruit him. However, this episode did not mark the beginning of Vygotsky's entry into psychology, as he had already established a laboratory and was teaching psychology at Gomel (Yasnitsky, 2018). At the time, he was already well acquainted with the congress, and Van der Veer and Valsiner (1991) posit that his critical stance towards Pavlov and Bekhterev's reflexology may have contributed, at least as much as the strong impression he made at the congress, to the invitation to join the Moscow Institute of Experimental Psychology.

The term *'reflexology'* refers to the study of reflexes based on the work of the physiologist Pavlov and the psychiatrist and neurologist Bekhterev. The Russian contribution to this field is the theory of conditional reflexes. Unlike unconditional reflexes (e.g. patellar reflex), conditional reflexes are acquired during life. Although it was introduced in Pavlov's work on the nervous system as early as 1903 (particularly in his famous work on dog salivation), it was Bekhterev who introduced the term reflexology. Reflexology, like its American alter ego, Watsonian behaviorism, refers to the connection between a stimulus and a behavioral response. The basic scheme is as follows:

$$S \rightarrow R$$

In his 1924 paper, Vygotsky mobilized the concepts of reflexology to develop a critique of the limitations of the methods employed by this science of reflexes in studying the phenomenon that, in his view, should be the key object of psychology: consciousness. At best, the well-known formula of causality between a stimulus and a behavioral response explains elementary psychological functions but cannot account for specifically human behavior or the organization of these reflexes into systems. As Blunden (2010, p. 13) notes, '*If everything was a reflex, then consciousness was not a reflex but the organization of reflexes, a process with a social origin, and which the subject themself can control*'. In other words, consciousness can be understood as the reflex of reflexes, as Vygotsky put it.

At the heart of his argument is a critique of the reductionism of Pavlov's and Bekhterev's reflexology. Reflexes cannot be considered in isolation; rather, they exist within a system of reflex regulation and organization. Because reflexes do not work in isolation, they interact and become a stimulus for another reflex system. For Vygotsky, reflexology has made significant contributions to the study of lower-level processes, but it has not provided insights into uniquely human behavior and higher-level psychic functions. This critique illustrates the importance that Vygotsky attached to the idea of psychological regulation of behavior and foreshadows the instrumental method to which we will return later (in this chapter and in Chapter 10).

After his arrival in Moscow, Kornilov's reactology served as a framework for Vygotsky in the early years of his career (he adopted its vocabulary), as did the goal of founding a truly Marxist psychology (Ratner & Silva, 2017).

1927–1928: The Crisis in Psychology and its Resolution on the Basis of Marxist Principles

Vygotsky distanced himself from Kornilov and his approach from 1926–1927. The intermediate period is distinguished by the writing of the work entitled '*The Historical Meaning of the Crisis in Psychology*' (Vygotsky, 1997c). Continuing his project to elaborate a psychological science, Vygotsky diagnoses in this work the crisis of the various psychological schools and the fragmentation of the psychology of his time. Despite representing a major turning point in Vygotsky's career, the work is paradoxically little cited in academic circles (Goertzen, 2008).

With Veresov (1999), several approaches to analyzing '*The Historical Meaning of the Crisis in Psychology*' can be identified in current scientific literature. The first analysis examines the book's essential contribution to the development of a Marxist psychology (Ratner & Silva, 2017). The new framework for a general psychology capable of resolving the contradictions he analyzes in the book is '*necessary for revealing the essence of a given domain of phenomena, the laws of their change, their qualitative and quantitative characteristics, their causality, for creating the categories and concepts that are appropriate for them, in short, for creating one's own Capital*' (Vygotsky, 1997c, p. 330). The second orientation situates the book within the context of historical and cultural psychology. This represents a significant shift in Vygotsky's approach to the problem of consciousness (Veresov, 1999). In this second orientation, Van der Veer and Valsiner (1991, p. 143) highlight that '*Vygotsky's analysis of the 'state of the art' in psychology can be seen as the prelude of his and Luria's later cultural-historical theory.*' In this sense, Vygotsky's cultural-historical theory is a way out of the crisis he analyzed in the book he wrote in 1927–1928.

Vygotsky's analysis of the crisis is historical in nature. For Vygotsky, the field of psychology is a battleground where different schools of thought clash: gestalt, psychoanalysis, and behaviorism. Each of these schools mobilizes an incommensurable explanatory framework, along with a central concept and a primary abstraction that shapes the phenomena it studies: consciousness, behavior, and the unconscious. The result is an amalgam of research findings with no unifying ideas. A synthesis is required, rather than the eclecticism he so vigorously criticizes. In this context, Vygotsky advocates for a unified psychology, which he terms '*general psychology*.' He also proposes a unifying methodology and a common object for psychology.

Based on a historical analysis of the generalization and expansion of scientific concepts (Dafermos, 2014, 2019), Vygotsky (1997c) demonstrates that the expansion logic of scientific concepts progresses through five distinct phases.

- In the initial phase, a scientific discovery is made in a limited field. For instance, the discovery of Pavlov's conditional reflex based on the dog's salivary reflex.
- In the subsequent phase, the initial discovery is extended to neighboring domains in which the procedure is deemed relevant. Pavlov's

procedure is thus deemed relevant to reflexes other than the dog's salivary reflex.

• The third period saw the domination of one current of psychology over neighboring subdisciplines. The notion of reflex was thus extended beyond the narrow confines of animal psychology to embrace an explanatory character for humans as well.

• In the fourth stage, the main idea, detached from the initial facts that gave rise to it, is used as an explanatory principle for other disciplines.

• In the fifth stage, the idea is widely criticized and definitively replaced. Additionally, criticism will be directed at the initial factual basis from which a new idea emerges, fueling a new cycle.

In this analysis, Vygotsky posits that extending an idea beyond its original context of emergence leads to a loss of meaning. Consequently, he advocates for the necessity of a general psychology.

Furthermore, in opposition to empiricism, Vygotsky rejects the idea that the starting point of all research should be direct methods. For Vygotsky, there is no distinction between the natural sciences and the humanities, including psychology. All of these disciplines employ some form of interpretation of facts to convey meaning. However, at the time of Vygotsky's research, psychological inquiry relied heavily on direct methods, both subjectively and objectively. In subjective psychology, the direct experience of the subject's conscious thoughts during introspection served as the foundation for theorizing. In contrast, behaviorists confined themselves to the direct recording of observable external facts. Vygotsky criticized the direct method as the sole possible method in psychology. Instead, he employs examples from the natural and historical sciences to demonstrate how the interpretation of traces and the reconstruction of facts are objective methods for reconstructing a phenomenon. Using the example of the thermometer, he exemplifies the indirect method:

> The use of a thermometer is a perfect model of the indirect method. After all, we do not study what we see (as with the microscope)-the rising of the mercury, the expansion of the alcohol-but we study heat and its changes, which are indicated by the mercury or alcohol. We interpret the indications of the thermometer, we reconstruct the phenomenon under study by its traces, by its influence upon the expansion of a substance (Vygotsky, 1997c, p. 273).

What are the driving forces behind the crisis, the main contradictions that need to be overcome? For Vygotsky, this driving force must be found in practice rather than in the theoretical sphere. This is an extremely important idea in understanding the interventionist dimension of Vygotsky's proposal (see Chapter 10 in particular). For Vygotsky, practice represents the most rigorous test for any theory, as it compels researchers to reconsider their perspectives. This process of reconsideration is precisely what renders practice a valuable contributor to scientific progress. As Vygotsky (1997c, p. 306) notes, '*Practice transforms the entire scientific methodology.*' It serves as the primary criterion and precludes the possibility of a single '*winner*' emerging from the opposition between different schools. This emphasis on practice does not, however, signify a departure from theory. In contrast, theory and philosophy can only inform research methodology. In this sense, practice without theory is incomplete, but theory without practice is mere speculation.

1928–1934: Building a Cultural-Historical Theory of Psychology

As posited by Veresov (1999) and Van der Veer and Valsiner (1991), the genesis of cultural-historical theory can be traced to the late 1920s. The initial work to systematically present Vygotsky's ideas was a treatise on pedology, recently translated into English (Vygotsky, 2019). The ideas of instrumental methods, mediation, and different lines of development are presented and discussed in the context of child development.

Following the publication of his work in 1928, Vygotsky collaborated with Luria on a book that remained unpublished during his lifetime. Entitled '*Studies of the History of Behavior. Ape, Primitive, Child*' (Vygotsky & Luria, 1992), the book explored the relationships and differences between humans, animals, and children. The central argument is that to understand human behavior, it is essential to grasp the evolutionary transition between animals and humans, between primitive and civilized humans, or between children and adults. These three essays constitute the core of this book.

Regarding the transition from animal to human, Vygotsky draws upon Köhler's experiments with chimpanzees to highlight two key points. The first point is that in the chimpanzee's use of tools, it is possible to perceive the beginnings of cultural development. However, it must be acknowledged that the use of a stick by the ape is merely a form of passive adaptation to the external environment. The stick is only used if it is placed in the chimpanzee's field of vision at the same time as the fruit to be caught. In this manner, the utilization of the instrument remains exceedingly rudimentary in the ape. While a stick may be employed in the present, it is not prepared, used, or designed for the future. Consequently, there is no evidence of mastery of the external environment in the chimpanzee. The evolutionary distinction between chimpanzees and humans is that the tool is not a component of a work process.

Vygotsky additionally posits that the chimpanzee is devoid of the capacity to utilize another category of instrument, namely signs. The ape's adaptation can be characterized by the absence of control over one's own behavior by means of these artificial signs, which constitute the essence of cultural development of human development (Vygotsky & Luria, 1992). In other words, what distinguishes humans from animals is precisely this ability to master their own psychological functions using signs. And it is precisely through the use of signs, the mastery of one's own psyche, that a real, forward-looking mastery of the environment opens up. As Sève (2008) indicates:

> The invention of artificial procedures based on signs gave men control over their psychic activities, both their own and those of others, and thus facilitated a further evolution of tool-based control over nature (Sève, 2008, p. 313).

In the book *'History of the Development of Higher Mental Functions'* (Vygotsky, 2014), the results of empirical research into higher psychic functions are presented, as well as an exposition of the instrumental method in the history of higher psychic functions, including attention, memory, and other topics.

The title of the book indicates that Vygotsky distinguishes between two forms of psychic functions: elementary psychic functions (basic forms of attention, perception, associative memory) and higher psychic functions (linguistic thought, voluntary attention, rational will, etc.). The higher psychic functions are irreducible to their primitive antecedents, as they are qualitatively different. These higher psychic functions do not simply develop from the elementary functions, as if the latter contained them in an embryonic state.

The two forms of psychic function do not follow the same developmental trajectory. The first form of psychic function undergoes a natural maturation process, while the higher psychic functions undergo a cultural development. To fully comprehend the qualitative transformations that give rise to the mature mind, it is essential to examine external factors, as the higher mental functions are distinguished by their mediation and therefore by external means. It is through external means that humans control their own psychic functions. The most straightforward illustration of this mediation, as elucidated by Vygotsky, is the act of tying knots to enhance memory. This represents the utilization of the sign as a tool in the process of memory retrieval (Vygotski, 2014, p. 404).

These forms of mediation are fundamentally social in nature, and the development of higher psychic functions is therefore based on the internalization of cultural means. The primary idea underlying the development of higher psychic functions is that all higher psychic functions are social in origin: first external, then internalized.

Vygotsky's third period can be further subdivided into several periods. The first of these is the instrumental period, which is finalized by the writing of '*The History of the Development of Higher Psychic Functions.*' The second period saw the emergence of a more holistic and systemic approach, as evidenced by the publication of Thought and Speech (Vygotski, 1987), which focused on the relationship between thought and language.

Vygotsky's Cultural-Historical Approach: A Basis for Further Development

The following section presents some of the key features of Vygotsky's cultural-historical theory of psychology. For each of the themes presented, we will also seek to identify how these themes will be further developed in the evolution of the CHAT.

Mediation and the Concept of the Psychological Instrument

Vygotsky's analysis of mediation is essential to understanding his contribution to psychology (Prenkert, 2010; Roth, 2007). As Vygotsky himself points out, '*The central fact of our psychology is the fact of mediation*' (Vygotski, 2002, p. 139). Indeed, this is the key to his approach to understanding how human mental functioning is linked to institutional, cultural, and historical contexts, since these contexts shape and provide the cultural tools mastered by the individuals who form this functioning.

The concept of the psychological instrument was developed in the book '*History of the Development of Higher Psychic Functions*.' The thesis he defends in this work is that all higher psychic functions originate with the assistance of psychological instruments, which consequently mediate these functions. The introduction of this category of mediation by psychological instruments is undoubtedly revolutionary in that it brings '*society*' into individual psychic functioning. Furthermore, it displaces the previous analysis proposed by reflexological approaches of a link between a stimulus and a behavioral response S→R to consider the psychological instruments serving as mediation.

To illustrate this idea of mediation and psychological instrument, consider the example of memorization. Let us suppose that I am driving to England in a left-hand-drive car. To remind myself to drive in the right direction, I will place an object on my dashboard to remind me that I need to change my habit of driving on the right, despite using my usual car. This object placed on the dashboard will act as a psychological instrument to remind me of the need to reverse my driving habits. Between the stimulus and the behavioral response lies a psychological instrument whose function is to enable me to control my behavior. The concept of a psychological instrument should not be regarded as an aid that merely facilitates existing mental functions, leaving them qualitatively unchanged. Instead of leaving mental functions unchanged, the psychological instrument develops and transforms them qualitatively.

In introducing the concept of the psychological instrument, Vygotsky rejected popular attempts to locate the organizing principle inside the human psyche and suggested looking for it outside. In this context, Vygotsky proposed an analogy with the tools that stand between the hand and the object on which a person acts. These tools may be pen, pencil, or other writing implement; hammer, saw, or other tool for working with materials; or any other object that is used to perform a specific task. Like material tools, psychological tools are artificial formations: they are man-made. By their very nature, then, both material and psychological tools are social: they accumulate the social and practical experience of humanity. However, Vygotsky's analysis diverges from this point onwards. While technical means are designed to regulate the processes of nature, psychological tools (signs) facilitate the regulation of the individual's natural behavioral processes. '*The sign is a means of psychological* action on behavior, one's own or that of others, a means of internal activity aimed at mastering man himself; the sign is directed inward.' (Vygotski, 2014, p. 207). In other words, in the instrumental act, humans master themselves from the outside, by means of psychological tools.

Examples of psychological tools and their complexes include signs, mnemonic techniques, and various counting systems. In '*The Instrumental Method in Psychology*', Vygotsky lists these instruments:

> Examples of psychological tools and their complex systems include language, various forms of numeration and counting, mnemonic devices, algebraic symbols, works of art, writing, diagrams, charts, maps, plans, all possible kinds of signs, etc. (Vygotski, 2014, p. 567)

Despite this divergence between material instruments oriented towards the transformation of nature and psychological instruments oriented towards the interior, there would be a mutual relationship between these two categories insofar as when humans transform nature through their activity, they transform themselves. In this context, and later, Leontiev eliminated the distinction between psychological and material instruments, grouping them together in the same category. Cole (1999) and Engeström (1999b) have also eliminated this distinction. For Cole (1999):

> One of the fundamental principles of the cultural-historical school is that the process of historical development of human behavior and the process of biological evolution do not coincide; one is not a continuation of the other. Rather, each process is governed by its own laws. The key to this difference lies in the concept of the artifact, a material object that has been modified by human beings to regulate their interactions with the world and with each other. Artifacts carry with them successful adaptations from an earlier era (in the life of the individual who made them or in previous generations). In this sense, they combine the ideal and the material. Therefore, in adopting the artifacts provided by their culture, human beings adopt at the same time the symbolic resources they embody (Cole, 1999, p. 90).

For Engeström (1999b):

> The mediating artifacts include tools and signs, both external implements and internal representations such as mental models. It is not particularly useful to categorize mediating artifacts into external or practical ones, on the one hand, and internal or cognitive ones, on the other hand. These functions and uses are in constant flux and transformation as the activity unfolds. An internal representation becomes externalized through speech,

gesture, writing, manipulation of the material environment – and vice versa, external processes become internalized. Freezing or splitting these processes is a poor basis for understanding different artifacts. Instead, we need to differentiate between the processes themselves, between different ways of using artifacts (Engeström, 1999b, p. 381).

The basic schema of any instrumented action can therefore be represented by Figure 4, which illustrates what can be described as the first generation of CHAT work stemming from Vygotsky's approach:

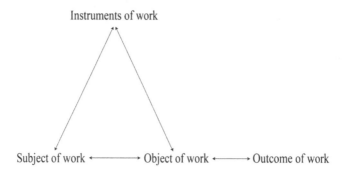

Figure 4: Mediated action as a unit of analysis for CHAT first generation.

In this section, we have used Instrument and Artifact, and sometimes Tool as a synonym, as is often the case in the literature. However, it would be important that, following the work of Rabardel (1995), we make an important distinction between artifact and instrument. Instruments don't immediately stand between subject and object. Following Rabardel, there is a process of internalization and externalization, of instrumentation and instrumentalization, so that the artifact can become a resource for action. In this context, instrumental genesis explores the transformations and development of these three poles, which never remain totally unchanged: by appropriating an instrument to act on an object, the subject transforms himself, never leaving the artifact totally unchanged, which he modifies to make it an instrument of action, just as the object and the meanings attributed to it changes.

The Instrumental Method

The instrumental method has its origins in the 1924 conference. It was further developed in the writings of the late 1920s and early 1930s. This method is variously referred to as the genetic method, the instrumental method as in the note above, or the double stimulation method. This method will serve as the basis for the writing and investigation of higher psychic functions, as published in the book *'History of the Development of Higher Psychic Functions'* (Vygotski, 2014). It will be referred to as the double stimulation method in the remainder of the book, as this is the name widely used in recent work.

Vygotsky's dedication to practice, the conviction that practice is the ultimate arbiter of theory, is evident in the methodology he developed in the late 1920s. It represents a departure from the objectivist and positivist tenet that investigative methods should strive to mirror reality as closely as possible. In contrast, Vygotsky asserts that the strength of experimentation lies in its artificiality. Rather than attempting to replicate reality, the researcher must strive to create the artificial conditions necessary to generate the objects of research in experimentation. As Stetsenko (2016b) suggests, this method extends well beyond the typical boundaries of both classical experimental approaches and descriptive methods relying on a contemplative stance. In accordance with the philosophical stance espoused in his work on crisis, the foundation of the methodology devised by Vygotsky and his colleagues in Moscow is the *'active co-creation of the investigative situation, including the very objects of investigation'* (Stetsenko, 2016b, p. s 36). It is essential to grasp the nature of the subsequent discussion. Stetsenko (2016b, p. s 36) asserts that *'pedagogical intervention'* represents the paradigmatic form of this method. This is exemplified by teaching-learning experiences where the learner is provided with the necessary tools to solve problems in collaboration with others. It is therefore evident why the Change Laboratory methodology presented in the third part of the book is classified as *'formative intervention'* by Engeström, and how it is inextricably linked to Vygotskian theory (Engeström, 2007b). Rather than viewing the development of higher psychic functions as a natural process, Vygotsky posits that it is a cultural process that he seeks to initiate, support, and amplify through the use of mediation tools. In this orientation, the traditional question of what psychological processes are in themselves is transformed into the question of how these processes are possible and what are the conditions that make these processes possible (Stetsenko & Arievitch, 1997). In other words, it is only by seeking to construct the conditions of emergence of phenomena that we are likely to grasp them.

This methodology situates Vygotsky within the field of transformative research as described by Bronfenbrenner (1977) and Sannino (2011). Transformative research aims to transform reality in order to gain a deeper understanding of it. The essence of these methodologies is action rather than contemplation and description. These methodologies are activist in that they are grounded in an ideal of social justice and a conception of the holistic educability of children, whether they have disabilities or not. It is important to note that Vygotsky worked for a long time with students with disabilities and that his contribution to defectology is significant. Indeed, in a notebook entry retranslated by Zavershneva and Van der Veer (2018), Vygotsky emphasizes the importance of this method, which he calls the double stimulation method, for teaching students with disabilities.

> Why the Instrumental Method is important for teaching, for the abnormal child, etc.

> We find in the instrumental function of sign use the common root of all cultural (=higher) intellectual development. Who is incapable of the instrumental function, is also incapable of arithmetic, language, writing, mnemotechnics and so on, and so forth. Let us call this X, this function, volition, i.e., intellect that has reached such a level that it can be applied to itself.

> Cf. Spinoza: Intellectus et voluntas idem.

> 2. The root of all investigations of volition is to create a situation where the volitional operation is necessary, just like Köhler created a situation in which the intellectual reaction is necessary, and adjustment cannot be accomplished without it (refrain from instinct and training). This is the 'will to remember something' (three years, Stern) the need to master one's behavior (Zavershneva & Van der Veer, 2018, p. 118).

A case in point is Leontiev's doctoral thesis, which was supervised by Vygotsky and Luria. This thesis was published in 1931. In this study, subjects of different ages were presented with a series of cards bearing images of simple everyday objects. The task was to memorize the images. This was a direct voluntary memorization task. In a second part of the experiment, participants were simultaneously presented with two sets of cards. The initial set of cards was analogous to the set utilized in the initial study. The subsequent set of cards was designed to facilitate the resolution of memory issues. To this end, participants were required to establish connections between the images on the two decks of cards. They were then permitted to utilize the second deck of cards to recall the images on the first deck. The findings presented in this study, conducted with three age groups of children and adults, demonstrate a notable increase in recall efficacy with age. Additionally, the results demonstrate that recall performance in mediated situations was comparable to that of adults and markedly superior to that achieved in the unmediated condition.

Defectology: The Promise and Prospects of the Vygotskian Approach

This section on Vygotsky's work in defectology serves to illustrate the two lines of development (natural and cultural) that he puts forward, along with the subsequent developments of this idea within the CHAT framework. It also illustrates how Vygotsky's work is rooted in practice. Finally, it highlights the need for an expansion of the unit of analysis through contemporary work on inclusion and disability.

Vygotsky was the founder of the Moscow Institute of Defectology (Vygodskaya, 1999). He remained engaged with this field throughout his career, even returning to medical studies in his later years. Defectology is defined as the study of physical and mental deficiencies that prevent a normal life. However, against this broad definition of the field of defectology, Vygotsky reversed the perspective to study how conditions enable children with disabilities to live normal lives.

In alignment with the Marxist tenets of his methodology and the transformative experiments conducted within this framework, the challenge for Vygotsky and his colleagues in their research on disabled children was to assist them in rectifying their social context, thereby enabling them to transform their environment and control their behavior (Bal, Waitoller, Mawene, & Gorham, 2020). Vygotsky's work on disability was translated relatively late in the English-speaking world (Vygotsky, 1993b) and in France (Vygotski, 1994). It should be noted here that this work is not separate from its theoretical development. Conversely, the opportunity to work with disabled children provided Vygotsky with the ideal laboratory for the elaboration and foundation of a developmental psychology with a Marxist orientation (Ratner & Silva, 2017). Although defectology is a misleading term, in Vygotsky's approach it refers to a grand conception that comes close to the recent concept of inclusion (Giest, 2018). Vygotsky makes a clear distinction between deficiency (biological) and handicap (social):

> A blind person will remain blind and a deaf person deaf, but they will cease to be handicapped because a handicapped condition is only a social concept; a defective condition is an abnormal extension of blindness, deafness, or muteness. Blindness by itself does not make a child handicapped; it is not a defective condition, an inadequacy, abnormality, or illness. Blindness becomes these things only under certain social conditions of a blind person's existence (Vygotsky, 1993b, pp. 83–84).

Vygotsky distinguishes between two lines of development in children: a biological line of maturational development and a cultural line of development in which children acquire cultural tools through participation in social practices. This distinction enables him to account for the complex structure of disability. In natural circumstances, the biological and cultural lines of development are mutually supportive. However, the fusion of natural and cultural lines does not occur in disabled children: there is an incongruence between these two lines of development. In this context, biological deficits impede children's ability to participate in social activities and acquire essential cultural tools. In other words, it is the incongruence between social situations and the axis of biological development that tends to result in disability, or the incompatibility between the child and their social conditions of development.

Vygotsky's dialectical psychological understanding of disability offers a useful approach to overcoming the dualism between the disabled student and society (Bøttcher & Dammeyer, 2012). In accordance with this dialectical perspective on disability, the most significant distinction between disabled and non-disabled children is their access to the cultural tools of learning. The typical institutional settings and activities may be unsuitable for the majority of disabled children (Bøttcher & Dammeyer, 2012, p. 436).

In addition to the aforementioned promise, this conception also contains a caveat and a problem with inclusive approaches to schooling children with disabilities without changing institutions and institutional practices. Gindis (1995) formulates this important question in relation to this conception:

> Vygotsky never wrote or implied that handicapped children should attend the same schools as their nonhandicapped peers; he insisted on creating a

learning environment that would supply disabled students with alternative means of communication and development and would develop those psychological tools that are most appropriate to compensate for their particular disability. Handicapped students need specially trained teachers, a differentiated curriculum, special technological auxiliary means, and simply more time to learn. How realistically can these demands be met in a regular classroom situation? (Gindis, 1995, p. 79)

As previously stated, implementing inclusive practice necessitates transforming the institutions in which it occurs, as these institutions were not originally designed for it. Additionally, it implies broadening Vygotsky's original definition of disability and extending the unit of analysis from the disabled student to the institutions in which these students' learning occurs.

In their literature review on disability research and cultural-historical approaches, Bal et al. (2020) note a paradigm shift in special education research and interventions. As part of this paradigm shift, the unit of analysis has been extended to the analysis of a collective activity system. The reasons for this paradigm shift are well summarized by Daniels (2006):

However, much of the post-Vygotskian research conducted in the West has focused exclusively on the effects of interaction at the interpersonal level, without paying sufficient attention to the form of collective social activity with specific forms of interpersonal communication, and to the interrelationships between the interpersonal and sociocultural levels. The way schools are organized and forced to organize themselves is seen as having an impact on the possibilities for collaboration and peer support, both at the teacher and the student level. However, the theoretical tools for analyzing these kinds of organizational effects are somewhat underdeveloped in the post-Vygotskian framework (Daniels, 2006, p. 106).

This criticism will be revisited at the conclusion of the chapter, where it will be demonstrated that the necessity for an expanded unit of analysis arises.

The Social Origin of Higher Psychic Functions

One of Vygotsky's most influential concepts is that higher psychological functions originate in social relations. To put it another way, to comprehend the individual, it is essential to grasp the social dynamics in which they are embedded. This perspective aligns with Marx's sixth thesis on Feuerbach (see previous chapter), as evidenced by the following:

> Changing the well-known thesis of Marx, we could say that the mental nature of man represents the totality of social relation internalized and made into functions of the individual and form his structure. We do not want to say that this is specifically the meaning of the thesis of Marx, but we see in this thesis the most complete expression of everything to which our history of cultural development leads (Vygotsky, 1981, p. 164).

Despite his engagement with Marx, Vygotsky did not address societal and institutional mechanisms directly. Instead, he concentrated on interpsychological processes that cannot be equated with societal processes (Wertsch, 1985). His famous law of development exemplifies this focus on the interpsychological dimension:

> Every function in the child's cultural development appears twice: first, on the social level, and later, on the individual level; first, between people (interpsychological) and then inside the child (intrapsychological). This applies equally to voluntary attention, to logical memory, and to the formation of concepts. All the higher functions originate as actual relationships between individuals (Vygotsky, 1978, p. 57).

In this framework, social relations serve as the foundation for the development of all psychological functions, and internalization represents the primary mechanism for understanding the evolution of higher psychic functions.

Internalization can thus be conceptualized as the transformation of social phenomena into psychological ones. This thesis has clear implications for teaching and pedagogy. Vygotsky's historical-cultural view that higher psychic functions are internalized historical constructs underpins a pedagogical optimism that contradicts the pessimistic view based on innate gifts. Development is always possible under specific, adapted conditions. His work in defectology until his death, although rarely mentioned, is undoubtedly the specific proof of this optimism.

Vygotsky's most promising insights into the development and social origin of higher psychic functions can be found in his well-known notion of the zone of proximal development (ZPD). This notion posits that development is not limited to actual capabilities but rather encompasses potential capabilities. It also highlights the relationship between teaching/learning and development. Although this concept emerged in the context of a critique of aptitude tests, it is a heuristic concept for thinking about potential development. Engeström (1987) used it in a different, reworked form to think about the development of activity systems (see Chapter 9).

One error that is commonly made when measuring development is that it is assumed that the current capabilities or performance of an individual represent the full extent of their potential. This is why, in a developmental approach, we are not concerned with the outcomes or results of development; instead, we focus on the potential for development (Dafermos, 2020). As Clot (2001, p. 256) notes, citing Vygotsky, *'Man is full every minute of unrealized possibilities.'* It is therefore necessary to discern the potential in the real to inform educational interventions and transformative methodologies in the workplace. Consequently, it is not the actual that should determine educational practices, but the potential.

In other words, if a child's level of development is determined by observing what he or she can do independently of a more advanced peer, only what has reached maturity is taken into account, and potential development is not considered.

> The state of development is never defined solely by what has ripened. If the gardener chooses to evaluate only the ripe or harvested fruit of the apple tree, he cannot determine the state of his orchard. Ripening trees must also be considered. The psychologist must not limit his analysis to mature functions. He must consider those that are still maturing. To fully assess the child's developmental state, the psychologist must take into account not only the current level of development, but also the zone of proximal development (Vygotski, 1987, pp. 208–209).

This undoubtedly calls for reflection on the means we use to analyze activity. Activity analysis must equip itself with the methodological means to shed light on the potential development of activity, as we will return to later. However, it is worth noting here that there is a very clear difference between the idea that activity analysis involves describing (phenomenologically or through observation) what *'subjects do'* in a work situation by the means of direct methods, and the idea that activity analysis should highlight the potential development of activity by the means of indirect methods. To paraphrase Vygotsky, the individual is full of unrealized possibilities every second. It is therefore evident that it is impossible to account for potential development solely by observing or describing the realization of an action.

Analysis by Unit Versus Analysis by Element

Unit analysis is undoubtedly one of Vygotsky's most significant contributions and occupies a pivotal position in the literature (Veresov, 1999). Unit analysis represents a challenge for CHAT and an object of debate and controversy. Each generation considers a qualitatively different unit of analysis as activity theory targets new issues. Nevertheless, the concept of analysis by unit represents a significant contribution made by Vygotsky in the latter part of his career:

> The requirements for units were formulated during the last period of Vygotsky's work, in Thinking and Speech (1934), but not before. That was a result of complex process of development that could be expressed as a development from dualism to monism in the methodology of analysis (Veresov, 1999, p. 193).

In fact, at the end of the 1920s, Vygotsky (1929) proposed a methodology that would break down the object of research into natural elements, in other words, an analysis by elements. This methodology was based on the comparison of humans to machines:

> Every cultural method of behavior, even the most complicated, can always be completely analyzed into its component nervous and psychic processes, just as every machine, in the last resort, can be reduced to a definite system of natural forces and processes. Therefore, the first task of scientific investigation, when it deals with some cultural method of behavior, must be the analysis of that method, i.e., its decomposition into component parts, which are natural psychological processes (Vygotsky, 1929, pp. 418–419).

Yastnisky notes the influence of Gestalt on Vygotsky's shift to unit analysis (Yasnitsky, 2018). However, Blunden (2023) argues that the idea of unit analysis and the germ cell (which he conceives of as synonymous) was taken from Marx's political economy analysis in '*Capital*.' For Marx, the commodity is the '*unit and germ*' of value. The understanding of how value arises from the commodity of productive labor is the foundation of the dynamics of capitalism. In this sense, the commodity is the smallest unit that allows us to understand the development of capitalism, as it contains a contradiction between exchange value and use value. Vygotsky refers to such an analysis in '*Thought and Speech*' (1934/1987). For Vygotsky, a unit of analysis following a holistic principle possesses the properties of the whole.

By basic units, we mean products of analysis such that, unlike the elements, they possess all the fundamental properties of the whole, and are living parts of this unity that can no longer be decomposed. The key to explaining the unique properties of water is not its chemical formula, but the study of molecules and molecular motion. Similarly, the true basic unit of biological analysis is the living cell, which retains all the fundamental properties of life inherent in the living organism (Vygotski, 1987, p. 54).

Consequently, these units of analysis must retain the qualities of the whole. To illustrate this point, Vygotsky draws upon an analogy from chemistry, wherein he questions the element-by-element method of analysis. He compares a unit to a water molecule, demonstrating that a unit cannot be understood by analyzing it element by element. A water molecule contains both oxygen and hydrogen atoms, and in order to understand its properties, a researcher must analyze it as a whole, as an indivisible unit. Otherwise, if we were to treat it by the elements of which it is composed, it would no longer be water, but a simple sum of two distinct substances with properties far removed from the whole formed by the molecule.

The scientist would be astonished to discover that hydrogen itself burns and that oxygen sustains combustion and would never be able to explain the properties of the whole from the properties of these elements. In the same way, psychology, which breaks down verbal thought into individual elements in order to explain its most essential properties, which characterize it precisely as a whole, will then search in vain for these elements specific to the whole. In the course of the analysis, they have evaporated, vanished into thin air, and all that's left is to look for an external mechanical interaction between the elements in order to reconstruct with its help, by a purely speculative route, the vanished properties it wants to explain (Vygotski, 1987, pp. 51–52).

Rather than the '*dismemberment*' (p. 51) that Vygotsky deems not to be '*an analysis in the true sense of the word*' (p. 52), it is necessary to resort to basic units that '*possess the fundamental properties of the whole and are living parts of this unity that can no longer be decomposed*' (p. 53). For Vygotsky, two characteristics define this fundamental unit: its indivisibility and its movement. Consequently, '*The key to understanding the distinctive properties of water lies not in its chemical composition, but in the study of molecules and molecular motion*' (p. 54).

In '*Thought and Speech*', Vygotsky proposes that the meaning of a word can serve as a unit of analysis for studying the relationship between thought and speech. Indeed, meaning is the domain of language insofar as a word without meaning is just a sound. However, meaning is also a psychological phenomenon, insofar as the meaning of a word is already a form of generalization. To illustrate, when a young child verbally refers to a dog, he or she is referring to an exemplary, singular animal belonging to the category of dogs in general. Meaning is thus both language and thought and is a useful unit for investigating the development of the relationship between thought and speech.

However, the units of analysis are not universal and must be specified in relation to the phenomena under study. For instance, Vygotsky's concept of 'Perezhivanie' (Blunden, 2016a, 2016b; Jornet & Roth, 2016; Veresov & Fleer, 2016) can be identified as a unit of analysis in his work on pedology (Vygotsky, 2019) pertaining to the relationship between a child and the environment.

The Need to Expand the Unit of Analysis?

The unit of analysis is also a point of contention among those who continue Vygotsky's work or claim to adhere to this orientation. For instance, Wertsch (1994) proposes that the unit of analysis for a sociocultural approach seeking '*The ways in which human action is intrinsically linked to cultural, institutional, and historical contexts*' (p. 203) should be mediated action. Instrument-mediated action represents a manageable unit of analysis that addresses the limitations of Vygotsky's proposal to make the meaning of the word the appropriate unit of analysis for investigating the development of consciousness (Wertsch, 1985).

> It becomes clear that Vygotsky's account of word meaning is not a good unit for analyzing the development of human consciousness. It does not provide the theoretical mechanisms needed to understand how the natural and social lines of development enter into emergent interactionism. Rather, Vygotsky used it primarily to explain the onset and development of the social line (Wertsch, 1985, p. 198).

In light of the fact that cultural, institutional, and historical contexts provide the instruments that shape human mental functioning, mediated action (through instruments or signs) constitutes a unit conducive to pursuing the Vygotskian project, as well as being more coherent with Vygotsky's overall project, according to Wertsch (1994).

The essence of mediated action is that it involves a kind of tension between the mediational means as provided in the sociocultural setting, and the unique contextualized use of these means in carrying out particular, concrete actions. In this view, any attempt to reduce this basic unit of analysis to the mediational means or to the individual in isolation is misguided (Wertsch, 1994, p. 205).

In a similar vein, Engeström, although not employing the same unit of analysis, also considers mediated action to be the unit of analysis for a first generation of Vygotskian-inspired work. However, this unit of analysis remains focused on the individual and interpersonal relations. In this vein, Bakhurst (2023, p. 224) notes somewhat harshly that '*despite its emphasis on the socio-cultural foundations of psychological development, Vygotsky's thinking remains centered on the individual subject conceived as a discrete, autonomous person.*'[5] In the same way, Engeström (2015, p. xiv) notes that the limitation of the first generation was that the unit of analysis remained centered on the individual.

Let us now add an important point that will allow us to make the transition to the next chapter. In proposing instrument-mediated action as the unit of analysis, Wertsch (1985) draws on Leontiev's distinction between the levels of activity, action, and operations. However, while Wertsch relies on this breakdown of activity into levels of analysis, he does not take activity as the '*molar*' unit of analysis. This discrepancy is likely to be perceived as ironic by those who adhere to Leontiev's approach. As noted by Leontiev's son, quoted by Blunden:

Throughout, even within the framework of activity theory itself, an ambiguous understanding of the units and levels of activity organization can be seen… As is well known, A. N. Leontyev does not provide an explicit definition of it; as a rule, he puts the term '*unit*' within quotation marks, and in so doing, '*determines*' it. And this is justified: after all, as it applies to his point of view, the concept of unit has little applicability to activity, action, or operation, since it presumes their discrete nature. In A. N. Leontyev's conception, the only thing that can be called a '*unit*' in the strict sense is activity (an activity act). (N.N. Leontiev quoted in Blunden, 2010, p. 211)

Consequently, Leontiev's work and the theory of activity he proposes can be readily identified as a means of addressing this issue by

---

[5] We find Bakhurst's phrase very harsh in that, while Vygostky's work remains focused on individuals and social interactions, the individual does not seem to us to be at all discrete or totally autonomous.

extending the unit of analysis from instrument-mediated action to the activity traversed by the division of labor. In the following section, we shall provide evidence to support this position: activity, as understood by Leontiev and then Engeström, constitutes the unit of analysis for three main reasons.

Firstly, activity is both an *'elementary brick'* of human society as a whole and a constituent of individual life. We share Stetsenko's (2017) ontological view that the social world, society, is made up of activities interacting with each other. Moreover, it is in activity and active participation in activity systems that subjects acquire the instruments and tools of culture and shape themselves. Thus, activity is the interface between society and the individual, enabling individual development.

Secondly, activity is historical in nature and develops over time. It carries within it the roots and seeds of both individual development and the development of society as a whole.

Thirdly, as we shall see, activity is a molar, indecomposable unit that evolves and develops via relationships between different levels. The analysis of activity needs to apprehend these levels and the contradictions that bear within them the seeds of future developments. Consequently, a unit of analysis cannot do without contradictions as an analytical concept for identifying future developments. Here again, the influence of Vygotskian experimentation is important: an analysis of activity aims to shed light on what the activity may become, its potential development, in other words, its future functioning based on its historical trajectory, rather than to explain why the activity is what it is, in other words, its present functioning based on its past historical trajectory.

Finally, it should be noted that expansion of the unit of analysis does not mean rejection of the principles underlying its definition. Vygotsky's concept of basic unity derived from dialectical thinking is based on the idea of an elementary *'brick,'* which is indivisible, riddled with contradictions and as a result in motion.

Chapter 3

The Second Generation of CHAT: Leontiev's Work

Nowhere was activity marked as to which science it belongs to (Leontiev, 1978, p. 55).
Leontyev made it possible to take Activity Theory from the domain of psychology into social theory as such, even though he himself remained a psychologist and his own incursions into social theory were miserable (Blunden, 2023, p. 31).

When Cultural-Historical Theory Becomes Activity Theory: The Kharkov School

The early 1930s constituted a pivotal moment in the development of the CHAT. Stalinist repression spread to all spheres of society. The initial group formed in Moscow by the '*Troika*' (Vygotsky, Luria and Leontiev) disbanded, and numerous Vygotsky associates and students relocated to Kharkov in Ukraine (then the capital of Soviet Ukraine) under Leontiev's guidance. This group became known as the '*Kharkov School of Psychology*,' which refers to a group of post-Vygotsky scholars and research carried out not only in Kharkov but also in Moscow and Leningrad over a period stretching from the early 1930s to the Second World War. Yasnitsky and Ferrari (2008) posit that the role of the Kharkov School is pivotal, given the significant theoretical advancements of the 1960s and 1970s (with authors such as Davydov, Lektorsky, and Ilyenkov).

Vygotsky, although maintaining contact with Kharkov researchers, remained in Moscow, and the divergence between Vygotsky and Leontiev was not only geographical but also theoretical. Yasnitsky (2018, pp. 116–117) relates the following episode. In December 1932, Vygotsky organized an internal conference with his collaborators, calling for the elaboration of a new psychological theory of consciousness. In contrast to the work of the Kharkov School, which focused on children's practical activity, Vygotsky's proposal to reorganize the research program was perceived by his colleagues as a '*radical theoretical step backwards*' tinged with idealism. This same criticism led to the banning of Vygotsky's work until the end of the Stalinist period[6].

Leontiev, who had been Vygotsky's student in Moscow, gradually diverged from the Vygotskian orientation and sought to develop his own theory. The concept of activity became central to the theoretical orientation of the Kharkov School, although it should be noted that the concept had already been introduced earlier by Rubinstein (Mironenko, 2013) independently of Vygotsky and the Kharkov School.

The divergence between Leontiev and Vygotsky can be succinctly summarized (Bratus, 2022). For Leontiev, it was a question of revisiting the initial theses of the Moscow group and developing them in new directions to study practical intelligence, that is, objective action. In contrast, Vygotsky remained focused on the study of consciousness, revisiting the traditions of affect and emotion, and turning more towards Spinoza in the latter period of his life (Roth & Jornet, 2016) to overcome the separation between intellect and affect, thought and speech.

This opposition between the Vygotskian and Leontievian approach serves as the backdrop for a recent controversy between Clot and Schwartz in the '*Revue Philosophique de la France et de l'étranger*'. For Clot (2015, p. 206) '*Yves Schwartz misplaces the psychological tradition opened up by Vygotski. He is too hasty to place him solely within the intellectualist lineage of German Tätigkeit (2007), whereas he borrows the essentials from Spinoza*'. In response, Schwartz (2015) asserts that it is reasonable to posit that the Marxian reconceptualization of Tätigkeit permeated the entirety of Soviet psychology, with varying content contingent upon the author, including Vygotsky.

Ultimately, Leontiev continued the Vygotskian line while distancing himself from it (Nechaev, 2022). He developed it by reappropriating the concept of productive social activity (Tätigkeit) in his materialist interpretation:

---

[6]   This banishment of Vygotsky's work is discussed in current literature. In one chapter, Fraser and Yasnitsky (2015) question the idea of an official ban on Vygotsky's writings, while Maidansky (2021) strongly criticizes this position in his review of the work.

By introducing the concept of activity into the theory of knowledge, Marx gave it a strictly materialist meaning: for Marx, activity in its initial and fundamental form is the sensible practical activity by which man comes into practical contact with the objects of the surrounding world, experiences their resistance and acts upon them by conforming to their objective properties. Therein lies the radical difference between the Marxist theory of activity and the idealist theory, which conceives of activity only in its abstract, speculative form (Leontiev, 1975/2021, p. 23).

By adopting the concept of activity as the central concept of their theory, Leontiev and his colleagues asserted the necessity of focusing on practical, material activity to comprehend and analyze the genesis and emergence of higher psychic functions. As stated by Kozulin (1984, p. 23): '*Vygotsky's thesis that the psychological tool is a point of mediation between objects of action and mental functions was replaced by the thesis that physical action mediates between the subject and the external world*'. After Leontiev's departure from Moscow and his break with Vygotsky, the concept of activity gained conceptual consistency and gradually differentiated itself from that of action:

> In contrast to Vygotsky, who concentrated his attention on the study of the role of the interaction between speech and thinking (and meaning making) for development of consciousness, the Kharkov school members emphasized the investigation of human practical activity. In fact, the members of the Kharkov School proposed a version of activity theory as an endeavor to investigate external, objective activity and its influence on the development of mental actions (Dafermos, 2018, p. 201).

To fully comprehend the distinction between the usage of the notion of activity and the evolution of its conceptual content during this period, it is essential to identify the obstacles to interpretation in Russian and the ensuing translation challenges. Mironenko (2013) notes that Leontiev's theory of activity is the recognized translated form of *Dejatelnost theory*, but that the branch of studies from Rubinstein through Vygotsky to Leontiev is called the *Sub'ekt approach* in Russian literature (p. 378). Additionally, there is a third term that can be related to the notion of activity and is sometimes translated as such: *Aktivnost*.

The use of these three terms suggests different meanings and underpins important differences between the main authors of activity theory. The term *sub'ekt* is used to indicate that the psyche is produced through an individual's active interaction with their environment. Vygotsky, for example, suggests that the child actively enters culture, appropriating elements from the outside for their own needs by internalizing them. This process is therefore referred to as the self-determined nature of human behavior.

Roth (2014) makes a clear distinction between the terms *dejatelnost* and *aktivnost*. *Dejatelnost* constitutes a unit of analysis insofar as it contains all the characteristics of society. In contrast, *aktivnost* refers to a vital activity devoid of object. Leontiev uses the German equivalents of the two terms (*Tätigkeit* and *Aktivitat*, respectively) to clarify these differences. For instance, he critiques the two-term Stimulus-Response scheme of behaviorism as an abstraction that excludes activity as a process linking the subject to the material world:

> The deficiency of this scheme lies in its exclusion of the content-bearing process that establishes the subject's real connections with the world of objects – his object-type activity (*Tatigkeit*, in contrast to Aktivitat). Such an abstraction from the subject's real situation is justifiable only within the narrow limits of a laboratory experiment seeking to clarify elementary psychophysiological mechanisms, and we have only to go beyond these narrow limits to see its groundlessness (Leontiev, 1974, p. 6).

Veresov (2005) notes that, while Vygotsky occasionally employed the term *dejatelnost* prior to 1927, he did so in a manner derived from Pavlov's physiology, specifically in its sense of *aktivnost*. The distinction between the two concepts is of paramount importance to Leontiev and subsequent generations of the CHAT.

With Leontiev and the work of the Kharkov School, the scope of the problems dealt with was extended beyond the limits of psychology in the narrow sense, explicitly taking societal phenomena into account. The Kharkov School's efforts focused on a version of activity theory that could explain and analyze objective external activity and its influence on the development of the psyche. Accordingly, they conducted a substantial body of experimental research under Leontiev's supervision, employing novel theoretical frameworks to investigate the problem of activity. The principles that emerged during this period are as follows:

- (1) Psychological functions are the result of the internalization of external activity processes. It is a derivative of the external process, the internalized external process.
- (2) The structure of psychological processes is isomorphic to the structure of external activity, of which the psyche is a derivative.

These two principles are not fully shared by Vygotsky and Rubinstein. This is undoubtedly the reason for the intellectual rift between Vygotsky and Leontiev, on the one hand, and Leontiev and Rubinstein on the other (Martins, 2013).

It is not necessary to delve into the specifics of the opposing views to emphasize that Leontiev and the Kharkov Psychological School were developing a line of research that was partly independent of the work initiated in Moscow under Vygotsky's supervision (Mironenko, 2013). This change of direction complicated the relationship between Vygotsky's early work and the Kharkov School. Moreover, Vygotsky's position became untenable in the social and political context of the 1930s in the USSR, where his work and its emphasis on sign and language could be suspected of idealism (a view that is, of course, highly debatable).

Against this backdrop, the work of the Kharkov School and Leontiev revisited the work of the late 1920s in Moscow, while extending it in a new direction with the concept of activity. Blunden (2010) notes that Vygotsky's mobilization of the concept of instrumented action played a role in the construction of the concept of activity in Leontiev's psychology:

> Vygotsky did not develop the differentiation between action and activity which we owe to Leontyev, but Vygotsky did have a concept of action and his concept of action shall play a crucial role in the critique and reconstruction of the concept of activity (Blunden, 2010, p. 189).

Researchers working in this direction have sought to avoid two dangers that could be considered antagonistic: on the one hand, subjectivism, by seeking to move psychology away from the boundaries of consciousness or a focus on it, and on the other, behaviorism. These two dangers are avoided by recourse to the materialist concept of activity.

> To avoid subjectivism it was necessary to keep constantly in mind the idea of the primacy of external activity; and so as not to fall into behaviorism, it was necessary to determine the psychological components in external activity itself. What unquestionably psychological components can be singled out in activity that is sense-bearing although objective? (Gal'perin, 1984, p. 59).

These psychological components of practical external activity are based on the distinction between the external objective goal and the actor's actual desires, which determine the actor's specific modes of action, i.e. his motive. In this theoretical orientation, goal and motive do not coincide, and the relationship between motive and goal constitutes the meaning that an activity has for the actor.

This consideration and focus on practical external activity distinguish Leontiev from Vygotsky. For Haenen (1995), Leontiev complained that it is impossible to find the cause of the development of meaning in social interaction itself, and devoted himself to discovering what lies behind social interaction, concluding that the origin of consciousness must be found in external activity.

However, a comparison of Vygotsky's contribution with that of Leontiev is not entirely accurate from a historical perspective. Several positions need to be highlighted here. The first position is to highlight the discontinuities and differences in direction of these approaches. The second position highlights the continuity between the two approaches, emphasizing, for example, the extent to which Vygotsky's historical-cultural theory was an essential condition for the development of activity theory, which is its continuation. The term *'Cultural-Historical Activity Theory'* (CHAT) has been chosen to designate a line of research that avoids opposing the two approaches.

> It has been common in recent years to emphasize differences between Vygotsky and Luria, on the one hand, and Leontiev on the other (Van der Veer & Valsiner, 1991). According to such interpretations, Vygotsky and Luria are best associated with the principle that the distinguishing characteristic of specifically human psychological functions is that they are culturally mediated: *'The central fact of human existence is mediation'* (Vygotsky, 1997c: 138). By contrast, so the story goes, Leontiev believed that his colleagues overemphasized the cultural mediation of thought and underemphasized the embeddedness of thought in human activity. It might be argued that a significant disagreement exists to this day among those who consider Vygotsky and his colleagues as a starting point for construct-ing a theory of human development and those who start with Leontiev (1978) [...] The basic impulse underlying a CH/AT approach is to reject this either/or dichotomy. Instead, adherents of a CH/AT perspective argue that whatever their disagreements, Leontiev (1981) readily acknowledges the constitutive role of cultural mediation in his account of activity while Vygotsky insisted on the importance of activity as the context of mediated action (Cole & Engeström, 2007, p. 485).

In this orientation, which consists in not opposing Leontiev's approach to that of Vygotsky, Leontiev's son notes that Leontiev's entire approach to activity theory is contained in the germ of Vygotsky's approach. He notes that all the fundamental tenets of Leontiev's activity theory are encapsulated within Vygotsky's theory. However, in the psychological dictionary he co-authored with Varshava, Vygotsky does not utilize the term *'activity,'* instead employing the terms *'action'* and *'operation'* in alternation. He adds:

> In one way or another, in 1930 Vygotsky indisputably was on his way to the creation of activity theory; hence, any attempt to oppose his views to the views of his school, in particular, the Kharkov group of psychologists, is quite groundless (Leontiev, 1995, p. 36).

The analysis presented by Bakhurst (2023) in a recent essay is noteworthy for elucidating the relationship between the Kharkov group and the work of Vygotsky, who passed away in 1934. Despite the 1936 decree of the Central Committee banning *'pedology'* and outlawing Vygotsky's work, the Kharkovites were unable to evade official criticism. This was a matter of survival and existence. However, by addressing criticism of Vygotsky's work as a form of defense against the Stalinist climate of the time, they produced a critique of the supposed weaknesses of their master's work that, paradoxically, gave Vygotsky a voice and enabled his work to survive a period of banishment.

> The concept of activity was brought to prominence by Vygotsky's students as part of an attempt to defend the general Vygotskian framework against this objection. To save the paradigm, and themselves, his followers rebuilt his psychology around the notion of predmetnaya deyatel'nost', usually translated as *'object-orientated activity'* (Bakhurst, 2023, p. 309).

In accordance with the second perspective, which perceives continuity between Vygotsky and Leontiev, this chapter has been designated as a *'second generation'* of CHAT. However, this position is not universally accepted. Iaroshevskii (1995) asserts that Vygotsky is regarded as the founder of activity theory, even though he never explicitly mentioned it in his work (cited in Nechaev, 2022, p. 45).

Leontiev's Stages in the Formation of the Activity Concept

Chaiklin (2019) identifies four periods in the construction of the concept of activity (Table 1). The first period corresponds to the work undertaken with Vygotsky and Luria in Moscow, whose main features we described in the previous section. This underlines the roots of Leontiev's work in the principles developed during this period, as well as the theoretical continuity between the two authors.

As evidenced by the historical record, the concept of activity was already being utilized in Russian psychology in the early 1920s. Introduced in the early 1920s by Rubinstein, it represented a novel approach at the time, introducing the principle of the (dialectical) unity of consciousness and activity. At this time, Leontiev was engaged in collaborative research with Luria and Vygotsky at the Moscow Institute of Psychology, where Kornilov had replaced Chepanov as director in 1923. The Institute's primary objective at the time was to develop a Marxist psychology. González Rey (2020, p. 81) notes that during this period, the concept of activity was only embraced by Rubinstein, who consistently opposed Kornilov's stance. It was during the subsequent period following Leontiev's departure for Kharkov that his work was formalized, from which the renowned example of primitive hunting was derived. This example will be presented in the following section, along with a detailed analysis of its structure. Upon initial examination, this example appears to be an attempt to describe the structure of external work activity and to differentiate it from that of animals. Two characteristics of human work activity are highlighted: on the one hand, its instrumental character, and on the other, its collective nature, based on a division of labor functions.

The third period is a stagnant one, during which no new qualitative ideas are introduced. However, it was during this period that '*The Development of the Mind*' (Leontiev, 1959/1976, 1981) was published.

Finally, the fourth period saw a reformulation of the central concepts of activity. It was marked by numerous publications that preceded the formulation of the theory of activity in Activity, Consciousness, Personality (Leontiev, 1975/2021).

Table 1: Four main periods in the development of the concept of activity in Leontiev's work, after Chaiklin (2019, p. 18).

PERIOD	NAME GIVEN TO THE PERIOD	MAIN EVENTS
1925–1931	Initial period.	Engagement with the general problem of realizing a Marxist psychology and overcoming the crisis in psychology.

Table 1: Continued

PERIOD	NAME GIVEN TO THE PERIOD	MAIN EVENTS
1932–1949	Conceptual period.	Explicit formulation of the activity structure.
1950–1968	Stagnant period.	Minimal development by Leontiev.
1969–1979	Final formulation period.	Introduction of personality-centeredness.

For Leontiev (1981), activity can be understood as a hierarchical system comprising three interdependent levels: activity, action, and operations. In *The Development of the Mind* (1981), Leontiev traces the development of human activity, differentiating it from, or contrasting it with, animal activity. For him, work is characterized by two main features that clearly distinguish it from animal activity. The first is the manufacture and use of tools. The second is that work is always a collective activity, mediating man's relationship with nature:

> The second feature of the labor process is that it is performed in conditions of joint, collective activity, so that man functions in this process not only in a certain relationship with nature but also to other people, members of a given society. Only through a relation with other people does man relate to nature itself, which means that labor appears from the very beginning as a process mediated by tools (in the broad sense) and at the same time mediated socially (Leontiev, 1981, p. 208).

Leontiev's Specific Features of Human Activity

As previously discussed in Chapter 2, Vygotsky and Luria conducted a comprehensive analysis of the transition from animal to human in the late 1930s (Vygotsky & Luria, 1992). In this chapter, we revisit the thesis from another angle, focusing on the concept of Tätigkeit, which is '*central to Leontiev*' (Sève, 2008, p. 356).

The Centrality of the Concept of Tätigkeit

The concept of *Tätigkeit* (or productive activity) is central to Marx's work. A concept of German idealism, it is repositioned within a materialist framework by Marx. For Sève, Marxian thought is a '*materialism of Tätigkeit*' (Sève, 2014, p. 196). For Marx, it is not the tool that defines the essence of Tätigkeit, but its integration into social labor and its social division of labor. One branch of this division is toolmaking. In other words, the tool-making actions inherent in one activity extend into a new, interdependent activity that is distinct insofar as it does not have the same object.

Roth (2008) employs the example of primitive hunting, described in this chapter, to illustrate this process. The production of spears for the purpose of hunting is a moment prior to and included in the collective hunt. However, for reasons that are not entirely clear, hunters who no longer participate in the collective hunt or are unable to do so engage in tool-making. This tool-making tends to become autonomous, becoming an activity that produces the means of production for the hunting activity. The tool-making activity becomes autonomous from the food-producing activity (hunting), while at the same time they are interdependent. The interdependence of these two activities implies exchange actions (originally bartering, for example), which can themselves become an autonomous activity: trade. The primitive form of exchange (barter) gives rise to the distinction between exchange value and use value. In this sense, exchange value is a property of the commodity that enables it to be exchanged, even though the two commodities have different use values.

This is the context in which we can understand Leontiev's subsequent remark, which introduces the example of hunting:

> Already at the earliest time in the evolution of human society, a division of the previously single process of activity between the separate participants in production inevitably arose. Originally this division seemingly had a chance, impermanent character. In the course of subsequent evolution, it took shape already as a primitive technical division of labor (Leontiev, 1981, p. 209).

For Sève, the centrality of man's productive activity allows for the explanation of the revolution in human efficiency, the equally exponential development of human capacities, and finally the constitution of a cultural world (Sève, 2014, pp. 286–287).

The concept of Tätigkeit, or activity, is therefore defined by a dual mediation: firstly, by the tool (or means of production) and secondly, by the social relationship. This dual mediation is also a central tenet of Vygotsky's work, as previously highlighted. It is evident that mediation through the instruments at the heart of his method is of significant importance, but it is also evident that mediation through others in the zone of proximal development is equally crucial. His emphasis on the individual does not negate the collective; rather, it represents its superior form:

> The individual and personal are not in opposition, but a higher form of sociality. To paraphrase Marx: the psychological nature of man is the totality of social relations shifted to the inner sphere and having become functions of the personality and forms of its structure (Vygotsky, 1989, p. 59).

By focusing on the sign, Vygotsky generalizes and distinguishes the idea of mediation by tools. If the tool is turned outwards, the sign is turned inwards (Vygotski, 2014). Thus, historically inherited cumulative mediations in tools and signs make possible the development of human subjective capacities. However, there is a difference between Leontiev and Vygotsky in this regard. The latter's emphasis on communication, the first on external practical activity. As Blunden emphasizes:

> Vygotsky always focused his scientific work on interactions between individuals, rather than using representations of societal phenomena and institutions abstracted from their constitution in specific forms of the activity of human beings. This is his strength and does not detract from the significance of his work for understanding societal activities. After all, societal institutions exist only in and through individual actions and interactions between individuals. All the essential aspects of the concept of activity are present in Vygotsky's concept of joint artifact-mediated action (Blunden, 2010, p. 199).

Leontiev's approach was to reintroduce the concept of Tätigkeit at the core of his psychology, clearly differentiating it from that of Aktivitat. Ultimately, he proposed a materialist theory of Tätigkeit in psychology. With Leontiev, the distinction between activity and action is paramount. If actions are the fundamental element of activity, activity must be distinguished from the actions that comprise it, as two distinct realities that do not coincide. For Leontiev, '*Properly psychological research cannot dispense with the study of external activity itself, of its structure*', and '*it is not possible to explain scientifically the nature and peculiarities of psychic reflection other than by relying on the study of these external processes*' (Leontiev, 1975/2021, p. 190).

In the subsequent sections, the external processes will be elucidated. Initially, the use of tools will be examined, followed by an investigation of collective mediation through the division of labor.

First Feature: The Use of Tools

On the use of tools, we choose here to begin with an example borrowed from Latour (2010)[7] to understand how the use of tools is a specific feature of human activity. Latour is a philosopher and sociologist whose work is difficult to categorize. He is particularly interested in technical objects and innovations. In his book *Cogitamus,* he engages in a dialogue with a student who did not attend his lecture. The student's task is to summarize the lecture in his absence. In the second of his lectures, he endeavors to direct his students' attention to the material dimension of their existence. To this end, he employs a thought exercise after a presentation of videos of baboons. Baboons are highly social animals. In humans, as in baboons, there is no course of action that is not social, yet does not mobilize a technical device:

> To make them feel this contrast, I ask the students, after I've shown them the films, to think of themselves there in the amphitheater, and to mentally remove, one by one, all the objects they have to pass through in order to communicate with each other, until they are in the same state of destitution as the baboons in the film […] And when I ask them how they are going to feed themselves now, they are all stunned and forbidden: everything that comes their way has to be fetched. And when I ask them how they're going to feed themselves now, they're all stunned and forbidden: everything that comes their way, they have to fetch, and sometimes very far away […] disciplines that don't take technical detours into account may be very interesting, but […] they're about baboons, not people. The humanities without technology are nothing but baboons (Latour, 2010, pp. 58–59).

Beyond the extreme technical complexity of our everyday actions, the difference between the use of tools by animals and humans lies in the fact that this use of tools is part of a collective activity and to some extent regulates the relationships between the beings that make it up.

> Even with an artificial specialized human tool, an ape therefore acts only within the narrow limits of the instinctive modes of its activity. In the hands of man, on the contrary, the simplest natural object often becomes a real tool, i.e., realizes a genuinely implemental, socially developed operation

---

[7] However, when considering Latour, it is important to note that his network actor theory differs from CHAT. For a detailed examination of the key distinctions between network actor theory and CHAT, please refer to the works of Engeström (1996c) and Miettinen (1999).

[…] A tool is thus a social object, is the product of social practice and of social labor experience. The generalized reflection of the objective properties, too, of the instruments of labor, which are crystallized in it, are thus also the product of social rather than individual practice. Even the simplest human knowledge that still comes about in a directly practical labor action, in an action by means of tools, is consequently not limited to man's personal experience, but comes about on the basis (Leontiev, 1959/1976, pp. 75–76).

In Leontiev's conceptualization, tools and artifacts are the product of a historical past as much as the material foundation of present-day activity. The utilization of tools by human beings differs significantly from the auxiliary means employed by animals. This theme is central to Galperine's 1938 thesis in Kharkov (Galperine et al., 2023), which reveals the research program of the Kharkov School conducted under Leontiev's supervision. In this thesis, which was rediscovered in 2020 and published only very recently, Galperine suggests that the difference between the use of tools by humans and animals lies in the functional significance of the tools used. Tools created and used by humans contain a cultural and historical experience that must be mastered in order to use the tool properly. Human engagement with these tools reorganizes existing psychological functions and encourages the development of new ones.

In the Vygotskian tradition, whose themes he had mastered by the early 1930s, Galperine nevertheless develops the Vygotskian line of research insofar as he inaugurates an extension of the internalization process and a focus on external practical activity and tool use. In this sense, Galperine's work can be seen as the missing link between Vygotsky's and Leontiev's work. Galperine's emphasis on tools mobilized in external practice and actions in the formation of the psychological mechanisms of human activity, which became the basis of his activity theory, aligns with Leontiev's emphasis on tools in external practice and actions. This is a crucial point, as previously mentioned in the preceding chapter, in which Vygotsky, in contrast to Leontiev, did not consider the tool to be equivalent to the sign. In fact, he was even opposed to it from a certain perspective. The tool is directed outward and toward the object, functioning as a means of action. In contrast, the sign is directed inward and serves as a means of affecting internal activity to gain self-control.

Second Feature: Work as a Form of Collective Activity. The Example of Hunting

Comparing animal activity to human activity, Leontiev notes that:

> However complex animals' '*tool*' activity, it never has the character of a social process, is not performed collectively, and does not itself govern a relationship of community among the individuals performing it. On the other hand, however complicated the instinctive contact between the individuals who make up an animal association, it is never built on the basis of their 'productive' activity, does not depend on it, and is not mediated by it. In contradiction, human labor is a social activity from the beginning, based on the co-operation of individuals, assuming a technical division, even though rudimentary, of labor functions; labor consequently is a process of action on nature linking together its participants, and mediating their contact (Leontiev, 1981, p. 209).

To illustrate this specificity of human work activity, Leontiev (1981) uses an example that has become famous and discussed in international literature, namely that of primitive hunting (Lémonie, 2023). We will summarize it in a few lines by producing an extract, before drawing some consequences for the analysis of work activity:

> Leontiev (1981, pp. 201–211)
>
> It is sufficient, in order to comprehend the concrete significance of this fact for the development of the human psyche, to analyze how the structure of activity is altered when it is performed in conditions of collective labor. Already at the earliest time in the evolution of human society, a division of the previously single process of activity between the separate participants in production inevitably arose. Originally this division seemingly had a chance, impermanent character. In the course of subsequent evolution, it took shape already as a primitive technical division of labor. It now fell to the lot of some individuals, for example, to maintain the fire and to cook food on it, and of others to procure the food itself. Some of those taking part in the collective hunt fulfilled the function of pursuing game, others the function of wailing for it in ambush and attacking it.
>
> This led to a decisive, radical change in the very structure of the activity of the individuals taking part in the labor process. [...] Let us now examine the fundamental structure of the individual's

activity in the conditions of a collective labor process from this standpoint. When a member of a group performs his lab our activity, he also does it to satisfy one of his needs. A beater, for example, taking part in a primeval collective hunt, was stimulated b y a need for food or, perhaps, a need for clothing, which the skin of the dead animal would meet for him. At what, however, was his activity directly aimed? It may have been directed, for example, at frightening a herd of animals and sending them toward other hunters, hiding in ambush. That, properly speaking, is what should be the result of the activity of this man. And the activity of this individual member of the hunt ends with that. The rest is completed by the other members. This result, i.e., the frightening of game, etc. understandably does not in itself, and may not, lead to the satisfaction of the beater's need for food, or the skin of the animal. What the processes of his activity were directed to did not, consequently, coincide with what stimulated them, i.e., did not coincide with the motive of his activity; the two were divided from one another in this instance. Processes, the object and motive of which do not coincide with one another, we shall call 'actions.' We can say, for example, that the beater's activity is the hunt, and the frightening of game his action.

How is it possible for action to arise, i.e., for there to be a division between the object of activity and its motive?

It obviously only becomes possible in a joint, collective process of acting on nature. The product of the process as a whole, which meets the need of the group, also leads to the satisfaction of the needs of the separate individual as well, although he himself may not perform the final operations (e.g. the direct attack on the game and the killing of it), which directly lead to possession of the object of the given need. Genetically (i.e., in its origin) the separation of the object and motive of individual activity is a result of the exarticulating of the separate operations from a previous complex, polyphase, but single activity. These same separate operations, by now completing the content of the individual's given activity, are also transformed into independent actions for him, although they continue, as regards the collective labor process as a whole, of course, to be only some of its partial links.

In order to illustrate Leontiev's example, we must first define the term 'action.' According to Leontiev, an action is defined as a process whose object and motive do not coincide. This definition is derived from Leontiev's 1981 work, in which he states, '*We shall call actions those processes whose object and motive do not coincide*' (p. 210).

In Figure 5, the animal's object is the bush. It makes noise to produce food. It should also be noted that the object and expected goal of the reel do not coincide with the underlying motive of the collective activity. The production of food implies actions other than the mere killing of game. For Leontiev, and in accordance with the principles of his theory, '*Action is only possible within a collective process acting on nature*' (Leontiev, 1981, p. 210). This collective process is an activity.

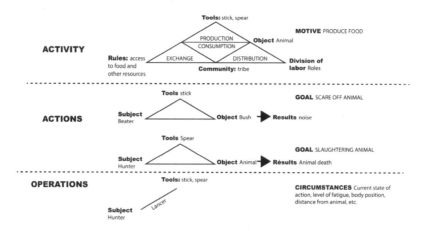

Figure 5: Representation of the three hierarchical levels of activity (collective), actions (individual) and operations in the example of hunting (Leontiev, 1959/1976) according to (Roth, 2008).

Leontiev's example of primitive hunting helps us to grasp the hierarchical structure of activity and the relationship between the level of collective activity (hunting), the level of individual actions (killing the game), and the level of operations that carry them out. Motivated activities are concretely realized through conscious, goal-oriented actions.

The relationship between these two levels is mutually constitutive (i.e. dialectical). On the one hand, goals and actions exist because they realize a particular activity; but, activity exists only in and through its realization through a sequence of actions. In other words, each level exists only in relation to the other levels.

In other words, the meaning of an action is related to the activity it partly performs; if the same action performs a different activity, it has a different meaning. There is a second constitutive relationship: between conscious actions and unconscious operations. An action exists only if it is performed by a sequence of operations; these operations are produced only because there is already a conscious goal.

This distinction between activity and action is important, even fundamental, for CHAT (Greeno & Engeström, 2014). Activities are formations that persist but also evolve over time. Actions, on the other hand, are limited in time and oriented towards conscious goals. This is where the fundamental difference between situated approaches, which take the situation as the unit of analysis, and activity theory comes into play. The situation is a concept that is both spatially and temporally limited. Temporally, it refers to series or sets of actions and interactions. Spatially, it refers to what is significant for an actor at a given moment. However, actions take place within institutions and organizations that have a historical trajectory and are subject to change and transformation over the course of their history.

Thus, for CHAT, the unit of analysis is not the individual action, but the activity, which has a structure, a history, and possibilities for future transformation. In this orientation, the activity is a '*molar, non-additive unit*' (Leontiev, 1975/2021). The context of an action is thus not the (work) situation, but the activity as a historical formation in which actions are inscribed and to which they contribute. Activity is thus the unit of analysis, the elementary building block for the analysis of life in society.

For Leontiev, activity is seen as a collective, historical formation and provides the objective material basis for actions that would otherwise become meaningless and totally unjustified. The hierarchical representation of the structure of activity can be seen graphically in the Figure 6 below:

Figure 6: Representation of the activity's hierarchical structure.

Let's look at operations: They depend on circumstances, on the situation. From this point of view, operations are not mediated but directly related to the objective relations of the situation (Roth, 2007). This direct relationship makes it possible to mobilize approaches derived from theories of nonlinear dynamic systems to analyze them (Lémonie, 2019), to the extent that these frameworks prove to be fully compatible with CHAT (Thelen & Smith, 1996). Indeed, nonlinear dynamic approaches build on the early work of the renowned activity physiologist Bernstein, who was part of the first Vygotskian circle in Moscow (Yasnitsky, 2011) and emphasize the variability of the operations that perform actions (Lémonie, 2019). We'll return to this point in this chapter.

As with the relationship between activity and actions, the relationship between operations and actions is dialectical: actions are realized by operations, just as actions are forms of attractors for operations that depend on circumstances (fatigue, body positioning, distance from the game, state of the game, etc., to take just a few examples related to primitive hunting).

Human Activity Is Collective. The Multiplicity of Interpretations of the Hunting Example

It should be noted that this interpretation of the famous hunting example is widely debated within the community. While the authors who have continued Leontiev's work (Engeström, Bødker, see next section) rely on this example to define activity as necessarily collective, other authors (e.g. Kaptelinin, 2005) points to the need to reintegrate this example into Leontiev's project, namely the development of a psychology that does not cut the subject off from society. In this interpretation, activity is not collective, but primarily individual-social. For Kaptelinin (2005):

> The focus on the individual is determined by the fact that Leontiev developed activity theory within a primarily psychological framework and the category of activity was introduced and explored by Leontiev in the context of psychology (Kaptelinin, 2005, p. 9).

But we don't agree with this claim. Just because Leontiev is a psychologist doesn't mean that he focuses '*primarily*' on individual activity. On the contrary, for Leontiev, human activity is collective because it involves a division of labor. In this context, his aim is to reinstate activity (and especially productive and collective activity) as a psychological category, insofar as it makes it possible to introduce into psychology units of analysis that carry within them the psychic reflet in its inseparability from the elements of human activity that generate it and are mediated by it (Leontiev, 1981). For Leontiev, in the example of hunting, it is indeed the collective activity, traversed by a division of labor, that is the objective material basis linking the actions of the beater and the hunter.

By viewing the activity through the prism of the individual-social, Kaptelinin reinterprets the hunting episode in a different way. He makes arguments that may seem convincing, but to which we will respond below. Kaptelinin (2005, p. 16) provides us with the premises that allow us to define activity as a collective category, without, however, pursuing the analysis by remaining focused on a form of individual activity and de facto limiting hunting to an individual activity. Leontiev's central division of labor suddenly disappears in the following lines:

> Consider a hunting activity that is shaped by a number of motives. Let us mention just two of them: food and self-preservation. If both motives are strong enough – for instance, getting food is a matter of life and death, but the prey is dangerous – a hunter can be in a state of confusion and hesitation. One of these motives can take over and the hunter would either flee with the risk of starving to death, or recklessly assault the animal with the risk of being killed. It is more likely, however, that hunter's activity is going to be directed to – wards a desired outcome, which will make it possible to attain both motives. For instance, the hunter can decide to chase the animal until it gets tired and no longer presents a danger. In that case, both food and self-preservation are influencing the hunter. The object of the hunting

activity, however – safely obtaining food by chasing the animal and making it tired – is what gives the activity structure and direction (Kaptelinin, 2005, pp. 16–17).

In this example, the motives are purely individual: to obtain food and to preserve oneself. These motives are not linked to a community in this example: it's about feeding oneself, not producing food for the community as in Leontiev's example. If everyone acted as individually as in the example of the Kaptelinin hunter, there would certainly be no tribe left after a few weeks, since the children would logically not be able to participate in the hunt. The insistence on '*individual activity*' is also problematic insofar as Kaptelinin suggests that there is an individual possibility of extricating oneself from the conflict of motives that he identifies (feeding oneself – preserving one's physical integrity). He gives the example of '*hunting to exhaustion*.'

However, examples of hunting to exhaustion are reported as forms of ancestral hunting in which hunters run after their prey until the latter is in a situation of hyperthermia (notably practiced by the Tan people of the Kalahari Desert). Biologically speaking, humans differ from animals in that they have a homeothermic system that allows them to dissipate heat in a particularly efficient way, mainly by sweating. The animal, on the other hand, must expel heat by panting, which forces it to make long stops. However, unlike the example presented by Kaptelinin, this type of hunting is not individual. On the contrary, it involves collective organization, division of roles, and collective management of fatigue. This little excerpt from MacDougall (2009) in a book on endurance racing should convince us:

> '*That's how it's done*,' Nate said as Louis caught up with them, panting. The four hunters ran fast but effortlessly behind the bouncing blankets. When one of the animals moved into the shade of an acacia tree, one of the hunters separated from the others to lead it back into the sun. The herd broke up, reformed, and broke up again, but this time the four Bushmen stayed behind one of the wagons, preventing it from joining the others and taking cover to rest. [...]. To his astonishment, Louis, who had been huffing and puffing at the back of the group, found himself on a par with Nate, the strongest and most skilled of the hunters. He wasn't carrying a canteen, unlike the others. After an hour and a half of hunting, Louis discovered why: when one of the tired runners fell behind, he passed his gourd to Nate, who drank it all before swapping it for a half-full one when a second runner slowed down (MacDougall, 2009, pp. 346–347).

We can see from this example that the best way to pursue the conflict of motives identified by Kaptelinin (food – self-preservation) is to resort to a form of '*exhaustion hunting*'. But this is not a hunt led by a solitary individual, but a collective hunt that itself has a rudimentary form of division of labor. In fact, it seems to us that Kaptelinin's analysis falls short of Vygotsky's. The individual is not isolated, alone in the desert, struggling to survive. He is always in a specific historical context. Vygotsky said nothing else.

> Already in primitive societies, which are only just taking their first steps along the road of their historical development, the entire psychological makeup of individuals can be seen to depend directly on the development of technology, the degree of development of the production forces and on the structure of that social group to which the individual belongs (Vygotsky, 1994).

Thus, for Vygotsky, psychology is not the psychology of an isolated individual, but that of an individual embedded in a social group formed by relations of production. What can we learn from this example of hunting to exhaustion? That the collective activity of hunting certainly appears throughout history as a solution to the conflict of individual motives. Far from being individual, the activity is collective.

Although Leontiev acted as a psychologist, his task was to establish theoretical categories that would allow us not to extract psychic elements and study them separately, but to elaborate categories that would allow us to study psychological development without separating it from the forms of collective activity that determine it. So just because Leontiev theorizes as a psychologist doesn't mean that he doesn't think of human activity (and work in particular) as a collective activity.

Let's take this argument one step further, using an example that Leontiev himself gives, concerning the perception of an object's elasticity. Perceiving the elasticity of an object is not a purely contemplative act. It takes place via an external motor process that has a practical goal: to deform the object. It is by deforming the object that we can perceive its elasticity.

For Leontiev, the '*subjective image*' and thus the sensation of object deformation is undeniably an object of psychology. But, he adds, in order to understand the nature of this image, We need to study the process that gave rise to it and, in this case, considered '*The process is external, practical*'. On the basis of this example, he considers it necessary to include in the object of psychological research '*the external, concrete action of the subject*'. Here he does indeed mean '*concrete action*', not '*activity*', inasmuch as this action (deformation of the object) is not related to the activity it performs. But if concrete action can become a unit of psychology, although at first sight it shouldn't be, why shouldn't concrete, practical, external, collective activity be included? Leontiev logically adds that:

> This means that it is incorrect to think that although the external, objective activity presents itself for psychological investigation, it does so only to the extent that it includes internal psychic processes and that psychological investigation advances without studying external activity itself or its structure (Leontiev, 1978, p. 56).

As we can see, just because Leontiev thinks within psychology and as a psychologist, the concept of activity does not necessarily have to be an individual-social concept. It is above all a concept that refers to a collective whose relations are produced by the division of labor.

The concept of activity refers to a system of actions in pursuit of an object determined by society, i.e. an object whose motive lies in the reproductive needs of society rather than in the needs of the individual (Blunden, 2010). Activity is defined by an object… not by the subject. It's common to read expressions like '*the activity of teachers*', '*the activity of fishermen*', '*the activity of cultural mediators*', and so on. These expressions refer to a common, scientific conception of the concept of activity, which defines the activity by the subject who wears it (Chaiklin, 2019).

Critically reviewing his own doctoral work, Leontiev (1975/2021) notes that the work initiated during his first period in Moscow dealt with activity '*in general*', but that the researcher always deals with '*particular activities*'. For him, what essentially distinguishes one activity from another is the difference in its object, and this object is the real motive, insofar as it responds to a need that ensures the continuity of a community:

> The main thing that distinguishes one activity from another, however, is the difference of their object. It is exactly the object of an activity that gives it a determined direction. According to the terminology, the object of an activity is its true motive. It is understood that the motive may be either material or ideal, either present in perception or existing only in the imagination or in though. The main thing is that behind an activity should always be a need, that it always answers one need or another (Leontiev, 1978, p. 62).

The Hierarchical Structure of Human Activity

The hierarchical structure is all too often overlooked in many activity reports, yet it is essential to their analysis. First, because this hierarchical structure gives the activity an explanatory dimension (which is why we can speak of activity theory). Second, explanations at one level are not necessarily valid at another level. Let's take a quick look at an example (albeit controversial) from another science: physics. Explanations at the infinitely small level are not yet compatible with explanations at the infinitely large level. In this sense, researchers are trying to find the theoretical key that will reconcile theories that do not apply to these different scales.

In the context of human activity, this theoretical key is provided by Leontiev through the system conception of human activity and work on the relationships between the level of activity, actions and operations. As he points out:

> [We must realize] the analysis of the working of the system of objective activity as a whole in which is also included the functioning of the physical subject – his brain, his organs of perception and movement. The laws that control the processes of this functioning are, of course, apparent only as long as we do not proceed to the investigation of the objective actions that are realized by these processes or of images that can be analyzed only by investigating human activity at the psychological level. No different is the situation in a transition from the psychological level of investigation to the wholly social. Only here the transition to the new, that is, the social laws, takes place as a transition from investigating processes that realize relationships of individuals to an investigation of relationships that are realized by the common activity of individuals in society, the development of which is subordinated to objective-historical laws. Thus a systemic study of human activity must also be an analysis according to levels. It is just such an analysis that will make it possible to overcome the opposition of the physiological, the psychological, and the sociological, as well as the reduction of any one of these to another (Leontiev, 1978, p. 74).

The two key ideas that emerge are that:

- Activity analysis is necessarily a multilevel analysis. However, just because this analysis is multilevel doesn't mean that activity is not the unit of analysis for Leontiev. Activity is the elementary unit that contains all the complexity inherent in social life, the building block of social life.

- However, this analysis requires a clear distinction between activity, actions and operations.

In the following sections, we return to the question of the relationships between these different levels, which are essential for a *'systemic'* analysis of activity.

The Relationship Between Activity and Actions

Human activity only really exists in the actions of individuals who reproduce it by enacting it. Activity and action are therefore inseparable and at the same time two different realities. The emergence of action is linked to life in society and the need for the division of labor to satisfy the needs of the community:

> The appearance of goal-directed processes or actions in activity came about historically as the result of the transition of man to life in society. The activity of participators in common work is evoked by its product, which initially directly answers the need of each of them. The development, however, of even the simplest technical division of work necessarily leads to isolation of, as it were, intermediate partial results, which are achieved by separate participators of collective work activity, but which in themselves cannot satisfy the workers' needs. Their needs are satisfied not by these *'intermediate'* results but by a share of the product of their collective activity, obtained by each of them through forms of the relationships binding them one to another, which develop in the process of work, that is, social relationships (Leontiev, 1978, p. 64).

In other words, if activity is the basic unit of human life, activity is constituted and embodied in a set of actions. The concepts of activity and action are not mutually exclusive but need to be distinguished. Another definition of action is that it is a process *'subordinated to the representation of the result that must be attained, that is, if it is subordinated to a conscious purpose'* (Leontiev, 1975/2021, p. 99).

If activity consists of a set of actions, actions and activity do not coincide: the same action can carry out different activities, and conversely, activities can give rise to totally different goals and thus be carried out by means of different actions.

The Relationship Between Actions and Operations

Just as we must distinguish activity from action, Leontiev clearly distinguishes action from operation.

> There is frequently no difference between the terms action and operation. In the context of psychological analysis of activity, however, distinguishing between them is absolutely necessary. Actions, as has already been said, are related to goals, operations to conditions (Leontiev, 1978, p. 65).

Operations realize actions. They are unmediated, i.e. context dependent. And they are unconscious. For Leontiev, actions and operations have different origins: while actions arise from the *'exchange relations'* of activities, operations arise from a form of automation of actions. He gives another famous example that of learning to change gears. At the beginning of learning to drive, shifting gears is an action that, once incorporated into a more complex action (changing the car's speed), becomes an operational component. What's more, operations are ultimately destined to be crystallized in machines and instruments. To continue with the example of driving a car, shifting gears is integrated into the so-called *'automatic'* transmission.

In what follows, we will elaborate on this level of operation based on current work on motor control within the theory of nonlinear dynamical systems. In the example of primitive hunting, the success of the collective activity is conditioned in part by the hunter's gestural control in killing the prey. This level of operation has been studied extensively in current motor control research, particularly since the work of Kelso and the emergence of nonlinear dynamical systems theory in this area (Kelso, 1995). We therefore present the operational level of activity, drawing here on work from activity physiology, starting with Bernstein (1996), rather than psychology, to reflect the claimed transdisciplinary nature of CHAT.

Bernstein's (1996) original work is part of the Russian activity tradition. He was one of the first members of the Vygotskian circle when it arrived in Moscow (Yasnitsky, 2011). But more than that, Bernstein's work inspired Leontiev in the development of his activity theory, as Leontiev saw in it a *'psychophysiological foundation'* for his own work (Feigenberg, 2014). Bernstein's work was particularly inspiring for Leontiev at the level of the processes of realization and regulation of intentional action in a multilevel hierarchical system, insofar as it brought the idea of goal-directed action into the field of physiology:

> Goal... determines the processes that should be united in the concept of goal-directedness. The later includes all motivations in the organism's struggle to achieve the goal and leads to the development and strengthening of the relevant mechanisms of its realization. And all the dynamics of the goal directed struggle via the goal directed mechanisms represent a complex that can best be encompassed by the term activity[8] (Feigenberg, 2014, p. 59).

The importance of Bernstein's ideas survived the Stalinist purge and his expulsion from the university, only to be revived in the early 1990s in the current of dynamic approaches to nonlinear systems, based in particular on the work of Kelso (1995) on motricity and Thelen on motor development (Thelen, 2000). Thelen and Smith (1996), for example, note that their work follows in the footsteps of Vygotsky, Luria, and Leontiev. Closer to home, Sève (Sève & Guespin-Michel, 2005) demonstrates the philosophical links between the materialist-dialectical tradition and this particular approach to complexity.

In this chapter on Leontiev's theory of action, we think it's important to present two main characteristics of movement and operations. The first is the variability of the operations required to perform an action.

Contrary to popular belief, dexterity or skill in performing an action does not consist in reproducing the same movement identically. In the field of work, Clot and Béguin (2004) point out that '*The analysis of work [...] has taught us that the same most repetitive gesture of the assembly line worker is always unique*' (Clot and Béguin, 2004, p. 43). In each repetition of a movement, there is variability: the operator's movement is not identical to itself and cannot be, even under highly standardized conditions. It therefore varies constantly. Let's take an example. Let's put an operator on a conveyor belt. In this locomotion task, the operator is to some extent affected by the speed of the conveyor belt. He is also constrained by the width and length of the belt. And yet, even within these constraints, his motion will vary constantly. This example was studied by (Hausdorff et al., 1996), who showed that although the step duration is relatively stable (between 1.1 and 1.4 s), it fluctuates considerably around its mean in a seemingly unpredictable way.

---

[8]   Bernstein uses the term Aktivnost, not Dejatelnost, as Leontiev used in his theory of activity.

This example teaches us that one of the essential properties of movement is its variability. The classical, cognitivist approach to motor control cannot account for this variability except in terms of random error in movement programming. Indeed, the traditional, centralist approach to movement control views variability as a form of error (Komar, Seifert, & Thouvarecq, 2015; Stergiou & Decker, 2011), reflecting inability to predict the parameters necessary to use the underlying motor program (Schmidt, 2003). Conversely, dynamic models of nonlinear systems that follow Bernstein's work make it a hallmark of complex systems and assign it an important functional role in the production of movement.

So why do the operations required to perform an action vary constantly? In the first place, the variability of operations is the result of changes in the interaction between the environment and the subject. As we have already emphasized, operations depend on the circumstances and constraints imposed on the organism.

The notion of constraints, as proposed by dynamic approaches, has profound implications for understanding the production and control of movement (Davids, Glazier, Araújo, & Bartlett, 2003). Indeed, they can be defined as boundaries or functionalities that limit the search for optimal organizational solutions in complex biological systems. Newell (1986) identifies and characterizes the system of constraints from which motor behavior emerges.

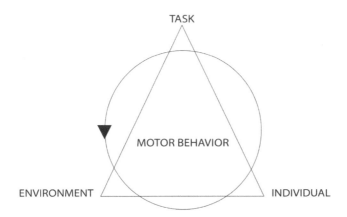

Figure 7: Systems of constraints underlying the emergence of motor behavior according to Newell (1986).

In this theorization, there is no need to define a set of external or internal constraints from the point of view of the system (here we return to Vygotsky's idea of basic unity). Motor control, like motor behavior, emerges from interaction within a system of constraints formed by the dynamic interaction between the environment, the task, and the organism.

But the importance of variability as a characteristic of actions goes beyond variation in the characteristics of the environment, it goes beyond simple adaptation to changing circumstances. The variability of operations is not purely '*reactive-adaptive*', it is an exploratory dispersion, an active analysis of the environment and the search for an optimal direction of action (Durand, 1993). In this way, each operation is always a partially singular response to a problem space defined in relation to a '*desired future*', to use Bernstein's terms.

In this sense, the analysis of activity is an analysis of the relations between different levels of activity structure, of the movements of these different levels and of their qualitative development. This seems essential to us, especially in the context of interventions that aim to intervene in musculoskeletal disorders (Lémonie, 2019). A first approach identifies MSDs as a multifactorial disease, paradoxically equating social, psychological, and physiological factors. This perspective is doomed to failure in that it is impossible to know which factors to act on to prevent MSDs, except by some form of random chance (for a critique of the factor-based approach, see the section on the presentation of the dialectical approach in terms of moving from the abstract to the concrete). A second perspective is one in which MSDs are understood as a disease of the organization, ignoring gestures, operations, and their variability.

The essential question overlooked by these two approaches is that of the relationship between levels, in order to understand how the performance of an activity can produce MSDs. What is the relationship between activity and action? How are goals formed? What is the relationship between actions and operations? How is the reduction of motor variability related to the history and transformations of the activity performed by the subject's actions and operations? Answering these questions requires theoretical and empirical work that looks at '*things*' in motion. Again, dialectics is essential. It requires a historical and genetic vision that grasps the transformations of an activity in two distinct movements. This historical and genetic vision thus constitutes a multilevel analysis because it looks at activity as a hierarchical system on three levels. These two movements are outlined below.

The Dual Dynamic of Activity Development

There are two dynamic aspects of activity that are perhaps underemphasized in the current literature. The first dynamic concerns the movement between hierarchical levels of activity. We'll call this dimension the vertical dynamics of activity development. To this vertical dimension, we need to add a second dynamic, which refers to a horizontal or historical dimension of activity development. According to Leontiev (1978, p. 50), *'activity is not a reaction and not a totality of reactions but a system that has structure, its own internal transitions and transformations, its own development'*.

In addition to this vertical dynamic, there is a second dynamic that we'll call horizontal. This refers to the historical nature of the activity and its evolution. Recalling the importance of the historical evolution of human activities allows us to escape from a static view of human activity, while at the same time linking several levels of development. As Scribner (1985) points out:

> Psychologists, for example, tend to conceive of the individual as a dynamic system while assuming, in their research plans, that history at the societal level is static; anthropologists often make the opposite assumption (Scribner, 1985, p. 140).

This horizontal dimension can be divided into three hierarchical levels of activity, as shown in the following table. At the level of activity (as a historical, social, collective and cultural formation, traversed by the division of labor, as Leontiev emphasizes), it is possible to follow the history of activity: far from being static, it develops over time. In terms of action, this level is characterized by diversity, including catachresis. Finally, at the level of operation, it is variability (or repetition without repetition) that accounts for this movement.

Table 2: Intermediate concepts to account for development at each level.

LEVELS	INTERMEDIATE CONCEPT TO CAPTURE 'HORIZONTAL' DEVELOPMENT
Activity	Historicity, developmental period
Action	Motor diversity
Operation	Motor variability

Presented in this way, these three levels could be understood independently of each other. This is not the case. For Leontiev, activity is a non-additive, molar unit.

However, we agree with Stetsenko (2005) when she points out that:

> Metaphors of space do not capture the dynamics of human development even if such zigzags or horizontal dimensions are added to the description, the latter proposed by Engeström, 1996a; however, this helps us to see it as a nonlinear and polydirectional process (Stetsenko, 2005, p. 85).

However limited this metaphor of the vertical and horizontal dimensions may be, it allows us to think the polydirectionality of the development of human activity and to inscribe intermediate concepts that allow us to grasp this polydirectionality: the concepts of motor variability (or repetition without repetition), motor diversity, and the development of meaning and efficiency (Clot, 2008) are all intermediate concepts that allow us to account for it.

Leontiev's Contribution To CHAT

Although Leontiev is considered the father of activity theory, he actually extended and developed the principles developed in Moscow with Vygotsky and Luria. Paradoxical as it may seem, this is a paternity within a paternity. One of Leontiev's undeniable contributions is to have made possible the development of a theory that, although developed within psychology, is inherently transdisciplinary and integrative, allowing a plurality of disciplines to interact. We have described in part how this theory was developed by drawing inspiration from Bernstein's work on the physiology of activity, but also how Leontiev's contributions, by placing the concept of activity (in the sense of Dejatelnost) at its core, make it possible to link man to society and to place society at the center of psychology. In this sense, the theory of activity that he produced as a psychologist is indeed transdisciplinary in nature. Of course, this is not without ambiguity. As Leontiev's students and collaborators point out in an article:

I think that at one time we confused the psychological with the nonpsychological, i.e. with some sort of logical, sociological characterization of activity, of its basic components and the structural interrelations that occur therein, etc. (Zaporozhets, Gal'perin, & El'konin, 1995, p. 12).

The formulation of a unit of analysis that is human activity leads Leontiev to distinguish activity from actions and to introduce the division of labor as a new mediator between the subject and the object of human activity (Spinuzzi, 2018a). However, the analysis of human activity is a systemic and dialectical analysis that studies internal relations and their development, insofar as activity is a process characterized by constant transformations, both vertically, in the passages between levels of activity, actions and operations, and horizontally, insofar as actions carry out activities that evolve historically, in the elaboration of a plurality of goals that allow the same activity to be carried out, or in the variability inherent to operations.

Thus, although he was a psychologist, Leontiev's activity theory paves the way for an interdisciplinary approach that necessarily involves a systemic analysis of human activity:

Thus, a systemic study of human activity must also be an analysis according to levels. It is just such an analysis that will make it possible to overcome the opposition of the physiological, the psychological, and the sociological, as well as the reduction of any one of these to another (Leontiev, 1978, p. 74).

Leontiev's contribution obviously leaves a number of problems to be solved (Davydov, 1999), but clearly constitutes an important programmatic orientation, as reported by his son (Leontiev, 1995):

The '*new system of psychological knowledge*' that Leont'ev expected by the year 2000 [...] must be constructed not 'from bottom to top', but from 'top to bottom'. In other words, from man-in-the-world to the-world-in-man, and from this latter to individual mental processes that sustain this image of the world, and then, ultimately, to their new synthesis. Further, it should be chronotopic in its origins: it should be able to describe man's existence not in abstract knowledge, but in real space and time, in 'major experience'. Finally, this major experience should be the actualization not only, and not so much, of the individual soul as, so to speak, of a 'collective' soul. Living in the world, I, a human being, 'find or have my "ego" not in myself (others

find it in me!), but in others, in another, existing outside of me, in an inter-
locutor, in a lover, in nature, and even in a computer, in the System': My
cognition is a process of internalization. My being is a process of externalization, embedded in an endless dialogue with persons and things (Leontiev,
1995, p. 44).

Some Criticisms of Leontiev's Approach

Given the international influence and dissemination of Leontiev's position, it makes perfect sense to write that the critique of activity theory is
first and foremost a critique of Leontiev's theorizing (Mironenko, 2013).

Several lines of criticism can be identified. They mainly concern
the homology between the structure of internal activity and the structure of external activity, and the conservative, reductionist character of
Leontiev's theorizing. Thus, for Toomela (2000, 2008), from the point
of view of cultural psychology, the unit of analysis cannot be activity,
insofar as he rejects the correspondence between external and internal
activity.

González Rey (2020) argues that Leontiev's position is reductionist
and conservative because it fails to emphasize the creative and generative
character of subjectivity. In fact, activity theory focuses almost exclusively on the process of internalization to explain how external practical activity is transformed into internal activity. Moreover, according to
Leontiev, the structural identity between external and internal activity
makes internal activity an epiphenomenon of external activity and, in
his theoretical conception, leads to 'the complete subordination of the individual to the dominant order within which the structure of activity emerges'
(González Rey, 2020, p. 87).

Stetsenko (2005) elaborates on the same criticism and sees an internal
contradiction, noting that Leontiev's theory places great emphasis on
transitions from the objective to the subjective world through a double
transition (a) from the objective world to activity; (b) from activity to
human subjectivity. Thus, Leontiev sees the historical-cultural experience of previous generations as the main mechanism of development,
to the detriment of the emphasis placed on the fact that individuals,
through their actions, also contribute to this experience and to the transformation of the world. This imbalance leads to an internal contradiction in Leontiev's work (Stetsenko, 2005):

Taken together, these imbalances in A. N. Leontiev's (1978) account (for a similar analysis, see Engeström, 1999) can be summed up as positing society above the individual and seeing the latter as produced by, subordinate to, and molded by reality, and especially society, at the expense of emphasizing individual agency–the ability to produce, create, and make a difference in social practices. Ironically, this shift away from the centrality of individual contributions to the world (though not a complete absence of a relevant discussion), contradicts the broad premises of activity theory itself. Namely, A. N. Leontiev himself called attention to the transformative practices as the foundation of human mind, for example, by quoting the following words by Engels: '... *the transformation of nature by humans, rather than nature itself, is the most significant and immediate basis of human thinking*' (Stetsenko, 2005, p. 78).

Finally, Blunden (2019, p. 271) points out that Leontiev conceived of activity in functionalist terms rather than as a project capable of reproducing, but above all of changing or transforming, society. Lektorski (1999) partly shares this criticism, but qualifies it to the extent that, in line with Vygotsky's ideas, activity involves not only processes of internalization (about which Leontiev wrote), but also processes of externalization:

Humans not only internalize ready-made standards and rules of activity but externalize themselves as well, creating new standards and rules. Human beings determine themselves through objects that they create. They are essentially creative beings (Lektorski, 1999, p. 66).

As we will see later, the work of the Finnish activity theory school, which draws on expansive learning theory (Engeström, 1987) and has developed formative intervention methods such as the change laboratory (Engeström, 2007b; Lémonie & Grosstephan, 2021; Virkkunen & Newham, 2013), seems to us to go beyond the critiques of Gonzales-Rey, Stetsenko, or Blunden. Engeström and Miettinen (1999) note that research inspired by activity theory has been mainly rooted in the internalization paradigm, with early research in Moscow by Vygotsky, Leontiev and Luria focusing not only on '*the role of given artifacts as mediators of cognition, but also interested in how children created their own artifacts to facilitate their performance*' (Engeström, 1999a, p. 26).

The dominance of the internalization paradigm in activity theory seems to be largely related to the political climate of the Stalinist Soviet Union. In Lektorski's (1990) book on the concept of activity, almost everyone points to the creativity of activity and its ability to overcome given constraints as key characteristics of the concept. Engeström and

Miettinen (1999) see the role of perestroika in this work, just as Leontiev and Luria's 1956 critique of Vygotsky's work can be seen as the weight of an ideological context:

> The frightening effect of the ideological officialism within which Soviet intellectuals were forced to think from the 1930s onward was that the stimulating achievements of Vygotsky's work were transformed into a violation of the doctrine's immaterial truth, with such invasive force that it affected even the most intimate evaluations of thought. Are Leontiev and Luria serious in their severe criticism of Vygotsky? There's no reason to doubt it, in the sense that under such conditions the dominant ideology thinks in them (Sève, 2008, p. 351).

However, ideological weight does not explain the differences of opinion within the first Vygotskian circle in the early 1930s. Leontiev's position cannot be interpreted as an alignment with the official doctrine. This was hardly the case in the early 1930s (Sève, 2008). Although Leontiev's position is based on the ideas of Vygotsky and Rubinstein, it differs both theoretically and in terms of the object of study. These different orientations were certainly the source of the rift between Vygotsky and Leontiev, which developed into a deep enmity between Leontiev and Rubinstein from 1947 (Mironenko, 2013).

Chapter 4

Third Generation of CHAT: From the Development of Mind to the Development of Activity in Engeström Work

The theory has to be spelled out concretely in each text to provide (a) a description of what is there and (b) a pedagogy for learning how to read the diagram (Roth, 2008, p. 181).
Activity theory has the conceptual and methodological potential to be a pathbreaker in studies that help humans gain control over their own artifacts and thus over their future. (Engeström, 1999a, p. 29).

As in previous chapters, we present some contextual elements to introduce CHAT developments in Engeström's work. These developments originated in the 1980s. They were developed in response to then-dominant cognitivism and as a methodological elaboration for interventionist research with the objective of transforming practices, initially those of teachers.

With Engeström's work, the focus shifts from the development of mind or higher psychological functions to the development of activity as a historical, systemic, cultural, and collective formation. Engeström is not a psychologist; his work is initially rooted in the field of adult education and training and is subsequently extended and taken up in a variety of disciplines and fields of study.

The following sections will demonstrate the evolution of Engeström's work and the underlying motivations that inform it, specifically the transformation of educational practices. Additionally, it will be shown that the framework he develops brings a fully 'disruptive' orientation to the then-dominant cognitivism of the 1980s.

When Engeström's work is referenced in the literature, the diagram representing an activity system is often cited. However, despite its heuristic value, this diagram is interpreted and used in different ways by different authors. A model is not a theory. In this chapter, we will devote a significant portion to explaining this model and its potential applications. Unlike a static model, this model is used to account for the movement of an activity system. As Roth (2008) suggests in the introductory quotation to this chapter, we propose a pedagogy for reading this activity system diagram.

Finally, this chapter will conclude with a few criticisms of Engeström's approach and its contribution to CHAT.

Context: The Difficult Transformation of Teaching Practices

Sannino et al. (2009a) identify four main phases in Engeström's career as an activity theorist. His trajectory provides insight for those engaged in research on the relationship between intervention and theory, given that Engeström's theoretical work seems to stem from frustration over the challenges of changing teachers' pedagogical practices. These difficulties are the underlying reasons for the development of the theory of expansive learning and the expansion of CHAT that he proposes in his thesis, published in 1987 under the title '*Learning by Expanding*'. The first period of Engeström's work emerged in the context of the student movements that swept the globe in the late 1960s. Engeström published his first book at the age of 21 (Engeström, 1970). This book, entitled '*Education in Class Society: Reflections on the Problems of Education in a Capitalist Society*' (in Finnish), offers a robust critique of education in capitalist society, without reference to CHAT and without offering any alternatives to what it criticizes. Engeström's initial period of activism and criticism fostered his awareness of the necessity to cultivate alternative perspectives. This led to a period of intensive work on appropriating activity theorists (translated into German at the time), particularly the work of Leontiev, Davydov, and Ilyenkov, which was widely cited and reintroduced as part of the development of his expansive learning theory (Engeström, 1987).

In a subsequent period, he sought to transform educational practices by '*applying*' Davydov's ideas on generalization and concept formation (Davydov, 1990b, 2008). Recently, Engeström (2020a) recalled in an article on conceptualization and the principle of ascending from the abstract to the concrete (see chapter 14) the important influence of Davydov on his own work:

Reading Davydov and interacting with him in person had a decisive impact on my thinking and research since the early 1980s up to his untimely death, and his ideas have remained a central influence for me (Engeström, 2020a, p. 32).

However, attempts to transform teaching practices encountered significant challenges, prompting Engeström to seek a theoretical framework to address these difficulties. As Sannino et al. (2009a, p. 49) observe, 'This work with teachers and the "Davydovian" pedagogical experiments also renewed Engeström's initial frustration about the difficulty of influencing school practices.' These difficulties in transforming pedagogical practices on the basis of scientific proposals are not unique to the Finnish context. They are also particularly highlighted in French-language works (e.g. Houssaye, 2011) in essays with a sometimes-pessimistic tone. It is therefore necessary to pause for a moment to consider these difficulties and their possible explanations in order to understand Engeström's subsequent path and the reasons behind his orientation.

Why does change not occur in the context of pedagogy? Why does the day-to-day work of teachers resist any possibility of transformation? It is easy to dismiss this as a form of corporatist conservatism. If teachers' work does not appear to evolve, it is not because they are unable to appropriate a scientific framework or theory, however, relevant or 'revolutionary'. Rather, it is primarily because teaching practices are not embedded in an institutional context conducive to its development. This limits the scope for change. Thus, Houssaye (2011) notes, citing Vygotsky (Thought and Language), that pedagogical changes, and in particular interactive pedagogy, are diluted into minimal practices. With regard to interactive pedagogical practices, he notes that they inexorably contract into a form of interrogative pedagogy, a form that he unquestionably considers unsuitable for the acquisition of concepts at school.

Interactive teaching has become the dominant form of traditional pedagogy in the contemporary era. Despite Vygotsky's assertion in 1934 that pedagogical experience and theoretical research were converging, it is evident that this is not the case. Let us consider his words: 'From the theoretical standpoint, there is no room for doubt: the thesis that the child acquires ready-made concepts in the school learning process and assimilates them in the same way as any other intellectual skill is totally unfounded.

Pedagogical experience teaches us, no less than theoretical research, that the direct teaching of concepts always proves practically impossible and pedagogically unprofitable' (1987, p. 277). It is evident that interrogative pedagogy is unlikely to be an effective solution in this regard. In essence, the model proposed by interrogative pedagogy is merely an extension of the existing pedagogy, which is already widely prevalent (Houssaye, 2011, p. 18).

However, what limits the implementation of a truly '*interactive*' pedagogy is not only a lack of understanding or misinterpretation on the part of teachers, but certainly an unfavorable institutional, organizational and human context (think of the role of parents in this process). As Houssaye points out:

> The constraints imposed by the teaching context (the nature of the students, the textbooks, the content, the image to be defended, the administrative environment) play an essential role in the construction of teachers' '*mental plans*' and severely limit the possibilities for evolution. To realize a pedagogical intention is to reverse priorities, in other words, to make the project take precedence over the context (Houssaye, 2011, p. 18).

But what does it mean to '*put the project above the context*'? Houssaye's expression is nebulous, to say the least, and we offer an attempt at interpretation.

We see the context as a stable, given, unchanging container. Or we can see it as the product of human activity, in constant motion, evolving historically and interactively with other forms of activity. In the first case, we will always observe that change is not taking place, and we will attribute the '*pedagogical dilution*' or contraction of a scientifically established pedagogy to external, contextual, or organizational factors. This approach is pessimistic, to say the least, and comes to a screeching halt in the face of the inability to transform pedagogical practices in the long run. In the second case, we might think of '*taking the lead*' as in some way '*bringing the context into line*', i.e. transforming the context on the basis of a new object of activity. Here, the very object of the teacher's activity can transform the context. In other words, transforming work or teaching practices here means developing (qualitatively reorganizing) the activity system (the context) in which the daily actions of teachers are taken up and given new meaning, i.e. '*making the project take precedence over the context*'.

It is clearly this second option that opens the third period of Engeström's work. This period, it should be remembered, was undoubtedly born out of the frustration of not being able to change teachers' pedagogical practices and of not finding in the school the conditions for a learning activity that radically transforms the context and the teachers' work. This third period is therefore an opportunity to develop developmental research in the field of work and to support workers in transforming their own work. The main question of this third period is: can we learn to transform our work context, i.e. our activity system? In other words, can people learn to master the future of their work?

This is indeed a question of learning. This kind of learning necessarily refers to a collective process: it's never an isolated individual who can transform a context (or an activity system), insofar as this context is itself made up of other individuals. What's more, this type of learning is clearly different from training or school-based learning in that the content is not known or determined in advance, as in training programs or curricula. In short, this learning is learning '*what does not yet exist*' (Engeström, 2016). These two aspects led Engeström to develop the theory of expansive learning. This development extended the analysis of learning beyond the walls of the school and was based on research-intervention work.

For Engeström, activity systems (understood as the context of actors' situated actions) develop historically. The main mechanism for the development of activity systems, and thus for cultural evolution, relates to a learning mechanism he calls expansive learning. Engeström's idea is to try to explain these expansive learning processes in order to develop a methodology for accelerating or supporting these processes of cultural transformation.

By developing the theory of expansive learning published in his now-classic 1987 book (Learning by expanding an activity-theoretical approach to developmental research) and by expanding the field outside the school, Engeström extends CHAT from a focus on the appropriation of predetermined cultural content to the construction of new content and practices in expansive learning theory. Rather than being placed in the position of acquiring a predetermined culture, participants become creators of a new culture by transforming their activity system and expanding the horizon of their possible actions.

Davydov's theory was constructed to transform teaching and learning in schools. Thus, it is to a certain extent confined to the notion of learning as assimilation and appropriation of culturally given contents. [...] The fact that Davydov's theory is oriented at learning activity within the confines of a classroom where the curricular contents are determined ahead of time by adults probably explains why it does not contain the actions of critical questioning of the given contents, on the one hand, and implementing and consolidating new concepts in practice, on the other hand. These are actions that imply the construction of actual culturally novel ideas and practices (Engeström & Sannino, 2020, p. 51).

This third period of theoretical and practical development bears the seeds of the fourth period, marked by efforts to create, and consolidate an international community of researchers. The worldwide dissemination of CHAT beyond its original disciplines and geographical areas owes much to the efforts of this community of researchers. This fourth phase saw the development of the Change Laboratory method (see Chapter 10). Initially, Engeström's work was based on what he called 'developmental work research' (e.g. Engeström, 1996b, 2005). However, the rapid changes required to develop work organizations in a context of economic crisis linked to the collapse of the Soviet bloc led the Finnish researcher to develop a method for accelerating and condensing the expansive learning process.

Beyond these developments, Engeström's scientific career (like that of his predecessors in the field of CHAT) is strongly rooted in practical problems of transforming human practices. The scientific dimension is strongly articulated with a militant dimension that serves as a guideline for the development of his work:

> For Engeström, as for the founders of activity theory, theoretical developments require activist involvement in concrete human practices. In constant dialogue with the activity-theoretical classic heritage – in particular that of Vygotsky, Leont'ev, Ilyenkov, and Davydov – Engeström's work addresses the pressing societal challenges of change and learning in work activities (Sannino, Daniels, & Gutierrez, 2009b, p. 15).

The four stages of CHAT development in the work of Engeström and his team are summarized in Table 3 below.

Table 3: Periods of development of Engeström's work, according to Sannino et al. (2009a).

FIRST PERIOD	Activism – Criticism of the capitalist school.
SECOND PERIOD	Appropriation of the Cultural-Historical Activity Theory. Davydonian experiment to transform teaching practices. Extension to work practices outside the school institution.
THIRD PERIOD	Development of expansive learning theory. Developmental Work Research.
FOURTH PERIOD	Creation and consolidation of an international community of researchers. Development of a formative intervention methodology – Change Laboratory

A Response to Mainstream Cognitivism

In scientific terms, the 1980s were marked by the dominance of the cognitivist paradigm in the cognitive sciences. It was also marked by the emergence of serious alternatives to this reductionist, mentalist understanding of cognition[9]. Thus, in the late 1980s and early 1990s, intense editorial activity and the emergence of a number of concepts and theoretical frameworks offered or began to offer serious alternatives to the then-dominant mentalist orientation.

Let's briefly summarize the cognitivist orientation, its difficulties, and some of the theoretical alternatives that emerged during this period (for a more detailed approach, see Steiner, 2005).

Cognitivism is a mentalist approach in that it assumes that the brain, conceived as an information-processing system, processes information from the external environment and controls behavior on the basis of representations of this external world. In this orientation, the functioning of the brain is compared to that of a computer or supercomputer. Cognitive processes are purely internal: '*Cognitivism assumes that the mind and its*

---

[9] This conception is still dominant, even in the field of labor analysis. But the late 1980s and early 1990s saw a break with this paradigmatic approach, as a number of texts appeared that built an alternative theory based on a critique of this paradigmatic approach that confines mental processes to the brain. We are thinking in particular of approaches to situated action and communities of practice (Lave & Wenger, 1991; Suchman, 1987); the enactive approach to cognition (Maturana & Varela, 1994; Varela, Thompson, & Rosch, 1991); approaches to nonlinear dynamic systems (Kelso, 1995); and distributed cognition (Hutchins, 1995).

capacities (language, perception) are internal, that is, that they stop where the external world begins' (Steiner, 2005, p. 17). Consequently, the notion of mental representation occupies a central place in the conceptual edifice of cognitivism (Varela et al., 1991). This mentalist vision is still widely present today, including in approaches that claim to be activity-based, despite strong criticism (for a critical account of cognitivism in the field of work and organizations, see Lorino, 2019; Theureau, 2004a).

A divergent approach to cognition sees the brain, body, and environment as interacting to form a single, complex cognitive system. In this framework, it is no longer possible to study cognition outside of an action context, since *'cognition is distributed'* in the environment (Hutchins, 1995). In the field of motor control, for example, the control of movement is no longer linked to a central instance, but emerges from interactions between the organism and the environment (Kelso, 1995), as we saw in the previous chapter when we dealt with the relationship between action and the operations that carry it out.

For cognitivism, cognitive mechanisms are universal and should be studied as such. Cognitive processes are thus seen as independent of bodily involvement in a situation and of culture. To give an example, decision making in sports has been studied in the laboratory in front of diodes of different colors (Temprado, 1991), i.e. independent of an athlete's actual involvement in a sporting encounter. As we saw with the theses on Feuerbach, this postulate favors a contemplative approach that does not link cognitive processes to action (recall Leontiev's example of the rubber band in the previous chapter). Cognitivism sees perception as a passive process of receiving external information. But perception is itself an action.

> Seeing is… a bodily activity. Seeing is not something that happens in us. It is not something that happens to us or in our brains. It is something we do. It is an activity of exploring the world making use of our practical familiarity with the ways in which our own movement drives and modulates our sensory encounter with the world. Seeing is a kind of skillful activity (Noë, 2009, p. 60).

The question that remains unanswered is how this action or skillful activity is acquired. However, it is not possible to think about these acquisitions without going through the necessity of a process of internalization of a culture (Arievitch, 2017). This is the important contribution of CHAT. In this sense, there is no universal mechanism of cognition, insofar as these cognitive processes are inscribed in necessarily cultivated actions. Thus, cognitive processes and their development are essentially social and cultural phenomena and not strictly biological, as cognitivism and some current neurophysiological approaches tend to claim (see Arievitch, 2017).

For cognitivism, cognitive functioning is unconscious: it is said to be subpersonal. More specifically, this means that the computations of the brain-computer to represent a reality outside the cognitive system take place outside the field of consciousness. The mind as described by cognitivism thus seems strange in that everything that makes up human experience or consciousness is not part of cognitive functioning. Thus, most of the criticisms of cognitivism relate to the neglect of consciousness and human experience in its elaboration. In this sense, Varela et al. (1991, p. 139) reject the notion of cognition as arising from a dualistic logic of opposition between exterior and interior. On the contrary, cognition and '*the world*' emerge together: '*It is not a matter of opposing the system and its world in order to find the winner. From the point of view of autonomy, the system and its world emerge simultaneously*'.

The presuppositions of cognitivism, its relevance, and limitations in the study of cognition, were fundamentally challenged in the late 1980s, during Engeström's years of theoretical development. The processes that cognitivism studies are abstract processes, unrelated to the concrete, cultural, embodied, experiential character of our everyday actions and their inscription in historically evolving practical and collective activities. Engeström's work (1987) is thus part of the movement to critique cognitivism. As he himself points out in the preface to the reprint of his work (Engeström, 2015):

> [Learning by Expanding] was written in order to formulate a strong alternative to the dominant Cartesian views of cognition and learning that depicted the human mind as if it were a computer, isolated from the cultural context. In the 1980s, notions such as '*everyday cognition*' (Rogoff & Lave, 1984), '*situated action*' (Suchman, 1987), and '*cognition in practice*' (Lave, 1988) began to emerge and challenge the dominant views. Learning by Expanding was part of this emerging new groundswell.

The book offers a real alternative to the computational approach to cognition and learning. For example, Engeström sees learning as a collective process rather than an individual one, as in traditional cognitive psychology. By seeking to characterize the processes of externalization and development of activity systems, he also opposes a fixed vision of action contexts that can be grasped outside of any activity[10]. For CHAT, it is culture that shapes our cognition and our actions, and contrary to the cognitivist hypothesis, our actions cannot be explained by the way the brain works[11]. At the end of the 1980s, for example, there was a clear convergence of different types of work that challenged the foundations of a cognitivist approach. As Theureau (2004a) puts it:

> All these works showed the inadequacy of the hypothesis and notions of man as a symbolic information processing system and provided empirical descriptions of human activities in a variety of situations. Some of them, notably Engeström (1987), proposed a return to the then largely forgotten psychology of Vygotsky, who had emphasized the mediation of tools, signs and culture in the study of '*higher psychological functions*' (Theureau, 2004a, p. 8).

In addition to offering an alternative to cognitivism and a '*simple return*' to Vygotsky's psychology, the 1987 work also represents an important development in CHAT in that it proposes to analyze learning less as the internalization of a defined form of culture than as a form of externalization and creation of culture. From the beginning of his book, he argues against the '*futility*' of learning when it is conceived as a reactive response to problems already constituted (or conceived as such) in defined and stabilized contexts. We reproduce here the argument used by Engeström (2015), which is essential for the rest of the book:

> Symptomatically enough, Norman ends his book with a tirade on how badly modern technology matches human capabilities. According to him, system designers misuse and ignore the users: 'They start with the machine, and the human is not thought of until the end, when it's too late: witness the control panels in the nuclear power plants' (Norman, 1982, p. 115).

---

[10] On the links between perception and action, and on the perception of the environment as an opportunity for action, see Gibson (1979/2014).

[11] In the CHAT approach, psychological processes do not take place in the brain, but are constituted and emerge from an agent's activity in the world. Accordingly, CHAT distinguishes between mind and brain because the latter cannot explain the former (Arievitch, 2017). Ilyenkov (2002, p. 98) notes this in a provocative formula: "*The substance of mind is always external activity ... and the brain with its inborn structures is only its biological substrate. This is why studying the brain tells you as little about the mind as analyzing the physical properties of gold, silver, or banknote paper tells you about the nature of money*" (quoted in Arievitch, 2017, p. 10).

Norman's solution is that technological systems should be designed so as to make learning easier. Pleas like this follow the traditional patronizing approach: The poor learners must be helped to cope with the tasks given to them. The approach is self-defeating. Norman himself points out that it takes a long time to learn the mastery of a complex skill. At the same time, the contexts of the tasks and skills are going through profound qualitative changes, which often render previous tasks and skills obsolete. Norman himself says, 'when it's too late'. This lag can never be overcome by patronizing, by asking designers to plan more 'user-friendly' systems. It can only be overcome by enabling the users themselves to plan and bring about the qualitative changes (including the design and implementation of technologies) in their life contexts. If learning has nothing to offer in this respect, we have good reason to talk about the futility of learning. Both in theory and in practice, human learning actually seems to be doomed to the role of running after those qualitative changes in people's life contexts (Engeström, 2015, p. 2).

As we can see, Engeström's (radical, to say the least) critique is that artifacts and devices cannot be better thought of in terms of activity and learning. This approach is doomed to failure, and the only way to overcome this difficulty is to provide the means for individuals to change their life contexts (not just their action situations) and to imagine their futures differently. In doing so, it is necessary to focus on a different type of learning that is less reactive and more prospective (i.e. future-oriented), which he calls expansive learning (see Chapter 8 for more on this process).

Collective Activity as Unit of Analysis

In his seminal theoretical work, Engeström (1987, 2015) builds on and extends the early work of Vygotsky and Leontiev:

This third lineage, from Vygotsky to Leont'ev, gives birth to the concept of activity based on material production, mediated by technical and psychological tools as well as by other human beings. This is the lineage I will try to continue and develop (Engeström, 2015, p. 59).

Engeström's (1987, 2015) continuation and expansion of CHAT consisted in developing the concept of activity that had previously been elaborated by Soviet psychologists, in particular by Leontiev (1975/2021, 2009). In doing so, he broke with the tradition that had made activity a concept of psychology and extended it to other disciplines.

As we have seen, there are several reasons for this collective orientation. In his work, Engeström develops a theory of expansive learning to explain the mechanisms of cultural development within communities of practice (Engeström & Sannino, 2010). Both learning and development are analyzed as collective processes through which a community learns and develops (Hefetz & Ben-Zvi, 2020).

Thus, for Engeström, activity is a historical, collective, systemic and cultural formation that responds to societal needs. In this, it is close to the concept of practice developed by Chaiklin (2019) from an example on education. Below we provide an excerpt from this example, which will clarify Engeström's acceptance of the concept of activity if we replace the term practice with activity.

> There is a societal need for educated persons. Educational practice refers to the tradition of action that aims to produce such persons. The organizational and physical form of school provides a common setting or arena where this practice can be carried out. In the current historical organization of school, individual teachers are not able to produce educated pupils by themselves. A division of labor is needed, where each teacher contributes to realizing this objective. The object of the practice – educated pupils – serves as the motive for teachers. It is this object which gives meaning to their activity. The practice is greater than what individual teachers can achieve, but their activity is organized by this practice (Chaiklin, 2019, p. 21).

However, it is important to distinguish between the concepts of practice and activity. The concept of practice refers to the ideal form of a collective organization that crystallizes in the form of routines and recurring patterns of activity (Greeno & Engeström, 2014, p. 128). Activity is the concrete, enacted, and collective form of a practice with a structure or anatomy that Engeström calls an '*activity system*'.

To introduce the different generations of CHAT, Spinuzzi (2018a) describes the historical evolution of CHAT between the work of Vygotsky and Engeström as follows:

> Throughout history, activity theory and the notion of activity have been redefined to go beyond the development of psychic functions to address the development of social systems. As the focus of analysis has shifted, so too has the emphasis. Whereas for Vygotsky, the extraordinary lies in the individual, for Engeström, the extraordinary lies in collective activity (Spinuzzi, 2018a, p. 138).

The shift in CHAT's perspective (and disciplinary focus) has concrete implications for the way social phenomena are viewed. For example, for Engeström, expertise, like learning and development, is no longer seen as an individual process, but as a collective one. In the introduction to his book on expertise, Engeström (2018) contrasts traditional approaches to expertise, which seek to explain the exceptional performance of singular individuals through the idea of a solitary mind and universal (context-independent), self-sufficient cognitive mechanisms, with approaches that view expertise as a collective process. He notes that in the first approach, research has ultimately shown (logically) that the most important factor in expertise is the amount of practice. However, these individual approaches to expertise fail to account for expertise in constantly changing organizations, or to understand how changes within organizations themselves are the product of the expertise of the workers practicing within them. In other words, in challenging the idea of expertise as an individual process, Engeström postulates that expertise resides in collective, object-oriented activity systems and cannot be reduced to individual skills.

For Lektorsky (2009), this focus on external collective activity is fully justified insofar as it is the latter that takes precedence over the inner reality experienced by the individual:

> From the point of view of activity theory, consciousness and 'the inner' are social and cultural constructions and exist, first of all, in forms of collective activity […] Nevertheless, the idea of '*the inner world*' is very important in cultural and social contexts. The subject as the unity of consciousness, the unity of an individual biography, and the center of making decisions can exist only as the center of '*the inner world*'. But the appearance of '*the inner world*' is possible only when the idea of '*the inner*' arises in culture, in other words, when it is realized in forms of collective activity […] In reality, the '*inner space*' of consciousness is a result of individual appropriation of certain kinds of external collective activity. So we may say that the so-called inner space first exists in outer, external actions as a part of collective activity. Internalization is impossible without participation in external mediated activity… (Lektorsky, 2009, pp. 80–83).

Thus, far from turning away from the Vygotskian origins of CHAT or offering a simple return to them, Engeström is a continuator of Vygotsky, integrating him but modifying the unit of analysis to focus on activity conceived as a systemic, collective, historical formation that includes, beyond tools, a plurality of other mediators (rules, division of labor, community). This shift in the unit of analysis is also accompanied by a reduced focus on processes of internalization (the passage from the collective to the individual) in favor of processes of externalization that set in motion and transform the activity system within expansive learning processes. Indeed, Engeström's interventionist approach involves the development of a methodology that enables individuals to transform, repair, or redesign their own activity system.

The Activity System

Based on a historical-genetic analysis of activity, Engeström (2015, pp. 59–63) defines and models an activity system, that is, the structure of human activity. This activity structure fulfills four prerequisites, which, according to him, are necessary to define a viable model of activity (Engeström, 1987, 2015):

(1) The activity is simply defined as the smallest unit of analysis that preserves the unity and essential quality behind any complex activity. Such a unit of analysis is the activity system. It should be remembered that Vygotsky's notion of a unit of analysis refers to his opposition to the kind of analysis that divides things into elements (see the example of the water molecule in the section on the first generation of CHAT).

(2) Activity must be analyzed in its dynamics and transformation, in its evolution and historical changes. This is a fundamental point: it's not so much the analysis of an activity system that needs to be carried out, but the analysis of the qualitative transformations of this activity system. This type of analysis makes it possible to determine possible developments on the basis of the history of transformations, without falling into arbitrary proposals or proposals at odds with the history of the activity system. Here we need to be able to analyze what causes these transformations in activity systems. The concept of contradiction will be essential here (see Chapter 7). But again, we can see the analogy with Vygotskian thinking.

(3) Activity must be analyzed as a contextual and ecological phenomenon. In this sense, laboratory studies are ill suited to account for

this kind of learning, which takes place '*in the wild*' but can still be supported by formative interventions (see Chapter 10)[12].

(4) Activity must be analyzable as a culturally mediated phenomenon. In this sense, dynamic models of the dyadic relationship between environment and organism are clearly insufficient to account for the triadic relationship. Engeström's systemic model of activity is a systemic model of complex mediations. It represents a form of culture in the sense that the transformation of an activity system constitutes a cultural transformation.

The following figure (Figure 8) shows a simplified graphical representation of an activity system. An activity system consists of several interrelated elements.

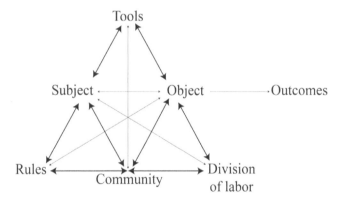

Figure 8: Schematic representation of an activity system from Engeström (1987).

This activity system is a heuristic describing the anatomy of activity, showing the mediating role of tools, rules, community and division of labor.

Let's quickly define each of the different poles, bearing in mind that in this systemic framework each of the poles defines the other (for example, the subjects define the object, but at the same time the object defines

---

12 Expansive learning is not just the product of formative interventions. They are explanatory processes of cultural change. In this sense, they exist in nature. Creating and accelerating these processes "*artificially*" is the goal of formative interventions.

the subjects of this collective formation: we will illustrate this internal dialectical dimension in the next examples).

The following table defines each element of an activity system through a series of simple questions:

Table 4: The main elements of an activity system.

ELEMENT OF THE ACTIVITY	Question	DEFINITION
OBJECT	What is transformed or produced in the activity?	The material and conceptual entity that directs and gives meaning to actions.
SUBJECT	Who is involved in the activity?	The individuals or collective group engaged in the activity; from whose vantage point the analysis is conducted.
TOOLS	How does the subject carry out the activity?	In this process, both physical and symbolic artifacts were mobilized.
RULES	Are there cultural norms, rules, laws and regulations governing the activity?	Regulations, standards, and conventions, both explicit and implicit, that constrain or govern activity.
DIVISION OF LABOR	Who is responsible for what when carrying out the activity, and how are roles organized?	The way tasks are allocated, as well as the structure of roles and hierarchies.
COMMUNITY	What is the environment/ who are the actors in which the activity takes place?	Individuals or groups other than the subject who share a similar objective with the subject and with whom the subject interacts.
OUTCOME	Quels sont les résultats (souhaités ou non) de l'activité?	Activity results.

Let's just highlight one change we've made and the reasons for it. In the previous proposals, outcomes are usually defined in the singular. We have used the plural because outcomes can be so complex to grasp when you want to intervene. They are not only desirable but can also be undesirable. For example, a work organization or activity system may produce a desirable result, but at the cost of very high staff turnover. In this context, turnover is analyzed as an undesirable result of an activity system. To illustrate this, let's mention a recent discussion with the Human Resources Director of a large French company, who mentioned the large number of employees who were unfit for the job. He stressed the need to find them a new job, because '*we must not forget that it is the company that has produced this incapacity*'. In this case, disability is in fact an undesirable result (just like accidents at work or occupational diseases) produced by an activity system. Lopes, Vilela, Querol, and de Almeida (2020, p. 134) also share this vision, in that they mention expected and unexpected results (in this context, fines, delays, high staff turnover, etc.) in their presentation of an activity system oriented towards the construction of an airport.

Let's now illustrate the different components of this activity system with an example related to the research activity. Before going any further, let's remember that for Leontiev (Chapter 3), what distinguishes one activity from another is its object. Activity is defined not by the subject who performs it, but by the object. In what follows, we speak of research activity (i.e. a historically evolving social practice), not of the activity of researchers. This research activity is enacted and exists concretely only through the actions of researchers… and through those of other protagonists who are part of this activity.

An Example: Research Activity

Research is an essential activity for society. The result of such an activity is undoubtedly the production of scientific articles, to the extent that the adage '*publish or perish*' has become commonplace. But research is not an 'individual' activity, even if it is carried out by an isolated researcher. A researcher's actions are social from the outset and thus take their place in a collective activity system. Marx (1844/1972) reminds us of this when he points out that:

> But even if my activity is scientific, etc., and I can seldom carry it on in direct community with others, I am social because I act as a man. Not only is the material of my activity—such as language itself, through which the thinker exercises his—given to me as a social product, but my very existence is a social activity; so is what I do with myself, what I do with myself for society, and with the consciousness of myself as a social being (Marx, 1844/1972, p. 89).

So who is involved in the division of labor? The editors who check the article and ask for corrections, the publisher, and also the readers. In order to produce his or her research, the scientist (or team of scientists) must follow a certain set of rules and norms: ethical and deontological rules (e.g. all research must be published), rules set by the journal, rules for citation or presentation of the work (e.g. rules set by the American Psychological Association), but also norms (an article can only be presented in a journal that allows it to be published, so you wouldn't present a humanities article in a theoretical physics journal). The researcher or group of researchers mobilizes conceptual and methodological tools to carry out their research. Finally, they place their work within a community that shares at least part of the object of their work (e.g. learning). Inspired by Roth (2001), we can represent this system of research activity as follows (Figure 9):

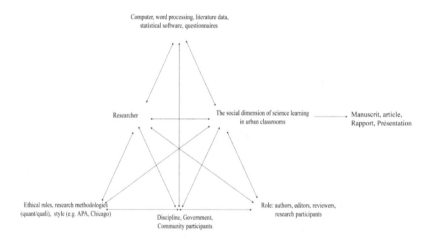

Figure 9 Schematic Representation of an Academic Research Activity System from Roth (2001).

But What Are the Four Sub-triangles for?

In the previous example, we have simplified the analysis. The use of the triangle focuses on its structural elements and not on its systemic and dynamic dimension. Moving to a systemic view means taking a closer look at the relationships that exist between the different poles of the activity system.

As mentioned earlier, the triangle of an activity system (Figure 8) is simplified at first glance because it does not include any subsystems that would allow us to consider the dynamics of the system. Thus, the activity triangle consists of 4 interdependent subsystems:

- (1) The production triangle, which links the subject/object/instrument poles.
- (2) The consumption triangle, which links the subject/object/community poles.
- (3) The distribution triangle, which links the community/object/division of labor poles.
- (4) The triangle of exchange, connecting the poles of subject/community/rule.

Roth (2008) notes this simplification, found in a number of publications as follows:

> Although the original triangular representation of the structure of human activity includes the terms production, consumption, distribution, and exchange (Engeström, 1987), these terms are seldom found in the theoretical articulations of (Western) authors who pledge allegiance to cultural–historical activity theory. This is unfortunate because these concepts are central to the elaboration of third-generation cultural–historical activity theory and therefore are intrinsic to its functioning (Roth, 2008, p. 179).

These four sub-triangles within the Activity System are shown in the following figure (Figure 10).

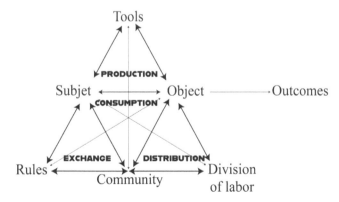

Figure 10: Representation of the sub-triangles of production, consumption, exchange and distribution within an activity system.

Let's take the example of primitive hunting to illustrate how these different sub-triangles are interdependent within an activity system. When the hunting collective performs a hunting activity (production triangle), it consumes energy (consumption triangle), but the very activity of hunting is to produce food to compensate for the energy consumed. Thus, the consumption and production triangles are consubstantial: consumption is the flip side of production.

Let's take this analysis one step further. The community also includes women and children who have not directly participated in the productive activity. The proceeds of the hunt must be redistributed to these individuals to ensure the survival of the community. Distribution, then, is a consequence of production, but it is also a precondition for production, since it ensures the distribution of roles and tools and, more generally, the distribution of functions related to productive activities. Here again, distribution is the essential other side of production. Finally, exchange is both a necessity for production and the consequence of a fair and just distribution of production.

This analysis can, of course, be applied to any productive and collective activity. In research, for example, the production of a scholarly article implies an act of consumption, insofar as it is necessary to draw on existing literature. But at the same time, the production of a scholarly article aims to be read and, above all, cited. Thus, in this activity as well, production and consumption presuppose each other.

As we can see, the activity system constitutes a '*unity*' in that it contains different '*moments*' that are consubstantial with each other (production, consumption, exchange, distribution). It is the consubstantiality of these different moments that ensures the robustness and durability of an activity over time. For Engeström (2015, p. 65), '*The model is actually the smallest and most simple unit that still preserves the essential unity and integral quality behind any human activity*'.

The Activity System as a Context for Situated Actions

Roth's depiction of research activity (2001), as well as his understanding of the consubstantial link between the different sub-triangles of activity, underscores the importance of the principles of dialectics in the construction of this model representing an activity system.

The upper triangle (that of production) represents the tip of the iceberg. It is what can be observed and analyzed in a work situation. Let's imagine that you are a researcher who wants to observe my work as I write this book. You will observe me in my usual work situation, sitting at my desk, rereading notes, typing, occasionally thinking, and so on. But what you observe, and what you may discuss with me during an interview, is just the tip of the iceberg. All the actions described taking place within a collective activity that involves a division of labor (and production), regular exchanges with colleagues within a community, and so on.

Thus, to focus on the tip of the iceberg, i.e. the triadic relationship between a subject, an object and instruments, is to carry out an analysis that can be described as '*decontextualized*'. Even if my actions could be finely resituated in my work situation in order to understand, for example, the instrumental genesis behind the writing actions (how I appropriated and at the same time used software like Scrivener to organize my manuscript), the analysis would, paradoxically, be incomplete because it would not integrate a context in which there are readers, colleagues with whom I have discussions, rules to respect, time to allocate, and so on. In a sense, although the analysis resituates my actions in the work situation, it is necessarily decontextualized in relation to the human activity in which my actions take place. For Karanasios, Nardi, Spinuzzi, and Malaurent (2021, p. 2):

> Human activity cannot be explained simply by the interaction of subject-mediating tools-object (the top part of the activity system) because the activity is thereby decontextualized. Rather, contextualized collective activity includes all elements of the activity system (Prenkert, 2010).

To illustrate what we mean by contextualizing analysis within an activity system, we give an example below. In a research seminar, a colleague presents a cross-case self-confrontation (Clot, Faïta, Fernandez, & Scheller, 2002) between two gravediggers as part of an intervention in the clinic of activity (Clot, 2006). During this interview, a controversy arose between the two gravediggers about the best way to break a tombstone with a sledgehammer. For one, the gesture should be made with the edge of the sledgehammer. For the other, the gesture should be performed by dropping the sledgehammer flat on the gravestone. Faced with the difficulty of agreeing on the best technique, the two gravediggers decided to carry out a simulation of the two techniques in the field, filmed by the intervening researcher.

In the film shot by the researcher, it is possible to observe the two gravediggers testing the two techniques and arguing based on their sensations and the product of their actions. But we can also observe another operator with a wheelbarrow collecting pieces of gravestones. In other words, limiting the analysis to what one operator does in performing a task (in this case, breaking a gravestone) seems necessarily decontextualized in that it denies the collective dimension and division of labor necessary for the analysis. This division of labor makes it necessary to look at the gesture in a different way. It's not just a matter of going fast and breaking the tombstone with ease. It's also about producing pieces that are neither too large nor too small, so that they can be easily and comfortably transported by the operator in charge of the removal.

Let's go one step further. In this excerpt, the material object of the activity is *'the gravestone'*. The real motive behind the gravediggers' actions is the 'reassignment of a burial plot'. However, this activity, which meets an obvious social need, implies a much broader division of labor than can be observed in the situation: for example, administrative work carried out according to well-established rules, decisions taken by the mayor of the commune, and so on. Here, as with Leontiev (1978), the goal of the action and the motive do not coincide (reassignment of a grave plot →breaking of a gravestone). And if we want to understand what the operators are doing in a work situation, we have to recontextualize the analysis within an activity system: they're not just breaking a gravestone with a sledgehammer, they're taking part in the collective activity of reallocating a grave plot, not in the reprehensible action of organized gang vandalism. The activity system is logically important for the analysis, because otherwise it would be impossible to distinguish between actions that are useful to the community (breaking a gravestone →reassignment a cemetery plot) and actions that are harmful to society (breaking a gravestone → vandalizing a cemetery).

Thus, an activity system constitutes the spatially and temporally distributed context of an observable work situation. The lower part of the triangle is the tip of the iceberg. Only the analysis of an activity system enables us to understand the actions or operations of operators in a work situation. In other words, the activity system is the invisible context of an operator's situated actions.

This very particular conception of an activity system as a context contrasts with more traditional conceptions of this notion rooted in formal logic. Indeed, contexts or environments are often considered in terms of hierarchically organized static concentric circles (see Figure 11 for a representation). They are hierarchically organized in that the outer circles seem to '*determine*' and '*control*' the innermost circles. For example, writing this book is part of a work situation (micro context), which is part of an academic institution (meso context), which is part of a national policy of the Ministry of Higher Education and Research (macro context).

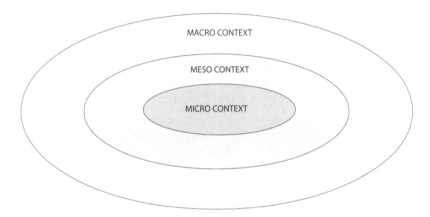

Figure 11: Classic representation of the notion of context.

This type of representation is what Davydov (1990b) calls empirical generalizations (Engeström, 2016, p. 103). However, this type of generalization (and representation) turns out to be limited because it does not allow us to account for the dynamics and origins of the phenomena under study. Engeström (2009a, p. 20) goes further and formulates the idea that this type of representation '*becomes an empty shell, a place that can be filled with any number of dimensions or variables used to classify other elements that seem to fit into the general category in question*'. In this way, empirical generalization is the way to fill boxes with factors that are more or less distant from the situation we want to study. In our view, the notion of determinants is consubstantial with this kind of contextual representation and empirical generalization, and does not (logically) depart from a factor-based approach.

The activity system is an alternative in that it shows the mechanisms at work in productive activity and their interrelationships. It provides an explanatory unit for understanding the genesis and roots of actions. It also points to a different interpretation of context. In the framework of activity theory, the term context refers to another meaning, closer to the Latin root of the term 'contextere', which means 'to weave together' (Cole, 1996, p. 135). Thus, context is seen as dynamically created by the weaving together of 'fibers' of action that together form a rope (a collective activity system) that is sufficiently strong and stable over time. The fibers of action are themselves created by threads of action. Understood in this way, context is not something external, but a qualitative relationship between at least two distinct, hierarchically organized units of analysis.

Finally, this metaphor of threads, fibers, and cords makes clear that in activity theory it is human activity that creates its own context. The figure of an activity system represents the anatomy or structure of this context, making it an analytical tool for understanding situated actions and operations.

What are the implications of this metaphor? For us, it's an important one because it allows us to reposition or even redefine terms commonly used in the work of science literature. For example, this organization is not a context external to activity. On the contrary, it is constitutive of activity, just as activity is constitutive of organization. This is clearly seen by Lorino (2017), who suggests a double meaning in the relationship between organization and activity:

> The concept of activity is not always clearly identified, especially in its relationship with organization, and this raises significant methodological problems that are rarely satisfactorily resolved. […] The relationship between organization and activity is not one of container and content: certainly, as is generally admitted, activity is always situated in an organization, but as we shall see, the organization is just as much situated in activity (Lorino, 2017, p. 921).

Thus, it is not possible to understand a situated action without relating it to its social and historical extensions, structurally inscribed in an activity system.

Activity System as an Ideal Type

Let's return to Roth's research example. It would be possible to formulate the critical idea that the analysis presented by Roth (2001) proves to be largely incomplete, beyond being speculative (it is not based on empirical data in his article). Regarding the dimension of incompleteness, we would like to make a very important point. This model does not serve to describe reality: it is a tool for analyzing reality. In addition to the fact that reality always exceeds the models that attempt to describe it, we would like to point out that the activity system is not intended to represent reality, but to circumscribe its essential features for analysis. The activity system is therefore both a tool for analysis, in that it provides a heuristic; the expression of a dialectical conception of human activity; and a result, in that it reveals only a qualitative part of reality. As a result of analysis, the activity system functions as an ideal type in Weber (1992) sense.

> An ideal type is obtained by unilaterally accentuating one or more points of view and stringing together a multitude of isolated, diffuse, and discrete phenomena, sometimes in large numbers, sometimes in small numbers, and sometimes not at all, which are ordered according to the previously unilaterally chosen points of view to form a homogeneous picture. Such a picture in its conceptual purity is nowhere to be found empirically (Weber, 1992, p. 181).

Thus, the activity system as an ideal type is no more than an abstract, 'ideal' form that accentuates certain features of social practice to reveal its anatomy or main anatomical features.

An activity system as a collective formation is not a homogeneous entity. Thus, within an activity system, and naturally, each individual has his or her own meaning of the object of the activity system in terms of his or her own position in the division of labor. For example, during an intervention in a *'priority education network'*, a district coordinator put forward the idea that working in priority education means working in a different way from the classical school form and that network projects should enable a more horizontal operation between primary and secondary schools. For the principal, on the other hand, working in a network meant working on the links between primary and secondary education (Lémonie et al., 2021). So, for Engeström (1993):

An activity system is not a homogeneous entity. To the contrary, it is composed of a multitude of often disparate elements, voices, and viewpoints. This multiplicity can be understood in terms of historical layers. An activity system always contains sediments of earlier historical modes, as well as buds or shoots of its possible future. These sediments and buds – historically meaningful differences – are found in the different components of the activity system, including the physical tools and mental models of the subjects. They are also found in the actions and object units of the activity (Engeström, 1993, p. 68).

This historical dimension is important. Indeed, the examples given so far could lead one to think that activity systems are typical ideal models, instruments for analyzing the functioning of an activity system. On the contrary, they are instruments for analyzing the potential development of an activity system. That's what we're going to do now.

The Dynamic Dimension of an Activity System

To be interested in functioning is to situate it at a particular point in time. Analyzing functioning is not the same as analyzing dynamics, let alone the evolutionary process of a system. Thus, if we believe that the activity system is a tool for analyzing the functioning of an activity, we run the risk of slipping into a static, fixed representation of an activity and preventing ourselves from understanding future evolutions or developments in practice. In the example of research activity borrowed from Roth (2001), he himself defines his representation as 'static'. It doesn't take into account the sedimented history within an activity system or potential developments.

In fact, Roth's (2001) approach violates the very principle of activity and its analysis, as he himself acknowledges. Indeed, activity is a process, and accounting for it implies accounting for at least the form or direction of that process. This dynamic dimension of the model is not recognized by many researchers. As a result, one of the recurring criticisms of the model is that it is precisely 'static'. For example, Bakhurst (2009) criticizes the representation of the activity system as follows:

> The moral is that you must be very cautious about given, stable, structural representations where you aspire to understand dynamism, flux, reflexivity, and transformation (Bakhurst, 2009, p. 207).

However, this model as such has no meaning outside of a developmental orientation. It is a tool for analyzing the historical development of an activity system, not for analyzing its functioning. In other words, the goal of the activity system model is to capture the '*developmental functioning*' of an activity system through the history of its transformations. Indeed, activity is a self-moving phenomenon. Activity is a minimal unit of change (because it consists of the same entities before, during, and after change). To account for this self-movement is to account for the internal contradictions of the activity system. However, Roth's figure representing research activity contained nothing contradictory to account for the dynamics of activity. Thus, the risk of trying to analyze activity with this model in the manner of Roth (2001) is to '*construct a sterile representation of interconnected abstract elements*' (Sannino, 2011, p. 580).

Thus, in constructing a model of activity, we must combat the positivist tendency to freeze it in stable characteristics that do not evolve historically, thereby erasing the dialectical dimension inherent in CHAT:

> The representatives of the positivist approach largely concerned with the analysis of an object into its constituent elements and stable characteristics, rather than to reveal its internal contradiction. In a rapidly changing world, filled with dramatic conflicts and contradictions, the reductionist and elementalist approaches are doomed to fail due to their inability to understand complex, developing systems (Dafermos, 2020, p. 24).

Thus, in Engeström's own multiple representations of an activity system, he seeks to account for the internal contradictions of the system he is analyzing. Let's take Roth (2001)'s example of research and contrast it with Engeström's (2016, p. 5) model of learning research (see Figure 12).

Based on the dilemmas highlighted in the editorials of learning science journals, Engeström states that the system of research activity is traversed by contradictions that are internal to each pole and present themselves in the form of alternatives. What Roth (2001) presented as a rule ('*publish or perish*') leading to an expected result (scientific production) is presented by Engeström as inscribed in an alternative between academic commitment and commitment to the transformation of social practices.

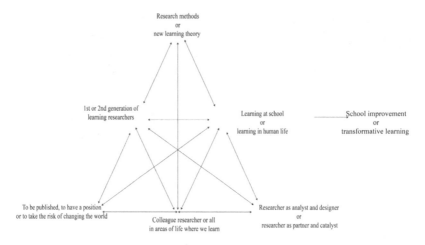

Figure 12: Representation of research activity for Engeström (2016, p. 5).

If, as Roth notes, the object of activity is constructed out of a societal need, it is not the publication or research as such that constitutes a need, but the use that can be made of it at the societal level. Engeström's diagram thus highlights the primary contradiction between use value and exchange value. In the first case, we produce scientific research to change or improve certain situations. In the second case, research is produced to '*make a career*'. Clearly, and rather surprisingly, Roth (2001) takes it for granted that research is done primarily for its exchange value, not its use value.

Highlighting these internal contradictions allows us to define the very principle of the self-movement of an activity system. It allows us to explain the internal dynamics of the activity system. As we can see here, the aim of an activity system analysis is not to account for the components of an activity system, according to the elementary approach denounced by Dafermos (2020). On the contrary, it is to focus the analysis on the internal contradictions of an activity system to understand its movement. These contradictions are historically inherited within an activity system. They also allow us to delimit a space of possible developments for this activity system.

Let's put it another way: the aim of the analysis is not to focus on the functioning, but on the possible development of an activity system. In this respect, fixed representations (as in the example of Roth, 2001), '*elementarist*' approaches and situated ethnographic approaches (which forget the context of an activity system) are unsuitable for providing a perspective on future transformations of activity systems, as Engeström (2000c) points out:

> Ethnographic studies have traditionally been preoccupied with observing and understanding stable orders, routines and repeatable procedures. The issue of change has been relatively alien to them. In this regard, they seem to be inherently handicapped in dealing with the turbulent worlds of work and technology (Engeström, 2000c, p. 151).

Four Uses of the Activity System

Four different uses of the activity system model can be identified. The first of these is the identification of the poles of the activity system. Very often this type of use refers to the researcher using the system to study actions. He then '*fills*' the activity system with what he sees. This use is possible (Engeström, 2000a), but it does not distinguish between actions and activity. It doesn't really belong to a system thinking approach that considers the links between the different elements of the activity system. This is what we might call descriptive-elementarist use (USAGE 1). For example, for the example of gravediggers in the cemetery *Père Lachaise* in Paris, this model could be used to describe the instrument used (the sledgehammer), the object that is assimilated to a goal (breaking a gravestone), the division of labor (one who breaks, the other who collects), the community (reduced to the craft), and the rules (completing the task within the allotted time).

To move to a second type of use, it is therefore necessary to (1) differentiate actions and activity; (2) think about the relationships between the different elements of the activity system. If we continue with the example of the gravediggers, what they do in a situation is not an activity, but a series of actions that carry out an activity. This activity aims to create new space in the cemetery without expanding the cemetery. It responds to a community need, just as it responds to certain administrative rules. Finally, the division of labor goes far beyond the cooperative processes that can be observed in the work situation: it includes administrative workers, the mayor, etc. This second type of use, which we call ahistorical systemic (USAGE 2), allows us to understand the meaning of actions by resituating them in an activity system at a given moment in time.

The third type of usage is historical, which allows us to look at the historical development of an activity (USAGE 3). It provides an account of the historical evolution of the activity. Still taking our cemetery example, in Paris, after the Revolution, funeral rites were forbidden in cemeteries, the Parisian inner cemeteries were closed and communal burial became the rule. Napoleon's decree of 1804 settled the issue of sanitation by creating funeral concessions and banning mass graves. The work of gravediggers evolved: they are the only people who can handle a corpse years after death. Their work is essential to ensure that the dead can be buried in conditions of health and respect for their families. This type of analysis allows us to understand the history of the activity, the historical role of gravediggers, and the evolution of rules and tools. But it does not yet allow us to explain the logic of development.

The fourth type of use allows us to identify the driving forces of historical development in the form of contradictions. This is a dialectical use of the activity system model (USE 4). The creation of concessions was a response to the public health problem associated with mass graves and the distance of cemeteries from city centers by creating a new object: the funeral concession. As a result, the activity of cemeteries evolved, as did the tasks entrusted to gravediggers. Cemeteries became places for visitors and public spaces. The Père-Lachaise cemetery opened its doors in 1804 and today welcomes more than 2 million visitors a year. The issue of the reallocation of burial plots is linked to the contradiction of creating space in an area (the cemetery) that cannot be expanded. The analysis must allow us to locate the historical contradictions that allow us to understand both past and future developments: it's a dialectical use of the activity system (USAGE 4). What might the future hold for gravediggers? Societal trends certainly point the way. The increase in cremations (50 % of funerals in France in the coming years) and environmental issues are changing our relationship with the grave and the funeral. Techniques such as 'aquamation' and 'humusation' are being developed in North America to reduce the carbon footprint of funerals, while at the same time contradicting the rules of current funeral systems, which require the deceased to be placed in a coffin.

These four uses are important to distinguish. At the same time, they represent a progression in the appropriation of the activity system and the CHAT. We depict these four uses in the following diagram. The transition from USAGE 1 to USAGE 2 is made by differentiating the actions of the activity and studying their links, and by adopting a systemic logic to identify the relationships between the elements of the activity system. The transition from USAGE 2 to USAGE 3 is made by adopting a descriptive historical logic that identifies developmental periods in the activity system. The transition from USAGE 3 to USAGE 4 is made by adopting a dialectical perspective that identifies the contradictions at the source of changes in the activity system.

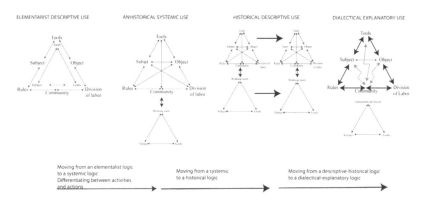

Figure 13: Four uses of the Activity System model and the logics of transition between uses.

Extending Activity Theory to the Third Generation

It wasn't until the 1990s that a third generation of activity theory really emerged, although the premises were laid out in Learning by Expanding. In this third generation, the unit of analysis is no longer limited to a single activity system. Instead, it encompasses one or more interacting activity systems. Nevertheless, the hierarchical structure of activities, as proposed by Leontiev (1981), remains:

> In activity theory, a collective, artifact-mediated, and object-oriented activity system, seen in its network relations to other activity systems, is taken as the prime unit of analysis. Goal-directed individual and group actions and action clusters, as well as automatic operations, are relatively independent but subordinate units of analysis, eventually understandable only when interpreted against the background of entire activity systems. Activity systems realize and reproduce themselves by generating actions and operations (Engeström, 2018, p. 14).

Within this framework, as shown in Figure 13, the unit of analysis of the third generation of activity theory can be modeled as two interacting activity systems.

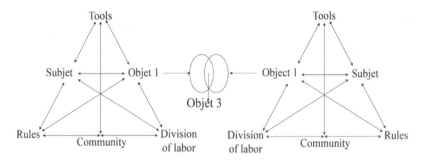

Figure 14: Two interacting Activity Systems as a minimal unit of analysis for the third generation of CHAT.

In terms of evolution, the object becomes 'fragmented': it is partly shared by another activity system, but since the determination of this object is historically constituted, it goes without saying that this sharing risks inducing *'contradictions'* between activity systems.

This broadening of the unit of analysis is particularly useful for understanding developments in work that involve the collaboration of activity systems that have been historically constituted separately. This is the case, for example, in the implementation, following the 2005 law and the 2013 orientation law on disability, of the desire to get schools, families and departmental health centers to work together to create an *'inclusive school'*. However, this interprofessional work is not self-evident, as the inclusive school is a boundary object (Star & Griesemer, 1989) likely to bring together the worlds of school, family and care, but also to come into contradiction with the modes of operation historically constituted within each of these systems. In fact, the education system was built and developed on the basis of an operating model that was historically quite different from that of *'special education'*. And so,

> The inclusive school is therefore, above all, a project that requires the transformation of the school, a project to be shared that could allow the long-awaited rapprochement of the worlds of school, medical-educational services and families (Thomazet & Mérini, 2015, p. 2).

Lémonie and Grosstephan (2022) present the inclusive school as an object shared by three institutions: the school, the family and the departmental house for the disabled (MDPH).

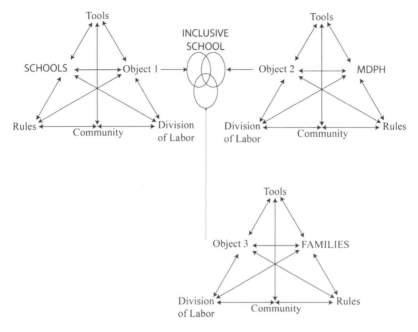

Figure 15: The inclusive school as an object shared by several activity systems, according to Lémonie and Grosstephan (2022).

Benefits and Risks of Extending the Analysis Unit

This expansion of the analysis unit has both advantages and risks.

The Benefits of Expansion: A Better Understanding of Social Phenomena

Analytically speaking, social phenomena are much better explained when we don't isolate an activity system from the network of activity systems that produce it or share the same object. Let's take three different examples to illustrate this point.

First example: First, an activity system does not exist in isolation in a '*vacuum*'. There are always related activity systems that produce the subject(s), rules, instruments, or division of labor of another activity system. Using Roth's (2001) example of research activity, it is possible to identify the activity systems that are related to the activity system that is central to the analysis. For example, Figure 15 shows that researchers (subjects of the research activity system) are produced by the university, that rules are produced by ethics committees, and so on. This network of activity systems further reinforces the stability of an activity system (recall the rope metaphor: here a network is made up of ropes knotted together).

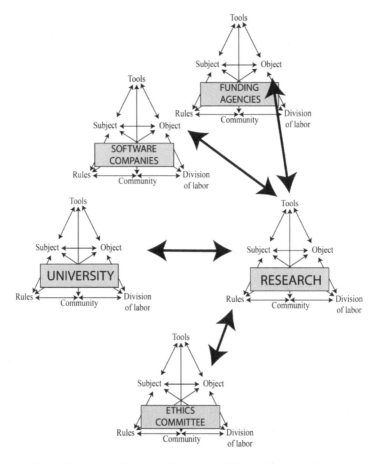

Figure 16: A Network of Activity Systems stabilizes the central Activity System (in this case, the research activity).

In this first example, however, the network of activity systems is generated by relations between activity systems. But it may be that an activity system is a subsystem of a larger activity system: either the division of labor begins to constitute a new activity system, or an activity system integrates an autonomous activity system as a new component of the division of labor. Thus, within a work organization, it's probably best to analyze management as a subactivity system within a company. Engeström (2009b) proposes a unit of analysis that links the '*company*' activity system, which consists of two subsystems (the management subsystem and the work unit subsystem), with the customer activity system.

Second example: Beyond the dimension specific to ease of analysis, it is possible for an independent activity system to become a subsystem of a larger activity system. Let's take the example of an intervention in a university teacher training institute (INSPÉ). Historically, these INSPÉs evolved from teacher training colleges (*écoles normales d'instituteurs*), which became IUFMs in 1989. Between 1989 and 2009, the IUFMs were responsible for initial teacher training. In 2009, with the '*mastérisation*' reform of teacher training, the preparation for the civil service recruitment exam was integrated into the master's program and the ESPÉs were integrated as a component of the university. This integration as a component took place mainly at the administrative level and had a clear impact on the daily work of the various actors (teachers and administrators alike). For example, one of the directors of an INSPÉ department feels that the university is not a real partner. This view can be explained historically: when the ESPÉs were integrated into the university, they lost their administrative and hiring autonomy. The parts of the ESPÉs that are located in areas that are sometimes far away from the university have been neglected because historically the university was not established there. This history has consequences for everyone's work: the secretaries juggle between sometimes contradictory rules (those of the University and those of the Ministry of Education), the directors of the INSPÉ components try to find projects to revitalize their structure and attract students (insofar as their budget is the consequence of the number of students enrolled), and the students find themselves in an unequal situation: they pay for services (libraries, the University Sports and Activities Service – SUAPS –, the University Cultural Activities Service – SUAC –) even though there is no access to these services in the areas neglected by the University.

Third Example: As you can see, a system doesn't exist in a vacuum. But this illustration does not justify the claim that social phenomena are much better explained when we try to take into account the interactions between several activity systems. To validate this claim, let's take a third example of an ergonomic intervention carried out by Master students.

The intervention takes place in a laboratory that produces silicone breast prostheses. The request to which they responded concerned an explosion in the number of musculoskeletal disorders (MSDs). However, the two ergonomists quickly realized that it would be impossible to consider the movements of the operators without taking into account a rapidly changing context.

Every year, 1.7 million breast implants are placed worldwide for aesthetic or reconstructive purposes. Whether filled with saline or silicone gel, breast implant shells can have smooth or textured surfaces. Breast implant-associated anaplastic large cell lymphoma (BIA-ACLL) is a rare form of non-Hodgkin's lymphoma recognized in the 2017 World Health Organization (WHO) classification. This cancer has been linked to the use of textured implants. In late November 2018, a global investigation by the International Consortium of Investigative Journalists (ICIJ) revealed major lapses in the regulation of medical implants, particularly breast implants. These revelations come less than 10 years after the PIP implant health scandal and the condemnation of the French state, with the courts finding that the French state had not taken '*the necessary control and investigation measures*'. A few months later, France became the first country to ban the textured implant linked to BIA-ACLL: the French National Agency for Medicines and Health Products (ANSM) banned textured breast implants from several manufacturers on April 2, 2019 (Vaysse, Laurent, Ysebaert, Chantalat, & Chaput, 2019).

This new regulation has an immediate impact on the production of silicone breast implants at Laboratory X. Prior to this regulation, the production of textured implants represented 95 % of total production, compared to only 5 % for smooth implants. Between the journalists' revelations and the ANSM's ban on textured implants, production quickly dropped to 25 % textured implants and 75 % smooth implants.

In addition to the qualitative change in production, the work of the operators who make the implants has become more difficult. In the case of shells produced by the dipping process, the scrap rate is around 25 %, which is considered normal in the manufacture of implants, the quality of which must be extremely controlled and beyond reproach. Over time, the reject rate has steadily increased and reached 50 %, following the

ANSM recommendation to give preference to smooth implants. As of February 2019, this rate is around 35 % to 40 %.

Figure 17 below illustrates the interactions between different activity systems. Understanding the activity system and its evolution, represented by Laboratory X, cannot be understood outside of a broader analysis that includes other interacting activity systems. Neither can actions and operations. The increase in MSDs within the lab is related to the historical evolution and interactions between the activity systems.

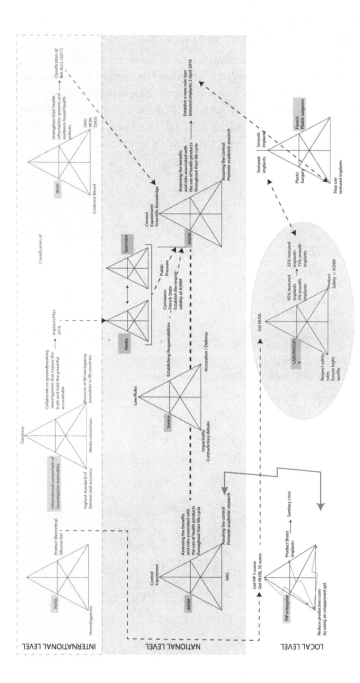

Figure 17: Representation of a network of activity systems to understand the rapid transformations within Laboratory X, the failures in production and the significant increase in MSDs.

Risks: Difficulty in Circumscribing Activity Systems and Loss of the Bodily, Experiential and Subjective Dimension

From the point of view of the risk, this expansion of the unit of analysis to multiple interacting activity systems is likely to lead to the loss of sight of the sensitive dimension embodied in operations and actions, and in the end to the analysis of only the evolution and development of activity systems, without taking into account their concrete embodiment in the realization of actions and operations. However, as Leontiev (1975/2021, p. 91) says, *'Activity is a molar, non-additive unit of the life of the real, concrete subject'*. Understanding the history of interaction between several activity systems does not mean forgetting the concrete dimension. On the contrary, we would say that the history of the evolution of activity systems helps us to better understand everyday actions, as well as the reasons for the problems encountered by professionals.

Nevertheless, this risk of a disembodied analysis is described by Engeström (2015) as a form of schism to be avoided, as it goes against the very principles on which activity theory was founded.

Third-generation activity theory expands the analysis both up and down, outward and inward. Moving up and outward, it tackles multiple interconnected activity systems with their partially shared and often fragmented objects. Moving down and inward, it tackles issues of subjectivity, experiencing, personal sense, emotion, embodiment, identity, and moral commitment. The two directions may seem incompatible. Indeed, there is a risk that activity theory is split into the study of activity systems, organizations, and history, on the one hand, and subjects, actions, and situations, on the other hand. This is exactly the kind of split the founders of activity theory set out to overcome. To bridge and integrate the two directions, serious theoretical and empirical efforts are needed (Engeström, 2015, pp. xv–xvi).

With the third generation of the CHAT, the macrostructure of analysis is expanded to include a fourth level. According to Tkachenko and Ardichvili (2017), this expansion, or qualitative transformation, of the primary unit of analysis results in four structural and hierarchical levels: (1) network of activity systems, (2) collective system of local activities, (3) actions, and (4) operations.

They further note that while an analysis that would include all four levels is rare (but not impossible), CHAT researchers have extensively analyzed the interaction between two adjacent levels, primarily the action and activity levels, in development work research (e.g. Engeström, 1996b, 2000c, 2005).

The emphasis on this interaction between two levels of the activity system, namely activity and action, probably explains why the second and third generations of activity theory are presented as macro studies of an evolving historical activity system, closer to an *'organizational sociology'* (Spinuzzi, 2011), as opposed to micro approaches that focus primarily on actions and operations situated in a local context: *'In order to simplify, Situated Learning Theory might be characterized as an agency-driven micro approach to practice, while Activity Theory can be conceived as a historically relevant macro approach'* (Arnseth, 2008, p. 300).

In the light of our account and the examples we have given, we obviously disagree with this account by Arnseth (2008). Third generation activity theory is about integrating different levels of analysis: an activity system can only be understood in relation to other activity systems; an action can only be understood in relation to an activity system; an operation can only be understood in a work situation.

In this respect, the third generation of activity theory is an integrative, systemic and dialectical approach. Its mobilization for empirical analysis is certainly a challenge, but it provides the theoretical keys for the analysis of the relationships between the local and the global, and the global and the local.

Let's be clear: in this view, it is not the global that determine the local, but the two that determine each other. And let's add that the global isn't just *'outside'* the local, it's *'within'* the local as well.

In our example of breast prosthesis production in laboratory X, if changes in the interaction between several activity systems lead to both musculoskeletal disorders (MSDs) and a high scrap rate, then the work gestures of the operators (the operations) inevitably also determine the future development of the activity system and its place within a network. But to mobilize the activity triangle, it is necessary to abandon forms of reasoning in the form of linear causality that are present in both quantitative approaches and much qualitative research and analysis (Maxwell, 2004). In short, we must abandon formal logic in favor of a dialectical approach.

Some Criticisms of Engeström's Approach

Here we present some of the criticisms that have been leveled at Engeström's activity system model.

In presenting the CHAT and Engeström's work in particular, Nicolini (2012) argues that the main weaknesses of the approach proposed by Engeström paradoxically lie in its strengths. For him, the activity system and its graphic representation constitute a powerful '*mediator*' of theory, which has effectively supported the circulation and adoption of activity theory. But a model is not a theory. Reducing CHAT to a model of the activity system runs the risk of losing sight of the processual nature of activity. As a result, in practice, the activity system is often reduced to "*a* "*thing*", *a real entity* "*containing*" *the different elements (objects, rules, etc.) that someone will, before long, try to measure or reduce to a series of factors. The signs are already there*' (Nicolini, 2012, p. 120). Nicolini's (2012) criticism is not directed at the model itself, so to speak, but at how it is likely to be used if attention is not paid to the theory underlying it. In particular, we agree with Nicolini (2012, p. 119) when he points out that the strength of the CHAT comes from '*combining a radically processual approach to the study of practice with a sensitivity for contradiction, development, and change derived from the Marxist tradition*'.

In the developments of this chapter, we have tried to present the activity system through numerous examples, not as a tool for analyzing the functioning of an activity system (and even less its composition), but as a means for understanding the historical developments of the activity in which the actions take place. In our view, the notion of contradiction, which will be discussed in more detail in Chapter 7 of this book, is crucial to overcoming this risk. Finally, Nicolini's (2012) criticism concerns the simplicity of the use of the activity system model, which allows for uses or interpretations that are in profound contradiction with the CHAT.

Among these interpretations that detach the activity system model from the theory in which it is embedded, we could mention Bakhurst (2023, p. 316), who focuses his critique on the static and structural character of the activity system model. Again, to be valid, criticism should not be directed at the model itself, but at its use in research; otherwise, the question posed by Bakhurst becomes unavoidable:

Engeström speaks confidently of the triangular structure of activity. But what is the rationale for that (apart from the supposed authority of Vygotsky)? Why not just have a list of factors? (Bakhurst, 2023, p. 315).

To reduce the activity system to a list of factors or elements is to lose sight of the central role that contradictions play in the transformation of an activity system. In this chapter we have tried to show how contradictions are central to the representation of an activity system. It is possible to point to numerous counterexamples of research that mobilizes or quotes the activity system but does not represent it in its movement or in its transformations. To give just one example, the study by Liaw, Huang, and Chen (2007) on the design of e-learning modules reduces the activity system to a list of factors concerning students' attitudes, which are investigated by means of questionnaires. The processual and dynamic dimension of activity is lost in favor of a factorial and elementarist conception.

While the concept of contradiction seems essential for understanding the idea that an activity system contains the sources of its self-movement, it remains vague for Bakhurst (2023, p. 315): *'In terms of understanding the dynamics of the activity system, a fair load is carried by the idea of a contradiction, but this notion is conspicuously vague.'* We'll return to this concept of contradiction in more detail in Chapter 7, but we want to emphasize that it is a central concept in dialectical thinking, from which it derives its meaning. In the context of CHAT, the concept of contradiction refers to opposing tendencies that pull the activity system into opposing positions. For Ollman (2005, p. 30), contradiction is defined as *'the incompatible development of different elements within the same relationship, i.e. between elements that are at the same time interdependent'*. And it's precisely because CHAT analyzes systems in motion that the concept of contradiction proves crucial. For Ollman (2005):

> It is contradiction, more than any other concept, that enables Marx to think accurately about the organic and historical movements of the capitalist mode of production, to grasp how they interact and evolve together from their origins in feudalism to what lies just beyond our horizon. According to common sense, the concept of contradiction applies to the ideas we have about things, not to the things themselves. It's only a logical relation between propositions (if I assert 'X', I cannot at the same time assert 'non-X'), not a relation that exists in reality. This interpretation [...] is based on a conception of reality divided into separate and independent parts [...]. While non-dialectical researchers in all fields of knowledge are constantly

on the lookout for an 'external agitator', a cause external to the problem under study, dialectical thinkers attribute the primary responsibility for any change to the internal contradictions of the system or systems in which it occurs (Ollman, 2005, p. 31).

Another recurring criticism of the activity-system model is its limited character, i.e. it is particularly relevant to the analysis of work activities but potentially inappropriate for accounting for other forms of activity. Thus, Blunden (2023) attempts to account for the limited and overly narrow nature of Leontiev and Engeström's conceptions of activity (p. 66) by critically presenting a number of research studies in activity theory. However, Blunden ends up presenting a taxonomy of activities that seems radically at odds with the fundamental principle of activity theory, i.e. its object-oriented character. We might therefore question the fact that we can find in the author's taxonomy a category of *'objectless activity'* (p. 215), even though for Leontiev there can be no such thing as objectless activity. It is possible to glimpse a form of incoherence in situating oneself in the CHAT *'family'* without ultimately endorsing its founding principles, even though these are presented in the first part of the book.

This potential incompleteness of the activity system is also emphasized by Bakhurst (2023):

> But does the model capture the general structure of activity systems? It looks too true to be good. It is pretty much impossible to find something recognizable as an activity that does not fit the model. What is wrong with that?!, you might reply. Isn't universality an advantage here? Not obviously so. The fact is that the model seems to work particularly well for the sorts of activity systems that activity theorists typically study: healthcare, work settings, some educational contexts [...] It is much less plausible for activities like, my writing and delivering this paper, or [...] for modest activities such as having dinner with colleagues, walking the dog, visiting one's invalid relative. The point is not that you cannot make the model fit these activities – you can. It is just that it has no explanatory value for activities like this: they need to be understood using methods that are remote from the conceptual apparatus presupposed by the schema. This suggests that what we have here is a universal, but generally vacuous schema, that turns out to be a useful heuristic in reference to certain kinds of activity (Bakhurst, 2023, p. 311).

In his critique, Bakhurst (2023) confuses *'modest activities'* with actions, which has been a crucial theoretical distinction in activity theory since Leontiev. If this distinction is crucial, it's because it allows CHAT to propose an integrative approach based on levels.

In formative interventions (see Chapter 10), the analysis of an activity system begins '*in the middle of things*', as (Nicolini, 2012, p. 118) puts it. More specifically, the starting point of any analysis is at the level of action as experienced by participants in order to understand the systemic causes in activity systems (i.e. to highlight contradictions). In this type of analysis, there is a need to combine an experiential and lived perspective with a systemic perspective (Spinuzzi, 2018b): what actors do in an activity system and the problems, dilemmas, and conflicts they encounter are simply the expression of historically inherited systemic contradictions. Learning to develop an activity system collectively involves linking the action level to the activity system level. Confusing the levels of action and activity is therefore detrimental to the successful analysis of an activity system, unless the model is abstracted from the overall theory of which it is but an expression. Put another way, it seems impossible to conceive of any form of activity analysis without distinguishing actions from activity and relating actions to the activity system.

Similarly, Langemeyer and Roth (2006) point out that the model favors a functionalist and systemic reading at the expense of a subjective and intersubjective vision:

> We acknowledge that models always exclude some aspects and interrelations to highlight others. But if we follow the subject-object-axis, the triangular model favors a third-person perspective, rather than a subjective or an intersubjective view. This inherently implies that the logic of the system is that of the analyst, the 'neutral observer', rather than that of the participant (Langemeyer & Roth, 2006, p. 30).

We concur with Langemeyer and Roth (2006) on this criticism. However, it is essential to add that fostering a systemic vision is what gives the activity system model its strength when mobilized as an instrument in an expansive learning process (see Chapter 8). Indeed, it is precisely by enabling participants to relate their lived experience to this systemic or system view that formative interventions can enable actors to regain control over the destiny of their activity system. The model enables the construction of a body of knowledge that transcends the actors' immediate experience but is nevertheless firmly anchored in it. This knowledge is not merely descriptive but seeks to develop the activity system in which it is embedded. The comments of Langemeyer and Roth

(2006) are presented here as critiques, if we extract the activity system from the CHAT and abstract it from an intervention project aimed at emancipating actors by transforming their activity system.

A potentially interesting approach to relating a work psychology model rooted in Vygotsky's psychology and the activity system was carried out by Kloetzer, Clot, and Quillerou-Grivot (2015). The tetrahedron model developed by Clot and his team (Kloetzer & Clot, 2016) is compared with the activity system (Figure 17):

> Comparing our model with Engeström's activity system (Engeström, 1987), we can in a mental exercise reduce the larger triangle of the activity system to the simpler version by folding its corners (Fig. 3.2). This mental exercise highlights that the collective dimensions, which are explicitly stated in the activity system, are present as mediations in the psychological activity of the subject which is our 'entry door into the analysis' (Kloetzer et al., 2015, p. 59).

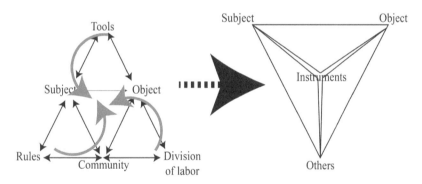

Figure 18: Transition from the Engeström model activity system to Clot's tetrahedron model of activity according to (Kloetzer, Clot, & Quillerou-Grivot, 2015).

The core of Clot's (2008) model, as we understand it, is the concept of an actor's *'social'* subjectivity. In contrast to the view that occupational psychology is a form of *'psychological crutch'* (Clot, 2010), he draws on the Vygotskian tradition to promote psychological development, extend the reach of professionals, and revitalize the work experience. The transition from one model to another, as outlined here, indicates that there is, in fact, a relationship between the two models, rather than incompatibility.

The question of referential or point of view is essential in this context. In our view, this transition between the two models indicates that the subjectivity involved in individual actions incorporates elements of the activity system: individual action incorporates activity. Consequently, by incorporating it, it inevitably expands the professionals' possibilities for action. In other words, actions are not only embedded in the activity, but the activity is also, on a subjective level, embedded in individual actions. This is also Leontiev's perspective. In the clinic of activity, dialogue therefore becomes an instrument for revitalizing these relationships between collective activity and actions.

> The idea of the work collective becomes essential: it is not a question of saying that collectives are a 'shield' for health. The objective is for the collective to become part of each individual, for each person to make it their own, in order to enhance their capacity to be alone and unique. Furthermore, it is essential that each individual be, in a sense, this collective, and that the collective is available to each individual for their own activity. This is not a method of manufacturing the collective as a mold or model to be applied by each individual. Rather, it is the idea that if one wishes to be very singular, one must be very collective, beyond the collective (Clot & Stimec, 2013, pp. 116–117).

In addition to promoting a potential dialogue between two cultural-historical traditions, this schema responds in part to the critique formulated by Langemeyer and Roth (2006). The activity system is indeed a tool that guides towards a 'systemic reading', but in formative intervention, this systemic reading becomes for participants an instrument for dialogue with their own experience. And it's precisely by collectively reconceptualizing an activity system that professionals can establish new links between collective activity and their own actions. In other words, for Clot, dialogue and addressee change constitute an instrument. Conversely, the alternation between subjective and systemic points of view, together with the plurality of addressees involved in the intervention – as highlighted by Engeström (1990b) – is a valuable resource for both the development of activity systems and the development of the '*horizon*' of actions.

In this chapter of his book, he illustrates the necessity for the actor to adopt a systemic point of view and for the researcher to adopt a personal point of view (p. 171). In a study conducted in a hospital in the mid-1980s, Engeström employed Wartofsky's categorization of artifacts into primary, secondary, and tertiary categories (1979) to illustrate the necessity of not only the construction of a new horizon for actions but also the establishment of a new horizon and direction for the activity as a whole in the context of the adoption of new artifacts:

> In other words, demanding changes in tools are hard to accept and imple-ment when an overall analysis and vision of the future form of the activity system – the 'where to' artifact – is missing (Engeström, 1990b, p. 194).

In this context, the activity triangle is indeed a *'where to artifacts'*, enabling professionals to collectively construct the direction of the activity system in which they find themselves. In other words, Langemeyer and Roth (2006) criticize the fact that the activity system is oriented towards a third-person reading. However, it can be argued that it is pre-cisely because it is oriented towards a third-person systemic reading that the activity system is an instrument for developing activity and the rela-tionship between actions and activity.

A final criticism is the relative neglect of the operations level in Engeström's approach[13]. Most intervention research considers actions and the activity system in their relations, without investigating the level of operations in depth. In the example given for laboratory X, the focus on MSDs implies linking operations and multiple interacting activity systems in the analysis. The results show that, faced with the difficul-ties encountered in the production of breast prostheses, managers are seeking to increase output and standardize processes. A comprehensive examination of operations and actions reveals that these decisions are counterproductive, as they result in a reduction in the variability of oper-ations performed by workers and an increased risk of musculoskeletal disorders (MSDs). Rather than merely critiquing these decisions, we view this as an area for potential development. Empirical intervention work is undoubtedly necessary at this level.

Finally, we will address other criticisms in the next chapter, which is devoted to a fourth generation of work. This chapter will demonstrate

---

[13] This focus appears to be largely linked to the demands that gave rise to the inter-ventions in question. To illustrate, an intervention focusing on physical autonomy among the elderly in a homecare service is an example of this level of operations being perfectly integrated. Indeed, it is at the core of proposals for integrating physical exercise into the daily activities of the elderly (Engeström, Kajamaa, and Nummijoki, 2015; Engeström, Nummijoki, and Sannino, 2012). We will revisit this intervention in greater detail in Chapter 10.

how the fourth generation of work responds to the criticisms previously formulated by other authors.

Engeström's Contributions to CHAT

Before going any further, it is necessary to summarize Engeström's contributions to CHAT. For the moment, these can be summarized in four main points.

First, he provided a graphical heuristic for representing Leontiev's activity system. These activity systems are historically evolving collective formations. At the heart of these systems is the concept of mediation. Thus, in the triangle of exchange (not to take the usual example of production, and even though this triangle seems central), a subject's relationship to the community is mediated by rules.

This triangle is a unit of analysis. It cannot be broken down; otherwise, we lose the unity and quality of the human activity we wish to analyze. However, it may be useful to focus on a particular sub-triangle, but this would mark a form of reduction, and here, we want to emphasize, any '*reduction requires conscious justification in order not to become a distortion*' (Engeström, 2015, p. 65).

To this heuristic dimension of the model of an activity system, he integrated the theorization of contradictions, especially from the work of Ilyenkov (1982/2008), making it crucial for the analysis of an activity system. We'll return to this difficult-to-understand concept later (Chapter 7), but let's emphasize right away that the contradictions running through an activity system are the main mechanism of its self-movement. Thus, by incorporating them into his model of activity, he is able to account for the dynamic character of an activity system, as well as to envisage future developments of these systems based on the history of these historically accumulated contradictions.

He has also extended the unit of analysis to multiple interacting activity systems. This broadening of the unit of analysis provides a better account of the social and societal phenomena at work, but also runs the risk of disembodying the analysis. Nevertheless, the levels of action and operation are not abandoned. But the keys to understanding these levels must be sought in the hierarchically superior levels (activity systems and the interaction between multiple activity systems). The analysis made possible by third-generation activity theory is therefore not a '*macro*' analysis of activity, as some formulations suggest (e.g. Arnseth, 2008; Zouinar & Cahour, 2013). Nor is it a '*micro*' analysis. It does, however, allow for an analysis that enables us to understand the relationships between levels. From a dialectical point of view, the macro does not exist without the micro, and vice versa. By adopting a dialectical point of view, CHAT has the potential to respond to the problem of change of scale identified by the approaches in the introductory work of the book: for us, change of scale is not a change of focus, but a movement that allows us to understand hierarchical shifts and relationships between different levels of analysis.

Finally, motivated by a desire to transform pedagogical practices, he has extended his fieldwork to work organizations. Here, Davydov's principles are not abandoned, but developed to focus on processes of externalization rather than processes of internalization of predefined cultural content. We'll return to this dimension in more detail when we discuss the principle of moving from the abstract to the concrete (Chapter 10).

Chapter 5

Towards a Fourth Generation of CHAT? Sannino and Real Utopias

The crisis of humanity will not be solved by pharmacology or surgery
(Blunden, 2023, p. x)
The apocalypse is exciting! (Bruno Latour, 2019)

As previously stated, CHAT is a theory oriented towards the future, not the past or the present. Dafermos (2020) further emphasizes this by formulating the idea, in metaphorical form, that in CHAT, the emphasis is on the '*buds and flowers*' of development rather than on the 'fruits' produced by development. However, what is the future of a theory born in a different context and in the previous century? What is the future of CHAT? How can it develop without denying its cornerstones?

In its principles, the CHAT is a theory oriented towards practice, aimed at transforming the world and carrying ideals of social justice and human emancipation. However, in order for such a theory to be developed in today's context, it is necessary to determine which issues it should address.

This chapter seeks to address these questions by presenting the most recent works in CHAT, which outline a fourth generation of work that has been emerging for approximately ten years.

Current Social Issues… And Their Systemic Causes

A moment's reflection reveals a plethora of pressing concerns. These include the pervasive issue of fake news, the alarming phenomenon of global warming, the looming threat of mass extinctions, the rapid pace of digitization, the widening inequalities, the alarming rise of famines, the surge in migrations, the mounting pollution and poverty, the growing marginalization of communities and individuals, and so forth. All these issues are interlinked and are the unintentional consequences of human activity and our modes of production. Therefore, their solution lies in the development of human activity, or to put it another way, in sustainable transformations of productive activity. The necessity for a reinvention and a transformation of human activities to ensure the sustainability of society has never been more pressing. The demand for expansive learning has arguably never been more urgent. In a succinct formulation that we share, Blunden (2023) notes that:

> Regrettably, human activity is threatening to destroy the capacity of our natural inheritance to any longer provide the conditions for human life. The task of modifying human activities so as to guarantee not only social justice but the very conditions for human life is pressing (Blunden, 2023, p. x).

While CHAT and expansive learning have proven their worth in resolving systemic crises that arise from contradictions between connected activity systems or within an activity system, current and future crises are much more global, unpredictable, and widely distributed (Lémonie, 2022). In order to effectively address these crises, theoretical and methodological evolution are necessary, as well as the overcoming of the contradictions that gave rise to them in the first place.

One can cite the example of global warming and the changes in ecosystems that are threatening the very existence of our societies. There can be little doubt that human activity is the cause of accelerated global warming, to the point where scientists speak of the Anthropocene. However, there is no consensus on this term. Malm (2019), the inventor of the '*Capitalocene*' concept, posits that it is not humanity that is responsible for global warming, but rather the capitalist mode of organization of society. The question thus arises as to whether CHAT constitutes an adequate theory and practice to take charge of the transformations that are likely to erode capitalism in such a way as to be able to transform not just one or a number of interconnected systems, but society as a whole.

In two critical articles (2007, 2009), Avis denounces what he considers to be the potentially conservative nature of CHAT. Mobilizing Gramsci's distinction between transformation and transformism, he argues that formative interventions, as conveyed by Engeström's work, focus more on secondary contradictions within activity systems, rather than on primary contradictions. These primary contradictions are considered by Avis to be peripheral in formative intervention, which is seen as a conservative practice safeguarding the interests of capital:

There is a rupture between Engeström theorizations and the practical application of activity theory. For whilst his underpinning Marxism holds progressive possibilities, it is nevertheless limited through the enactment of developmental work research, which is no more than a form of consultancy aiming to improve work practices (Avis, 2007, p. 169).

In response to this criticism, Engeström and Sannino (2010) demonstrated how a revised activity system was linked to an analysis of alternative scenarios for the service's activity in a home care service in the city of Helsinki. The participants of this CL intervention identified a potential risk, namely, that of the commodification of home care and its privatization, which could lead to cost savings but also to the abandonment of the elderly and their families to the market.

Accordingly, Miettinen (2009) posits that the acknowledgment of primary contradictions must be undertaken at two levels to facilitate the emancipatory potential of formative interventions and CL:

> The contradictions of capitalism as a source of change in work activities need to be analyzed on at least two levels, as Engeström did in *Learning by Expanding*. On the one hand, we need analyses of the development of capitalist production and social institutions in order to recognize the primary contradictions in the elements of a local activity system. The development of new forms of contradictions in capitalism may be only partially or in a preliminary way expressed in a specific activity system. That is why the comparison of many empirical studies can contribute to a more profound analysis of the evolving contradictions of a field of activity. On the other hand, the recognition of contradictions presupposes an analysis of what is happening in other productive activities and institutions (such as intellectual property right regimes) of capitalist society. Such an analysis is important for constantly reconceptualizing the 'gray', contradictory zone of threats and emancipatory possibilities in the development of work (Miettinen, 2009, p. 167).

Avis (2007) further develops this argument by examining the tension between the localism of developmental interventions and the need for broader interventions. Whilst Engeström argues '*The mightiest, most impersonal societal structures can be seen as consisting of local activities carried out by concrete human beings with the help of mediating artifacts*' (1999a, p. 36). This insight fails to be translated into wider societal interventions that challenge capitalist relations (Avis, 2007, p. 163).

The development of a fourth generation of work in CHAT is intended to address the limitations of previous approaches, as critiqued by Avis (for a similar critique, see Warmington, 2008). This new generation of work aligns itself with movements to transform society and aims to take charge at another level of global issues that are obviously expressed within activity systems.

A number of scholars have proposed the need to elaborate a fourth generation of activity theory, with arguments that focus less on the Marxist roots of CHAT, such as those put forward by Avis (2007), but more on the profound transformations associated with new technologies (Karanasios et al., 2021; Lompscher, 2006; Rückiem, 2009). It is first necessary to examine the arguments put forward by these authors before considering the path followed by Engeström and Sannino in developing and proposing work that moves beyond the localism criticized by Avis.

New Information and Communication Technologies: An Opportunity to Transform CHAT?

The contemporary era is distinguished by the advent of revolutionary advances in information and communication technologies. These technological transformations are engendering novel societal, organizational, and individual prospects. However, they are also accompanied by a range of challenges, including the influence of algorithms on decision-making, the '*uberization*' of work, the blurring of boundaries between public and private life, and so forth.

If we accept Vygotsky's and Leontiev's assertion that tools change human nature, we must consider whether CHAT should acknowledge the profound change brought about by the changing nature of the tools used. According to Rückiem (2009), CHAT was created at a time when new information and communication technologies did not exist. He laments the fact that CHAT researchers pay too little attention to digitization, even though it undoubtedly poses the greatest conceptual and methodological challenges for CHAT. Indeed, for him, the theorization of mediation is historically outdated and inscribed in a world dominated by Gutenberg and '*book culture*' rather than in an information society and Web 2.0. In his critique of the lack of development of CHAT in relation to the evolution of technologies in Engeström's recent proposals, he argues that for Engeström the Internet is an instrument like any other:

Engeström refers to collective activity systems embedded in capitalist societal structures as described by historical materialism. His methodology does not allow him to interpret the Internet as a basic transformation factor, let alone as a framework for perceiving our present reality as a qualitatively new emerging societal formation. Because there is no theoretical possibility for distinguishing between different dominating media, Engeström is hardly able to tell the difference between activity systems determined by an old medium and those processes formed by a new medium. That means that he deals with local changes and limited developments of activity systems within the boundaries of a society coined by a traditionally perceived dominating medium (Rückiem, 2009, p. 95).

Rückiem's (2009) perspective suggests that CHAT can reach its full potential by reexamining and revisiting the concept of mediation as originally outlined by Vygotsky (see Chapter 2). However, the notion that contemporary technological innovations have the capacity to generate new theoretical challenges that require new theoretical developments needs further examination.

For example, Tikhomirov (1999, p. 347) notes that the delegation of certain human functions to computers presents new challenges to activity theory. He further asserts that the advancement of computers and information technology not only leads to significant changes in human activity, but also necessitates the evolution of activity theory (p. 358). From our perspective, the transfer of certain human functions to technologies is not an entirely new phenomenon in the context of CHAT. As noted above, Leontiev himself refers to this dimension in his book Activity, Consciousness, Personality (1978), where he discusses the future of operations and their potential crystallization in tools. This idea is further explored in another quote that is particularly relevant in the context of AI development:

> Nonetheless, an operation does not in any way constitute any kind of '*separateness*', in relation to action, just as is the case with action in relation to activity. Even when an operation is carried out by a machine, it still realizes the action of the subject. In a man who solves a problem with a calculator, the action is not interrupted at this extracerebral link; it finds in it its realization just as it does in its other links. Only a '*crazy*' machine that has escaped from man's domination can carry out operations that do not realize any kind of goal-directed action of the subject (Leontiev, 1978, p. 66)

It is accurate to say that new technologies have brought about significant societal changes. In fact, these technologies have permeated all aspects of life and have influenced every aspect of an activity system. This includes the creation of online communities, the emergence of new activities, the introduction of new rules, and so on. While the nature of the tools may be changing, it is still unclear whether this requires a change in CHAT.

Furthermore, Rückiem's approach demonstrates a form of *'Internet centrism'* in the sense understood by Morozov (2013), in that his argument is based on the firm conviction that we are living in a unique era where everything is changing, and previous truths are no longer relevant. The idea that the Internet represents a revolution in human activity needs to be questioned and perhaps even historically challenged. Crowdsourcing, for example, is often presented as a new phenomenon associated with the advent of the Internet, in which a large number of anonymous actors contribute to funding a particular activity. However, historical evidence suggests that the practice has a long history. For example, the British government used crowdsourcing techniques as early as 1714 to improve maritime navigation and find a reliable way to calculate longitude (Spencer, 2012).

The changing nature of tools is also the focus of the recent article by Karanasios and al. (2021). Based on a literature review of studies dealing with new technologies, the authors find that CHAT is a powerful tool for conceptualizing current technological tools, although new technological tools differ from traditional tools in their *'generative'* character. Nevertheless, in their view, these new technological tools pose a challenge to the analytical delimitation of the poles of an activity system. In the case of Facebook, for example, they note that:

> We don't even know how to analytically separate *'tool'* and *'community'* within use of these artifacts. [...] Such separation is a mainstay in versions of activity theory like Engeström's triangle. For example, a Facebook group can be considered both tool and community in that it acts upon an object, but it also constitutes a community (Karanasios et al., 2021, p. 7).

While this kind of argument is undoubtedly compelling, it can be debated. For example, when using an activity system to conduct an analysis, it is not possible to discern the poles of tools and community without first situating them in the context of a real analysis of the use of *'Facebook groups'* by real users. Furthermore, an activity system is a graphical representation of a process. It is not static but animated by the contradictions that set it in motion. Consequently, the analytical attribution of a pole is not fixed once and for all in the movement of the activity. An object or result can become an instrument, an instrument can become a community, and so on. For instance, Engeström (1996c) discussing the actor network theory (Latour, 2005), provides an illustration of the diversity in the role of a '*wall*' within the life of an activity system:

> The wall begins its life as an object to be created (1) for the owner of a house by means of hiring a carpenter. When the construction is finished, the wall momentarily appears as an outcome, a product (2). For a while, the owner of the house sees the finished wall as a mediating artifact, a tool with which he reaches the purpose of rearranging his living space (3). Soon enough, the wall ceases to be a tool; it becomes an aspect of the tacitly assumed community infrastructure (4) for the family living in the house and for the friends visiting it. As a designated space, e.g. as the study of the husband, it begins to define the division of labor in the family (5), and the associated rules – e.g. children are not allowed to play in this room (6). Once it has taken root at this community level of the activity, the wall is on its way to becoming a constitutive element in the makeup of the subject's identity (7) (Engeström, 1996b, p. 260).

The arguments put forth by Karanasios and al. (2021) regarding the relationship between agency and new technologies are more compelling. Technologies have consistently influenced human behavior, particularly through their affordances (Kaptelinin & Nardi, 2018). However, this influence is becoming increasingly significant, to the extent that it is interfering with decision-making processes and even threatening a society's democratic processes[14].

> The manipulations of big data suggest that activity theorists need to consider how technology influences the subject, both magnifying subjects' intentions and manipulating them [...] We must speak to the ways millions of people can rather quickly adopt, and act on, bizarre messages that seem capable of providing relief to lonely and confused minds (Karanasios et al., 2021, p. 8).

---

[14] The Brazilian presidential elections are a case in point. See, for example, (Cesarino, 2020; Ricard & Medeiros, 2020)

The argument presented here raises two key questions. First, it is essential to understand not only how technology influences the subject, but also how this influence is constructed through the network of decision-making that led to the design of a technological tool[15]. Second, from an interventionist perspective, if we take this issue seriously, we must ensure that subjects are able to influence technological developments, rather than being forced or simply adapting to them.

With regard to the first point, and without going into the details of a discussion that would undoubtedly go beyond the scope of this chapter, it is illustrative to consider an application designed to track users' health data and offered by an insurance company. In exchange for providing a connected watch, the company adjusts the insurance premium based on the data obtained from the watch. Essentially, if users walk 10,000 steps a day and maintain a physically active lifestyle, their insurance premium will be reduced. At first glance, this may seem like a mutually beneficial arrangement: the company can adjust its rates, while the user gains access to a free tool for tracking his or her health data. In reality, however, the use of a watch in this context fundamentally changes the purpose of physical activity. Instead of being performed for its intrinsic value (maintaining health), it is now performed for its exchange value (obtaining a lower insurance premium).

The implication of this example is that new technologies are not the 'cause' of changes in human activities. In fact, identifying technologies with a cause undermines the purposes and objects they serve. The discourse on new technologies often fails to address the object of activity and the primary contradictions of objects. Consequently, while new technologies contribute to the intensification of the primary contradiction between use value and exchange value, they are not the sole cause of this intensification (Engeström & Sannino, 2010). Therefore, if the nature of the instruments changes, CHAT seems to be an appropriate framework for discussing and understanding the role of these new technologies in the transformation and development of productive activities under capitalism. Nevertheless, calls to modify CHAT in light of the evolution of artifacts are not persuasive. In our view, the most compelling

---

[15]   To take an example outside of new technologies and related to homelessness, which we'll come back to later, French municipalities spend a lot of effort designing street furniture in a way that harms the homeless. For example, benches are designed so that people can sit on them, but not lie down (Mestdagh, 2021).

argument is the intensification of the contradictions between use value and exchange value, the challenge of navigating the influence of these new technologies, and the need for an activist, interventionist perspective to empower subjects to regain control over the future development of technologies.

Bødker and King (2018) discussed in more detail in Chapter 11, represent an extension of this basic activity-theoretical perspective, which posits that subjects construct a desirable future guided by principles of social justice and human emancipation. An illustrative example is Blanc's work (2023), which shows how a community of designers is using web technologies to regain control over their work tools and no longer have to endure the necessity of using proprietary software.

The 'Runaway Object'

In addressing today's challenges, it is necessary to move beyond the limitations of a conceptual approach tied to the nature of the instruments employed. Instead, we need to consider a broader perspective on the object of activity, as proposed by Engeström and Sannino (2020):

> In the current phase of capitalist globalization, such interconnected objects as poverty, climate change, and pandemics cannot anymore be treated as isolated issues to be brought under control by technical means; they influence and pervade the objects of innumerable activities and call for radical revisioning of the ways our societies and lives are organized (Engeström & Sannino, 2020, p. 13).

The concept of object is central to CHAT (for more details on the concept of object, see Chapters 3 and 7). These objects are the foundation of an object-oriented activity theory. They give meaning to actions, justify and define an activity system, and underpin the motivation of actors. As new needs arise, these objects evolve. However, they are not simply the product of one or more activity systems; rather, they are sometimes the effects or unintended products of the interaction between a variety of activity systems. Engeström (2009b) refers to these objects as 'runaway objects', in reference to Giddens' sociological approach (2003). They are 'runaway' because they are potentially uncontrollable, have potentially escalating and destructive effects, and can spread on a global scale. Runaway objects are objects that generate opposition and controversy.

The characteristics of the COVID-19 virus are consistent with those of a runaway object. Despite numerous attempts to control it, including varying degrees of impact on individual freedoms, the virus remains uncontrollable. Its consequences are also unpredictable, including a shortage of raw materials and an increase in inequalities that the NGO Oxfam has described as unprecedented. The report points to an increase in situations of extreme poverty, especially in countries with informal economies. This situation threatens our security and our health, generating resistance (for example, the introduction of the '*health card*' in France, followed by the '*vaccination card*') and controversy (especially scientific and public debate). However, these uncontrolled phenomena do not appear and grow without human activity. There is no more activity without an object than objects without activity, as postulated by Leontiev. The rapid spread of the virus and the inability (and attempts) to control it, as observed in the case of zoonoses, do not exist without human activity. Researchers at IBSES and the IPCC have identified a number of factors that contribute to the emergence of new viruses, including disruption of ecosystems, global warming, and intensive production methods. They have also highlighted the significant costs associated with reactive measures, noting that responding to diseases only after they have emerged, with public health measures and technological solutions, is a slow and uncertain path, punctuated by human suffering and costing tens of billions of dollars each year. There is a dialectic here: runaway objects are the unintended consequences of human activity, and they in turn affect human activity. The fourth generation of activity theory aims to intervene in such runaway objects..

In addition to the above examples, other cases of runaway objects can be identified. These include global warming, extreme poverty, and social inequalities in access to educational success (Lémonie et al., 2021), occupational accidents and diseases (Boudra et al., 2023). All of these objects are the unexpected and unintended consequences of human activity and represent the primary contradiction between use value and exchange value inscribed in activity systems. These objects evolve and change over time yet remain uncontrollable due to the lack of a clearly defined system for managing them. While these objects are not entirely negative, they do have the potential to transform human activities. In fact, they necessitate action to transform human activities. In an interview with *Le Monde* published in 2019, Latour stated, '*Apocalypse is exciting*'.

CHAT's approach to these issues involves both theoretical and methodological development.

- From a theoretical standpoint, dealing with these runaway objects involves defining and, above all, articulating levels of analysis that range from the local to the global. These levels of analysis must be articulated in a way that allows for the integration of different forms of expansive learning (see Chapter 8 for a detailed account). Finally, these theoretical contributions must be consistent with the orientation of an emancipatory social science.

- From a methodological standpoint, it is necessary to implement developmental interventions at different scales, thus creating the conditions for the formation of heterogeneous coalitions of actors.

Inclusion in an Emancipatory Social Science: Real Utopias

As has been demonstrated, in the context of contemporary challenges, the identified threat is capitalism as a mode of organizing human activities. The 4th generation must facilitate the transformation of human activities as possible alternatives to capitalism. The positioning of the CHAT's fourth generation is therefore explicitly political. Indeed, as Stetsenko (2021, p. 34) asserts, capitalism is *'unfit to meet today's challenges, which require cooperation, planning, equality, and solidarity on a global scale'*. The work by Sannino (2020) that we shall present draws part of its positioning from the work of the American sociologist Wright.

Wright (2010) rehabilitates the notion of utopia in the social sciences, thereby overcoming two antagonistic attitudes. On the one hand, there is a form of skepticism that claims that the possibility of changing the world has lost all meaning. On the other hand, there is an imaginary utopianism that is out of touch with reality and its history (see figure below). Positioning real utopias requires a deep understanding of activity systems, their interactions and contradictions. As Wright explains in response to an interview: *'As long as we do not confuse science fiction and literary imagination with rigorous scientific analysis, these approaches can together contribute to the development of new ideas'* (Farnea & Jeanpierre, 2013, p. 233).

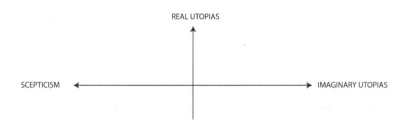

Figure 19: Positioning Wright's (2010) real utopias as overcoming two antagonistic postures.

The concept of a real utopia is based on the adjective '*real*'. In essence, these utopias are real because they have already been implemented. By bringing these utopias to light, we challenge the certainties associated with skepticism. They are not mere pipe dreams; they are real insofar as, in the spirit of dialectical thinking, we must recognize the prefigurations of a utopian future that we can collectively build and democratize today. The concept of a '*real utopia*' thus represents a practical approach to the realization of social change.

This notion of a '*real utopia*' is based on a systemic vision of society that is compatible with the ontological positioning of CHAT. According to Wright, society can be metaphorically represented as a pond containing a variety of species. Occasionally a new species is introduced into this pond, at other times it develops by creating a niche and then '*gradually displaces other species*'. This can be translated back into the CHAT framework. Society is conceptualized as a set of interacting activity systems. It is likely that the creation of a new species of activity as an alternative to capitalism will result in the formation of a niche, which will subsequently evolve and erode capitalism.

Wright (2010) cites several experiments to exemplify real utopias, including the Mondragon employee cooperative in the Basque Country (Morris, 1992), municipal budget management in the Brazilian city of Porto Alegre (Marquetti, Schonerwald da Silva, & Campbell, 2012).

Wright (2010) proposes three forms of transformation in the struggle against capitalism. The first type of transformation is '*transformations of rupture*'. The second type of transformation is referred to as '*interstitial transformations*', where citizens' initiatives exploit the inherent contradictions and fissures within the dominant economic and social system to progressively implement practices that will bring about significant, systemic changes. These initiatives aim to build emancipatory alternatives within the spaces of capitalist economies and advocate for the defense and expansion of such spaces. This is accomplished through the use of social democratic institutions that facilitate negotiations between workers and capitalists. Wright's proposals represent a model of emancipatory social science oriented towards action and social change. CHAT's contributions to this model are significant and warrant further study.

Eradicating Homelessness and Sannino's Work

Eradicating homelessness is a major challenge for social justice and equality in any society. Finland serves as a model in this area, with the goal of eradicating homelessness by 2027. The work of Sannino and his team at the RESET laboratory at the University of Tampere contributes to this goal.

Her work uses theoretical and methodological resources derived from the third generation of activity theory. However, it extends the analysis beyond the limitations of localism critized Avis (2007) and Warmington (2008). The eradication of homelessness requires the participation of many sectors and work organizations in the emergence of a genuine utopian society. On a theoretical level, it also implies the definition of a new unit of analysis in place of the minimal unit of the third generation.

> Time is now mature for the development of a fourth-generation activity theory. This should offer a unit of analysis able to grasp a qualitatively new type of activity formations and concerted efforts that can realistically meet the challenge of cross-sectoral service integration and interorganisational service production. As for the example presented in this article, this kind of service integration and service production are essential for eradicating homelessness (Sannino, 2020, p. 5).

Sannino's intervention involved three Change Laboratories (CL) on three different levels. The first level was carried out in a reception unit that housed about one hundred apartments for homeless people. Prior to the CL, two meetings were held in the unit, attended by representatives of the NGO in charge of the unit and staff members. A total of twenty interviews were conducted, and selected excerpts from these interviews were used as 'mirror material' in the CL sessions. Six CL sessions were held over the course of four months.

At the city level, two meetings were held with the senior administrator and nine interviews were conducted with key actors representing the main sectors of work on homelessness. These interviews informed the preparation of the CL, which was held six times over a six-month period and was attended by 19 participants representing 11 city organizations and different levels of activity. The study was informed by three meetings with the national Housing First policy manager and national network leaders. In addition, 18 interviews were conducted with national stakeholders. The CL took place over a period of six months, with six sessions.

These three CLs were designed to support the extensive learning efforts already underway. For example, the homeless reception unit had already started its transformation work in 2018. At the national level, the CL has been established as a means of changing public policy to facilitate the pursuit of this utopian ideal. These three CLs bring together actors from different sectors who need to work together to achieve the eradication of homelessness in Finland. The organization of these three CLs allows CHAT's 4th generation unit of analysis to extend both horizontally across different sectors and organizations, and vertically across different hierarchical levels within society.

The third generation unit of analysis is no longer a viable approach for such an undertaking. Instead, Sannino (2020) proposes a unit of analysis that allows us to capture the articulation and entanglement of multiple expansive learning cycles. These multiple cycles are both potentially interdependent and partially independent. We will make some suggestions along these lines in Chapter 9, which is devoted to expansive learning. Articulating Expansive Learning Levels as a Solution

In her article, Sannino identifies at least three broad cycles of learning. The central cycle (and arguably the starting point) consists of learning within reception units between residents and frontline workers. This cycle is articulated with a second cycle involving the NGOs responsible for these reception units. The first cycle is also articulated with a third cycle that supports learning in the neighborhood of the reception unit. These different cycles are articulated with a learning cycle involving municipal services (at the level of the City of Tampere) and finally at the national level. The unit of analysis can thus be represented in the following figure.

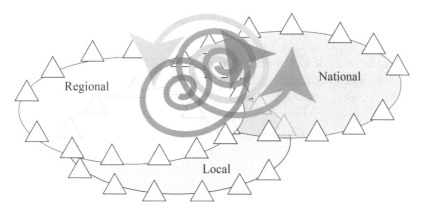

Figure 20: Schematic representation of the unit of analysis proposed for a fourth generation of CHAT proposed by Sannino (2020).

In the articulation proposed by Sannino, the learning cycle at the housing unit level continuously fed the learning cycles at higher levels. Consequently, the work within the housing units continuously feeds developments and reorientations at the NGO, municipal and national levels. In this way, it proposes the germination of expansive macro-learning cycles based on the soil formed by expansive micro-learning cycles[16]. It is crucial here to acknowledge the importance of this inter-relationship between expansive learning cycles at different levels. This will ensure that the fourth generation of CHAT does not become a form of social intervention divorced from the experiences and knowledge of frontline workers.

This point was elucidated by Engeström (2009b) in the context of the necessity for CHAT to be able to translate runaway objects into intermediate objects that are potentially transformable, visible, and accessible. These intermediate objects must transcend the limitations of the utilitarian profit motive:

> We need intermediate runaway objects that are less spectacular and more inviting. Various social movements try to meet this need. Organic farming, Wikipedia, open models of scientific research and publishing are examples. Most such attempts fail or remain marginal (Engeström, 2009b, p. 305).

---

[16] On the articulation of the different levels of expansive learning, see our proposals in Chapter 8.

The Notion of a Heterogeneous Coalition of Actors

The effective management of social issues requires the involvement of a wide range of stakeholders. Sannino's (2020) intervention involves a variety of actors, including NGOs, politicians, representatives of social and municipal services, residents of the host unit's neighborhood, front-line workers in the host unit, associations and activists.

The implementation of such an intervention requires the formation of a heterogeneous coalition of actors, as described by Sannino. This represents a significant shift from the third generation of activity theory, which emphasized the conflictual dimension inherent in the object within an activity system. In the third generation, formative interventions that support expansive learning bring together participants who occupy different positions within multiple activity systems. In the fourth generation, the activity systems involved in transformations are heterogeneous:

> These activities are heterogeneous because they represent qualitatively different types of work and because they operate at different hierarchical levels in the society. These activities require one another to enact the shared utopia and their actors must learn to operate on the basis of concerted initiatives rather than only within their individual sectors and organizations and by top-down orientations (Sannino, 2020, p. 5).

The concept of '*multi-voiced*' as used in the second and third generation of CHAT should not be confused with the notion of a heterogeneous coalition of actors. These two concepts have different scopes and are used for different purposes.

Critical Discussions on the Fourth Generation of Activity Theory

The article by Engeström and Sannino (2020) on the fourth generation of activity theory was discussed by Spinuzzi (2020a) and Stetsenko (2021).

For Spinuzzi (2020a), the fourth generation of CHAT requires the adaptation of CLs to the change of scale introduced by the new unit of analysis. In particular, greater consideration needs to be given to the way in which CLs are interconnected and articulated.

Stetsenko's (2021) discussion is more political in nature and is consistent with her previous work on CHAT concepts in terms of the political values that underpin this activist and interventionist research orientation (e.g. Stetsenko, 2019, 2020, 2022, 2023), which has been a leading proponent of this approach since its origins in Vygotsky (Stetsenko & Arievitch, 2014). In particular, she regrets the lack of t a contextualized, historically situated, and politically explicit critical diagnosis of homelessness in Finland:

> Combating and eradicating homelessness is a highly commendable goal, and the authors should be applauded for working on it (this effort follows with, and is in compliance with, the Programme of Prime Minister of Finland's Government, as the authors explain), yet a more contextualized, critical, and politically explicit analysis would have been beneficial (Stetsenko, 2021, p. 35).

According to this perspective, questions should be asked explicitly. Here are two examples: How do state policies contribute to homelessness? How is homelessness related to neoliberal trends in capitalism?

These two questions (among others) are of interest to us because they require a critical examination of the object of intervention. Consequently, having collaborated with other scholars on the topic of social inequalities in academic achievement, we considered it essential to contextualize the interventions within the historical trajectory of the struggle against educational inequalities and within a critical analysis that would allow us to elucidate the underlying causes of the production of educational inequalities within the French education system (Lémonie et al., 2021).

The asserted historicity of CHAT undoubtedly requires re-examination and development. The history of a specific activity system is not the only relevant consideration. The role of a broader system of loosely connected activity systems in producing and combating inequalities, or more broadly, runaway objects, also deserves attention.

Conclusion

One of the challenges of the fourth generation of CHAT is to provide support and guidance for expansive learning related to the major societal issues of our time. While it is true that the evolution of tools and the growing influence of new technologies are important, they are not the main driving factors behind the evolution of the framework initiated by Vygotsky, Leontiev, and Engeström and developed over three successive generations. Given the urgent need to address the emergence of novel objects that pose a significant threat to our existence, the development of both theoretical and methodological frameworks is of paramount importance.

In this context, the fourth generation of work in the field is beginning to emerge. This new generation of research raises new questions and calls for new ways of analyzing, for example, the degree of interdependence and independence of expansive, multilevel learning. It also calls for a dialogue between the histories of different levels and scales. In essence, this implies a comprehensive, interdisciplinary approach within the sciences with the aim of pursuing real utopias that challenge the capitalist organization of society.

Conclusion of Part 1

This first part offered a '*historical journey*' through the development of cultural-historical activity theory. This presentation was presented through the lens of the differentiation of work into different generations. At this point, it is crucial to return to the question of generational work for further discourse.

Are we not dealing with multiple theories and distinct projects? Or are they all developments of a unified theory? In this first part of the presentation, we have emphasized the characteristics that distinguish these generations. In this concluding note, we would like to emphasize the commonalities that unite these generations.

Back to the Idea of CHAT Generations

The concept of generation used in this first section is actually a metaphor. In the context of history and sociology, the term is used to categorize actors, their shared experiences, their habits, and so on. However, it is not typically used to describe generations of work. From a historical or sociological perspective, each generation is different from the previous one because it does not share the same social situation of existence.

> Men born in the same social environment at similar times are inevitably influenced by similar factors, especially during their formative years. Historical evidence shows that their behavior toward much older or younger groups is typically very distinctive. This is also true of their disagreements, which can be extremely sharp. To be passionate about the same debate, even in opposite directions, is still to be similar. This community of imprinting, arising from a community of age, constitutes a generation (Bloch, 1949/2023, p. 105).

In another sense, the term generation refers to a set of people descended from an individual at each degree of descent. Generation refers to the act of procreation. Each generation begets the next. This concept of generation is then more closely related to that of descent. According to Blunden

(2023), CHAT is '*a family of practices sharing the same grandparents, but having diverged over the years in terms of interests and characteristics*' (p. x).

The notion of generation implies a dialectic of change and permanence. Therefore, the occurrence of evolutions and qualitative changes in the unit of analysis does not negate the existence of common characteristics of CHAT. Furthermore, each generation gives rise to the next, although the generations can be clearly distinguished. According to Blunden's (2023) family metaphor, it is accurate to say that the grandson has '*inherited*' the traits of his grandfather, even though they belong to different generations. It is also possible to argue that the grandson can learn from his grandfather's experiences and make them his own, integrating them into his own projects. Despite the differences, there are some things that are passed on from generation to generation. The concept of a '*generation*' implies a form of heritage to be developed, rather than a work to be sanctified. In other words, each generation builds on the achievements of the previous one with regard to its own project and distinguishes itself from the previous one. For some, however, the question of generation remains open to debate. Bakhurst (2023) does not question the concept of generational identity but expresses reservations about this particular interpretation.

> The fact that this account of the nature of activity theory has become part of the self-consciousness of the tradition means that there is an important element of truth to it. A tradition is, after all, partly constituted by its understanding of itself. Nevertheless, there are aspects of this representation that I find unsatisfying (Bakhurst, 2023, p. 307).

He identifies two distinct branches of CHAT. The first is a philosophical branch, in which the concept of activity constitutes a general concept to explain human capacities. The second branch emerges from Leontiev's work, which, in his view, '*a method for representing activity systems with a view to facilitating not just understanding, but practice*' (Bakhurst, 2023, p. 313).

In our view, there is no fundamental contradiction between these two visions. They share the idea of generation. However, Bakhurst could be criticized for making a clear distinction between a philosophical branch dealing with philosophical questions and a more practical branch. The distinction is not so clear-cut: the work of the first branch informs the work of the second, and vice versa. Bakhurst's (2023) work demonstrates this, especially when he highlights Ilyenkov's involvement with Meshcheryakov's work in Zagorsk with multisensory impaired children (Meshcheryakov, 2009).

While the previous sections have shown the development of activity theory with its emphasis on difference, we will now return briefly to some elements of fliation to conclude this section. This will allow us to speak definitively of generations of the same cultural-historical theory.

Some Typical Features of a Common Parentage

Anchored in Practice, Responding to Societal Challenges and the Notion of Utopia

Each generation of work is distinguished from the previous one by a qualitatively new unity of analysis in relation to the need to confront issues specific to its time. However, each generation of work is rooted in a relationship with practice that makes it the very principle of knowledge elaboration. Practice is the place where knowledge and theory are elaborated, and thus it is useful not only for understanding and analyzing the world, but also for transforming it.

This is exemplified by Vygotsky, who saw pedology and defectology as essential contributions to the development of a new society. A similar perspective is evident in Leontiev's work. The Second World War was an important aspect of his career. The rehabilitation of the wounded was one of the most urgent tasks of the time. In response, Leontiev founded a rehabilitation center in Kaurovka with the goal of restoring motor function to limbs damaged by bullet wounds. At that time, the focus was on object-oriented activity. This work led him to study the effects of physical injury on body function and perception. With the growing internationalization of CHAT, there is a need to respond to issues with a more global scope. The support of social movements, the transformation of segregated cultures, and the promotion of genuine utopian ideals provide an ideal setting for the promotion of expansive learning efforts.

Orientation Toward the Future and the Question of Utopia

In keeping with this practical orientation, all generations of activity theory follow an epistemological orientation that differs from classical epistemology. Instead of trying to explain what is, the goal is to explain what could or should happen. In attempting to elucidate what has happened, an attempt is made to demonstrate the construction of the present from the past through a genetic methodology. Conversely, the attempt to elucidate what could or should happen is an attempt to demonstrate the presence of the future in the present.

All generations share this future orientation. Vygotsky's notion of the zone of proximal development concerns the separation between present and future development. To paraphrase Leontiev, Soviet psychologists of the 1st and 2nd generations were not interested in understanding how the child became what it is, but rather in determining how the child could become what it is not yet.

In Engeström's view, expansive learning is a form of learning that is oriented toward the future. This orientation involves the construction of what does not yet exist (Bound, 2022).

CHAT methodologies are those that give a place to utopia and the desirable future versus its opposite, dystopia; as well as the possible and its conditions. This is particularly evident in Vygotsky's work on defectology (1993b, p. 107), where he states that '*education must, in fact, make the blind child a normal and socially accepted adult, and must eliminate the label and the notion of deficiency that have been affixed to the blind*.' This is also evident in the author's work on pedagogy and psychology. Kozulin (1984) posits that scientific research is anchored in a utopian vision that it helps to bring about:

> The first generation of post-Revolutionary scholars largely shared the utopian program of their time. In their minds the Revolution was more than a political turnover that changed the ruling class and the economy. They envisaged it as a cosmic event that would transform everything from technology to the very nature of people, their conduct, and culture. Behavioral science therefore had to become a social instrument aimed at the dissection and transformation of human personality in a manner that might at once implement and realize the communist (Kozulin, 1984, p. 15).

In a similar vein, *Learning by Expanding* (Engeström, 1987) can be interpreted as a programmatic research program focused on tangible human activities undergoing transformation. The methodologies he employs are characterized by a clear orientation over the desired future.

Inclusion in the Dialectical and the Notion of Unity of Analysis

If CHAT approaches include the future and the possible in their conception of the history of human activity, it is because they are all based on dialectical logic. Dialectical logic enables us to look at *'things in motion'* and grasp the logic of their development. While each generation brings with it a qualitatively new unit of analysis, the idea of unity of analysis is nevertheless an achievement of the first generation of activity theory. It permits the abandonment of elementarist analyses and the examination of phenomena in terms of their relations and movement.

Overcoming Classic Dichotomies

CHAT is a *'strong theory'* (Nicolini, 2012) in that it transcends the classic dichotomies of others, arguably more traditional, approaches. Each of these approaches, in some way, transcends the traditional dichotomies of local and global, individual and society, inside and outside, change and permanence.

As has become clear, the concept of generation serves to elucidate the evolution of CHAT as well as its persistence. It allows us to account for the way in which one generation gives rise to another, each with different interests, which is precisely how CHAT is able to evolve while preserving its characteristics as a living tradition.

Part 2

FOUR CENTRAL CONCEPTS FOR ANALYZING ACTIVITY

Introduction to Part 2

Although CHAT is a relatively new theory, it has the capacity to travel, to spread and to expand. As such, we should speak of an interdisciplinary and international theoretical movement that mobilizes and develops activity theory. Let us begin by noting two possible ways of mobilizing it. CHAT can be mobilized as an explanatory framework of what actually happens in practice. The concepts are mobilized as a king of category. In this case, activity theory is not itself subject to development and runs the risk of becoming an unquestioned dogmatic orientation. In a second orientation, activity and its development can be considered an object of study in its own right. It is then legitimate to conceive the development of theory by putting it to the test in research aimed at capturing the development of activity. Barabanchtchikov (2007) notes that:

> As with all living theories, this conception is beset by problems, difficulties, and moments of crisis. For instance, the schematism of notions relating to the structure of activity, which has remained unchanged for many decades, raises many questions. Activity is most often considered not as an object of study, but as an explanatory principle. Empirical studies themselves focus mainly on a few specific actions and operations. Finally, as previously stated, it is the structural rather than the dynamic (though promising) level of activity analysis that remains of paramount importance (Barabanchtchikov, 2007, p. 58).

It has been demonstrated on numerous occasions that the error lies precisely in representing an activity as static, as a stable state that does not allow us to account for its possible development, for the seeds of novelty it contains. CHAT tries to give an account of processes, which means that it tries to capture the movement of things. As a result, documenting contradictions, expansive learning processes, and the evolution of an activity and its object pose significant challenges if one is to account for the dynamism and evolution of an activity beyond its functioning. Accounting for the potential development that internal contradictions inscribe in the activity thus promises possibilities for transforming the activity, avoiding the pitfall of arbitrary recommendations based on a diagnosis that ignores the fact that the future of an activity is already contained in the germ of the current activity.

Lompscher (2006) identifies five key features of CHAT as an analytical tool. These can be summarized as follows:

- Analyzing activity as a process and as a system (the two are interrelated, as we have endeavored to demonstrate throughout this chapter) as a theoretical and practical phenomenon, i.e. examining the components of an activity system and their interrelationships: the subject (mainly collective), the object and its transformation into a result or product, the means and potential rules, the division of labor and the community with the (practical) goal of finding solutions.

- Analyze the activity in question and its transformation in terms of the dependencies and interrelationships it has with other activities or activity systems, taking into account the socio-cultural and historical contexts in which it is situated.

- In considering activity systems as '*developing*', it is essential to include their history in the study and determine their zones of proximal development based on this history.

- This approach allows for the revelation of fundamental contradictions and the identification of potential solutions. It also stimulates and drives forward transformations that reveal the internal connections within the corresponding activity systems and their development potential.

- These transformations should be put into practice in the interests of people.

These principles demonstrate that the mastery and use of CHAT cannot be achieved without a thorough understanding of its central concepts. In his analysis of the historical significance of the crisis in psychology, Vygotski (1927/1999) presents two distinct perspectives on the relationship between concepts and scientific facts.

> In the first case, concepts do not constitute an object, a goal, or an objective of knowledge; they are instruments, auxiliary procedures, and it is the facts that constitute the goal, the object of knowledge. At the end of a search, the number of facts known to us has increased, but not the number of concepts; the latter, on the contrary, like any working instrument, weaken, alter with use, need revision and, often, replacement. In the second case, on the other hand, we study concepts as such; their correspondence with facts is merely

a means, a way, a procedure, a verification of their validity. As a result, we don't discover new facts, but rather acquire either new concepts or new knowledge about them (Vygotski, 1927/1999, p. 105).

In this section, we will examine the second posture proposed by Vygotsky. We will investigate four key concepts of CHAT to ascertain their potential utility for researchers engaged in qualitative analysis or formative intervention.

The choice of these four concepts is not arbitrary. They are central to the understanding of CHAT, and they are also polysemous and in need of clarification. However, a definition of these terms would be too convenient. It is in action, in use, that we can perceive their meanings. In this context, it will be useful to refer to empirical studies that allow us to perceive their use by researchers and the potential they open up for research. Taken together, these concepts are necessary for the analysis of activity as Lompscher understands it above. The first concept to be examined is that of the object of activity (Chapter 6). This term is polysemous, but it is central to understanding CHAT in that, as we saw in the previous section, it is the object that defines the activity. In our view, the distinction between the concepts of goals and objects is essential to an understanding of CHAT.

The concept of contradiction is discussed in Chapter 7. The concept of contradiction is often confused with its symptoms or with problems, conflicts and dilemmas. However, it is important to understand that contradiction is central to the movement or development of an activity system. An activity system is not a fixed context for action; it is an open context that sometimes goes into crisis when systemic contradictions escalate. However, contradictions are not only negative in that they precipitate a crisis in an activity system; they are also positive in that they offer potential for the development of the system. The expansive learning we will examine in Chapter 8 is object-oriented learning, a collective process that draws on the historically inherited contradictions in an activity system to redesign a new object. This chapter addresses the issues surrounding the articulation of expansive levels of learning in the context of CHAT's evolution toward a fourth generation of work. Finally, and arguably the most polysemous concept of all, development is addressed in Chapter 9. Here, development is conceived as a qualitative bifurcation, a collective, non-determined process that opens up to the generation of the new.

Chapter 6

The Object of Activity

[Feuerbach] fails to see how the sensible world around him is not a thing given directly from all eternity, remaining always the same, but the product of industry and the state of society; and, indeed, in that it is a historical product, the result of the activity of a whole succession of generations, each standing on the shoulders of the preceding one, developing its industry and its relationships, modifying the social system according to changed needs (Marx & Engels, 2012, p. 55).

Just as a horizon is forever unreachable, an object is in principle uncatchable (Foot, 2002, p. 132).

The Concept of Object and Its Importance for Chat

The concept of the activity object is one of the most important and controversial concepts in the research community today (Kaptelinin, 2005). It represents *'the most challenging theoretical construct in activity theory'* (Engeström, 2018, p. 15). The difficulty in conceptualizing this theoretical construct lies in its centrality to CHAT, the most fundamental aspect of the theory. CHAT is a theory of *'object-oriented activity'*. Consequently, the concept of the object and its understanding are of paramount importance.

As Stetsenko (1995) posits, the principle of object relation represents a foundational aspect of the development of activity theory. However, the content of the principle has not been fully explicated in a way that would preclude a reductive interpretation or a direct contradiction of the underlying meaning as advocated by Leontiev in the initial formulation of the principle of object relation. This observation is relevant to the understanding of the object relation principle as well as other principles within CHAT.

The heuristic potential of many of them has not been fully appreciated, and they have not become working principles, i.e. principles that can define, in real terms, a strategy for organizing concrete (theoretical, empirical, or practical) research. This has created the basis for what Leontiev termed 'an emasculation' of the activity approach (Leontiev, 1978). Let us repeat that some of the premises of this emasculation were contained in embryo in the theory of activity itself in that a number of its postulates were not fully stated or were reductive, which opened the door to numerous possible interpretations that often directly contradicted the original meaning (Stetsenko, 1995, p. 55).

In his work on the object-relation principle in Leontiev, Stetsenko (1995) distinguishes between two interpretations or understandings of this concept. The first of these interpretations, which she refers to as the '*broad interpretation*', is that activity is directed toward objects in the external world. Consequently, activity cannot take place without an object, which is primarily posited externally '*As something to which a living being relates and toward which the activity of that being is directed*' (Stetsenko, 1995, p. 56).

In this initial, broad interpretation, all activity (whether internal or external) finds its object in the external world of objects. Consequently, in Leontiev's theory of activity, the object-oriented nature of activity generates the object relation, but also the needs, feelings, emotions and perception: '*The object relation of activity is what generates not only the object character of images, but also the object character of needs, emotions, and feelings*' (Leontiev, 1975/2021, p. 87).

Several logical consequences follow from this broad conception of the object relation. The first consequence is the subjective outward transfer of the products of mental reflection. The effects of objects on the organs of perception are not perceived as subjective stimuli, but rather as the objective form of the object itself. This means that in perception, the subject does not establish a relationship between their image superimposed on the thing and the thing itself; for the subject the image is essentially the thing itself (Leontiev, 1975/2021, pp. 59–60). The second consequence is the potential for the subject to form '*images of integral objects that cannot be reduced to fragmented sensory impressions*' (Stetsenko, 1995, p. 57). Finally, the object-oriented nature of activity has the consequence that it is directed and regulated by the image of the object. Leontiev (1974) notes that:

An object of activity appears in two ways: primarily in its independent existence, and secondarily as a mental image of the object, as a product of the
subject's 'detection' of its properties, which is realized through – and only
through – his activity (Leontiev, 1974, p. 11).

The introduction of the category of object-oriented activity enables
Leontiev to move away from the famous behaviorist schema linking a
stimulus to a behavioral response (S → R), and the postulate of immediacy it presupposes. Activity is what links the object to the subject. In
other words, it is through practical contact with the external object that
the image of its properties is then used to direct activity. For Stetsenko
(1995):

Specifically, it amounts to the position that mental reflection is generated
not directly by external objects and influences, but by practical contact
with the world of objects, which must necessarily be subordinate to (and
even likened to) its properties, connections, and relations. A dual process of
mutual transition takes place here between the poles of subject and object
(Stetsenko, 1995, p. 58).

Leontiev's approach differs from that of Rubinstein in that it is oriented towards the object of the activity and interprets this relationship as
a way of overcoming the postulate of immediacy of the stimulus-response
schema. In his 1974 work, Leontiev strongly criticizes Rubinstein's position, which, in his view, does not allow us to go beyond the postulate of
immediacy of the S→R pair.

One approach was to emphasize the fact that the effects of external influences
depend on how the subject 'refracts' these influences on the psychological
'intervening variables' (Tolman and others) that characterize the subject's
inner state. S.L. Rubinshteyn express in a formula stating, 'External causes
acts through internal conditions'. Indeed this formula is quite indisputable.
If, however, we include those states evoked by an influence this formula
adds nothing new in principle, to the S →R formula (Leontiev, 1974, p. 6).

According to Stetsenko (1995), Leontiev's activity theory encompasses
two additional dimensions. These are based on a narrower interpretation
of the term 'object', which is understood to possess two distinct meanings. Kaptelinin (2005), highlights that the Russian language employs
two words that appear synonymous and interchangeable. However,
they are not considered to be equivalent in terms of their denotation.
In this sense, Objekt refers to a physical object that exists independently
of human thought. It designates objective material reality in general,

or '*things having existence*'. It is used to describe one pole of the '*subject-object*' opposition. In this context, activity is defined as a process of mutual transformation between subject and object (Leontiev, 1975/2021).

The term '*object*' in *Predmet*'s sense was used to designate a perspective that regards activity as '*object-oriented*'. In this context, the term '*object*' refers more to the content or target of thought and action. In contrast, the term '*object*' in the sense of *Objekt* refers to a '*thing*', or to an aspect of material reality that can be described using a combination of spatial and temporal characteristics. The term object, as it is understood in *Predmet*'s narrower concept, refers to a form that embodies a '*socio-historical experience of humanity*'. In summary, the essence of an object is not constituted by its physical properties, but rather by the specific connections and relations that emerge in the process of collective activity (Stetsenko, 1995, p. 59).

In this way of understanding the concept of an object, the principle of relation to the object is not only opposed to the postulate of immediacy (the original broad conception of relation to objects) but also to a solipsistic principle. The object relation is thus a fundamental characteristic of all human processes, which develop and are constrained by social norms. It is not the individual practice of a subject that forms the basis of cognitive processes, but rather the entirety of human practice. Consequently, the richness of the human perception and thought far surpasses that of the relative poverty of individual experience (Leontiev, 1975/2021, pp. 64–65).

In his initial theoretical work, Leontiev did not distinguish between these two meanings for the term object. In his book on the '*Development of the Mind*', he introduced the notion of objects immediately after defining the concept of activity. These concepts and ideas were subsequently presented in a more systematic manner in his 1975/2021 work titled '*Activity, Consciousness, and Personality*'. In this work, Leontiev employed both the terms '*Objekt*' and '*Predmet*', carefully distinguishing between them to emphasize the dimension of meaning described above.

In the context of the CHAT approach, the object is to be understood in the sense of '*Predmet*'. More specifically, the object is not something that acts upon and determines the subject. Rather, it is the object in the external world towards which activity is directed. Consequently, activity cannot exist without orientation towards this object, to the extent that activity without an object is meaningless. It is of paramount importance as a foundation for the CHAT approach to avoid falling into a reductionist and deterministic vision of the object in terms of activity (Stetsenko, 1995).

An another consequence, as elucidated by Stetsenko (1995), pertains to the fact that the image of an object does not merely refer to the external world, but rather unfolds within the external world. In this sense, the image does not belong to the subject's inner world, but rather to an outer, objective material world. Thus conceived, the mind is not situated within a subject's cranium, but rather situated in a space of interaction external to the subject. This allows for the mind to be studied through the objective analysis of its externalized activities. In his analysis of the extraction of a bullet from a wound, Leontiev illustrates how the sensations experienced by a surgeon are externalized in their actions.

> When a surgeon probes a wound, it is the tip of the probe that '*feels*', rather than the surgeon's own hand. This demonstrates that sensations are paradoxically transferred to the world of external things. They are not localized to the 'probe-hand' meeting point; rather, they are located at the '*probe-object*' meeting point. The same can be said of any analogous case: when we perceive the roughness of a piece of paper with the tip of our pen, when in the dark we feel for the road with a stick, etc. (Leontiev, 1975/2021, p. 61).

All the implications of the object relation of activity form the backbone of CHAT. It can overcome several classic oppositions, including those between the individual and society, between inside and outside, and between the subjective and the objective. Regarding perception, Leontiev highlights the implications of this object orientation of activity for psychology.

> The psychology of the past, which reasoned in terms of metaphysics, invariably analyzed perception in the context of two abstractions: the abstraction of man in relation to society and the abstraction of the perceived object in relation to objective reality (Leontiev, 1975/2021, pp. 67–68).

Differentiate the Object of Activity From the Goal of Actions

As Toiviainen and Vetoshkina (2018) point out, the object of activity does not refer directly to observable artifacts and infrastructure. Rather, the object represents the motive for the activity, responding to the reason why a given activity is needed and performed in society.

> The concept of object not only removes objectivist and subjectivist positions from analysis, it also helps us to understand not only what people do, but why they do it over the long term. It allows us to answer the question of why people do what they do in a particular situation (Engeström, 1995, p. 411).

In the view of Engeström (2018), the object of activity is a *'moving target'*. It may present itself as a raw material, or as a form of projection or anticipation of an expected result. He takes the example of a doctor's object, which initially takes the form of a singular patient, and then becomes a particular case. The process of transforming the object necessarily mobilizes instruments such as medical categories, disease classifications, and so on.

The differentiation between the conscious goals of actions and the object of activity is of particular importance for analysis, since it is the relationship between goals and object that gives meaning to action. The object of activity must therefore be distinguished from the goal of actions.

For Leontiev (1978), goals are conscious and direct actions. The difference between actions and activity lies in the temporality and collective dimension of the object. Thus, the goal of an action or an objective is something finite. Once achieved or not, we are aware of having succeeded or failed. In contrast, the object of activity is continually reproduced and unfinished. It is the *'why'* of an activity system: there will always be patients or students, and the *'why'* of a school or hospital lies precisely in this object. As Leontiev points out:

> Because the object of an action does not itself prompt to act, it is necessary for action to arise and to be accomplishable, for its object to appear to the subject in its relation to the motive of the activity of which it forms part. This relation is also reflected by the subject, moreover, in a quite definite form, namely in the form of awareness of the object of the action as a goal. The object of an action is therefore nothing other than its recognized direct goal (Leontiev, 1978, p. 401).

The object thus provides both the meaning of actions and their horizon of possibility.

> From a research perspective, the concept of the object of activity is a promising analytical tool providing the possibility of understanding not only

what people are doing, but also why they are doing it. The object of activity can be considered the 'ultimate reason' behind various behaviors of individuals, groups, or organizations. In other words, the object of activity can be defined as 'the sense maker', which gives meaning to and determines values of various entities and phenomena. Identifying the object of activity and its development over time can serve as a basis for reaching a deeper and more structured understanding of otherwise fragmented pieces of evidence (Kaptelinin, 2005, p. 5).

Alienation occurs when workers are unable to construct the object of their work as a meaningful motive. In modern labor, the separation of ownership of the means of production from their productive use, the complex division of labor, and the piecemeal segmentation of tasks to be performed and actions to be carried out for workers make it difficult to construct a motive. In this sense, the collective construction or reconceptualization of a new object is a powerful tool for emancipation.

This question of the object clearly distinguishes the CHAT approach from cognitivist approaches (see, for example, Lorino, 2019; Steiner, 2005) and situated approaches (In the context of work analysis see for example Theureau, 2004a, 2004b, 2005a, 2005b). Engeström (2018) identifies a limitation of both situated and cognitivist approaches: they restrict their analyses to actions in relation to tasks to be performed or situations to be analyzed.

From the perspective of activity theory, cognitivist and situated approaches share a common weakness. In both, the focus of analysis is restricted to actions, whether couched in 'tasks' or in 'situations'. Both are unable to account for what makes people act and form goals in the first place, what creates the horizon for possible actions, and what makes people strive for something beyond the immediately obvious goal or situation. What is excluded is objects and thus motives of activity – the long–term Why? of actions. Without this level, theories of situated cognition run the risk of becoming merely technical theories of How? – more elaborate and flexible than mentalist and rationalist models, but equally when faced with societal change and institutional contradictions that pervade the everyday actions of clinical practitioners and their patients. (Engeström, 2018, pp. 69–70).

It could be argued that situated action approaches constitute an important paradigm for activity analysis, i.e. in the field of Francophone work analysis (Wisner, 1995). Indeed, the work of Suchman (1987) has had a particular influence on the theoretical and methodological framework of the course of action. Nevertheless, it is important to recall how the object of analysis was defined within the framework of this approach:

> The activity of one (or more) actor(s) engaged in a situation that is significant for the actor(s), i.e. one that can be shown, told, and commented on by the actor(s) at any time under favorable conditions (Theureau, 2004b, p. 50).

The analysis proposed by Theureau concerns the meaningful activity of one or more subjects placed in favorable methodological conditions. These conditions typically include a self-confrontation interview procedure, which involves confronting the subject with video images of their work. This enables the subject to describe their achievements in a particular situation. In accordance with this theoretical framework, the methodology is founded upon the primacy of the intrinsic and employs an empirical phenomenology to account for the course of action through a description provided by the actor confronted with his own images. However, meaningful activity for an actor does not exhaust activity in the CHAT sense. This is because by investigating meaningful activity for an actor, the course-of-action methodology 'sequesters' (this is an image that has no pejorative value in my mind) the notion of activity in the work situation under analysis. As previously discussed in Chapter 4, activity analysis as understood by CHAT necessitates the integration of an intrinsic point of view with a systemic point of view on the activity system (for further insight, please refer to the chapter on expansive learning on this subject). This consequently requires the articulation of a point of view on situated action that gives rise to experience and a systemic and historical 'top-down' (Spinuzzi, 2018b) point of view accounting for the historical transformations of activity systems. Formulated differently and in relation to the concept of object, it is the relationship of actions to the objects of collective activity that explains the why, beyond the how of situated actions. Lorino (2017, p. 927) similarly asserts that *'we cannot understand situated action if we do not take into account its historical and societal extensions'.*

While acknowledging the value of situated analyses (which serve as a crucial starting point for analysis), CHAT posits that actions (guided by conscious objectives) occur within activity systems that evolve over time and are never perfectly stable. This perspective aligns with Spinuzzi's (2005a) assertion that the object is not merely a material entity with a singular experience, but rather, it is the conduit for a socio-historical experience intertwined with human practice.

If actions shape the development of activity systems, they are also shaped by these historical developments. This historical development of activity systems is conceived as the '*resolution*' (in the dialectical sense) of contradictions between or within activity systems. The influence of these systemic contradictions on actions in work situations is a theme that has been neglected by both situated and cognitivist approaches, which often remain at the level of actions and operations in the analyses that these frameworks are likely to propose. For Clot and Béguin (2004):

> The operation of development does not fit easily into the frameworks of situated theories of action, which stage an alternation – and even an antagonism – between the stabilized routines of ordinary life, on the one hand, and event-driven, uneventful creation on the other. On the one hand, repetition, which becomes routine, is taken literally. Conversely, the act of creation is perceived as a rupture, manifesting in various forms of 'creationism' (Clot & Béguin, 2004, p. 45).

If such a phenomenon as creationism exists, it is likely due to the fact that the concept of the object of activity is overlooked in the analytical process. Focusing on the manner of situated action ignores the rationale behind these actions. We concur with the authors' conclusion that '*Actions are best situated within the context of activity development, with goals and objects being linked. This approach preserves the virtues of creativity and inventiveness that Francophone work analysis recognizes in action*' (Clot & Béguin, 2004, p. 46).

From a CHAT perspective, goal-directed actions must be distinguished from activity and its object. However, actions must be interpreted in relation to the historical evolution and object of the activity of an activity system. This inclusion of history in the situation can transform contradictions into a resource. While they give rise to disruptions and failures at the level of actions, they also give rise to innovative solutions that signal possibilities for systemic change within activity systems.

The Characteristics of the Object of Activity Through Six Principles

We build upon previous discussions to identify six principles for characterizing the object of activity. The first principle is to emphasize that humans engage in activities for which the object is the primary motive, and the reason for the existence of this activity lies in a societal need. The idea of object-oriented activity enables us to overcome the opposition between the individual and society. This opposition is often expressed as the view that society is merely an '*external environment*' to which man is forced to adapt. For Leontiev (1975/2021)

> The individual is not only influenced by external social conditions that shape their activity, but these social conditions also provide the motives and aims of their activity, the means and modes of its expression. In other words, society produces the activity of the individuals who compose it (Leontiev, 1975/2021, p. 82).

The second principle is that the object of activity is presented on two planes. The first plane is material and '*objective*', while the second is ideal. For Leontiev, the object of activity is present on two levels.

> Firstly, it exists independently and acts upon the subject, transforming their activity. Secondly, it is an image of the object, a product of the subject's psychic reflection of its properties. This image is realized by the effect of activity and cannot be realized otherwise (Leontiev, 1975/2021, p. 83).

The third principle is that the object of activity is in a state of constant change. In contrast to time-bound actions, activity is a more enduring systemic form of training. However, this does not imply that the object of activity is fixed; rather, it evolves and develops over time. The evolution of the object of activity is driven by the relationship between personal meaning and significance, which evolves, develops, or comes into conflict in space and time. This process makes the object of activity more durable over time. Querol (2011) provides the example of a house-building activity. This activity cannot be reduced to the construction of a single house. However, the experience gained in building a house can be utilized to open up new perspectives and evolve the concept or object of the activity. This could include building houses that are more ecological, more economical, more comfortable, and so on.

The fourth principle is that the object of the activity can only be pursued collectively. As Leontiev suggests, the object of activity responds to the needs of a community. In modern societies, the object of activity cannot be achieved individually; rather, it involves a joint collective activity. To illustrate this point, consider a seemingly mundane example from a book on social inequality (Robichaud & Turmel, 2014): the production of a toaster. The object in question may appear mundane, but its production is the result of a historical legacy and relies on a highly specialized division of labor. This encompasses everything from design to the manufacture of the various components to the extraction of resources. Each action relies on highly specialized skills and knowledge that cannot be acquired by a single individual. Distribution also requires shared infrastructures and rules. It is evident that the production of a seemingly mundane object such as a toaster cannot be accomplished without the application of a division of labor and a significant socio-historical heritage. It is implausible that a single individual, even one residing on a remote desert island, would be capable of manufacturing a toaster independently.

The fifth principle posits that the object of activity is inherently polyphonic (Huotari, 2008). The relationship to the object is not uniform for all participants within an activity system. Each actor within an activity system develops a particular relationship to the object, which of course depends on their position in the division of labor. The object is thus *'multi-perspective'*. This implies that, in order to be discovered, the object of activity (in *Predmet*'s sense) must take into account the multiple perspectives to which the object refers for different people within an activity system:

> When we talk about the object, we need to distinguish between the generalized object of the historically evolving activity system (compare G. H. Mead's [1934] 'generalized other') and the specific object as it appears to a particular subject, at a given moment, in a given action. […] The particular, situationally constructed objects are unstable mixtures and partial manifestations of the generalized objects (Engeström, Puonti, & Seppänen, 2003, p. 181).

This principle has significant implications for formative interventions, which will be discussed in greater detail in Chapter 10. However, it is important to note immediately that the multiplicity of perspectives and functions within an activity system represents a crucial aspect for analyzing the object of activity and reconceptualizing it (Engeström, 2001).

The sixth principle is that the object is traversed by a contradiction between use value and exchange value. This fundamental (primary) contradiction of the object can be found within each of the elements of the activity system (instruments, rules, etc.). However, it is central to the object of activity. Leontiev repeatedly insisted on this contradictory dimension of the object of activity, and on the need for psychology to take it into account, so as not to make a psychology of an abstract man or a man '*in general*'. He gives the example of a doctor:

> The doctor who buys a practice in some little provincial place may be very seriously trying to reduce his fellow citizens ' suffering from illness and may see his calling in just that. He must, however, want the number of the sick to increase, because his life and practical opportunity to follow his calling depend on that (Leontiev, 1981, p. 255).

The next chapter (Chapter 7) will examine contradictions in empirical research. Miettinen (1998) places particular emphasis on this dimension in explanations of the historical evolution of a research object. Readers are invited to refer to his presentation at the end of this chapter.

There Is No Objectless Activity: From Object to Activity Delimitation

The delineation of an activity system, or the identification of the geographical and personal limits of activity, is not an arbitrary action. Frequently, and erroneously, authors identify or define activity in terms of subjects (e.g. teachers' activity, school heads' activity, etc.). This approach is inappropriate, as activities are defined first and foremost by their object. Consequently, the identification of an activity system is, in essence, the identification of an object in perpetual motion, towards which an activity system is oriented. This simple aspect undergoes a profound shift in perspective when viewed through the lens of analysis and its scope. To illustrate this shift, we may consider the doctoral thesis of Lahoual (2017), which examined mediation activities within a museum. In this work, the author did not study '*the activity of cultural mediators*', which would have been a reductionist approach. Instead, the author studied the activity of cultural mediation, which involves not only cultural mediators, teachers, and the researcher involved in the study, but also the children who were engaged in cultural mediation with their parents on their way back from the museum. The activity is thus distributed across multiple subjects, places, and temporalities, and necessarily implies an act of delimitation for its analysis.

This raises a significant methodological issue in the act of delimiting an activity system. The object is required to delimit the activity system, yet the object of activity is not immediately apparent during the research process. Consequently, Vetoshkina and Paavola (2021) emphasize that:

> The classical conceptualization of the *'object is the true motive of activity'* was developed as an abstraction, from which one needs to ascend to the analysis of concrete activities in empirical research (Kaptelinin, 2005; Vasilyuk, 1991; Vetoshkina, 2018). Originally a theoretical abstraction, it is utilized as both a practical and a theoretical concept with multiple functions pointing towards the different time scales and layers, tensions and contradictions around activities. In a specific research case, the object of activity cannot be taken for granted; it unravels during the research process (Vetoshkina & Paavola, 2021, p. 134).

In particular, while the definition of objects may be relatively straightforward in certain activities, it can be more challenging to identify in others. As Engeström and Escalante (1996) observe, the objects of certain types of activities, such as manual labor, are relatively straightforward to discern and articulate due to their observable materiality. In contrast, the objects of *'intellectual work'* are more difficult to identify.

> It is much more difficult to envisage and define the objects of activities such as commerce, administration, play, leisure or scientific research. A closer look at these activities reveals the slippery, multifaceted nature of their objects. Yet it is clear that these activities are oriented towards something and motivated by something. This something – the object – is constantly in transition and under construction and manifests itself in different forms for different participants in the activity (Engeström & Escalante, 1996, p. 30).

In introducing the concepts of Russian psychology to the French-speaking world, Savoyant (1984/2010) recognized the necessity of a methodological approach that would enable the analysis of collective activity. This approach necessitates the delineation of the activity process from the object.

> The delimitation of the collective activity process appears to be a necessary prerequisite for the psychological analysis of collective activity. This is because it is this delimitation that will make it possible to define the composition of the team or work group. This group or team includes all participants in the defined activity process. It is crucial to note that the composition of the team is not predetermined but rather derived from the delineation of the activity process. This aligns with our overarching perspective, which is focused on the activity of a group rather than the groups themselves. This leads to the conclusion that the activity process must be defined first, followed by the composition of the group carrying it out. It is

not possible to define the group first and then identify the activity process it carries out (Savoyant, 1984/2010, p. 110).

Identifying and delimiting this collective activity process is not straightforward, as it frequently does not align with the organization chart or the formal breakdown of the organization. As Witte and Haas (2005) posit, each of the potential strategies for delimiting an activity system is inadequate, as they are either arbitrary or tautological.

> A related problem for the researcher is strategic: If every human engagement with the social or material world is part of an activity or an activity system (and all such engagements may well be), as a researcher I am left with two equally unsatisfactory research strategies, given the two writers' theoretical models. Either I can offer a description of some activity around which I've drawn some arbitrary boundaries, knowing that my description is not in and of itself an explanation, or I can explain activity in terms of activity, in which case the object of analysis becomes indistinguishable from the analysis itself (Witte & Haas, 2005, p. 141).

The solution to this predicament can be found in a return to the notion of the object, insofar as:

- It can be posited that there is not such thing than an objectless activity.
- The object of an activity is the defining characteristic that distinguishes one activity from another.

As previously stated, defining the object itself can be challenging. Spinuzzi (2011) offers an interesting methodological perspective for delineating one or more systems of interacting activities around an object. Noting the expansion of the object inherent in the transformation of work, he proposes a method of progressive contraction of the object in several stages.

The initial step in identifying the object is to provisionally delimit a site. The identification of a site is a preliminary step that only provisionally delimits the case. As Spinuzzi (2011, p. 473) notes, '*the boundaries overflow in some places and will shrink in others*'. For example, if the objective is to investigate the activity of reprocessing household waste, the first step is to identify a dedicated site, such as a recycling plant.

The second step is to identify a common object. On the site, there is no guarantee that all employees will have the same understanding of the intended output of their work. When one initiates an interview with a subject, the subject will typically provide an account of their current activities, their intended outcomes, and the rationale behind their approach. This process allows for the identification of differences and similarities and the initiation of the identification of different visions of the object.

The third step is to document the multiplicity of the object through the results that are expected to be produced, which will be different for the multiplicity of actors in the activity system.

The fourth step is to delineate the system and describe its principal characteristics, including rules, division of labor, community, and so forth. In certain instances, however, it may be necessary to extend the analysis. To illustrate, in the case of the recycling plant, it is necessary to consider the perspectives of other potential participants in the activity system who are not physically present at the identified site. For example, the supermarket customers of the recycling plant are part of the division of labor, as they sort plastic and cardboard upstream. For the recycling plant, the plastic and cardboard represent a raw material that it will subsequently recycle. For customers, the plastic and cardboard represent waste that must be disposed of. Nevertheless, both the customers and the plant are likely to be part of the same activity system. Nevertheless, it is not straightforward to see how Spinuzzi's delimitation method could be used to extend the boundaries of the activity system beyond the limits initially set in step 1.

It is crucial to acknowledge that if the object of activity is the '*sense maker*' (Kaptelinin, 2005), it must be identifiable as that which provides logical meaning to the actions of the various actors within an activity system. To illustrate, consider the gravediggers presented in Chapter 3. When two gravediggers embark on the task of '*breaking a gravestone*,' they inevitably do so with conscious awareness. The objective of the gravediggers is to engage in a dialogue with a well-defined goal: the tombstone. Nevertheless, this action itself is devoid of meaning. The reason for this is that the object of their work is not the grave or the gravestone. Rather, the object of their actions is the grave plot, and their actions are driven by a motive that corresponds to a societal need to reallocate the grave plot. Once the meaning of the object has been identified, it is possible to delimit the activity directed by the object, which is the funeral plot. This activity extends far beyond the boundaries of the cemetery, due to the division of labor. It encompasses a diverse range of individuals, including families, administrative staff, the mayor of the municipality in which the cemetery is located, and others.

The activity system, as a unit of analysis, necessitates the integration of the system's perspective and the subject's perspective. The analyst constructs the activity system as if viewing it from a position above. Concurrently, the analyst must select a number of different members of the local activity, through whose eyes and interpretations the activity will be delineated, and the general object identified. This dialectic between the systemic and subjective points of view prompts the researcher to engage in a dialogical relationship with the local activity under study(Engeström, 1990b).

The Controversy Over the Notion of Object

From the perspective of activity analysis, the concept of object can be considered an analytical instrument insofar as it represents both a material object and the reflection of that object. This duality serves to orient activity and to imbue the actions of subjects engaged in activity systems with meaning.

As with the concept of activity, translation problems have largely contributed to the diversity of interpretations. It should be noted that the intention is not to provide the most accurate interpretation. Nevertheless, in this section, we have drawn upon the work of Leontiev and Engeström in order to elucidate the meaning of the concept of object. For the purposes of this discussion, the conceptual frameworks developed by Leontiev and Engeström are considered to be closely aligned. However, Kaptelinin (2005) posits that Leontiev and Engeström do not fully share the same concept of object, given their disparate perspectives. He presents his position in the following table:

Table 5: Differences in object conception between Leontiev and Engeström, according to Kaptelinin (2005, p. 11).

FACETS OF THE ACTIVITY	Leontiev	Engeström
Activities are carried out by...	Individuals	Communities
Activities are performed by...	Both individually and collectively	Collectively

Table 5: Continued

FACETS OF THE ACTIVITY	Leontiev	Engeström
The subject relates to...	Motivation, need (the true motive)	Production – what is transformed into the outcome
Field of application	Psychology	Organizational change

We take exception to the manner in which Kaptelinin presents his argument for a number of reasons. Firstly, we have previously argued in this book that Leontiev, when he speaks of activity, does so in the context of the concept of dejatelnost. This is defined as a practical, collective formation traversed by the division of labor and constitutes the unit of analysis of social life. In contrast to this interpretation, Kaptelinin does not share our understanding of Leontiev's position.

Kaptelinin posits that Leontiev's concept of activity is primarily an individual phenomenon. Consequently, there is a divergence in his interpretations of Engeström's and Leontiev's conceptions of the object. While Kaptelinin acknowledges the two distinct meanings of the term 'object' in Leontiev's work, he does not emphasize the implications of this distinction. The fact that Leontiev anchors this concept in psychology does not significantly alter the matter. For Leontiev, it is of paramount importance to develop a psychology that is not isolated from real productive processes. In his analysis of alienated labor, its development in capitalist society, and its significance for the psychology of consciousness, he notes:

> The traditional psychologist, of course, refuses to consider them, seeing in them only a relation of things. He demands that psychology should, come what may, remain within the context of the 'psychological', which he understands purely as subjective. He even reduces psychological study of man's industrial activity to investigation of its 'psychological components', i.e. of those psychic features for which engineering presents a demand. He is unable to see that industrial activity itself is inseparable from people, social relations, which are engendered by it and determine their consciousness (Leontiev, 1959/1976, p. 112).

In his analysis, Kaptelinin adheres to a broad conception of the concept of object. However, for Stetsenko (1995), it is precisely this narrow conception and its implications that distinguish Leontiev's work from that of other authors. *A narrow conception of the relation to the object*

204   The Object of Activity

is the dividing line between Leontiev and other psychological tendencies' (Stetsenko, 1995, p. 58).

With regard to Kaptelinin's interpretation of the object in Leontiev, it is challenging to comprehend how activities can be *'realized'* by individuals and yet *'performed'* by individuals or collectives. This distinction between realization and effectuation appears to be opaque and paradoxical.

The third reason for our disagreement with Kaptelinin concerns his presentation of Engeström's conception of the object. For him, the object in Engeström refers to the transformation of a product into a result. In this analysis, Kaptelinin places a strong emphasis on the material aspect of activity, which significantly narrows the scope of Engeström's position. Similarly, Engeström defends the dual material-ideal dimension of the object of activity, maintaining that it is both a given and an anticipated entity. It is therefore essential that Engeström recognizes this duality of the object if he is to intervene in modern work organizations. Engeström builds upon Leontiev's analysis of alienation in class society to highlight the challenges of constructing the object in modern work organizations:

> As Leontiev (1978; 1981) emphasizes, the true motive of activity is its object. The motive of the blacksmith's work activity resides in the iron – in the societal meanings and relations embodied and molded in each piece of iron the blacksmith makes his or her object. The notion of alienation implies that the workers, the subjects of work activity, cannot construct the object of their work as a meaningful motive. The separation of ownership and the practical productive use of the means of production, interwoven with an intricate division of labor and the increasing abstractness of the object, make motive construction exceedingly difficult in many complex work organizations. And it is seldom possible to revitalize traditional motives simply because the object of work – what is actually produced and for what kind of uses – must be continuously questioned and redesigned under market, technological, and legislative pressures. (Engeström, 2018, p. 36).

This duality is essential insofar as it is motives that need to be revitalized. This can be achieved by enabling actors to reconceptualize collectively the object of their activity. Engeström's way of conceptualizing the object of activity does not seem to us fundamentally different from that developed by Leontiev.

Identifying Objects and Their Evolution in Empirical Research

As previously stated, while the identification of the object of work in manual labor may appear straightforward, particularly in the case of the craftsman, it is a more complicated process in the context of '*intellectual*' work, or in the context of modern work organizations. Consequently, the identification of an object necessitates an investigative approach, whereby the multiple perspectives held by participants in the activity system within which they work are considered in relation to the historical evolution of the object's significance in relation to societal needs.

The following three studies (among numerous others) illustrate the construction and historical evolution of the object of an activity. These studies represent a posteriori reconstructions of the evolution of the object of an activity system or a network of activity systems. These reconstructions are based on archival data, interviews, and, in some cases, observations. All three studies demonstrate the historical evolution of an object and an activity. As they reconstruct a process historically, they are unable to account for the fine-grained level of expansive learning actions engaged in the reconceptualization of the object of activity by groups.

This type of research has been conducted on an ongoing basis, and it demonstrates how Change Laboratory participants utilize secondary and tertiary artifacts to redefine the object of their activity. Further details on the methodology of the Change Laboratory can be found in Chapter 10. For the sake of brevity, we have chosen not to present this type of research here, in advance of the chapter devoted to this methodology. For this reason, the examples presented below are limited to the historical evolution of an object, while demonstrating how researchers construct and identify the object and its evolution.

In their own way, all three studies focus on the characteristics of the object and its development. For Miettinen (1998) it is the object's inherent contradiction (between use value and exchange value) that drives its evolution. Concurrently, the reconstruction of the object implies the reconstruction of new artifacts. In contrast, Foot (2001) places greater emphasis on the fragmented dimension of the object, which she approaches through the lens of meaning and personal motives for engaging in the network. Finally, for Vilela et al. (2018), the analysis of contradictions by professionals in a workplace accident prevention network enables the object to develop in the form of an expansion.

The Evolution of a Research Object

In his 1998 work, Miettinen examines the way a community of cellulase researchers establishes a shared research object through the mediation of cultural artifacts.

The construction of an object is part of a process in which a subject (in this paper, a cellulase research group), an object (ethanol production by enzymatic degradation), the means and tools of construction (microbes, methods, apparatus, and models) and social relations (a network of activity systems participating in the construction) are simultaneously established and transformed. The evolution of the group's research object is linked to its dual nature. On the one hand, the objective is to develop industrial applications for ethanol production from cellulose degradation. On the other hand, the objective is to generate high-level knowledge on the mechanisms of complete cellulase degradation, with the aim of enabling industrial applications. This dual nature of the project is the primary reason for its evolution.

In the early 1980s, the cellulase research program and the complete hydrolysis of cellulose entered a crisis due to several reasons. The first challenge was the resistance of forest industry waste to enzymatic action. From the mid-80s onwards, the price of oil began to fall. In this context, the use of wood as a substitute raw material for oil in fuel production became unprofitable. However, to produce fuel from cellulose degradation (an industrial application), it was important to be able to degrade all the cellulose economically. This presented a contradiction between exchange value and use value. The socially and ecologically desirable production of fuel from wood became economically unviable due to falling oil prices and the resistance of oil industry waste to enzymatic action. The principle of total wood utilization of the previous period was reformulated in a new direction of pulp production in a more cost-effective and environmentally friendly process, as it did not use sulfur or chlorine by mobilizing enzymes. At the same time, cellulose was being studied using cell biology techniques. This technique permitted the production of enzymes for a variety of industrial purposes. The transformation of the research object, which involved the transformation of the application aspect, transformed the epistemic aspect. At the same time, the structure of the research changed considerably beyond the object.

During the third period, a novel network of researchers and industrial clients was established to facilitate the development of cellulase research applications. The objective was to develop industrial applications with a dedicated enzyme catalog. Moreover, concerns regarding the environmental impact of pulp bleaching and dioxin production led paper producers to engage in a network seeking a *'responsible'* method for bleaching paper.

Although Miettinen's (1998) research is relatively technical, it enables us to trace the evolution of the object in detail and to characterize the processes of evolution and historical transformation of a research object with a dual nature (the production of knowledge and the production of industrial applications). Moreover, the study illustrates the pivotal role of artifacts and models employed by researchers in the construction of a vision of the future. This evidence clearly indicates that the object is perpetually oriented towards the future, with an anticipatory perspective. In addition to its dual nature, the internal contradictions (between use value and exchange value) that exist within this research group's activity serve to set the object in motion.

The Gradual Construction of the Object of a Conflict Monitoring Network

In her 2001 and 2002 publications, Foot examines the historical development of the object of a network for monitoring and preventing ethnic conflicts on the territory of the former Soviet Union (the EAWARN network). To this end, she draws on a variety of sources, including oral and textual discourses of the network (documents, reports, emails, etc.), observations of interactions within the network during the period of this study, and interviews with EAWARN participants. In analyzing the interview transcripts, Foot places particular emphasis on the articulation of the interviewees' aspirations for the EAWARN project, their respective motivations for joining, and their perceptions of the Network's objectives. Despite the multiplicity of perspectives on the object under consideration, Foot (2001) demonstrates that there is a shared object that motivates the construction and activity of the network. Two main conceptions of this object emerged across all data types:

- Monitoring ethnic relations and conflict early warning (A).
- Building an epistemic community (B).

The results obtained by Foot demonstrate the great complexity of the object and the importance given at certain times to certain dimensions of this equally dual object

With regard to the monitoring and early warning of ethnic relations (A), Foot identifies three distinct conceptualizations that accord varying degrees of importance to the question of early warning in relation to ethnic relations monitoring.

With respect to the construction of an ethnic community (B), Foot demonstrates that there are four distinct conceptualizations of the object, depending on whether the community is comprised of academics and researchers or activists, and on whether this community is situated within the borders of the former USSR or forms part of a broader international community. It is evident that Foot's findings illustrate the fragmented nature of the network's object.

Changes in the Object of an Industrial Accident Prevention Network in Brazil

Vilela et al. (2018) employ a historical analysis based on interviews, observations, and documents to examine the expansive learning cycles of an occupational accident surveillance and prevention system in Brazil (SIVAT) within the Occupational Health Reference Center (CEREST). The article identifies two complete expansive learning cycles, each comprising two sub-cycles.

From 1997 to 2016, the primary objective of the SIVAT surveillance was to enforce regulations on companies. In a second learning sub-cycle, the interventions were extended to all companies in the same sector, given that there were similarities between companies. The interventions were focused on ensuring compliance with regulations and understanding the causes of work-related accidents, which could be identified by labor inspectors. Nevertheless, the interventions implemented and targeted at specific identified companies did not result in a reduction in the rate of workplace accidents. The discrepancies identified can be attributed to differences between the instruments used for surveillance (an epidemiological surveillance network, then information from a sector) and the object (the application of regulations by companies), as well as between this object and the result (stagnation in the rate of occupational accidents).

The second period commenced with an aspiration to transcend an approach that was exclusively focused on the overt nature of risk factors and instead centered on the legislation that was in force. The initial sub-cycle permitted the expansion of our focus to the organization of work as a source of occupational accidents and illnesses through the mobilization of ergonomic intervention tools. A preliminary model (MAPA) was developed to elucidate the genesis of an accident based on typical work practices, their variability, and the strategies employed by workers. This approach facilitated the discernment of organizational factors that had remained concealed when utilizing conventional tools, such as standards-based inspection, during the initial period. However, this methodology encountered limitations in the domain of diagnosis. Labor inspectors observed that the diagnosis conducted using the MAPA tool and the resulting recommendations required extensive learning to be effectively implemented. Consequently, it was not uncommon for companies to disregard the recommendations made following an inspection, as they involved significant collective learning. The second subcycle presented an opportunity for the network to introduce the tools of the change laboratory and CHAT as a preventive measure aimed at overcoming the identified limitations of the transformations introduced by the MAPA tool.

Vilela et al. (2018) represents the expansion of the surveillance network's object via a matrix crossing two axes. The first horizontal axis concerns the agency of the actors involved in the process, while the second vertical axis concerns the span of intervention, which ranges from aspects targeted at visible risk factors to the organization of work. The movement of the object is represented in the table below (Table 5).

Table 6: Object trajectory of the monitoring network according to Vilela and al. (2018).

	INDIVIDUAL AND EXTERNAL. LOW AGENCY	COLLECTIVE AND INTERNAL
FOCUS ON SOCIO-TECHNICAL SYSTEMS AND WORK ORGANIZATION WORK	3. MAPA and ergonomic analysis	4. Change laboratory
FOCUS ON VISIBLE RISK FACTORS AND REFERENCES IN LEGISLATION	1. State order. Inspection visit	2. CAST NET Sector-wide operations, training initiatives

This matrix delineates a proximal zone of development for the SIVAT network, where formative interventions constitute an expansion of the object of their activity. This enables them to overcome the limitations of interventions based on external diagnosis (3), the agency introduced by the CASNET operation, but limited to visible risk factors (2), and the low agency and low reduction of work-related accidents to compliance with current regulations (1). In this example, the identification and recognition by professionals of the contradictions historically inherited from their activity system enables a reconceptualization and expansion of the object.

Chapter 7

The Concept of Contradiction

To say that activity is dialectical is to appreciate something of the synthetic work that the performance of contradiction always accomplishes (Parker, 1999, p. 64).

Contradiction is the key to all other concepts and categories of dialectical development. Contradiction is to dialectics as matter is to materialism (Elhammouni, 2015, p. 274).

Activity systems are not static entities but rather evolve historically. As previously stated in Chapter 4, the concept of contradiction is essential for accounting for the self-movement of activity systems. Activity systems do not exist in isolation; they are interconnected with other activity systems and susceptible to being influenced by alterations in the activity systems of the network within which they exist, persist, and evolve. In this sense, activity systems can be considered open systems. Furthermore, they are susceptible to external elements that enter the activity system and exacerbate contradictions between the new element and older elements of the system. For example, Bonneau (2013) employs ethnographic research to examine the tangible manifestations of contradictions resulting from the introduction of a technological platform (Moodle in this case) in higher education in Quebec, particularly the ensuing redefinition of work organization. These concrete manifestations of the introduction of new technologies are problems, conflicts, dilemmas, or even local innovations identifiable at the level of professional action. It is therefore necessary to distinguish between the contradictions themselves and their manifestations.

The objective of this chapter is to provide a more precise definition of what is meant by contradictions and how they can be identified in research.

The Concept of Contradiction: A Dialectical Concept

The concept of contradiction as mobilized in CHAT is part of the Marxist tradition, which posits that social change is the result of contradictions inherent in the capitalist economic system. As the quotations presented in the introductory section of this chapter illustrate, the concept of contradiction is a pivotal concept within the field of dialectics. The concept of contradiction is a pervasive theme in the literature on organizational change. However, in order to fully comprehend its implications, it is necessary to contextualize it within the broader theoretical landscape. This entails delineating its relationship to related notions that are frequently employed synonymously in the literature. Engeström and Sannino (2011, p. 368) emphasize the necessity of this distinction, noting that '*there is a risk that contradiction becomes another catchword with little theoretical content or analytical power*'. They add that:

> In current organizational literature and research, contradictions tend to be watered down in three interrelated ways. First, they are not theoretically defined; instead they are equated with a number of other terms, the exact meaning of which is left vague. Second, contradictions are depicted ahistorically, as a universal feature of organizations, without embedding them in the socioeconomic formation of capitalism. Third, contradictions are commonly presented merely as constellations of competing priorities which need to be combined or balanced (Engeström & Sannino, 2011, p. 369).

It is of paramount importance to acknowledge that the concept of contradiction is fundamentally rooted in dialectical logic in order to prevent the misinterpretation of contradictions as mere problems, dilemmas, conflicting motives, contradictory demands, and so forth. In contrast to formal logic, which conceives of things solely as fixed, abstract entities, dialectical logic encourages us to avoid being constrained by the words that support concepts in the representation of abstract things. These entities are perceived as being self-contained and possessing their unchanging characteristics and metaphysical identity. Dialectical logic encourages the identification of the relationships in which the entities in question more deeply consist, their internal contradictions, and the source of their essential properties.

> This represents the initial '*nodal*' point in the comprehension of Marxism, a point that is frequently overlooked: the specific concepts of Marxism (or

earlier concepts taken in their Marxist context) are not concepts of things but of relations (Sève, 1980, p. 70).

By examining things in terms of their relations, it becomes possible to grasp their movement. The concept of contradiction plays an essential role in dialectics, as it constitutes the very source of this movement. For example, when discussing the problem of representation, Leontiev notes that representation is not '*fixed*', but rather living, in the form of a virtuality capable of realization. The concept of contradiction is central to him:

> Our generalized sensible images, like concepts, include movement and thus contradiction; they reflect the object in its multiple connections and mediations. This means that no sensible knowledge is a fixed impression. If it is indeed preserved in man's mind, it is not as something 'ready-made', but only virtually – in the form of physiological brain constellations that have formed and are able to realize the subjective image of the object, revealing to man in this or that system of objective connections. The representation of an object encompasses not only what is identical in objects, but also the various facets of that object, including those that do not overlap with others and are not in relationships of structural or functional similarity. Our sensory representations are therefore dialectical in the same way as our concepts; they are therefore capable of fulfilling a function that cannot be reduced to the role of a fixed model standard, corresponding to the actions exerted on receptors by isolated objects. Similarly, the subject's activity is inseparable from the representation, which enriches it in content, brings it to life, and makes it creative (Leontiev, 1975/2021, pp. 69–70).

As previously discussed in Chapter 4, the representation of an activity system without contradictions is meaningless insofar as it suggests that the activity system is stable and fixed. It can be argued that contradictions are the driving force behind the transformation of an activity system. It is therefore important to differentiate between the concept of contradiction and its common-sense acceptance. In everyday language, the term '*contradiction*' is often applied to ideas, rather than to things themselves. In contrast, dialectical logic considers contradiction to be inherent in things themselves, as relations. This perspective is in opposition to formal logic and the principle of non-contradiction. Those lacking in dialectical logic and a conception of things as processes and relationships are necessarily hindered in their ability to discern the two contradictory elements within a system. Furthermore, they are prone to misperceiving the mutual interaction between these elements as causal.

(Ollman, 2005, p. 32) Furthermore, they find it challenging to account for the movement of things as anything other than a dynamic, i.e. a succession of observable events, but whose underlying logic is difficult to characterize. As Ollman (2005) asserts:

> 'Non-dialectical thinkers', operating with a vision based on common sense, can only understand real contradictions as differences, paradoxes, opposition, tension, dislocations, imbalance, or if accompanied by open contestation, as conflict. However, without the dialectical notion of contradiction, they rarely perceive and are unable to fully comprehend the underlying forces responsible for these phenomena. Moreover, they are unable to comprehend the nature of the development or assess the strength of these tendencies until they have emerged to the surface of events (Ollman, 2005, p. 32).

We emphasize that the distinction made by Ollman between the surface of things and the underlying forces that explain their appearance is of paramount importance for an understanding of contradiction. In fact, contradictions can be perceived as forces that emerge from the relationship between contradictory elements within a system. These forces exert an attractive force on the system and its participants, yet simultaneously act as a source of resistance and opposition.

In conclusion, contradiction is a foundational concept of dialectical logic that cannot be ignored. Consequently, the concept of contradiction is of paramount importance in CHAT. Dialectics is the study of the logic of the development of activity systems. In this context, the logic of development must be sought within the system under analysis, and not in relation to a cause external to the system under consideration. As will be discussed, the elements of an activity system exhibit internal contradictions. It is crucial to recognize that these internal contradictions within the elements of the activity system (referred to as a primary contradiction) modify the relationships between the elements of the activity system, which can then enter into contradiction (referred to as a secondary contradiction), thereby influencing the system's development.

Finally, it should be noted that the ability to account for the logic of a system's development based on the study of its history enables the anticipation of the future. The concept of contradiction thus becomes central to the definition of a system's proximal development zone.

A more detailed examination of dialectics will be provided in Chapter 10, which is devoted to the Change Laboratory. In particular, the method of ascending from the abstract to the concrete will be discussed in detail. For the present, however, it is necessary to demonstrate how contradictions within an activity system are the driving force behind its development.

Contradictions as the Driving Force Behind the Development of Activity Systems

As previously discussed in Chapter 4, the act of analyzing an activity system does not entail merely filling in the corresponding boxes for each of the system's poles. Rather, the objective is to grasp the system's movement and underlying logic of development. This entails accounting for the logic of historical changes within the system. This is in contrast to the common misconception that analyzing an activity system means merely 'filling in' the boxes corresponding to each of the system's poles.

In this orientation, the concept of contradiction is fundamental, as it enables us to understand why qualitative and systemic changes take place within an activity system (Passage from USAGE 3 to USAGE 4). These qualitative and systemic changes (development) within activity systems can be understood as collective efforts to resolve and overcome historically accumulated contradictions within an activity system. This can be conceptualized as expansive learning (see Chapter 8).

In order to account for the significance of contradictions as an explanatory principle in the development of activity systems, it is necessary to analyze both the contradictions accumulated within a system and the transformative processes by which contradictions are resolved, leading to the formation of a new activity.

The following three examples from the literature illustrate the role played by contradictions in the historical evolution of an activity system in distinct ways.

Example 1: The U.S. Food Production System

In his 2020 work, Adamides provides a comprehensive account of the historical process of CHAT mobilization, which serves to elucidate the concept of contradiction. The illustration is based on a socio-technical system that is organized around food production and consumption in the USA. Adamides identifies three major developmental periods in this system: (1) the generalization of processed foods, (2) the 'nutritionalization' of foods, and (3) the development of medical nutrition.

In his analysis, Adamides (2020) distinguishes two interacting activity systems: food production activity on the one hand, and the family activity of producing a meal (referred to as consumption activity in his analysis) on the other. The two systems are linked by the fact that the food production system provides the instrument for the meal production system. For illustrative purposes, we will limit our discussion to the first historical period analyzed by Adamides (2020). During this initial period, processed foods (principally canned goods) were introduced into the American army due to their ease of transport and preservation. With men stationed at the front in Europe, women assumed a new role within the division of labor (Activity System No. 1 in Figure 1). This new division of labor (housewives versus women who work outside the home) necessitated the preparation of meals in a timely and straightforward manner.

As the object and subject of the production activity system undergo transformation, a contradiction arises between the new object (quickly prepared meals) and the instrument, i.e. the food used to prepare the meals. This contradiction is resolved by the introduction of processed foods into this activity system.

Nevertheless, the introduction of processed foods gives rise to further contradictions within the food production activity system. Firstly, on the object pole, this is resolved by introducing a qualitative change in the object of food production. Secondly, between the poles of subject, object, instruments, community, rules, and division of labor, these contradictions are resolved by qualitative and systemic transformations of each of the poles of the food production system, as shown in bold in Figure. For example, the community and division of labor incorporate a novel actor into the sales process of industrial production: supermarkets.

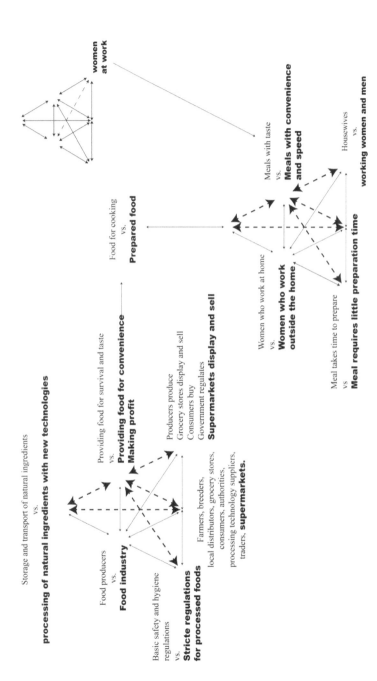

Figure 21: Evolution of food production in the United States according to Adamides (2020)

Example 2: France's Occupational Accidents and Disease Prevention System

A scoping literature review (Munn et al., 2018; Pham et al., 2014) was conducted by Boudra et al. (2023) to identify the primary contradictions within France's occupational injury and disease prevention system. The literature review identified four major contradictions in the French occupational injury and disease prevention system. One of these concerns the object pole of the prevention activity system in France. This is the contradiction between prevention and reparation. This contradiction has been present throughout the history of prevention in France, giving rise to new developments in the prevention system. At times, the prevention system has been oriented towards prevention, while at other times it has been oriented towards reparation.

Example 3: Developments in Coworking

The identification of contradictions implies the identification of developmental periods, i.e. profound qualitative changes in the activity system under analysis. The identification of these developmental periods can be relatively complicated when attempting to account for a widely distributed and highly heterogeneous activity system. This is exemplified by Ivaldi, Sannino, and Scaratti (2022) in their account of the development of coworking. Coworking initially emerged as a means of promoting forms of work and organization that require simultaneous, multidirectional, and reciprocal work, as opposed to forms of organization that incorporate an established division of labor, bounded communities, and formal and informal sets of rules. However, since its introduction, coworking has evolved and transformed itself in new directions. Based on a review of the literature, the authors identify these new directions of development in the conceptualization of coworking. While these developments cannot be reduced to periodization or unitary phases, the authors demonstrate the multiplicity of potential development pathways based on a matrix that brings two main contradictions into tension. The first dimension concerns the orientation of coworking, whether it is inward- or outward-looking. The establishment of coworking has been based on the creation of a network of actors that crosses the boundaries of each coworking space in an outward direction. Conversely, the evolution of coworking has been driven by the necessity to address users' needs. In this context, the focus has been on the internal aspects of the space. The second dimension of development concerns a contradictory orientation between the original socially oriented idea of coworking and a secondary idea of profitability. Initially, the social dimension was linked to the idea of coworking as emphasizing aspects of work not directly linked to profit. The original concept of coworking was to create spaces that would support workers in challenging the dominant orientations and the limits of domination by private institutions. With the spread of coworking spaces, additional needs in terms of profitability emerged, which translated into more activity-oriented orientations.

These two contradictory dimensions are described in a matrix that proves to be an important tool in the context of intervention to materialize what Engeström (1987) calls the proximal zone of development of intervention. We will return to this artifact in the chapter devoted to formative interventions and the presentation of the Change Laboratory (Chapter 10).

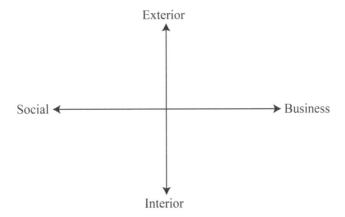

Figure 22: Developmental dimensions characterizing the historical evolution of coworking according to Ivaldi, Sannino, and Scaratti (2022, p. 47).

Observable Symptoms and Manifestations of Contradictions

The preceding analyses were conducted at the level of activity systems and their history, based on bibliographical research or literature reviews that employed several procedures and degrees of systematicity. The analyses demonstrate that contradictions are historically accumulated tensions within activity systems, which explain their historical transformation. The newly produced activity system can be seen as a means of overcoming historically accumulated contradictions.

It is, however, important to note that these contradictions cannot be observed in the same way that an activity system cannot be observed. It is therefore appropriate to inquire as to the manner in which these contradictions operate in a work setting or in the daily actions of workers. To put it another way, what is the relationship between contradictions as an active force and the surface of things that can be observed, as Ollman (2008) posits? In order to gain a deeper understanding of the relationship between contradictions and observable phenomena, it is essential to examine the specific manifestations or symptoms of these contradictions. It is also crucial to differentiate between the two.

> Contradictions are not the same as problems or conflicts. Contradictions are historically accumulating structural tensions within and between activity systems (Engeström, 2001, p. 137).

If contradictions cannot be observed, only their symptoms can be apprehended through observation. Indeed, systemic contradictions within an activity system have repercussions for situated action, since they can be analyzed as manifestations of an activity system (Engeström, 2008, p. 27). Consequently, contradictions are reflected in the form of recurring problems or local micro-innovations. They can also be apprehended through conflicts, dilemmas or recurring local problems.

The figure below illustrates the distinction between contradictions and their manifestations by linking the structural level of an activity to that of action. Consequently, if contradictions are historically inherited within activity systems, they necessarily manifest themselves in the actions that carry out that activity.

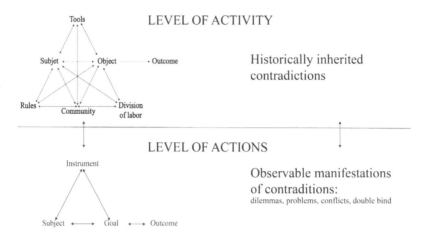

Figure 23: Differentiation between historically inherited contradictions operating at the level of the activity system and their observable manifestations at the level of action.

Conducting a field study often presents researchers with the challenge of swiftly grasping historically embedded contradictions. Consequently, researchers must approach these contradictions through their residual traces. As elucidated by Engeström and Sannino (2011):

> As contradictions are historically emergent and systemic phenomena, in empirical studies we have no direct access to them. Contradictions must therefore be approached through their manifestations. We may also treat manifestations as constructions or articulations of contradictions; in other words, contradictions do not speak for themselves, they become recognized when practitioners articulate and construct them in words and actions (Hatch, 1997). However, contradictions cannot be constructed arbitrarily. Their material and historical power is not reducible to situational articulations and subjective experiences (Engeström & Sannino, 2011, p. 371).

It is therefore necessary to investigate the history of the activity system in which we operate. The initial step in this investigative process is to identify the symptoms of contradictions that can be observed at the level of individual or collective action. As Engeström and Sannino (2011) note, contradictions are not limited to observable work situations. Observation of work situations represents merely the initial stage of an investigative process aimed at identifying and analyzing contradictions. To illustrate this point with a metaphor, reporting contradictions is analogous to being in the same position as a physician confronted with the symptoms of an illness. As proposed by Spinuzzi (2018b), describing symptoms does not generally lead to a diagnosis.

Let us continue with this metaphor of medical diagnosis to clearly distinguish between symptoms and the actual cause of these symptoms, and to account for the investigative work required to identify systemic contradictions within activity systems.

To illustrate, consider a scenario in which an individual has fallen and sustained an injury to their leg. They seek medical attention and inform the physician of their discomfort. The physician does not conduct a comprehensive examination but instead prescribes analgesics and anti-inflammatory drugs. What, then, is the physician's objective? It can be argued that the physician has merely alleviated the symptoms, rather than addressing the underlying causes.

Now, imagine that the individual has suffered a fracture. While pain relief may be beneficial, it is not a solution to the underlying problem. Furthermore, the alleviation of pain may result in the foot being placed in a position that exacerbates the fracture line.

What insights can be gained from this illustrative example? In the context of organizational dynamics, it is inevitable that individuals will encounter a multitude of challenges, conflicts, and dilemmas. These problems, conflicts, and dilemmas are indicative of systemic contradictions within the activity system. In the context of an intervention within a work organization, addressing the work problems will not resolve the underlying systemic contradiction. This is analogous to providing aspirin for a broken leg..

The symptoms and observable manifestations of contradictions are of different kinds. These include dilemmas, conflict, critical conflict, double-bind, and recurrent problems. It is crucial to distinguish between these symptoms and historically inherited systemic contradictions. Otherwise, the researcher runs the risk of identifying contradictions in all aspects of the situation without actually identifying any of them.

Engeström and Sannino (2011) propose a framework for the analysis of discursive manifestations of contradictions. This framework enables the researchers to distinguish four types of discursive manifestations, which are summarized in Table 7.

Table 7: Different discursive manifestations of contradictions for Engeström and Sannino (2011).

TYPE OF DISCURSIVE MANIFESTATION	FEATURE	LANGUAGE INDICATORS	RESOLUTIONS
DILEMMA	Moral reasoning, ideologies,	'On the one hand, on the other', 'Yes, but'	Denial or reformulation
CONFLICT	Disagreements, divergences, alternative behaviors, criticism	'No', 'I don't agree', 'That's not true'.	Finding a compromise
CRITICAL CONFLICT	Inner doubts, unsolvable contradictory motives for the subject	Personal, emotional, moral accounts living metaphors, 'I realize now that…'	Finding new personal meaning
DOUBLE BIND	Unacceptable alternatives in one's own activity system, dead end, pressure to do something/ impossibility of doing it.	'We', 'We must', expressions of powerlessness, 'Let's do it this way', 'we'll get there'.	Transformative practice and collective action

The first type of observable manifestation concerns dilemmas. A great deal of research has mobilized other theoretical frameworks to study dilemmas, particularly in the context of teaching or work. This research includes studies by Oliveira, Brito, and Lacomblez (2012); Ria, Saury, Sève, and Durand (2001). Dilemmas are situations in which two opposing options are presented to an individual, who is then challenged to choose between them. These situations are informed by socially shared, historically inherited beliefs. Discursively, they take the form of hesitations and formulas such as 'on the one hand, on the other hand', '*yes, but*'.

The second type of manifestation concerns interpersonal conflicts. Conflicts take the form of disagreements or criticisms. They pertain to a situation of opposition between individuals who feel negatively affected by antagonistic positions or behaviors. Discursively, conflicts take the form of open opposition, manifested in the utterances '*no*', '*I don't agree*', and *'that's not true'*. They are generally resolved either by submission to authority or to the majority.

The third type of discursive manifestation is critical conflicts, which are defined as *'situations in which people are confronted with inner doubts that paralyze them in the face of contradictory motives unsolvable by the subject alone'* (Engeström & Sannino, 2011, p. 374). These experiences are emotionally charged and involve contradictory motives. They can be highlighted through autobiographical accounts or expressed in the form of metaphors (Sannino, 2008).

Finally, the fourth and last type of discursive manifestation proposed by Engeström and Sannino (2011) refers to double-bind situations, which have been particularly studied by Bateson (Bateson, 1980; Wittezaele, 2008). A double bind refers to a situation in which an individual is subjected to two mutually incompatible constraints or pressures. A double bind is typically a situation that cannot be resolved by an individual alone. Thus, resolving a double constraint usually involves an attempt to make the transition from the individual *'I'* to the collective *'we'*, for example, *'we must. . .'*. The resolution of a double bind necessitates practical, collective transformative action that transcends mere rhetoric; however, such action is often accompanied by expressions such as *'let's do this'*, *'we'll get there'*.

Experiencing Contradictions

At the level of action, actors experience contradictions within or between activity systems. An actor is not an actor of a single activity system. Activity systems are therefore *'experienced'* (Vasilyuk, 1991). This can give rise to tensions in people's experience of participating in several activity systems. This phenomenon is particularly evident in adolescents, who are often divided between multiple social spheres, including school, family, and peer groups. This phenomenon is, of course, not limited to adolescents. Research by Engeström, Rantavuori, Ruutu, and Tapola-Haapala (2022) focuses on the tensions experienced by adolescents. It serves here as an illustration of how the authors use the framework of discursive manifestations of contradictions (Engeström & Sannino, 2011) to identify them and transform them into a resource for the development of an activity system.

The research presented here constitutes an initial study for a broader project designed to support adolescents with projects that are likely to facilitate the '*desencapsulation*' of school learning. Indeed, in the school institution, knowledge is often presented as an end in itself, rather than as instruments for carrying out activities that matter to adolescents (Engeström et al., 2023b). As part of this research, Engeström and al. (2022) sought to identify the developmental tensions between the different activity systems in which adolescents act. The researchers distinguished six activity systems: peer activity, school participation, family, digital activity, future activity, and civic activity. To this end, they conducted 12 semi-structured interviews with teenagers aged 14–15 who volunteered to participate in the study. Prior to each interview, the adolescents were requested to create a poster to introduce the themes of the interview. Each adolescent was requested to create a poster that introduce the issues that were important to them in relation to the different activity systems and the way in which they experienced these different activity systems and their potential contradictions.

The initial stage of the analysis involved the examination of the interviews to identify the discursive manifestations of contradictions (Engeström & Sannino, 2011) within the transcripts. The authors identified 147 discursive manifestations of contradictions. These manifestations were then classified according to the six activity systems identified.

(1) The world of school encompassed learning, teaching, and the social interactions that occurred within the school environment.
(2) The world of peers pertained to interactions with peers and leisure activities that occurred outside of school.
(3) The digital world referred to media and social networks.
(4) The family world was about the aspirations and challenges they had encountered in their family life.
(5) The future world was concerned with matters of concerns, aspiration, and personal issue.
(6) The civic world pertained to opinions on global events, climate, politics, racism, and the ways in which individuals could participate in and influence society.

In the third stage of the study, the researchers sought to identify the ways in which the different worlds experienced by the participants were intertwined. It should be noted that the different worlds are not entirely independent of one another. For example, in one interview, one of the teenagers interviewed by the researchers discussed the school year he had planned without being able to use his phone (school attendance – digital activity). The findings indicate that lived dilemmas and conflicts are the two most significant manifestations. The expression of dilemmas is more prevalent in relation to the future world, whereas conflicts are more common in the context of the school world and school policy, which fails to meet the needs and hopes of adolescents.

The school world is the most hybridized in the results, as the authors point out:

> For these adolescents, the challenge is not just moving from one world to another; dwelling in one single setting such as the school means facing tensions generated by hybridization. Tensions stemming from the intrusion into the school of other worlds cannot be suppressed but should be turned into drivers of expansive learning and development (Engeström et al., 2022, p. 1).

In conclusion, the researchers urge educators to assume a more active role in navigating the complex dynamics of school life. In light of these considerations, educators are encouraged to identify and address contradictions in their pedagogical practices.

With regard to methodology, the researchers employ interviews and discourse analysis to uncover contradictions and their manifestations. This is achieved through the analysis of both the discourse produced by students during interviews and a poster produced by students in response to an open-ended prompt.

Contradictions Are Not Problems, But Their Systemic Causes

The classification proposed by Engeström and Sannino (2011) is not exhaustive, as it primarily focuses on discursive manifestations. Consequently, an ethnographic approach can identify active traces of contradictions by observing behavior. Disruptions, deviations from the rules, or even local innovations can be considered examples of contradictions:

> By disturbances I mean deviations from the normal scripted course of events in the work process, normal being defined by plans, explicit rules and instructions, or tacitly assumed traditions. A disturbance may occur

between people and their instruments or between two or more people. Disturbances appear in the form of an obstacle, difficulty, failure, disagreement, or conflict (Engeström, 2008, p. 24).

The observation that both recurring problems and local disturbances can be understood as traces of contradictions can be explained by the fact that activity systems undergo relatively long cycles of qualitative transformation. As contradictions intensify, some participants in the activity system begin to challenge established practices and identify novel solutions. To illustrate this aspect, we may consider the intervention of Poulain (2017).

The initial request concerned workstation design in the automotive industry. The intervention concerned the dashboard assembly line. Following Lémonie (2019), Poulain (2017) observed the variability and diversity of the operations implemented, which led her to conclude that operators never performed the requested operations in the same order. Moreover, the number of operations varied according to the work cycles. In an effort to identify the underlying causes of this discrepancy, she discerned that the operators collaborated with one another. When an operator observed his colleague struggling on the downstream line, he would proceed to perform additional operations to assist him in catching up. The implementation of a new production rate on the assembly line (from 47 to 64 vehicles per hour) reinforced and legitimized this innovative local solution: to keep up with the pace, operators gradually instituted a three-shift rotation (one operator carries out operations at stations 1, 2, and 3, following the vehicle, then returns to station 1). The role of the ergonomist was to provide support and legitimacy to the '*module-based*' approach to management, as opposed to the '*shift-based*' approach. As evidenced by this example, the initial contradiction between the imposed cadence and the division of work by shift led the operators to devise an innovative solution, which then had to be integrated within the broader activity system.

As Ilyenkov (1982/2008) notes, innovations do not originate from a centralized authority. Rather, they emerge as deviations from existing norms, which subsequently become new norms:

> In reality it always happens that a phenomenon which later becomes universal originally emerges as an individual, particular, specific phenomenon, as an exception from the rule. It cannot actually emerge in any other way. Otherwise, history would have a rather mysterious form. Thus, any

new improvement of labor, every new mode of man's action in production, before becoming generally accepted and recognized, first emerge as
a certain deviation from previously accepted an codified norms. Having
emerged as an individual exception from the rule in the labor of one or
several men, the new for mis then taken over by others, becoming in time a
new universal norm. If the new norm did not originally appear in this exact
manner, it would never become a really universal form, but would exist
merely in fantasy, in wishful thinking (Ilyenkov, 1982/2008, pp. 83–84).

Consequently, the initial step in analyzing contradictions is to observe
both recurring issues and local innovations at the level of actions and operations. The Francophone tradition of work analysis, which distinguishes
between '*prescribed work*' and '*real work*,' provides an excellent foundation for understanding the symptoms of contradictions. Nevertheless,
it is crucial to distinguish between symptoms and underlying causes,
which are historically inherited contradictions within an activity system.
In the literature, there is often considerable confusion between problems
and contradictions. As previously noted in the metaphorical example
of medical diagnosis, this confusion carries the risk of exacerbating the
contradictions, or the underlying causes of the problems encountered.
This confusion is evident once again in the article by Detchessahar,
Gentil, Grevin, and Stimec (2015). The authors note that establishing
work discussion spaces can facilitate the activation of organizational and
strategic levels from below by delegating the design or redesign of sites
that arise from the observation of work tensions or contradictions (p. 83).
However, in the hospital intervention they describe, they are not referring to the discussion of contradictions within an organization, but to
a recurring problem[17]: The article states that health managers are over-
whelmed. On pages 72 and 73, the authors describe solutions and action
plans that were developed in discussion forums with operators. The solution found is to relieve the burden on healthcare managers.

The article does not specify which actors will assume some of the
duties typically performed by health managers. Moreover, the article does
not elucidate the historical reasons for this phenomenon or investigate
the underlying contradictions that result in the overloading of healthcare

---

[17]   To clarify that their analysis is not about systemic contradictions, but about a problem, is not to negate the significance of that problem. On the contrary. However,
identifying a solution to this problem necessitates the identification of the systemic
contradictions at its root.

managers. Additionally, the article does not examine the relationship between the healthcare managers' duties and the object of collective work, which in this case is the patient. The challenge of Detchessahar, Gentil, Grevin, and Stimec's (2015) intervention work was to implement '*discussion spaces*[18]' as an a priori solution within the organization.

However, by addressing the symptoms of these contradictions, rather than their underlying causes, there is a significant risk of exacerbating the systemic contradictions inherent to activity systems. In this regard, while we concur on the significance of discourse on labor, we must underscore the potential for these discussion spaces to become instruments for resolving localized issues, at best, and, at worst, to have the opposite effect, by exacerbating contradictions that are not recognized and not linked to the challenges faced by professionals.

From Manifestations to Contradictions in Activity Analysis

As can be observed, the distinction between symptoms and causes is of paramount importance in the analysis and identification of contradictions. The method therefore consists in identifying the symptoms in order to trace the contradictions. The example below, taken from the study by Lémonie et al. (2021), illustrates how it is possible to link a manifestation to a historically inherited contradiction. The research-intervention carried out was designed to facilitate the implementation of an educational policy to overhaul priority education. The objective of this policy was to establish Priority Education Networks (REP or REP+) comprising a middle school, elementary school, and nursery school. These networks are supervised by a primary school inspector (IEN) and the principal of the middle school. The steering committee for these institutions includes representatives from the two pilot institutions, network trainers, network coordinators (Coordo.), and, on occasion, principals of primary and nursery schools.

The conflict that emerged at the steering committee meeting concerned the implementation of a pedagogical action by the network

---

[18] Work discussion forums are solutions put in place by ergonomists in France to help build work collectives and develop activity. However, we are highly critical of these forums, which can have the opposite effect to that intended. We also discuss them in the chapter on change laboratories.

coordinator involving primary school teachers and secondary school mathematics teachers (Table 7). The principal objected to the involvement of secondary school teachers on the grounds that, although informed, he felt that the principal should plan and organize the work of the teachers. The primary school inspector, who is the network coordinator's direct supervisor, attempted to resolve the conflict by emphasizing the distinct regulatory frameworks between primary and secondary schools. While direct communication with primary school teachers is permitted, it is not with secondary school teachers. Such interactions must be initiated with the principal's approval.

Table 8: Discussion during a steering committee meeting in a REP+ network. Conflict arises.

Coordo (1): We received an e-mail from the math teacher. So the coordinator and 5 teachers want to take part in the math challenge, which concerns all X schools. And so the next steering committee meeting, i.e. finalizing the challenges, will be on Monday December 4, during the day, and so I'll be sending out a letter at the same time as to the teachers, to the teachers at your middle school (address to the principal).
Principal: Excuse me, you mentioned five teachers. Are they...?
Coordo (1): We're talking about 5 math teachers from... (turns to his colleague), from 6e.
Coordo (2): 6th grade
Coordo (1): 6th grade, yes. I can't remember who, but they seemed very interested, very involved, so they'll be invited to this work session on December 4.
IEN: All day?
Coordo (1): Yes, because for us it's REP+ time.
Principal: Yes, but would it be possible...?
Coordo (1): Yes, they're invited. We give them time slots and they come when they want.
Principal: Oh yes, but no. You have to check with us beforehand. It's not that we're against this kind of meeting, but we need to know in advance as soon as possible to know when they won't be at the school, because we're going to have duty hours. Let's say, for example, that on December 4, there are 5 maths teachers missing, which means 5 on-call sessions each time.
IEN: I think the idea here was to use out-of-class time.
Coordo (1): I'm not sure, because we only had their names...
IEN: Because the math project is common to all the X networks, and to the other two REP+ networks, so it poses fewer problems. Management has to be in the loop so that you can get organized.
Coordo (1): But the date can't be changed, but after the rest...
Principal: But after the rest... to make sure you understand, not every teacher is a free electron.

Table 8: Continued

Coordo (1): So it's up to you to define their availability on that day?
Principal: That's not what I'm saying either. You talked about the fact that you're going to offer them several slots…
Coordo (1): But it's all day!
IEN: But in fact you have to go through the management.
Principal: Yes!
IEN: And then see a delegation of teachers if they're all in class, you see… Or if they're not in class, they can come on a voluntary basis, you see. It's… it's absolutely essential that you're in the loop, that you're solicited for these questions. So that it doesn't disorganize the college and at the same time be a joint institutional effort, you really need to be in the loop.
Coordo (1): But it seems to me that you were in the loop when the math teacher sent out an e-mail on behalf of all the teachers. You were in the loop.
Principal: Mrs. X, as math coordinator, sent you the reply.
Coordo (1): yes
Principal: I was in that e-mail, but then

In their self-confrontation interviews following the steering committee meeting, all the actors involved mentioned this episode. The coordinator and the principal do not share the same object in working on the network. For the principal, working in a network in priority education means '*working on the articulation between levels of education*'. In his view, this means working on the articulation between primary and secondary education. This is why the steering committee's agenda almost exclusively concerns cycle 3 (8e, 7e, 6e classes). In contrast, the coordinator believes it is necessary to '*work on new teaching methods with primary and secondary school teachers who are not used to working together*'. While the coordinator endeavors to create a distinct space for teachers to collaborate, the principal endeavors to regulate the actions implemented on the network, as they must primarily pertain to cycle 3.

This conflict is 'resolved' through coercive action on the part of the principal. The principal and the primary school inspector, the two institutional leaders, are endeavoring to maintain the authority they were institutionally guarantors of. The extract is notable for the IEN's observation that the rules for primary and secondary schools differ. While the coordinator must inform the principal in advance, he is not required to inform elementary school principals. Consequently, the rules vary according to the level of the school, reflecting a form of hierarchy between primary and secondary schools. This form of hierarchy, which reproduces the two orders of education identified in the history of the school institution, serves as a resource for the action of the secondary school principal to control work in his school. However, it also presents an obstacle to the work of the coordinator.

This form of hierarchy is reinforced by the fact that the principal exercises a form of coercion that goes far beyond the legitimate authority conferred on him. Consequently, the network coordinator is unable to fulfill his duties, namely to facilitate the implementation of novel pedagogical approaches within a collaborative environment where teachers engage in horizontal collaboration. In contrast, the principal maintains direct hierarchical authority over teachers, a position he is reluctant to relinquish: '*At our level, we are the ones responsible for implementing changes within the secondary school. Mastery of change (…) and the use of effective working aids are essential for controlling this change. At the network level, we are responsible for initiating change, with the primary school inspector and I spearheading this effort. However, we are not the ones who implement the actions we suggest. This discrepancy represents a significant challenge that requires our attention*'.

The introduction of priority education networks has introduced a new dynamic into the French education system, challenging the historical construct of an implicit hierarchy between the primary and secondary levels of education. Several episodes in intervention research have reinforced this conviction. To fully comprehend the contradiction at hand, it is essential to undertake a historical analysis. For a detailed examination of this analysis, please refer to Lémonie et al. (2021). The foundations of the French republican school were established at the end of the 19th century through the implementation of the Ferry laws, which guaranteed the right to education for all through compulsory schooling (Prost, 1968). Nevertheless, despite the emancipatory project that underpinned the republican school, it was divided along class lines. Elementary school was regarded as the people's school, while secondary school was a school where the bourgeoisie trained the future elite (Dubet, 2019). This division between two levels of education gave rise to a form of implicit hierarchy between secondary and primary schooling, which the introduction of priority education networks overturned.

Observation of situated action enables the researcher to propose certain hypotheses, which can then be validated or corroborated through historical analysis of the system(s) of activity being analyzed.

Identifying Developmental Periods and Contradictions in Historical Analysis

The identification of contradictions necessitates the identification of developmental periods, namely, significant qualitative transformations in the activity system under examination. Querol (2011) defines a developmental period as follows:

> In order to grasp qualitative changes in the course of development, the concept of a period is needed. A period is a 'piece' of history in which something essentially new develops that can change the direction of development. A period is commonly understood as a time in which the principle and the direction of development is the same, and the period changes when the direction changes (Querol, 2011, p. 88).

Thus, historical analysis represents a form of inquiry in itself. The objective of historical analysis is to hypothesize about the contradictory processes that drive the evolution of the phenomenon being analyzed. Virkkunen and Newham (2013) provide indications regarding potential stages of such a historical analysis. The initial phase of the historical analysis is the collection of data on the changes that have occurred in the phenomenon under study, particularly at the level of the object. This data is then ordered on a timeline. The data collected may take several forms, including interviews, company documents, and research or studies previously conducted. The data sources may encompass periods of varying scope and length. For instance, Querol (2011, p. 84) notes in his thesis on biogas production that he gathered data on:

- Empirical studies covering the period from 1980 to 2008.
- Company documents (annual reports, newspaper articles) from 1998 to 2008.
- Staff interviews covering the period from 2002 to 2008.
- Observations and reports covering the period of his thesis from 2005 to 2008.

The second step is to identify developmental periods, which are defined as periods when the activity system under analysis is qualitatively different. One tool that can be utilized for this purpose is a change matrix, which organizes the data from the first stage in a double-entry table. The periods are identified on the ordinate, while the elements of the activity system are organized on the abscissa. Table 9 below describes such an analysis tool.

Table 9: **Example of a matrix used to identify developmental periods, inspired by Virkkunen and Newham (2013, p. 253).**

	OBJECT– OUTCOME	SuBjet	TOOLS	COMMU- NITY	Division OF LABOR	RULES	CENTRAL PROBLEMS ENCOUN- TERED
PERIOD 1							
PERIOD 2							
PERIOD 3							

This matrix can be mobilized to highlight the concrete history of the evolution of a problem central to the analysis. For example, in their Master's thesis, Cosseron and Treguier-Rosario (2021) sought to account for changes in absenteeism and staff turnover by relating them to changes in the activity system they were analyzing (a medical-educational institute in which they were working). The production of this change matrix (or a tool of this type) serves as a basis for identifying contradictions, thereby enabling us to understand the causes of changes in activity systems.

Four Forms of Contradiction

It is possible to distinguish different forms of contradiction. To do so, let us recall the roots of the concept in Marx's work as a starting point. The notion of contradiction is based on the bifid nature of the commodity (Marx, 1963/2017). Every object has a double value. A use value, which refers to the utility of the object for the user or users, and which is only expressed in the consumption process. An exchange value, which refers to the property of the commodity that enables it to be compared with other commodities for the purpose of exchange.

For Engeström (1987), following Leontiev (1959/1976), the primary contradiction refers to the contradiction between the use value and the exchange value of the object of production. it is essential to recognize this characteristic of the object of activity in order to conduct scientific studies of human activity and to create a psychology that is not isolated from its historical context. This psychology is distinguishable from a science of the psyche of an abstract man, of man in general.

This primary contradiction is therefore inherent in the object of activity, but it is also inscribed in each of the other elements of the activity system. This therefore refers to the dialectical nature of each of the elements of the activity system, as highlighted by Engeström (2006):

> This fundamental contradiction [between use value and exchange value, Y.L.] is evident in all other dimensions of human activity. The activity of general practitioners in the healthcare sector provides an illustrative example of this dual nature of use value and exchange value. This contradiction arises at every level of a doctor's professional activity. To practice medicine, a doctor has recourse to a wide range of medicines and remedies, which constitute his working tools. However, these remedies have more than just useful curative properties. Furthermore, they are consumer goods, costing money, aimed at a specific market, advertised and sold for profit. In their day-to-day decision-making, members of the medical profession are necessarily confronted with this contradiction in one way or another (Engeström, 2006, pp. 143–144).

Warmington (2008) critiques the dual nature of each component of activity systems, noting that while the dual and contradictory nature is readily apparent in the object or instrument pole, it is less clear how use and exchange value can be present in the other components of an activity system, such as community, rules, or subject, insofar as these poles are not commodities. Warmington's critique is of significant importance and necessity. However, his analysis is limited to a single isolated activity system. As previously discussed, activity systems are not isolated entities; rather, they interact with other activity systems that produce their components. For example, training systems produce the subjects of another activity system. As the subject is both a producer and a consumer, the dual nature of the activity system can manifest in both poles. This contradictory nature of each of the activity system's poles is exemplified, for instance, by Engeström in his description of learning research communities (Engeström, 2016, p. 5), which is presented in Chapter 4. The primary contradiction between use value and exchange value, present in each of the poles of an activity system, gives rise to other forms of contradiction. In addition to primary contradictions, Engeström (1987) defines three other forms of contradiction. Secondary contradictions are those that arise between the poles of an activity system. As activity systems are open systems, the introduction of a new element into the activity system is in contradiction with the other poles of the activity system. For instance, the implementation of a novel regulation or instrument is likely to be at odds with the other elements of the system. Conversely, the primary contradiction, which is inherent to the elements of the activity system, is likely to give rise to changes in the relationships between the different poles of the activity system. It is the primary contradictions that give rise to the secondary contradictions. The example presented by Adamides (2020) at the beginning of this chapter is particularly illustrative of this point.

A tertiary contradiction arises between an activity and a more advanced activity with a new, more extensive motif. This type of contradiction is particularly evident during the initial stages of intervention, when participants, having modeled a new activity, attempt to implement it. For example, during an intervention at teacher education institute (INSPÉ), the implementation of an activity system with a broader object, aimed at enabling student equity, clashes with the old activity system, and in particular with the instruments. While teachers desired to utilize hybrid forms of teaching in order to offer students distributed across multiple geographically distant sites the same choices, the administrative tools make the operation complicated, as they were initially designed to manage students and groups by site. The organization of schooling and the division of labor are also called into question. Finally, a quaternary contradiction emerges between the activity system being developed and neighboring activity systems interacting with this new activity system. The various forms of contradiction—primary, secondary, tertiary, and quaternary—are illustrated in the figure below..

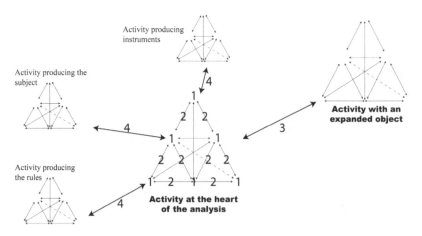

Figure 24: Illustration of the four types of contradiction, adapted from Engeström (1987, 2015, p. 71).

In this figure, (1) refers to the primary contradictions present in each of the poles of the activity system; (2) refers to the secondary contradictions between the poles of the activity system; (3) refers to the tertiary contradictions between the activity and a more evolved form of activity whose object is more extensive; (4) refers to the contradictions between one activity system and neighboring activity systems.

Continuing his medical example, Engeström (2015) illustrates secondary, tertiary, and quaternary contradictions as follows:

> A typical secondary contradiction in this work activity would be the conflict between the traditional biomedical conceptual instruments concerning the classification of diseases and correct diagnosis, on the one hand, and the changing nature of the objects, namely, the increasingly ambiguous and complex problems and symptoms of the patients. These problems more and more often do not comply with the standards of classical diagnosis and nomenclature. They require an integrated social, psychological, and biomedical approach that may not yet exist.

> A tertiary contradiction arises when, say, the administrators of the medical care system order the practitioners to employ certain new procedures corresponding to the ideals of a more holistic and integrated medicine. The new procedures may be formally implemented, but probably still subordinated to and resisted by the old general form of the activity.

> Suppose that a doctor, working on such a new holistic and integrated basis, orders or suggests that the patient accept a new habit or conception and change his way of life in some respect. The patient may react with resistance. This is an instance of the quaternary contradictions. The patient's way of life or his 'health behavior' is here the object activity. If patients are regarded as abstract symptoms and diseases, isolated from their activity contexts, it will be impossible to grasp the developmental dynamics of the central activity, too (Engeström, 2015, p. 72).

It is crucial for professionals to acknowledge these contradictions in order to facilitate the implementation of effective intervention strategies aimed at sustaining expansive learning processes. By acknowledging and then addressing the underlying contradictions, participants can focus on the expansive creation of a solution to overcome the identified contradictions.

It is also important to consider the types of contradictions that can or cannot be resolved within the framework of an intervention. Avis (2007, 2009) posits that the focus on secondary contradictions has led to a neglect of primary contradictions. Indeed, there appears to be a dichotomy between interventions aimed at 'tackling' primary contradictions and those that address other forms of contradiction. In other words, there is a clear distinction between genuinely transformative approaches that seek to support forms of activity governed by use value, and those that aim to adapt and improve activities governed by exchange value. Avis, following Gramsci, describes the latter as transformist (Gramsci, 1971).

This distinction is illustrated by Sawchuk (2006). For Sawchuck (2006, p. 251), activity systems and modes of participation can be classified as legitimate or illegitimate. The legitimacy/illegitimacy relationship is defined by a primary contradiction inherent to capitalist activity systems (between use-value and exchange-value). In capitalism, it is necessary to produce use-value while also producing exchange-value. Furthermore, he asserts that, insofar as expansive learning is ultimately defined by the progressive resolution of systemic contradictions, we may paradoxically engage in such processes by resolving a series of more peripheral contradictions up to the point of the most primary contradiction, namely that between use and exchange value.

Avis's argument (2007) hinges on the premise that the primary contradictions inherent in intervention strategies prevent the achievement of genuine transformation. He posits that the pursuit of emancipatory aims, which he deems to be the driving force behind such transformation, is effectively sidelined by the localism inherent in second- and third-generation CHAT interventions and research:

> Although the recognition of primary contradictions could herald wider emancipatory possibilities, these are effectively bracketed. This is a result of developmental work research's interest in 'grasping developmental potentials' and 'by initiating and supporting change' in practical work-based activity (Engeström, 1990a, p. 72), effectively evacuating the wider political context. It could be argued that Engeström's position has been traduced, in as much as his intervention starts from developmental work research which does not preclude the engagement in a wider politics. This is clearly the case but such an engagement is barely visible (Avis, 2007, p. 163).

Avis's critique was formulated in 2007, prior to the emergence of what Engeström describes as the fourth generation of CHAT. However, in order to transcend the limitations of localism within a single interacting activity system, it is necessary to implement interventions that can effectively address the societal scale. This is the objective of the fourth generation of CHAT (Chapter 6). While this represents an initial response, it is not a wholly satisfactory one. Localism in no way precludes an account of primary contradictions (Engeström, 1987; Leontiev, 1959/1976). Engeström's commitment to this position, which is *'barely visible'* to Avis, yet constantly recalled throughout his writings, is evident. The contradictions of the capitalist system are always expressed locally, and this perspective has remained consistent throughout Engeström's work. Engeström's perspective is to facilitate the emergence of local alternatives that are sufficiently generative to be taken up at other levels. If this position appears to be consistent throughout his theory of expansive learning, the fourth generation of activity theory represents a logical continuation, enabling these local innovations to be sustained at other levels. It should be noted that Avis's critique is based in part on Sawchuk's (2006) essay. For Sawchuk, CHAT should take greater account of the notion of power relations. He draws in part on Certeau's work to show the importance of illegitimate, often hidden social practices that are inscribed in the interstices of legitimate practices. This interstitial dimension is also essential for the fourth generation of CHAT, which draws on the work of sociologist Wright (2010). In his book, Wright presents a series of case studies that illustrate the potential for institutional innovation to offer emancipatory alternatives to dominant social organizations. The objective is to challenge the dominant capitalist paradigm by exploring alternative ways of thinking about the horizon of a post-capitalist world. The strategy adopted is to erode capitalism. Wright (2010) defines emancipatory alternatives as those which can be constructed within the confines of capitalist economies, and which must be contested in order to be safeguarded and expanded. He defines a real utopia as one that can be constructed in the present, foreshadowing an ideal world that can assist in achieving the objective of post-capitalism.

The necessity of a change in scale and the significance of interstitial spaces are fundamental to the construction and development of a fourth generation of CHAT. These elements permit a response to the criticisms made by Avis, Warmington, and Sawchuk. Nevertheless, these criticisms are crucial for any intervention or research endeavor that aims to adopt a broad emancipatory perspective.

To Sum Up

In this section, we will present a summary of some of the defining characteristics of contradictions. Contradictions represent a central concept in the field of dialectics. They facilitate the explanation of the movement and transformations of an activity system. In essence, contradictions can be defined as forces that act to pull the system into opposing positions. The resolution of contradictions can only be achieved through the generation of a third term, which enables the contradiction to be overcome.

The primary contradiction that drives the self-movement of an activity system is the contradiction between use value and exchange value. This primary contradiction gives rise to three other forms of contradiction: between the poles of an activity system, between an activity system and an activity system with an extended object (the example of the priority education network is illustrative of this type of contradiction), or between neighboring activity systems.

It is important to note that contradictions are not observable; rather, the symptoms of these contradictions are. These symptoms manifest as recurring problems (or micro-innovations that deviate from the usual action scripts), dilemmas, conflicts, critical conflicts, or antagonistic constraints.

It can be argued that contradictions are the source of observable symptoms. The resolution of problems during an intervention does not address the underlying structural tensions or contradictions in the activity system that give rise to these problems. A developmental approach to intervention aims to facilitate the construction of a novel activity system by enabling stakeholders to identify contradictions within their existing activity system.

From a methodological standpoint, contradictions are identified by identifying their manifestations. These manifestations can be classified into one of several categories, including problems, conflicts, dilemmas, situations of double constraint, or situations of local innovation. It is of the utmost importance to establish a connection between the observed symptoms and the underlying contradictions. This is accomplished through the use of historical analysis. These two stages represent the initial two phases of an expansive learning cycle. They are regarded as fundamental in numerous ways.

An activity system is in a state of constant flux. The objective of expansive learning is to transform an activity system. In order for this transformation to be sustainable, it must take into account the movement of the activity system and its underlying developmental logic. Ollman (2005) offers a metaphor to help us understand this idea:

> Imagine trying to get into a car that is still moving. How is this different from getting into a stationary car? One might inquire whether it would be possible to enter a moving vehicle if one were blindfolded. One might also inquire whether it would be possible to enter a moving vehicle without knowing in which direction the vehicle was moving or even at what speed it was moving (Ollman, 2005, p. 21).

An activity system can be likened to the vehicle in question. It has a direction, which must be identified, and a speed. The objective of analyzing contradictions is to comprehend the developmental logic and, consequently, the trajectory of the activity system. From our perspective, this represents the stage in expansive learning that we intend to present in the subsequent chapter.

Chapter 8
Expansive Learning. Learning What Is Not Yet There

The bread and butter of human development is collective learning III, gradual in form but profound in substantial effects (Engeström, 2015, p. 125).
Each of us accepts the reality of the world we face (Truman Burbanks, The Truman show).

For Engeström, expansive learning represents the primary mechanism involved in development, namely the qualitative transformation of activity systems (Engeström, 1987, 2015, 2016). The theory of expansive learning constitutes a central tenet of his work since the publication of his book, Learning by Expanding.

In this chapter, we delineate the principal characteristics of expansive learning, drawing upon empirical studies in each case. We commence by differentiating expansive learning from other forms of learning.

Expansive Learning Versus Other Forms of Learning

Expansive learning theory can be described as a '*non-standard*' theory of learning, insofar as it refers to forms of learning that are not usually considered in more conventional learning theories. Expansive learning theory may be described as non-standard in three main ways: the content of learning, the collective dimension of learning, and the metaphor used to account for learning. The three dimensions will be described in detail below.

Learning What Is Not Yet There

In the context of learning content, classical or standard learning theories posit that what is learned (generally knowledge or skills) refers to a relatively stabilized and identified content. The majority of training approaches are based on this orientation, which identifies the knowledge or skills utilized in the workplace to develop curricula or training instruments (Bourgeois & Mornata, 2012; Durand, 2008; Poizat, Durand, & Theureau, 2016). For example, professional didactics (Pastré, 2002, 2007; Pastré & Vergnaud, 2006) defines itself as *'the analysis of work with a view to training'*. The objective of this approach is to identify the schemas and concepts that support the actions of expert professionals in order to model the professional skills to be acquired in training. Professional didactics is concerned with learning on the job, yet it focuses on skills already acquired by operators, which constitute professionalism. In contrast, expansive learning theory refers to the process of learning knowledges that have not yet been identified because they reside in activities that do not yet exist. This is an innovation-oriented form of learning. Accordingly, Engeström (2018) posits that:

> In important transformations of our personal lives and organizational practices, we must learn new forms of activity that are not yet there (Engeström, 2016). They are literally learned as they are being created. There is no competent teacher, or there are many competing ones. Standard learning theories have little to offer if one wants to understand these processes (Engeström, 2018, p. 18).

In the view of Engeström (2016), who follows the CHAT orientation as set out by Vygotsky (Stetsenko, 2016a), human beings of all ages are the creators of a new culture. This specific perspective challenges the prevailing orthodoxy of constructivism, which posits that individuals are the primary agents of their own development. In contrast, the CHAT orientation posits that individuals are co-producers of societal and cultural development (Roth, 2014). In expansive learning, participants not only facilitate their own development but also contribute to the growth of the broader activity system in which they are situated. Thus, initially formulated in the context of the study of learning at work, expansive learning theory begins with the observation that, in contrast to institutions dedicated to training, the majority of learning at work concerns content that has not been defined beforehand.

> Many of the most intriguing kinds of learning in work organizations violate this presupposition. People and organizations continually learn something that is not stable, not even defined or understood ahead of time (Engeström, 2018, p. 18).

In Engeström's view, learning is a cultural process, whereby individuals and groups create new cultural knowledge and forms of expression. This understanding of learning does not, however, limit this type of learning to adults, although the original formulation of this perspective occurred in the context of adult and work-based learning. The concept of learning by expanding is evidenced by several examples from Engeström's work, wich demonstrate the creative potential of young people and adolescents. For example, the children's campaign for nuclear disarmament initiated by seven teenagers aged 12–17 (pp. 161–163) is illustrative of this phenomenon. While initiatives are often perceived as forms of disobedience to rules, they can also be viewed as potential innovations at the source of the creation of new cultures. William Webb Ellis, for example, seized the ball in his hand during a soccer match and initiated the sport of rugby[19]. Furthermore, one might consider the impact of the Friday school strike initiated by Greta Thunberg in Sweden, as well as the influence of hip-hop, which originated in the early 1970s in New York's Bronx ghetto[20].

In 2018, we were invited to contribute to the Physical Education (PE) high school national curriculum writing commission. The theory of expansive learning in mind, we argued for a more dynamic vision of the culture of Physical Sports and Artistic Practices (PSAP). It is therefore proposed that the challenge for PE should be to create and develop a PSAP culture, rather than merely acquiring a PSAP culture. In accordance with this perspective, both learning and human development are integral aspects of collaborative practices, rather than mere adaptation. To put it another way, what distinguishes us as profoundly human is not the perpetuation and preservation of a culture, but rather the initiation of that culture through expansive learning.

This approach to learning places greater emphasis on the processes of externalization and the creation of new cultural content, rather than the internalization of identified and stabilized cultural content. In this respect, the expansive learning theory represents a significant advancement of CHAT, while also building on Leontiev's work. However, it

---

[19] It's certainly a form of legend, but it has the merit of showing how a transgressive action gives rise to a new sporting activity.

[20] It's a remarkable story, and one that deserves to be analyzed through the prism of CHAT and expansive learning theory.

overcomes some of the limitations inherent in Leontiev's theory, particularly in the form of conservatism present in his theory (González Rey, 2020).

Nevertheless, in Leontiev's lineage, expansive learning remains 'object-oriented' learning, and is thus distinct from many definitions and theories of learning. For example, consider this relatively old definition by De Landsheere (1992):

> A process of varying degrees of permanence by which new behaviors are acquired or existing behaviors are modified in interaction with the environment (De Landsheere, 1992, p. 125).

In traditional learning theory, learning is presented as manifesting itself in transformations linked to a subject of learning: either a transformation of behavior or a transformation of cognition. In contrast, expansive learning manifests itself primarily in a transformation (an expansion) in the object of activity, the conceptualization of which results in the qualitative transformation of an entire activity system (see Chapter 6). The outcome of expansive learning is the formation of a new object, a new concept, based on the discovery and modeling of a germ cell (see Chapter 10). This then gives rise to the generation of a new activity and its concrete manifestations.

The Collective Dimension of Expansive Learning

In traditional approaches to learning, the individual is the unit of analysis and the focus of the process of learning. This is also true of both behaviorist and cognitivist approaches. Expansive learning theory diverges from these traditional approaches in that it places greater emphasis on the collective dimension of learning. In accordance with the tenets of expansive learning theory, the process of learning is conceived as an activity that engenders the emergence of a novel activity. This activity offers the potential for enhancing the quality of life and increasing the capacity to influence one's own living conditions.

Indeed, professionals' efforts to redesign their activity systems necessarily involve collective learning. The objective of this learning is to transform patterns of collective activity by transforming the very object of collective activity in order to broaden professionals' possibilities of action (Virkkunen & Ahonen, 2011). It is evident that an activity system cannot be sustainably transformed by an isolated individual. This necessitates collective endeavors that transcend the division of labor intrinsic to the activity system.

An illustrative example can be found in the research intervention of Bal, Afacan, and Cakir (2018). Their research responds to a request from a Wisconsin high school that has experienced racial disproportions in behavior and outcomes. While African-American students represented only approximately 7 % of the school's enrollment, they accounted for approximately 67 % of school exclusions. The restoration of a school climate conducive to learning and the overcoming of a segregated culture required collective efforts to rethink a dysfunctional disciplinary system that was at odds with the school's object of *'building a healthy and inclusive learning environment'*. The first steps in these efforts were to broaden learning efforts to include, beyond administrators and teachers, parents and students.

The fact that expansive learning efforts transcend the division of labor and involve multiple protagonists occupying different positions is of primary importance for two key reasons.

Firstly, the object of activity is always open to debate within an activity system. Any attempt to expand the object of activity must therefore build on its conflictual nature. Thus, expansive learning is a plurivocal and conflictual process. It implies a conflictuality between different relationships to the object of activity, linked to the different positions occupied in the division of labor within an activity system.

> Applied to expansive learning and research, this means that all the conflicting and complementary voices of the various groups and strata in the activity system under scrutiny shall be involved and utilized (Engeström, 2015, p. 247).

Second, when an activity system requires transformation, traditional forms of learning prove to be inadequate; development of such a system inherently involves collective and creative processes.

This emphasis on the collective dimension of learning has been the subject of criticism. Langemeyer (2006) posits that expansive learning theory fails to adequately address the individual, subjective dimension. However, as we shall describe later, while expansive learning theory emphasizes the collective nature of learning, it nevertheless draws on the experience and subjectivity of participants. The conflict of individual viewpoints and experiences represents a central dimension of the learning process. In this regard, it can be argued that expansive learning theory resolves the traditional dichotomy between the individual and society present in many traditional learning theories by articulating, as previously stated, an individual and subjective point of view and a systemic point of view.

Expanding as a Form of Metaphor

In the field of education, the acquisition and participation metaphors have traditionally been used to explain the genesis of new knowledge. These two metaphors have been the subject of debate between those who espouse a cognitive perspective and those who adhere to a situated perspective on learning.

In the acquisition metaphor, learning is conceived as '*the act of acquiring new knowledge*'. This view posits that the mind is a kind of knowledge '*container*', and learning is a process that fills the container by implanting knowledge. Consequently, knowledge is conceived as an inherent property or capacity of the individual's mind, and learning is understood as a process of construction and acquisition achieved during the utilization and application of knowledge in novel contexts.

> In contrast, the participation metaphor regards learning as a process of participation in a multitude of cultural practices. In this framework, the focus is more specifically on the activity than on the product of learning. Knowledge is not an entity existing in the world or in individual minds; rather, it is an aspect of participation in cultural practices (J. S. Brown, Collins, & Duguid, 1989; Lave & Wenger, 1991). It cannot be separated from the situations in which it is used. This metaphor supplements or, in some cases, replaces terms such as acquisition and accumulation with concepts such as discourse, interaction, activity, and participation (Paavola, Lipponen, & Hakkarainen, 2004, p. 558).

Despite the fundamental theoretical opposition between the first two metaphors of learning, they undoubtedly share more than they have differences:

> In fact, from the point of view of expansive learning, both acquisition-based and participation-based approaches share much of the same conservative bias. Both have little to say about the transformation and creation of culture. Both acquisition-based and participation-based approaches, the latter especially in the original legitimate-peripheral-participation framework (Lave & Wenger, 1991), depict learning primarily as one-way movement from

incompetence to competence, with little serious analysis devoted to horizontal movement and hybridization (Engeström & Sannino, 2010, p. 2).

The defining characteristic of expansive learning is its clear divergence from the conservative, past-oriented bias inherent to other learning metaphors.

The Expansion Metaphor

It must be acknowledged that, at the outset of our engagement with CHAT, we were initially perplexed by this metaphor. We sought to comprehend the rationale behind Engeström's use of the term *'expansive'*. He could have used other adjective to describe this type of learning: creative or generative learning for example, or productive learning, which distinguishes it from reproductive learning (Engeström, 2015). Why this expansion metaphor? This is a question that we have frequently been often asked. The following paragraphs will elucidate the metaphor of expansion.

Expansion as a Journey Through Hierarchical Levels of Activity

In our discussions with Engeström, he repeatedly posed the question, *'What is the big picture?'* Many approaches to activity describe in great detail *'what subjects do'* in a work situation. However, these detailed descriptions remain at the level of the actions and operations engaged by these subjects in these situations. While these analyses may be relevant, they struggle to situate these descriptions within an overall explanatory picture. In other words, the actions described in such detailed description are not situated by the analyst within an activity system that has a history and is riddled with contradictions. As Ollman (2008) has observed, despite their finesse, they remain on the surface of things.

Expansive learning means crossing the level that separates actions from the activity system, resituating actions within an activity system to grasp contradictions. This learning process is potentially explosive. In 2018, Yrjö Engeström was invited to present his book, Expertise in Transition, in Paris. During the event, a colleague, V. Grosstephan, posed a question regarding the Yellow Vests movement in France. As a reminder, this movement began following the introduction of a tax on petrol. In addition to the social and ecological implications of the tax, the movement of rural populations occupying traffic circles had given rise to an important and flagship demand of the movement: the shared-initiative referendum. This movement went from a personal problem (shared by many) linked to purchasing power and the need to use a car in rural areas to a questioning (and proposal) of institutions seen as no longer truly democratic. This expansive movement has the potential to be *'explosive'* in the sense that it implies a questioning and a will to transform institutions or activity systems.

Consequently, expansion entails a shift in analytical focus from the specific circumstances to the broader activity systems, with the objective of elucidating the underlying rationale behind the situated action.

Expansion as a Shift from an Experiential to a Systemic Viewpoint

In order to comprehend the expansion metaphor, it is essential to acknowledge the transition that occurs within the expansive learning process between an experiential and a systemic perspective, as described by Spinuzzi (2018b) as *'Top Sight'*. This transition begins with a sense of dissatisfaction with the recurring issues encountered in practice, which involves questioning the practice itself. These issues and conflicts are manifested at the level of action. These experiences are 'experienced' by real subjects at the level of their daily actions. Consequently, in expansive learning, the transition from an individual experiential perspective to a systemic perspective from above is of paramount importance (Engeström, 1990b; Hackel & Klebl, 2014). This transition between these two perspectives represents a form of expansion, occurring both vertically and horizontally. Neither of the two viewpoints taken separately – experiential and systemic – is sufficient to engage in expansive learning. This is because the experiential point of view tends to isolate actions and situations in work situations and the present. This perspective is succinctly encapsulated by Stetsenko (2015):

> The notion of experience used as central in many perspectives is too strongly tied to what is going on in the present and does not sufficiently engage future-oriented dimensions of human practices. Experience and related notions of interpretation, dialogue, and situativity of knowing have been important in challenging traditional *'objectivist'* models and accounts. Yet these notions require further critical elaboration to more resolutely break

away from the idea that individuals need to adapt to what is 'given' in the present in order to develop and learn (Stetsenko, 2015, p. 104).

Conversely, the systemic perspective is also inadequate, as it fails to consider the experiences of the individuals who are engaged in the learning process:

> The system view of an organization is blatantly insufficient when the researchers try to understand and facilitate qualitative changes by means of expansive learning. Changes must be initiated and nurtured by real, identifiable people, individual persons and groups. The interventionist researcher must find within the activity system flesh-and-blood dialogue partners who have their own emotions, moral concerns, wills and agendas (Engeström & Keruoso, 2007, p. 340).

This expansion from the individual, experiential to the systemic points of view is analogous to the concept of conscientization as espoused by the renowned Brazilian educator Paulo Freire. It is about the construction of knowledge that, while originating in immediate experience, emerges from it to produce a new culture. In this way, expansive learning can be seen as:

> A collective process of concrete elaboration (and not simply the acquisition or construction of existing knowledge) of a knowledge that goes beyond one's own concrete experience. This knowledge must take into account the needs of the people and become a tool of struggle, enabling them to be the subjects of their own history. The participation of the people in the creation of culture (…) breaks with a tradition which considers that only the elite is competent and knows what is necessary for society (Freire, 1991).

Expansion as Overcoming Contradictions

In CHAT, the developmental transformations of an activity system are understood as attempts to overcome historically inherited contradictions within that activity system. As previously stated in the previous chapter, these contradictions are not immediately apparent. Instead, they manifest themselves in the form of dilemmas, recurring problems, and local innovations. Nevertheless, it is not possible to resolve a contradiction by removing one of the two terms of the contradiction.

> To be resolved, a contradiction must be overcome. A contradiction can be resolved in a weak sense by an operation that reproduces it, or it can be

resolved in a strong sense by a development that goes beyond it by transforming or eliminating its foundations (Sève, 1998, p. 211, as quoted in Eloi, 2022, p. 32).

In this context, the metaphor of expansion refers to the effort of professionals to overcome the contradictions historically accumulated within an activity system by going beyond them. In this context, the metaphorical concept of expansion refers to the movement to overcome the systemic contradictions that have accumulated within an activity system.

Expansion of the Object of Activity

As previously discussed, the developmental transformation of an activity system occurs through the conceptualization of a novel, more extensive object and the reorganization of each of the activity system's poles. In other words, one of the fundamental elements of expansive learning is the expansion of the object. This new object represents the overcoming of a contradictory unit, namely the germ cell of the activity system.

The expansion of the object constitutes an overcoming of the contradiction present in it by a third term that enables it to be overcome. Engeström (2000c) identifies three forms of object expansion:

- (1) A sociospatial expansion concerns the enlargement of the people involved in the activity.
- (2) A temporal expansion relates to the enlargement of the object's temporal perspective.
- (3) Finally, a politico-ethical expansion concerns the societal consequences of the activity.

Theoretical Sources of Inspiration for Expansive Learning Theory

Three theoretical sources can be identified in expansive learning theory. These three theoretical sources are respectively (1) the levels of learning defined by Bateson; (2) the hierarchical structure of activity; and (3) the distinction between different forms of artifact. One of the theoretical inspirations for expansive learning was Bateson's (1980) proposal on levels of learning. Bateson defines three levels of learning (in fact, there are five, but only the first three are detailed here).

Level I corresponds to learning in which a link is established between experience and context. This is the level of reinforcement learning. It corresponds to the modification of response specificity through the correction of choice errors within a set of alternatives.

Level II corresponds to generalization. Level II corresponds to a change in the learning process, for example, a corrective change in the set of alternatives from which the choice is made, or a change in the way the sequence of experiments is punctuated. Level II corresponds to the introduction of context into learning.

Level III corresponds to a change in the learning process II, for example, a corrective change in the system of sets of alternatives from which a choice is made. It corresponds to a radical change in context. Bateson (1980, pp. 323–324) notes that '*it appears that such a phenomenon occurs from time to time, in psychotherapy, religious conversion, and other sequences that mark a profound reorganization of character*'. An illustrative example of how this radical change of context can be understood is provided by Tosey, Visser, and Saunders (2012), based on the film '*The Truman Show*'. The protagonist, Truman Burbank, is the subject of a television show from his earliest years. His surroundings, which include his neighborhood and even his own family, are essentially a vast, televisual construct. The film's central theme is the protagonist's discovery of the secret workings of his life. The world he discovers is radically different from the one he has known since childhood.

It is crucial to acknowledge that, according to Bateson's (1980) characterization of learning levels, each level is not isolated from the others. Rather, it corresponds to the resolution of contradictions at lower levels. Consequently, each higher level incorporates the lower ones.

If, as previously proposed, the living being is elevated to Level III as a consequence of the resolution of contradictions generated at Level II, it can be expected that this resolution constitutes the positive reinforcement at Level III (Bateson, 1980, p. 328).

Expansive learning is associated with Level III in Bateson's classification. It is of particular interest to note that while Bateson did not believe that learning III could be achieved by conscious, instrumental means (Tosey et al., 2012, p. 299), Engeström places the question of instrumentality at the center of his thinking and the development of expansive learning theory. From this perspective, Engeström's book, Learning by expanding, can be regarded as an inquiry and research work aimed at defining artifacts to support these expansive learning oriented towards understanding and transforming '*the context of contexts*', as Bateson formulated it.

Engeström (1987, 2015) relates the hierarchical levels of activity inherited from Leontiev, Bateson's levels of learning, and the artifacts required to pursue each level of learning, drawing on Wartofsky's (1979) classification[21]. The author of the book Models posits that models have a future orientation. They are therefore not mere artifacts that guide action; they have a more profound and future-oriented function:

> A model is not simply the entity we take as a model but rather the mode of action that such an entity itself represents. In this sense, models are embodiments of purpose and, at the same time, instruments for carrying out such purposes (Wartofsky, 1979, p. 142).

In this context, he distinguishes three types of artifacts: primary, secondary, and tertiary. Primary artifacts are defined as tools utilized in the production process, such as a hammer. Secondary artifacts are those used in the preservation and transmission of acquired skills or modes of action through which production takes place. In this sense, secondary artifacts may be understood as external representations of the aforementioned modes of action. Finally, tertiary artifacts are a class of artifacts that may come to constitute an autonomous '*world*' in which the rules, conventions, and outcomes appear no longer directly practical. These are representations embodied in real artifacts that express or illustrate an alternative mode of perception. Once the visual image can be perceptually '*experienced*', it can also color and modify one's perception of the 'real' world by envisaging possibilities that are not currently recognized Wartofsky (1979, p. 209).

Engeström subsequently modified Wartofsky's classification to distinguish four classes of artifacts (Engeström, 1990b). The first category, '*what-artifacts*', encompasses primary artifacts, which are the objects utilized in the activity. The second category, '*secondary artifacts*', is divided into two subcategories: '*how artifacts*', which are routines and procedures that guide the use of *primary artifacts*; and '*why artifacts*', which represent

---

[21] For a presentation and discussion of the tertiary artifact idea, see Cole (2019).

explanatory models and hypotheses. Finally, *tertiary artifacts*, or *'where to artifacts'*, represent an imagined vision of the future. These classes are not static; rather, they can undergo transformation in the process of use or depending on the user's perspective. A secondary artifact may, for instance, become a tertiary artifact.

> For example, what sort of artifact is a school textbook? From the perspective of a teacher, it might be a primary artifact for doing the work of teaching and thus surviving. But, from the perspective of the content, it is a secondary artifact meant to transmit cultural knowledge. Finally, from the perspective of a bored student it may be a basis for daydreaming and thus a tertiary artifact (Gillespie & Zittoun, 2010, p. 44).

The table below depicts the mapping between learning levels, activity levels, and Wartofsky's (1979) classification of artifacts by Engeström (1987).

Table 10: Relating the hierarchical structure of activity (Leontiev, 1957/1976) to levels of learning (Bateson, 1980) and Wartofsky's classification of artifacts (1979).

LEVEL OF ACTIVITY (LEONTIEV, 2021)	LEARNING LEVEL (Bateson, 1980)	ArtIfacts Wartofsky (1979)
Activity – Object	Learning III	Tertiary Artifact
Actions – Goals	Learning II	Secondary Artifact
Operations – Conditions	Learning I	Primary Artifact

In Level I learning, objects and instruments are provided. Learning is essentially the correction of the way an instrument is used to elicit a behavioral response. Artifacts are the primary artifacts. At this level, these primary artifacts crystallize operations (Leontiev, 1975/2021).

Level II learning corresponds to reproductive learning, mobilizing secondary artifacts. These secondary artifacts are, in a sense, instructions for the production and use of primary artifacts.

The first two levels are those typically studied in classical learning theories. They presuppose an individual subject. In contrast, the third level of learning presupposes a collective subject. This level of learning is concerned with the mastery of *'the context of contexts'*, as Bateson put it. Tertiary artifacts are tools that can help achieve this mastery. They are *'where to'* artifacts, as Engeström (1990b) put it, pointing the way for collective activity. In the Change Laboratories, the activity system model or the matrix modeling the zone of proximal development constitute such artifacts (see Chapter 10, the section devoted to artifacts mobilized in the Change Laboratories).

Expansive Learning as a Process: The Expansive Learning Cycle

Expansive learning theory is a processual theory of learning (Engeström & Sannino, 2012). The conceptualization and methodology of the ascent from the abstract to the concrete form the basis of this theory. A more detailed examination of this methodology can be found in Chapter 10, which is devoted to the methodology of the change laboratory and formative interventions. In conclusion, the method of ascending from the abstract to the concrete can be defined as a method of dialectical thinking. Expansive learning is an activity that occurs through learning actions. The theory of expansive learning is based on the propositions of Davydov (1990b). Nevertheless, Davydov (1990b) had developed a process for teaching and learning mathematics based on the method of ascending from the abstract to the concrete. His method was designed to facilitate the internalization of a culture rather than the creation of a new one.

Building on Davydov's work, Engeström (1987, 2015) proposes that the process of learning and conceptualizing a new object for a new activity is based on a series of seven expansive learning actions that, when taken together, form a cycle. This learning activity commences when individuals commence to question the activity system in which they operate and collaborate to analyze the historical circumstances (contradictions) at the root of their dissatisfaction. This analysis is conducted with the objective of establishing a zone of proximal development. The seven expansive learning actions are as follows:

- (1) Question, criticize, or reject certain aspects of accepted practice.
- (2) Analyze the situation through historical and cultural analysis to explain current practice and through current and systemic analysis to point out current contradictions within activity systems.
- (3) Model new relationships within an activity system to overcome the contradictions identified in (2).

- (4) Examine the model, implement it, and experiment with it to fully grasp its dynamics, potential, and limits.
- (5) Implement the model through practical applications, enrichments, and conceptual extensions.
- (6) Evaluate/reflect on the process.
- (7) Consolidate the results into a new, stable form of practice.

The following figure represents these seven expansive learning actions taken from a typical ideal cycle.

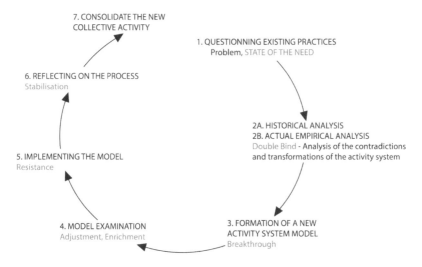

Figure 25: The seven expansive learning actions forming an expansive learning cycle.

Expansive Learning as the Construction of a Zone of Proximal Development

Expansive learning can be conceptualized as a process that enables a journey into a proximal zone of activity development. The seven actions that comprise the expansive learning cycle facilitate the construction of a zone of proximal development by linking the disturbances experienced at the action level to the contradictions historically accumulated in an activity system. The resolution of these contradictions paves the way for the emergence of a zone of proximal development. The notion of the zone provides a framework for the future orientation of the activity system. As a zone, it is not a fixed point that can be identified upstream of the expansive learning cycle. Engeström employs the concept of the zone of proximal development in a distinct manner from that of Vygotsky. In the case of Engeström,

> The zone of proximal development may be depicted as a gray area between actions embedded in the current activity with its historical roots and contradictions, the foreseeable activity in which the contradictions are expansively resolved, and the foreseeable activity in which the contradictions have led to contraction and destruction of opportunities (Engeström, 2000c, p. 157).

The figure below depicts the expansive learning process that underpins the development of an activity system.

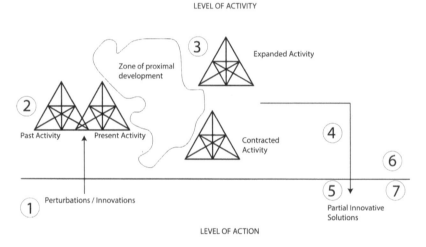

Figure 26: Proximal zone of development of an activity system and corresponding expansive learning actions.

Expansive and Defensive Learning

In their 2018 study of a care assistant service, Nummijoki, Engeström, and Sannino examine defensive learning and, paradoxically, provide an account of the nature of expansive learning. The introduction of a novel activity into an established routine can result in a contradiction, particularly at the level of routines, which can either be questioned or defended. This phenomenon is referred to as a '*tertiary contradiction*' (see Chapter 7). The act of defending established routines represents a form of defensive learning, which is the opposite of expansive learning.

The study builds upon and extends an initial intervention with a municipal home help service that led to the redefinition of the activity system and the implementation of an instrument to facilitate physical mobility exercises with elderly people. The introduction or implementation of this redefined activity by the careers generates both defensive and expansive learning at the micro level. Defensive learning includes '*actions of questioning the need for or feasibility of such exercises, reasoning about and arguing for the preferability of the existing script of home care encounters, and so on*' (Nummijoki et al., 2018, p. 3).

Such actions may be performed by either the caregiver or the elderly person. Consequently, Nummijoki et al.'s (2018) study entails categorizing and monitoring the learning of the caregivers and the elderly person during their encounter. The results indicate that the learning cycles are heterogeneous, with predominantly expansive cycles containing defensive learning actions and defensive cycles containing expansive learning actions.

The challenge inherent to implementing the mobility agreement lies in overcoming the fundamental contradictions inherent to the activities of the client and the homecare worker. From the perspective of the customer, the primary contradiction can be identified as that between autonomy and security. From the perspective of the worker, the primary contradiction lies between the saving of labor by adherence to the standard procedure, on the one hand, and a proactive and collaborative response to the customer's vital needs on the other.

Expansive Learning Scales and Their Articulation

The definition of expansive learning has consistently emphasized the collective nature of learning, oriented towards transforming activity systems. This has led to a consistent focus on the activity system as the level of analysis for expansive learning, with numerous researchers employing the activity system model to investigate the nature of expansive learning. In his recent publication (2020a), Engeström proposed a scale to categorize the levels of expansive learning, based on the dimensions of temporality and spatiality. The resulting scale comprises three levels: micro, meso, and macro. The following section will describe these levels and their respective characteristics.

Expansive Micro-Learning

Micro-scale expansive learning cycles refer to processes that take place over a limited timeframe and bring together professionals involved in expansive learning efforts that are spatially limited, but difficult to resolve individually. Peer-to-peer learning is fundamental at this level, as the three examples below illustrate. In their study of learning configurations in limiting the use of fertilizers and pesticides, Chantre, Le Bail, and Cerf (2014) identify one of the problems professionals are trying to solve as 'reducing nitrate levels in water and operational costs' (p. 11). While these authors do not explicitly utilize expansive learning theory to elucidate these learning configurations, they do analyze peer-to-peer learning in the creation of an innovative solution to this problem. Another example is Cuvelier's (2023) study of anesthetists, in which the author demonstrates the expansion of the object of their activity in discussions between peers. Finally, in the study by Rantavuori, Engeström, and Lipponen (2016), a group of Finnish beginning teachers aim to produce a short theatrical performance on the concept of time as part of a pre-service course. In all three examples, the reconfigurations that occur at this level of scale are associated with a spatially and temporally delimited work situation. This is also evident in the example presented earlier, namely that of care assistants working with the elderly (Nummijoki et al., 2018).

Expansive Meso-Learning

The second intermediate level (meso) is the most frequently studied level in studies of expansive learning, as it aims to achieve a global qualitative transformation of one or more activity systems. This level of learning is typical of studies employing the change laboratory methodology, as detailed in Chapter 10. This methodology was developed with the specific objective of accelerating expansive learning processes aimed at reconfiguring an activity system. The methodology has been adopted on a global scale, with research conducted in over 30 countries (Engeström, 2020a).

To illustrate the nature of this level, we may cite the study by Vänninen et al. (2015), which presents an intervention leading to systemic innovation in the context of integrated pest management in horticultural practices. The studies collected in the book by Vilela, Querol, Hurtado, and Lopes (2020) also focus on this level, demonstrating a diversity of interventions conducted in the field of occupational accident prevention.

Finally, Spante, Varga, and Carlsson (2021) study of an intervention to combat boys' failure at school in Sweden refers to the idea of transforming not simply classroom practices, but overcoming contradictions identified from historical analysis and thinking about school organization differently.

The three examples presented illustrate that the defining feature of this expansive learning process and level is the involvement of actors occupying multiple positions within the division of labor within an activity system. Conversely, if this is not the case, it can result in the reinforcement of the initial contradictions present in the activity system.

For instance, in the study by Launis and Pihlaja (2007b), the intervention was conducted with actors from a company, categorizing them according to their position within the hierarchical structure. The outcome was what the authors designated as *'organizational asynchronism.'* These asynchronisms are defined as differences in the object development that guide collective activity at each hierarchical level of the company. In their intervention, the workers collaborated with occupational health and safety services and researchers to develop a new production system based on partnership. The authors indicate that the implementation of the model was contingent upon managerial acceptance. In 2003, the aforementioned initiative aligned with the center's management policy. In 2004, however, management opted to reorganize services into three independent production lines: catering, building maintenance, and cleaning. This restructuring resulted in the center reverting to a mass service organization. Furthermore, the team members expressed frustration, stating that it would be more beneficial to focus on their daily work. From the outset of the project, it was evident that the management team would not be receptive to the workers' suggestions.

The majority of the asynchronisms identified by the authors are vertical in nature, stemming from the fact that each level of work organization employs distinct concepts and objects..

The majority of the asynchronisms identified by the authors are vertical in nature, stemming from the fact that each level of work organization employs distinct concepts and objects.

Finally, for the sake of completeness on this meso level, it is important to emphasize that while most studies have utilized change laboratories as their methodology, this does not imply that these learning processes cannot exist independently of an intervention. Conversely, this expansive meso-learning can also be analyzed in their natural setting (Engeström, 2000b; Hopwood & Gottschalk, 2017).

Expansive Macro-Learning

The third level is that of the macro. This level of learning is characterized by extensive processes that engage a diverse array of actors across a vast geographical area and over a relatively long temporal span. Caldwell, Krinsky, Brunila, and Ranta (2019) demonstrate, for example, how on the scale of New York City, learning processes are engaged by a coalition of actors to promote collective land trusts in the fight against gentrification and the displacement of the poorest populations. In Foot (2001), historical analysis and participant observation are employed to illustrate the expansive learning cycles involved in the establishment of a conflict prevention network in the former Soviet Union. These expansive macro-learnings are often analyzed retrospectively through historical analysis, which aims to trace the trajectory and cycles of expansive learning.

The challenges associated with the emergence of a fourth generation of work in CHAT involve the conceptualization of interventions that can support and articulate these diverse levels of learning (Sannino, 2020).

The various levels of expansive learning are illustrated in the following figure.

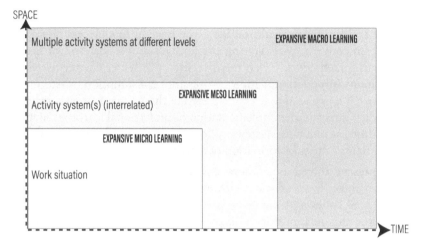

Figure 27: Different levels of expansive learning over time and space.

Challenges Associated with Articulating the Different Levels of Expansive Learning

The advent of a fourth generation of work on CHAT (see Chapter 5) necessitates a shift in perspective, moving away from the traditional compartmentalization of these learning levels and towards an integrated approach to their articulation. This represents a significant empirical challenge for expansive learning theory, as Engeström (2016) puts it:

> The ultimate test of any learning theory is how it helps us to generate learning that penetrates and grasps pressing issues the humankind is facing today and tomorrow. The theory of expansive learning currently expands its analysis both up and down, outward and inward (Engeström, 2016, p. 77).

This test for Expansive Learning Theory can only be met by analyses that extend and support the different levels of expansive learning and their articulations. Consequently, it is essential to examine the interconnections and integrations between the three previously delineated levels of learning. To illustrate, consider a hypothetical situation in which a transformation of food chains is required to adapt to global warming and to limit the impact of human production on the environment. This transformation of food chains is contingent upon learning at the territorial (macro) level within the framework of Territorial Food Projects (PAT), as established by the 2014 Avenir law in France. For a department like Seine-Saint-Denis, with the lowest income level in metropolitan France and limited agricultural land, the issue of food accessibility is a significant concern, necessitating the formation of a coalition of heterogeneous stakeholders. Given the diversity of activities encompassed by food chains (production, supply, processing, consumption, waste management), it is essential to transform each of the activity systems within a network. Moreover, the implementation of professional learning, such as those aimed at reducing waste in collective catering and school canteens, is essential for the transformation of activity systems.

At present, there is no comprehensive analysis of the interrelationship between these levels of scale. However, recent work aimed at addressing societal issues and involving diverse coalitions of actors has begun to explore this relationship. This is particularly evident in the work of Sannino (2020). Engeström and Sannino (2020) concur with this perspective, noting that a fourth generation of CHAT work entails contemplating the '*vertical and horizontal interaction between multiple expansive learning cycles*' (Engeström & Sannino, 2020, p. 17). Nevertheless, an attempt was made to model the articulation of expansive learning cycles by De la Torre (2022) in a study of the learning of a community coping with the contamination of a fluvial basin in Mexico.

Analyzing Expansive Learning

The objective of this section is to demonstrate the types of analysis that can be employed to account for expansive learning processes in publications. The examples presented will be drawn from a variety of fields. It should be noted that this is not intended to be an exhaustive representation.

It is crucial to acknowledge that the majority of the analyses presented in the studies below have concentrated on expansive learning within the context of formative intervention. To date, only a few studies have investigated expansive learning in its natural setting, apart from the studies presented here, which investigate expansive macro-learning a posteriori.

A Matrix for Investigating Expansive Learning

In the view of Engeström (2001), any theory of learning should address four key questions: (1) Who are the subjects of learning, how are they defined and located? (2) Why do they learn, what motivates them to make the effort to learn? (3) What do they learn, what are the contents and outcomes of learning? (4) How do they learn, what are the key actions or processes of learning?

Engeström (2001) cross-references these four questions with five CHAT principles to produce an analysis matrix (table below). These five principles are:

- 1. The activity system as the unit of analysis.
- 2. The multiplicity of perspectives.
- 3. Historicity.
- 4. Contradictions.
- 5. The expansive learning cycle.

In this section, we will not elaborate on these five principles, which the reader should be familiar with by this stage of the book. This matrix, although used in a theoretical article, can be used to account for expansive learning. The numbers in the matrix indicate the stages followed in the analysis.

Table 11: Analysis matrix of an expansive learning cycle from Engeström (2001).

	THE ACTIVITY SYSTEM AS A UNIT OF ANALYSIS	MULTIPLI- CITY OF PERSPEC- TIVES	HISTORI- CITY	CONTRA- DICTION	EXPANSIVE CYCLE
WHO'S LEARNING?	1	2			
WHY DO THEY LEARN?			3	4	
WHAT DO THEY LEARN?	5		6	7	8
HOW DO THEY LEARN?		9		10	11

The learning challenge presented in this example is to design a care pathway for children suffering from long-term illness and multiple pathologies. These children often move from one institution to another without anyone having an overview of the care provided. In order to answer the question of '*who learns*', it is necessary to identify the activity systems involved and the multiplicity of perspectives. In this case, learning occurs at the nexus of three discernible activity systems: the activity system of the children's hospital, the activity system of the primary care center, and the activity system of families with chronically ill children. Each of these activity systems is rife with internal contradictions. During the inaugural session, each practitioner, representing the activity system in which he or she operates, espoused defensive stances regarding the transmission or receipt of information from the hospital.

To answer the question '*Why do they learn?*', it is necessary to identify the historical processes that lead professionals to recognize a crisis or a deep-seated problem that needs to be addressed. In this case, patients who are transferred from the children's hospital to primary care become a new object (3), which is at odds with the tools and rules of the hospital (4).

To answer the question, '*What do they learn?*' it is necessary to identify the expansion of the object and the new concept constructed by the professionals (8), the resulting new activity system (5), and the contradictions between the old model and the new model of activity system (7). This last point is of particular importance, as it enables professionals to plan the implementation of the new activity system by anticipating certain forms of resistance.

Finally, to answer the question '*How do they learn?*' it is necessary to identify the dialogues, debates, and controversies between professionals (9), the gradual construction of contradictions (10), and the expansive learning actions throughout the learning cycle (11). This matrix is an excellent starting point for guiding a researcher wishing to investigate expansive learning, whether 'in the wild' or within a formative intervention, insofar as it enables the entire expansive learning process to be tracked and documented.

Analysis of Past Expansive Learning Macrocycles

The learning cycles in question are primarily highlighted in current literature through retrospective and historical analysis. This is notably the case in Foot's study (2001), which seeks to account for the development of a network for monitoring and preventing ethnic conflict in the former Soviet Union. Through participant observation, she collected data made up of meeting recordings, field notes, semi-structured interviews, official reports and e-mail exchanges between participants at conferences. This material enabled Foot to reconstruct the chronology of the construction of the surveillance network, the construction of the object and the instruments, and to identify contradictions based on the symptoms of these contradictions expressed by the participants.

In the study by Caldwell et al. (2019), the expansive learning cycle was employed to track the learning of a community comprising approximately two dozen associations engaged in opposing gentrification in New York City and rising real estate prices and rents. The researchers were not merely observers of the community, but rather were actively involved in the associations grouped together in this movement. The data analyzed included field notes, archival documents, and interviews with individuals involved in the movement. The expansive learning cycle spanned a six-year period, from the founding of a coalition of actors based on a need to regroup a fragmented associative landscape to the development of a business model to preserve affordable housing in a context of speculation and gentrification (Community Land Trust). The expansive learning cycle is therefore a tool for reconstructing the path of an activity system in the proximal zone of development.

Longitudinal Analysis of Expansive Learning Actions

It is only recently that researchers at CRADLE in Helsinki have sought to account for expansive learning processes by means of longitudinal analyses, thus enabling the apprehension and analysis of the fine composition of learning. As a reminder, these actions are:

- Questioning – criticism or rejection of aspects of current practice or suggested changes.
- Analysis – actions taken to explore the causes and explain the problematic situation.

- Modeling–ideation and construction of an explicit, simplified model that explains and offers a solution to the problematic situation.
- Examination–execution, exploitation and experimentation of the model to fully grasp its dynamics, potential and limitations.
- Implementation–preparation and practical application of the model, its enrichments and conceptual extensions.
- Reflection–evaluation and reflection on the expansive learning process.
- Consolidation–generalization of results and consolidation into a new, stable form of practice.

The following two examples of empirical research aim to account for the expansive learning process through the identification of discursive actions within a change laboratory. The expansive learning cycle is, in fact, a typical ideal. Therefore, it is important to be able to document how the process was really carried out. Documenting the real expansive learning cycle involves analyzing expansive learning actions throughout a learning cycle.

The first study concerns the investigation of the expansive learning cycle within a university library (Engeström, Rantavuori, & Kerosuo, 2013). The results indicate that six of the seven expansive learning actions were mobilized within the expansive learning cycle. The most represented action was situation analysis, while the action of consolidating the new practice did not appear in the results. In contrast, non-expansive actions were identified, including informing, clarifying, and summarizing. Expansive learning was observed as a process that occurred intermittently with frequent non-expansive actions, some of which were beneficial, some neutral, and some detrimental to expansion. By identifying the number and frequency of expansive learning actions, the authors were able to identify two interlocking cycles, as well as the presence of mini cycles within each session. This was evidenced by the fact that at least four expansive learning actions were present in each session of the change laboratory.

The same analysis strategy was used by Augustsson (2021) in a change laboratory involving teachers from a Swedish secondary school engaged in a participatory design project. The results demonstrated that the seven expansive learning actions served as analytical tools for mapping teacher learning and development. The analysis also revealed numerous deviations, disruptions, and occurrences of practical design actions in the process.

In the two examples presented above, numerical data were mobilized in an orientation of qualitative examination of expansive learning cycles. This represents a distinct approach from the first two analytical strategies employed with macrocycles by Caldwell and al. (2019) or Foot (2001, 2002). For Yanchar (2011), the utilization of numerical data in the research work of Engeström and his associates within explicitly interpretive and contextual inquiry demonstrates the potential for the use of numerical data derived from practical activities and contexts. These numerical data can be coherently merged with other data from qualitative methods, such as discourse analysis, to produce results that facilitate the transfer and naturalistic generalization, as opposed to statistical inference.

Highlighting the Emergence of Transformative Agency

One of the defining characteristics of expansive learning is the agency of the learning subjects (Sannino, Engeström, & Lemos, 2016). While Engeström considered research on agency an issue fifteen years ago (Engeström & Sannino, 2010), a number of analyses have since been conducted, notably thanks to the theoretical work carried out by Sannino on the transformative agency by double stimulation model (Engeström, 2007b; Engeström et al., 2015; Sannino, 2015a; Sannino & Engeström, 2018). A further discussion of this model will be presented in the Chapter 10.

The agency of participants in an expansive learning process is referred to as '*transformative agency*'. Transformative agency has been defined as '*breaking with the given framework of action and taking the initiative to transform it*' (Virkkunen, 2006, p. 49).

As with the previous analysis strategy, the analyses consist in quantifying discursive action categories to track the emergence of transformative agency. Haapasaari, Engeström, and Keruoso (2016) sought to account for discursive cues to analyze the evolution of transformative agency within CLs. The evolution of transformative agency (Engeström & Sannino, 2011) is reflected in the following actions: (1) criticism; (2) resistance; (3) explanation; (4) visioning; (5) concrete action; (6) consequential action to transform the activity system.

The results demonstrate a qualitative evolution of the main discursive indicators (see Figure 27).

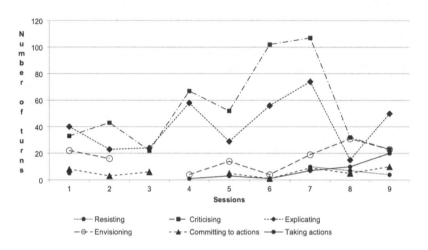

Figure 28: Evolution of discursive indicators of transformative agency according to Haapasaari, Engeström, and Keruoso (2016).

It is important to note that this analysis strategy, which focuses on speech acts, may inadvertently overlook the processes of instrumentalization and instrumentation of the secondary and tertiary artifacts provided by the interveners. By focusing on discourse, this analysis strategy may also fail to account for the use of the artifacts through which these actions are carried out. In other words, we posit that accounting for the emergence of transformative agency necessitates tracking the instrumental genesis (Rabardel, 1995) of the secondary and tertiary artifacts in use, since there can be no transformative agency without instrumental genesis (Lémonie & Bationo-Tillon, Forthcoming).

Transformative Agency as a Trigger for Expansive Learning

The final type of analysis pertains to the manner in which transformative agency initiates and facilitates expansive learning processes. In this analysis, the authors endeavor to elucidate the underlying mechanisms of expansive learning actions. To this end, they leverage Sannino's model of transformative agency by double stimulation, integrating it with the discursive indicators of transformative agency utilized in the preceding analysis.

The study by Morselli and Sannino (2021), like that by Kaup and Brooks (2022), analyzes a Change Laboratory by relating the five stages identified in Sannino's TADS model. The results indicate that the first four phases of Sannino's model are not strictly followed in the order of the theoretical model, but that these first four phases are present in all sessions of the Change Laboratory.

A more detailed examination of the TADS model will be presented in the chapter devoted to the Change Laboratory (Chapter 10).

Chapter 9
Development as Qualitative Reorganization

Before studying development, we need to explain what development is (Vygotski, 2014, p. 44).
Our research is not just about producing analytical academic reports. It aims to capture the potential and dynamics of development by initiating, supporting and recording qualitative changes in practical work activity itself (Engeström, 1990a, p. 72).

Although intervention is '*not a sport*' (Clot, 2017, p. 187), let us present the challenge of this chapter and foreshadow the third part of this book through an analogy. Seeking to adopt a developmental orientation in research and intervention without having sought to conceptualize what development is akin to playing a game without knowing either the rules or how it works. This chapter aims to conceptualize development CHAT. It is our contention that conceptualizing the concept of development is essential for reasons pertaining to contextual elements and the risk of immoderate use of the concept of development. In concluding a book that retraces a year of seminars held in his laboratory, Clot (2017, p. 188) notes the ambiguity and polysemy associated with the use of the notion of development in research work. He states, '*the word [development] often recurs in the preceding pages, as is often the case today in the literature. Yet it is difficult to find a precise conceptualization*'. We can only follow Clot on this critical path. For him, the study of concepts is of paramount importance, as interventions necessitate the development of resources outside the intervention itself.

The technical activity of researching the instruments used to produce results deserves to become a regular object of research in its own right, beyond 'action reflexivity'. This is undoubtedly a guarantee for regenerating this action with resources that are also constructed outside it (Clot, 2017, p. 186).

In the absence of this work, there is a significant risk that the concept of development will be transformed into a catch-all term. This term would operate '*blindly*', as Schwartz would say of the concept of activity (Schwartz, 2007), preventing scientific work from being guided. This observation is not new. Vygotsky made a similar observation almost a century ago:

> The concept of development is still vague and confused. The concept of development has not been differentiated from other related or neighboring concepts, and its meaning is often unclear. The content assigned to it lacks definition (Vygotski, 2014, p. 88).

Nevertheless, this risk is always present. In a special issue of a scientific journal devoted to '*developmental interventions*', we identified 265 occurrences of the term in just six articles. The analysis was conducted using *Nvivo* qualitative analysis software. The semantic diversity of the concept is particularly noteworthy in this issue. The term is sometimes used to refer to an increase (e.g. capability development), sometimes to a design process (e.g. artifact development), sometimes to a psychological process (e.g. subject development), and sometimes to a sociological process (e.g. organizational development). The semantic diversity of the concept is such that it is sometimes difficult to find a unity to the concept within the same text. Perhaps most problematically, no reference is made in this special issue to developmental science, developmental psychology, or the cultural-historical tradition, giving the illusion of a scientific concept without history. This chapter aims to respond to this identified gap by discussing the concept of development in the cultural-historical tradition of activity.

The Problematic Nature of a Polysemic, Totemic Concept

The semantic proliferation around the concept of development undoubtedly has its advantages. It is the reader who invests the concept with meaning, and any act of change in a work situation is considered to be developmental, making any intervention in a work situation a developmental intervention. Development is easily associated with change.

However, this situation is detrimental to research itself, as it risks conflating local, incremental improvement situations with developmental intervention situations. We have therefore decided to begin with a development that will allow us to differentiate the concept of development from related or often associated concepts in the literature.

Development, Improvement, Change, Transformation

Bryk (2015, 2017), in critical opposition to '*evidence-based education*'[22] propose to establish communities of practice and discussion forums on '*practice evidence*'. This approach is intended to enhance teaching-learning practices by focusing on the identification of effective strategies, rather than relying on scientific methods alone. Engeström (2017) critiques this perspective, highlighting potential dangers associated with the emphasis on improvement. The term '*improvement*', however, implies that the school (as an activity system) is doing things right and that any necessary changes can be made to improve efficiency and effectiveness. However, this type of approach does not address the content of the school's curriculum or the school's vision for the future, nor does it consider the school's role in addressing contemporary societal issues. In essence, Brik's approach substitutes technical discussion for discussion of the '*political-pedagogical*' project. Engeström's assessment of this approach is notably critical.

> I find this approach dangerous. It disregards the possibility that educational systems may in fact be coming to crossroads where qualitative transformations in their foundational assumptions and directional visions are necessary. By ignoring and suppressing this possibility, Bryk creates a situation in which improvement and transformation are seen as mutually exclusive alternative diagnoses and strategies (Engeström, 2017, p. 31).

Continuing his analysis, Engeström formulates the idea that the education system is riddled with contradictions, and that it is impossible to overcome these contradictions by simply looking to improve. Conversely, Engeström asserts that education systems require a profound qualitative transformation, rather than mere improvement. The title of the article in which he takes this position is notably explicit: '*Improvement Versus Transformation*.' In this context, transformation is defined as a qualitative development of the activity as a whole, based on a reorganization and

---

[22] On critiques of evidence-based approaches in education, the reader may refer in particular to (Barends, Janssen, ten Have, & ten Have, 2014; Biesta, 2010; Davies, 1999).

expansion of its object. Consequently, transformation is synonymous with development, as it signifies a profound qualitative change. It is necessary to clarify the meaning of the term *'transformation,'* which must be distinguished from the concept of *'change'* (Virkkunen & Schaupp, 2008). For Davydov, the concept of transformation is of central importance and is directly related to the object of activity.

> Many changes of natural and social reality carried out by people affect the object externally without changing it internally. Such changes can hardly be called transformations. Transformation means changing an object internally, making evident its essence and altering it (Davydov, 1999, p. 43).

Davydov (1999) specify the notion of essence that is altered in the transformation process :

> In dialectical logic, essence is an initial or universal genetic relation of a system of objects, which gives rise to its specific and individual characteristics. Essence is a law of development of the system itself (Davydov, 1999, p. 43).

In accordance with Engeström's (2017) perspective, the transformation of the school necessitates the transformation of its object, which can be achieved by recognizing its contradictory nature, its essence, or the laws of its development.

> Transformation is not a process of achieving preset goals; it is a process of resolving contradictions by constructing and traversing a collective zone of proximal development (Engeström, 2017, p. 34).

The two contradictions identified as significant in the context of the school are those between the object of the school and the primary contradiction between use value and exchange value. He distinguishes between:

- Knowledge as a good versus knowledge as a commodity.
- Student commitment to personal gain versus commitment to collective participation in favor of equity and sustainability.

To comprehend the law of system development is to acknowledge the contradictory nature of phenomena in order to grasp their essence. In the context of an activity system, this contradictory nature can be elucidated through historical analysis. By elucidating contradictions, it becomes possible to discern the essence of the phenomenon, its *'germ cell,'* or the fundamental contradiction from which the system under analysis develops (see Chapter 10).

However, in dialectical thinking, a historical analysis is not equivalent to a precise understanding of the temporality or dynamics of a activity system. Rather, it concerns grasping the logic of its development, that is, its historicity. Sannino (2024) offers a compelling summary of this distinction between temporality/dynamics and historicity in the context of educational literature.

> Temporality, however, is not the same as historicity. [...] An approach based on temporality, [...] has the virtue of bringing in a time perspective, which makes it possible to look at movements and dynamics. This approach, however, remains significantly limited as it cannot account either for the intrinsic dynamics of the historical development of structural contexts, nor for the extrinsic tool-mediated dynamics of individual and collective development (Sannino, 2024, p. 311).

The concept of development cannot be defined as a simple improvement or a simple or profound change, as these terms do not fully encompass the multifaceted nature of the concept. The concept of change is frequently employed in intervention approaches where the object of the activity is affected from the outside, without seeking to truly transform it from the inside in top-down, anhistorical approaches. In contrast, development is not merely a matter of changing something; it initiates the idea of an underlying logic that can be grasped.

Four Dimensions of Development to Discuss

The controversy initiated by Engeström in the pages of the journal '*Éducation et Didactique*' allows us to identify several points concerning the concept of development as apprehended by CHAT. In this chapter, we propose to develop and discuss these points.

The first point to be made is that improvement concerns a quantitative dimension (more effective, more efficient), whereas the concept of development refers to a genuine qualitative transformation, a change in the essence, vision, or object of the activity. To illustrate, consider the evolution of agriculture following the Second World War. This period saw a shift towards a form of intensification, characterized by increased mechanization, the use of chemical product and the standardization and expansion of plot size. This approach has had a significant impact on the environment. Nevertheless, it is possible to enhance this type of agriculture by limiting the utilization of chemical product to optimize a farm's economic performance. This is the concept of '*reasoned agriculture*.' From this perspective, the transition from intensive to reasoned agriculture represents an improvement without development. Another perspective is that of organic farming, which respects the natural cycles of the environment and aims to maintain or even improve the condition of soil, water, and air. This approach excludes the use of inputs or monocultures. The transition from intensive to organic farming represents a genuine qualitative transformation, rather than merely an improvement on the vision of intensive farming.

For Vygotsky, the transformation of quality represents the primary focus of his investigations in child psychology (Vygotski, 2014, p. 298). This transformation enables him to grasp the dialectical relationships between two stages of development. To illustrate this concept, he cites the transition from unconditioned to conditioned reflex, noting:

> Each successive stage in the development of behavior negates the preceding stage in the sense that the properties inherent in the first stage are overcome, eliminated, and sometimes transformed into an opposite, superior stage. In this way, each successive stage indicates the negation of the properties of the previous stage. On the other hand, the previous stage subsists within the preceding one. Its properties are identical to those of the unconditioned reflex; it is the same instinct, except that it manifests itself in another form, in another expression (Vygotski, 2014, p. 296).

The second point is that the development of an activity system necessitates the overcoming of historically accumulated contradictions within the activity system. The concepts of contradiction, crisis, and conflict therefore contain the seeds of development. In conclusion, CHAT postulates that contradictions and conflicts are the driving forces behind development. Vygotsky's perspective aligns with this view, stating that the conflict between the developed forms, the cultural forms of behavior that the child encounters, and the primitive forms that characterize his own behavior is the very essence of his cultural development (Vygotski, 2014, pp. 273–274).

In the context of the concept of '*improvement*,' the notion of contradiction in the dialectical sense is not a prerequisite. In contrast, the concept of contradiction in the dialectical sense is essential in an approach oriented toward transformation. Transformations necessitate an understanding of the logic of development, including the contradictions that underpin its genesis and rationale.

The third point is that development implies significant cultural change, which cannot be achieved without the active participation and learning of the participants. Consequently, the process of learning must precede the potential for development. Similarly, crises in the development of an activity system dialectically constitute the origin of the development of that activity system. This implies that development, like the concept of learning, is a collective process.

The fourth point is that development is not a process of maturation or teleology. The outcome of development is largely indeterminate, though bounded by the space of contradictions that gives rise to it. This indeterminacy is linked to its socio-historical nature. In this manner, it differs from a form of maturational development. Vygotsky subsequently elucidates that:

> In this process, novel forms emerge, and thus, they are not the links in a chain that has been pre-established and reproduced in a stereotypical manner (Vygotski, 2014, p. 274).

However, in children, the coexistence of maturational and sociohistorical development is observed, a phenomenon that is not present in adults (Prot & Schneuwly, 2013). For this reason, it is crucial to emphasize the sociohistorical nature of development, rather than the intersection of two lines of development, as is the case with children. As with the previous concepts presented in previous chapters (object, contradictions, expansive learning), it is evident that a simple definition of development is untenable. Such a definition would fail to capture the full depth and implications of the concept for analysis. In this chapter, we will therefore discuss the characteristics of the concept of development outlined above and the consequences we draw from it for activity analysis and intervention.

Development as Qualitative Reorganization

In his discussion of Vygotsky's concept of neoformations, Roth (2017) posits that the concept of development can be understood as a form of qualitative reorganization, a change in the essence of the observed phenomenon. This perspective is of central importance to the understanding of the concept of development in Vygotsky and the various CHAT authors. As Dafermos (2016) notes, for Vygotsky, development is not a gradual accumulation of quantitative changes; rather, it is a qualitative change that occurs as a result of internal conflicts and crises. The product of development is a qualitatively new form. This vision of development is based on the dialectical law of the transformation of quantity into quality (Sève, 1980). For Ollman (2005),

> The quantity/quality relationship is a relationship between two differentiated moments in time within the same process. At a certain point (which varies depending on the process under study), a qualitative transformation occurs, manifested in a change of appearance and/or function. The process has undergone a transformation, while its fundamental relations remain unchanged. Marx's approach to identifying this transformation is to examine the evolution of a process from its earlier to its later stages (Ollman, 2005, pp. 29–30).

Roth (2017) proposes that the emergence of qualitatively distinct forms of behavior is contingent upon the dialectical law of the transformation of quantity into quality. To illustrate this conception of development, the author presents the case of a Brazilian teacher, Leandro. Leandro employs an independent-lesson approach to sociology instruction, with each lesson addressing a distinct theme. In the early years of his career, Leandro refined his methodology, becoming more effective, more efficient, and more convincing as he implemented this teaching method. In essence, he is becoming more proficient. However, upon reading an article about a biology teacher who had engaged with his students in an action against the dumping of sewage in an ocean near a favela, Leandro experienced a crisis of conscience. He came to recognize that he had never encouraged his students to utilize their sociological knowledge to resolve their everyday issues. As a consequence of this epiphany, Leandro undertook a comprehensive reexamination of his pedagogical approach, embracing a more proactive role for students, integrating lectures into hands-on activities, and aligning topics more closely. From his role as a sociology instructor, he encouraged his students to engage in sociological research. The emergence of this novel form of student participation is illustrated in Figure below, which depicts the five phases described by Roth (2017). These five phases provide a framework for understanding the evolution of this new teaching method, which employs a *'genetic method'*.

In the first phase, Leandro gradually improves his teaching methodology until he reaches a crisis point, or *'phase 2'*. In this critical phase, the sociology teacher's teaching method conflicts with his own approach to teaching. This discrepancy makes it challenging for him to continue teaching in this manner (phase 3). Phase 4 represents a radical transformation of his teaching style. Phase 5 is a phase of gradual improvement.

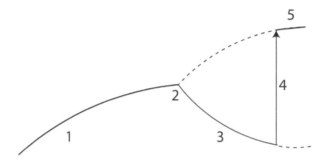

Figure 29: Development as qualitative reorganization and neoformation according to Roth (2017).

The following example serves to illustrate the qualitative changes that are associated with the transformation of tools. A method can be defined as an artifact. However, from Roth's example, it can be seen that the transformation does not result from the transformation of the artifact used by the teacher, but rather from the conceptualization of a new object. This is exemplified by the shift from the traditional approach of teaching as a form of transmitting knowledge about the main authors of sociology to a more contemporary perspective of teaching sociology as a militant instrument for transforming the world.

Similarly, with regard to the concept of an activity system, the development of an activity is perceived as a qualitative reorganization of the entire activity system, brought about by the expansion of the object of this activity. The notion of a developmental period is therefore necessary to account for historical development and to identify the contradictions that set the activity system in motion. Accordingly, Mukute (2015, p. 48) defines systems of activity as developing in terms of their movement and displacement, while implying a qualitative change or evolution from what was to what is.

This perspective on development is central to cultural-historical approaches and is also shared by approaches that employ theoretical frameworks other than those of quantitative improvement, such as non-linear dynamic systems approaches[23]. Accordingly, for Thelen and Smith (1996, p. xiv), '*Development is also non-linear and qualitative, since complexity calls for new forms and capacities*'. It should be noted here that, while this framework differs from that of CHAT, it is fundamentally compatible with it.

Engeström (1996a) employs a novel by Peter Hoeg (Borderliners) to challenge the developmental conceptions of both Piaget and Vygotsky. The story follows three young people from challenging backgrounds who find themselves at an elite school. The narrator, Peter, is 14 and has been abandoned. Auguste killed his parents, and Katarina lost her parents to illness and suicide. The narrative then proceeds to describe the actions undertaken by the three young people to ascertain the reason for their admission to the school in question. Their investigation is conducted in a series of actions that are specifically designed to disrupt the institution in which they find themselves and to test its limits. The objective of this disruption is to gain an understanding of the mechanism behind the school's strict order. Gradually, the three protagonists come to realize that they are participating in an experiment on a school-wide scale. The outcome of this experiment is either integration with normal students or placement in institutions for the mentally retarded.

This narrative exemplifies Engeström's three principles of development. Firstly, the process of development is not merely the acquisition of knowledge and abilities. In addition, it can be regarded as a form of resistance to and rejection of the existing order. This phenomenon can be observed in instances of rebellion, as exemplified by Hoeg's narrative. Such instances can be considered as forms of development, as they suggest a desire for change and the shaping of one's life trajectory.

---

[23] For a presentation of its interest in MSD prevention, see (Lémonie, 2019). This compatibility is noted by Thelen and Smith (1996, p. xxi), who state, "We recognize that our developmental approach is also compatible with the school of developmental theorists going back to Vygotsky." It is also important to note that this theoretical framework, which is widely utilized in the study of motor skills, is based on the work of the renowned Russian physiologist Bernstein (Bernstein, 1996; Feigenberg, 2014; Kant, 2016), Shvarts and Bakker (2019) demonstrated the continued influence of Vygotsky's work, citing his participation in the first Vygotskian circle in Moscow in the 1920s (Yasnitsky, 2011). Finally, the dialectical character of the non-linear dynamic systems approach is particularly highlighted in recent work (Sève and Guespin-Michel, 2005).

For Engeström, the challenge for development theory is to account for the negative, destructive, and explosive elements in development processes without reducing them to formulas that are perceived as patronizing and safe from the outset (Engeström, 1996a, p. 129). This challenge is addressed in the implementation phase of expansive learning theory, which occurs within the context of a novel activity system. In this phase, the previous system resists and contradicts the new one. Consequently, the successful implementation of a new activity system necessitates the partial destruction of the existing system.

The second principle is as follows: Development is not merely a vertical movement; it is also a horizontal movement that transcends limitations. In traditional theories of development, progress is viewed as a vertical movement from competence to incompetence, from primary to higher psychic functions. Hoeg's narrative illustrates that development is not solely a vertical phenomenon; it is also a horizontal movement of boundary crossing. The three protagonists of the narrative traverse the institution's boundaries in two distinct ways. Firstly, they are placed there by external forces. Secondly, they resist the institution and attempt to escape.

Thirdly, development is not merely an individual phenomenon. Furthermore, it is a collective phenomenon. This dimension will be illustrated in greater detail at a later point in the discussion. In historical context, the questioning of an institution cannot be carried out by a solitary individual. This process is inherently collective and cannot be explained by the history of each individual child. A discussion of the aforementioned characteristic of development will be presented at a subsequent stage of this analysis.

If development is regarded as a process of qualitative transformation, it would appear that forms of intervention designed to enhance work situations and/or facilitate the acquisition or improvement of skills could be regarded as examples of developmental interventions. The concept of 'professional development' is frequently understood to encompass the continuous improvement of skills through a process of reflexive reflection on practice. However, there appears to be some confusion surrounding the relationship between the notions of learning and development. This is exemplified by Postholm's definition (2012):

Professional development is defined as teachers' learning: how they learn to learn and how they apply their knowledge in practice to support student learning (Postholm, 2012, pp. 405–406).

Contradictions, History and Development

As previously discussed, contradictions are the driving force behind development. This concept has been present since the inception of CHAT. As elucidated by Brossard (2013) in his analysis of the role of the teacher in relation to the Vygotskian conception of development, the teacher's role is to design tasks that organize the contradictions between the student and his environment, assisting the student in overcoming them in order to generate a developmental transformation.

It is crucial to reiterate the significance of identifying contradictions for the development of activity systems. To illustrate this point, consider the following example. In the 1980s, my father, like many adult males, utilized disposable razors. At the time, these razors were considered a revolutionary innovation, as they made shaving safer and quicker than the 'cut and thrust' razors previously used. The act of shaving is an example of a self-presentation activity that is subject to a number of tacit or explicit rules of society. However, from the 1980s onwards, there was a growing awareness of ecological issues within society. Consequently, the object of this activity underwent a transformation, accompanied by a relaxation of the associated rules. This led to the emergence of the 'three-day beard.' It is no longer a given that shaving safely and quickly should be the object of an activity when the subject wishes to reduce their individual ecological footprint. In light of the significant environmental constraints posed by disposable tools, disposable razors are no longer viable instruments in view of the expansion of the object to include an environmental dimension that was barely present in the previous era.

To reconcile this contradiction between the new object and the instruments used, an increasing number of individuals are turning to ecological solutions. These solutions, however, necessitate a new learning curve. One individual who has participated in a website dedicated to the topic of 'ecological shaving' solutions has provided a description of his experience:

> The initial experience was challenging, requiring over a quarter of an hour and resulting in unsatisfactory outcomes. However, with continued

practice, I was able to refine my technique, reducing the time required to a mere few minutes. Additionally, I no longer incurred any self-injuries, the process was more efficient, and the final result was consistently clean.

This example illustrates the historical contradictions that arise between the extended object of an activity and the instruments that drive its development. These contradictions manifest as new rules, new instruments, new divisions of labor, and a new community. These qualitative bifurcations are referred to as development, as they represent a radical break with the preceding form. In contrast, incremental improvements are referred to as learning. Nevertheless, these forms of learning can be directed towards the development of an activity system. In this instance, we refer to expansive learning. The notion of contradiction is therefore of central importance in our understanding of the logic of development and the potential directions it may take. Nevertheless, even if dialectical analysis enables us to grasp the potential directions of development, development remains a largely indeterminate process.

The Indetermination of Development

The second characteristic of development that we address here is its indeterminate nature. In the CHAT framework, development is seen as a historical and cultural process. Bronckart (2013) distinguishes two forms of development based on a presentation of the notion of development in Vygotsky and Piaget. The first is a form of maturational development, which is biologically based and part of the continuity of life. The second form of development is linked to the internalization of signs; as such, it fundamentally transforms the nature of development and becomes socio-historical. In his 2014 work, *'The History of the Development of Higher Psychic Functions'*, Vygotsky (2014) outlines several orientations to be excluded from any investigation of development. The first orientation is an embryological conception that *'consists of a purely quantitative increase in the dimensions in the embryo of what is given from the beginning'* (p. 271). Vygotsky notes that this theoretical perspective, which has been discredited, persists in practice to the extent that psychological methods often portray the child and its development in a negative light, emphasizing deficiencies. However, when we analyze a behavior or activity in terms of lack, we are comparing the analyzed behavior or activity to an ideal form of the analyzed behavior. This ideal form of behavior is tacitly conceived as the predetermined endpoint of the development of the analyzed form.

The second orientation that Vygotsky deems necessary to overcome is that of '*latent evolutionism*', which posits that development is a gradual accumulation process. This evolutionary conception of development is understood to be analogous to the growth of a plant. However, this evolutionary conception ignores the '*revolutionary, critical, leap-like changes [...] so often encountered in cultural development*' (p. 273). This form of development is stereotyped and does not depend on external influence. In children, development is not a stereotyped process. It is always characterized by the appearance of the new, '*of ever-new forms*' (p. 274). Development is a creative process. Vygotsky distinguishes between growth or maturation, where each new stage results from the deployment of potentialities contained in the previous stage, and development, which '*consists in the fact that the new stage is born not from the deployment of potentialities contained in the previous stage, but from a real conflict between the organism and the environment, and from its living adaptation to the environment*' (p. 275). Consequently, development is not predetermined.

As Clot (2017) notes, drawing on Dewey, development is only unidirectional and predetermined in the abstract outside real situations. In contrast to this abstract notion, it is precisely real situations that transform the expected development into an incomplete story whose end is not known in advance and that can branch off (Clot, 2017, p. 188). This idea is shared by other researchers who do not necessarily adhere to the cultural-historical framework. Accordingly, Bullinger (2017, p. 23) asserts that '*we cannot provide an answer at the outset that we hope to find at the end of development, as this would be a perspective that denies development itself*'. For Thelen and Smith (1996) development doesn't '*know*' where it's going from the start.

The discussion must extend beyond the '*end point*' of the development to encompass the 'direction' of development. Schneuwly (2013) poses the question of whether the implicit '*hierarchy*' present in many proposals on adult development should be abandoned.

> Should we not abandon the presupposition of a kind of hierarchy, a cumulative progression in adult development? Such a progression is conceivable – and, in my opinion, should be – for child development, given that it is largely the result of education, an artificial development aimed at ideal

forms, as Vygotsky says. However, here too we need to be very careful: all development is always also involution, and all development always implies one possible orientation among others. This is particularly evident in the case of adult development, which we previously characterized, following Engeström, as '*development as breaking away and opening up*' (Schneuwly, 2013, p. 255).

If the ultimate outcome is not already known in advance, the direction of development is not itself determined in advance. It is both vertical and horizontal in nature.

In his 2017 work, Clot distinguishes two postures in accordance with the two previously outlined conceptions of development. In an embryological view of development, he posits that the key issue is to '*liberate the potentialities of a supposed power to act*' (p. 188). In contrast, a cultural-historical conception of development posits that the joint activity of subjects on the object must proceed from the known to the unknown, towards reversible concrete solutions that no one had previously considered. It is these solutions that confer effective power to act.

We concur with Clot (2017) on this final position, although the term '*march from the known to the unknown*' is open to debate. In the context of formative interventions, this march occurs within a territory that participants delineate as the intervention progresses. This territory is defined by the expansive learning process itself, which uncovers the systemic contradictions underlying the participants' problems, conflicts, or dilemmas. This territory is defined by the expansive learning process itself. Nevertheless, the outcome of the developmental process is always novel, representing a hitherto unidentified form of activity. This territory represents a zone of potential development.

Development as Formative and Collective Conquest

As noted by Schneuwly (2013), Vygotsky's notion of the zone of proximal development (ZPD) articulates two opposing or contradictory conceptions for conceptualizing development. On the one hand, development can be conceived as self-movement, and on the other, it can be conceived as a form of education in the broadest sense. The notion of the zone of proximal development as defined by Engeström (2015) also articulates these two contradictory dimensions. He reformulates it as follows:

It is the distance between the present everyday actions of the individuals and the historically new form of the societal activity that can be collectively generated as a solution to the double bind potentially embedded in the everyday actions (Engeström, 2015, p. 138).

As will be demonstrated in the chapter dedicated to the methodology of the change laboratory (Chapter 10), the development of an activity system is always a collective endeavor. However, this collective endeavor is achieved through the process of becoming aware of the contradictions at the source of the '*self-movement*' of activity systems.

Engeström extends and develops the notion of the zone of proximal development, as he believes that this concept fails to address the relationship between individual development and the development of society. As previously discussed, the Vygotskian school primarily focused on the acquisition and internalization of tools and signs from culture. In essence, the culture itself is perceived as immutable or stabilized. Consequently, the question of how an activity, conceived as a historical, cultural, societal, and collective formation, develops itself is largely overlooked.

In his view:

> Human development is real production of new societal activity systems. It is not just acquisition of individually new activities, plus perhaps individual creation of '*original pieces of behavior*'(Engeström, 2015, p. 138).

This position is consistent with that proposed by Stetsenko (2017) in her project to radicalize and develop Vygotskian work. For her, human beings are acting actors who co-create the world and their future through their activity. The central ontological assumption in her position is that the world is not '*given*' and cannot be considered as a fixed, static structure existing independently of us, to which we would have to adapt. In contrast, the world is constituted by activity systems that undergo constant evolution through the implementation of individual actions, which are simultaneously social. Alternatively stated, the world, society, is not a preexisting entity to which we must merely adapt; rather, it is a dynamic reality shaped by the actions of individuals within their activity systems. Within this framework, Stetsenko (2015) defines development as follows:

> Human development, in this approach, is a constant work-in-progress by people who simultaneously create the world and, in and through these creative acts of change, also bring themselves into existence. In other words,

development is a collaborative achievement of an activist nature in that it relies upon people forming and carrying out their future-oriented agendas and projects of social transformation. (Stetsenko, 2015, p. 108).

In the context of CHAT, the development of activity implies a form of collective power to act that these approaches refer to as *'transformative agency'* (Haapasaari & Kerosuo, 2015; Sannino et al., 2016; Vänninen et al., 2015, 2021). Transformative agency is oriented towards the qualitative transformation of a social practice, which is modeled and conceived in terms of an activity system.

The development of an activity system within this framework is conceived as a collaborative, *'multivoiced'*, and necessarily conflictual process. It is largely indeterminate, but it builds on the contradictions inscribed in this activity system. Its product is the qualitative reorganization or transformation of this activity system, which goes far beyond mere improvement.

Conclusion of Part 2

This second part of the study focuses on four central concepts. Without delving into the intricacies of each concept, it is imperative to demonstrate their interconnectedness in an analysis of activity, employing a dialectical approach to thinking.

Prior to analysis, it is necessary to identify the system to be examined. This system is oriented towards an object that serves to define it. Consequently, the concept of the activity object is of paramount importance in this initial stage of analysis.

The dialectical approach to analysis necessitates the identification of the contradictions that set the system in motion. These contradictions are the root cause of disorders, problems, dilemmas, or local innovations at the level of situated action. The distinction between symptoms and real contradictions between the surface and the underlying forces of the process is of fundamental importance in this context. Furthermore, it enables the differentiation between various interrelated activity systems.

The second stage of the dialectical approach to analysis is to identify the contradictions that set the system in motion and which are at the root of disorders, problems, dilemmas, or local innovations at the level of situated action. The differentiation between symptoms and genuine contradictions between the surface and the underlying forces is of paramount importance in this context. However, the identification of contradictions can only be achieved if the delimitation of the activity system has been properly carried out and a clear distinction has been made between the level of action and that of activity. In the second stage, the historical dimension is of paramount importance, as it enables the identification of developmental periods, thereby highlighting the systemic contradictions at work. Once the contradictions have been identified, a zone of proximal development is established within which the participants will learn in a comprehensive manner.

The objective of this type of analysis is to project a potential future for the transformation of activity systems. Nevertheless, this future is not solely dependent on the researcher's will or persuasive abilities. Furthermore, the success of this approach is contingent upon the willingness of professionals to engage in expansive learning. Having reached this juncture, it is necessary to delve deeper into the realm of interventionist research, which is designed to facilitate these expansive learning endeavors among professionals.

Part 3

THE INTERVENTIONIST DIMENSION OF CHAT: FORMATIVE INTERVENTION AND CHANGE LABORATORY

Introduction to Part 3

Qualitative research is frequently conducted using the CHAT framework. Indeed, this type of research is particularly prevalent in the educational sciences (Nussbaumer, 2012). To illustrate this usage, consider the following example from the management sciences. Canolle and Vinot (2021) aim to demonstrate how material and human interactions contribute to the generation of value in the doctoral thesis, which can then be employed in the non-academic sector (industry). Data were collected via interviews with 20 former doctoral students to study the progressive construction of the object during their professional trajectory between the start of the thesis and their employment in the non-academic sector. In this context, the CHAT framework is employed as a conceptual tool to inform both the design of the interview and its subsequent interpretation. It serves as an explanatory framework for understanding the processes involved in the construction of the value of the thesis on the non-academic job market.

In this research orientation, the researcher is the analyst. The researcher is responsible for designing the research, posing the research questions, collecting qualitative data (generally in the form of observation or interviews), mobilizing the analytical tools derived from activity theory, and carrying out a form of '*diagnosis*', which is the production of knowledge about the phenomena and processes the researcher wishes to investigate. This qualitative orientation of research provides access to the depth and singularity of phenomena and enables the researcher to understand the logic of development. However, it is constrained in its capacity to effect transformation of the phenomena under investigation. In addition to the understanding of reality, there is a necessity to effect transformation (in the sense previously elucidated in Chapter 9). The eleventh thesis of the '*Theses on Feuerbach*' thus serves as the foundation for the CHAT approach: it is not merely a matter of understanding reality, but rather of transforming it.

Even if qualitative research is conducted in an exemplary manner, it is not the researcher's results or proposals that will transform the activity from the outside. Even if the diagnosis has been meticulously crafted and the prospects for transformation are substantial, their concrete implementation necessitates expansive learning processes that engage workers in the analysis and resolution of the contradictions inherent to their activity. This necessitates a transformation in the researcher's posture. The researcher must adopt a more engaged and involved posture, which some might consider to be militant (Stetsenko, 2023). Conversely, transforming or developing activity systems in intervention constitute a testing ground for CHAT (Engeström, 1993) and a promising way to develop it.

Rehabilitating the role of intervention in the production of knowledge, far beyond the mere descriptive contemplation of the situations he encounters, CHAT inscribes transformations in a history oriented towards a future thought of as an indeterminate horizon of possibility.

As Clot (2008) points out in reference to Vygotsky, *'History is not the past'*. The transformation of the past into becoming, or the failure of this transformation, represents a crucial aspect of historical change. Mobilizing a lived history into a history to be lived, overcoming contradictions for the collective design of a new activity system, and design for new uses are all objects of intervention oriented towards a desirable, but nonetheless indeterminate, future. Bronfenbrenner (1977) cites Leontiev's description of Soviet approaches to activity as an illustrative example of this phenomenon.

> It appears that American researchers are consistently attempting to elucidate the manner in which the child has attained his current state; in contrast, Soviet psychologists are endeavoring to ascertain the means by which he may evolve into a state that he has not yet attained'. Soviet psychologists frequently discuss what they refer to as transformative experiments. The term *'transformative experiments'* is used to describe experimentation that radically restructures the environment, producing a new configuration that activates a previously unrealized behavioral potential of the subject (Bronfenbrenner, 1977, p. 528).

These experiments place the concept of development at the heart of their approach and make it possible to qualify developmental forms of intervention. This type of research aims to capture the potential and dynamics of development by initiating, supporting, and recording qualitative changes in the practical work activity itself (Engeström, 1990a,

p. 72). The forms and characteristics of these transformative experiments will be discussed in detail below.

In contrast to the idea of simple adaptation to an unchanging environment, CHAT seeks not to account for or facilitate adaptation to a constituted reality. Rather, it aims to go beyond the status quo. In opposition to what they perceive as a narrow and reductionist interpretation of Vygotsky's work, Stetsenko and Arievitch (2004) argue that one of the cornerstones of Vygotskian theory is the notion that human development occurs through the transformation of an existing environment and the creation of a new environment through the production and deployment of new instruments.

For the sake of brevity, we will not delve into the specifics of these various points at this time. However, it is important to note that cultural-historical orientations differ from other ethnographic approaches in terms of the role of the researcher and conceptualization. As Engeström (2000b, p. 151) states,

> Ethnographic studies have traditionally been concerned with observing and understanding stable orders, routines, and repeatable procedures. The question of change has been relatively foreign to them. Consequently, the researcher plays a secondary role in these developments, insofar as the question of development is largely excluded from their theorizations. Ethnographers have largely avoided theorizing development, perhaps fearing deterministic and evolutionary implications. Faced with the ubiquitous and often spectacular changes taking place in the workplace, such an attitude amounts to burying one's head in the sand (Engeström, 2000b, p. 151).

Once again, dialectics lie at the heart of interventions aimed at transforming activity systems. However, the aim of formative interventions is not to apply the categories of dialectics, but to make them an instrument enabling professionals to learn how to develop their activity system. In other words, dialectics is an instrument enabling professionals engaged in expansive learning to transition from future orientation to future construction (Engeström, Rantavuori, Ruutu, & Tapola-Haapala, 2023a). This entails mastering one's destiny by inventing something that did not yet exist (Engeström, Engeström, & Suntio, 2002).

The two chapters that comprise this section seek to elucidate CHAT's interventionist perspective in greater detail through the formative intervention methodology known as the Change Laboratory (Chapter 10). In

Chapter 11, we will contrast the Change Laboratory with other interventionist approaches widely present in the international literature, thereby enabling the reader to discern the distinctive features of the Change Laboratory.

Chapter 10

The Change Laboratory Methodology

Can people learn to master their future? (Engeström, 2000b)
It's not within the narrow confines of your personal life and personal
affairs that you'll become a true creator in the future (Vygotsky, 1997b,
p. 350).

The Change Laboratory (CL) is a formative intervention methodology designed to support the expansive learning efforts of participants
who wish to transform the activity system within which they operate. It
is a developmental intervention methodology conceived in the late 1990s
at the CRADLE laboratory in Helsinki, Finland, by Engeström and colleagues (Lémonie & Grosstephan, 2021; Virkkunen & Newham, 2013).

CL is comprised of a series of sessions during which professionals
from one organization (or several collaborating organizations) engage
in discourse about their work, analyze the developmental history of the
activity system in which they operate, identify the contradictions and
zone of proximal development of their activity system, define a new
model and object of activity, and finally take steps towards implementing the model.

CL's distinctive feature is its strong foundation in CHAT. In order
to gain a comprehensive understanding of the CL process and its implementation, it is essential to master the key concepts presented in the
second part of the book. As we have emphasized on numerous occasions
throughout this book, CHAT is an interventionist theory. In a clear
statement, Friedrich (2010, p. 53) asserts that *Vygotskian psychology is not
only about knowing, but also about intervening*. Given its roots, CHAT
must therefore be initiated by *transformative* interventions. However,
the literature often employs a *contemplative* approach to CHAT in qualitative research. For instance, in the book that presents CHAT in educational research, Yamagata-Lynch (2010) mobilizes the main concepts
(including that of activity system) in a qualitative research orientation.

Activity theory is indeed a theoretical frame– work that is compatible with qualitative research investigations, and since its introduction to the United States in the early 1990s, activity systems analysis has been commonly used as a supplementary analysis in qualitative investigations [...] Additionally, I agree that not all research using activity systems analysis contribute to practice. When activity theory was adopted in North America most scholars, including myself, used it exclusively as a descriptive tool in qualitative studies and not as a method for changing practice. Engeström's original works have focused on changing practice, but most North American scholars did not initially embrace this aspect of the methodology (Yamagata-Lynch, 2010, p. 31).

In contrast to this North American appropriation, CL constitutes *'perhaps the most visible program of contemporary interventionist research'* (Penuel, Cole, & O'Neill, 2016, p. 489). In recent years, there has been a notable increase in the amount of research utilizing CL in various fields and regions around the globe. Consequently, CL has been mobilized in higher education (Bligh & Flood, 2015, 2017; Costa et al., 2018), in the prevention of occupational accidents and diseases (Ferreira et al., 2023; Hurtado et al., 2020; Vilela, Querol, Almeida, & Filho, 2020), in the accompaniment of a public policy of secondary education in France (Lémonie et al., 2021), in agriculture (Lotz-Sisitka, Mukute, Chikunda, Baloi, & Pesanayi, 2017; Mukute, 2015; Mukute et al., 2018), university libraries (Engeström et al., 2012; Meyers, 2007), the refoundation of a policy to combat homelessness (Keruoso & Jokinen, 2023; Sannino, 2020, 2023a), and the education of children in crisis management in Japan (Yamazumi, 2021), among others.

Despite its use as a research methodology and the expansion of publications and experiments carried out across the globe, there seem to be obstacles to the use of CHAT as a valid interventionist research methodology. It is therefore necessary to return briefly to this chapter to discuss the epistemological legitimacy of interventionist research. Our view is that the main obstacle lies in the lack of understanding of this legitimacy.

The Epistemological Legitimacy of Interventionist Research

CHAT as an Interventionist Theory

For a significant period at the outset of my career, I believed that research conducted in close proximity to practices, resulting in a qualitative in-depth analysis of the actions of actors in a given situation, would likely lead to prospects for relevant transformations that would be taken up by the professionals I encountered and with whom I had to interact. Unfortunately, as Argyris and Schön (2001) have observed, professionals do not typically behave in the manner of consumers of scientific knowledge. Even when recommendations are implemented, the difficulty in doing so can result in a learning curve, which may not be avoidable.

During a one-day seminar, a renowned colleague stated that he wore two '*hats*': one as a trainer, which he put aside to wear his '*hat*' as a researcher. When he donned this second hat, he refrained from intervening in order to avoid '*distorting the work situations he was investigating*'. He did, however, admit to an instance in which he had to intervene when a situation was becoming unmanageable. He did not, however, provide any details regarding the use of these data in the research process.

The examples presented above demonstrate a recurring dilemma among researchers regarding the appropriate posture: to ensure the ecological integrity of the settings they analyze or to intervene. This dilemma can be traced back to a fundamental belief in the necessity of analyzing a work situation by way of observation, interviews with professionals, and maintaining an observational stance. This stance is believed to be necessary in order to ensure the ecological integrity of the situation being analyzed is not distorted.

However, in order to ascertain the properties of an object, it is necessary to act upon it. The process of understanding work is to transform it. Leontiev provides the following example of an an object's elasticity is perceived (Leontiev, 1975/2021). The perception of an object's elasticity is not a purely contemplative act. This occurs via an external motor process that has a practical purpose: to deform the object. Leontiev's perspective aligns with that proposed by Marx in his second thesis on Feuerbach. In Marx's view, it is through human practice that humans elaborate knowledge. Consequently, Marx wrote that:

> The question of whether human thought should be recognized as having objective truth is not a theoretical question, but a practical one. It is in practice that man must prove the truth, i.e. the reality, and the power of his thought, in this world and for our time. Discussion of the reality or unreality of a thought that isolates itself from practice is purely scholastic [Thèse 2].

In the Marxist orientation whose origin we have located, CHAT is an interventionist research approach (Sannino & Sutter, 2011). This approach justifies the use of interventionist approaches and indirect methods, which are central to Vygotsky's resolution of the 'crisis' in psychology (Dafermos, 2014, 2018). Vygotsky posited practice as constituting the foundation for the development of psychological research and knowledge. It is even presented as serving as the supreme judge in this regard:

> A psychology which is called upon to confirm the truth of its thinking in practice, which attempts not so much to explain the mind but to understand and master it, gives the practical disciplines a fundamentally different place in the whole structure of the science than the former psychology did. These practice was the colony of theory, dependent in all its aspects on the metropolis. Theory was in no way dependent on practice. Practice was the conclusion, the application, an excursion beyond the boundaries of science, an operation which lay outside science and came after science, which began after the scientific operation was considered completed. Success or failure had practically no effect on the fate of the theory. Now the situation is the opposite. Practice pervades the deepest foundations of the scientific operation and reforms it from beginning to end. Practice sets the tasks and serves as the supreme judge of theory, as its truth criterion. It dictates how to construct the concepts and how to formulate the laws (Vygotsky, 1997c, pp. 305–306).

This extract illustrates that Vygotsky's position is radical. It is not a matter of simply adding practice to theory or simply verifying theoretical ideas in practice. Rather, it is a question of developing a comprehensive framework that encompasses the entirety of his research. Consequently, in contrast to the traditional model of research, which is characterized by a distance and disinterest in the production of knowledge, Vygotsky proposes a model of research where practice and theory interpenetrate, inaugurating an innovative and transformative approach. As Stetsenko (2016b) suggests:

> The researcher, according to Vygosky, instead of striving to copy reality, should actively and consciously create conditions (by necessity, artificial) that permit to construct and generate the objects of investigation in the processes of studying and changing them. This method moved beyond the limits not only of the classical experimental paradigm but of the whole ideology of descriptivist methods coupled with contemplative stance and speculative metaphysics (Stetsenko, 2016b, p. s36).

Vygotsky and his followers consistently demonstrate an anchoring in practice and in the transformative ambitions of the concept of activity. This permeates the entire work of the school of thought. To put it another way, this school of thought places a strong emphasis on understanding by transforming reality. This epistemological motto significantly shifts the questions posed. Rather than focusing on understanding psychological processes in isolation, it is now understood that understanding the conditions of possibility and transformation of psychological processes is of greater importance. This represents a significant shift in perspective (Arievitch, 2017).

The formative interventions and methodology of the change laboratory are the direct descendants of these transformative experiments. However, they have somewhat deviated from the original aspirations of twentieth-century Soviet psychologists. In this context, the objective is not to alter a given situation or immediate environment, but to alter institutions in concrete terms by combating the entrenchment of research in a form of status quo. Bronfenbrenner (1977) provides a helpful framework for understanding this ambition when he discusses social systems that are relatively stable in developmental research:

> Most of our scientific ventures into social reality perpetuate the statu quo; to the extent that we include ecological contexts in our research, we select and treat them as sociological given rather than evolving social system susceptible to significant and novel transformation. Thus, we study social-class differences in development, ethnic differences, rural-urban differences [...] as the nature of these structures, and their developmental consequences, were eternally fixed and unalterable, except, perhaps, by violent revolution. We are loath to experiment with new social forms as contexts for realizing human potential [...] It is one thing to compare the effects on development of systems or system elements already present within culture; it is quite another to introduce experimental changes that represent a restructuring of established institutional forms and values. (Bronfenbrenner, 1977, p. 528).

Formative interventions and the methodology of the change laboratory are specifically designed to re-design existing '*institutional forms*', as defined by Bronfenbrenner.

This approach requires a focus on the future, rather than the past or present. However, there is still some uncertainty about how to investigate this future. How, then, can we effectively guide the transformation and reconfiguration of activity systems in a manner that truly enables the generation of novel potential? How can we anticipate and anticipate change in activity systems, while avoiding the risk of haphazard and unsystematic extrapolations?

As Ollman (2008) notes, the realization of a new potential requires a thorough analysis of the preconditions for that potential. Otherwise, the potential for transformation is open to chance, randomness, or luck:

> The notion of potential is mystified whenever it is applied to a part separate from its encompassing system, or when this system is separated from its origins. In this case, 'potential' can only refer to possibility in the sense of chance, because all the necessity derived from the relational and processual character of reality has been removed, and there is no longer any reason to expect one outcome rather than another (Ollman, 2008, p. 12).

These are significant inquiries, and their responses can be discerned through dialectics, particularly the method of ascent from the abstract to the concrete, which will be elucidated in greater detail in this chapter. This method represents Marx's operational approach to anticipating the future (Garrido, 2022; Ollman & Smith, 2008). Identifying contradictions is a crucial aspect of this method, but it is not the only element. The dialectic can be conceptualized as a four-step process that traverses the present, past, and future. This process accounts for the movement of reality as processes or relations:

- The first step is to analyze the connections between the whole and the parts in the present.
- The second step is to historicize the analysis by examining the preconditions for the most important present-day connections identified in the first step in the context of past contradictions.
- The third step involves projecting the main social contradictions from the past, through the present, to their resolution and beyond into the future.
- Finally, step 4 involves the organization of the actions necessary to achieve the future. This entails returning to the present through the future and examining the present conditions that would facilitate the realization of this future.

Subsequently, this chapter will demonstrate how expansive learning is a collective learning in dialectical thinking. This enables the anticipation of future developments by identifying and analyzing the contradictions inherent in the history of an activity system.

Here, it is crucial to emphasize the importance of dialectical thinking and the necessity of grasping the methodology of ascending from the abstract to the concrete in order to implement a formative intervention. In an interview (Ploettner & Tresseras, 2016), Sannino describes the difficulties involved in adopting this methodological principle:

> One difficulty that many students of activity theory find is the relation between expansive learning and the dialectical method of ascending from the abstract to the concrete [...] This is an important point because in change laboratory interventions aimed at promoting expansive learning what the interventionist does is actually invite the participants to think differently. To think differently about their activity means to think dialectically about their activity. So, in this way formative interventions are formative because they bring participants to acquire a different type of thinking about their work. This is done by mobilizing different theoretical tools without which you could not possibly talk about the Change Laboratory. That is why one must be very careful when initiating a Change Laboratory intervention. A Change Laboratory is not just a method that could be applied by reading a couple of methodological chapters in a book. It has a theoretical background without which the entire intention of promoting expansive learning and dialectical thinking would collapse (Sannino in Ploettner & Tresseras, 2016, pp. 91–92).

In this chapter on formative interventions, we seek to relate expansive learning to the dialectical method of ascending from the abstract to the concrete.

Between Planification and Agency

It is essential that interventionist research and interventionist research methodologies are based on a solid theoretical foundation to ensure effective planning, the selection of appropriate 'mirror data', the development of hypotheses that can be reconciled, and so on. However, if the planning of CL interventions and methodologies is comprehensive, this does not imply that participants do not take an active role in the transformation and expansive learning process.

Nevertheless, while CL interventions and methodologies are meticulously planned, this does not imply that participants do not engage with them and assume control of the process of transformation and expansive learning. As outlined by Engeström, Rantavuori, and Kerosuo (2013), there is a productive gap between the researcher's planning and the operators' implementation. This gap suggests the emergence of transformative agency and the need for negotiation between researcher and participants throughout the intervention. The reality of a CL thus reveals a genuine space for co-construction. As the intervention progresses, participants gradually adopt and create new tools to shape the future of their activity system.

In a critical review article, Sutter (2011) presents two positions regarding the concept of intervention within CHAT. A formative intervention can be conceptualized as an activity (collective, transformative) on another activity (e.g. teaching, prevention, etc.). This distinction allows for the identification of two positions.

The first position reflects only the researchers' support for the activity under analysis. Consequently, in research articles, the research activity itself is not subjected to analysis, and the unit of analysis only considers the supported activity. The second position views research activity through the lens of CHAT's third-generation unit of analysis, which comprises at least two interacting activity systems. In this orientation, the two activity systems establish a new joint hybrid activity, the development project, which aims not only to support the activity of the professionals involved in the CL, but also to support the research activity. While both positions share the idea that researchers and professionals participating in a CL co-construct the development of the target activity system, the second position is also able to highlight the participants' efforts in developing the research activity and transformative methodologies specific to CHAT.

Key Principles of Formative Intervention Methodology

Five principles guide formative interventions. For the sake of brevity, we will not delve into the details of these principles here, as they have been developed throughout the book. However, we believe it is useful to recall them here.

- Firstly, the unit of analysis is object-oriented collective activity systems (Chapter 6).
- Secondly, systemic contradictions are both motives and sources of systemic redesign (Chapter 7).

- Thirdly, members collectively engage in expansive learning actions to design new systems. The researcher's role is not to instruct participants; rather, it is to organize the intervention in a way that supports the definition and traversal of a potential zone for collective activity development (Chapter 8).
- Fourthly, a dialectical method is the key to mastering expansive learning action cycles. This is the method of ascending from the abstract to the concrete, as discussed in this chapter.
- Fifthly, an interventionist methodology is necessary to advance, record, and analyze expansive learning cycles, as discussed in Chapter 7 and this chapter.

Material Organization of the Change Laboratory

The CL method was initially implemented at five post offices in Finland in the late 1990s (Pihlaja, 2005). The typical CL program comprises six to 12 weekly sessions of two to three hours, withup to 20 participants per session.

Prior to the implementation of the CL, there is a phase of ethnography that lasts for an extended period. This phase is not intended for the diagnosis of a problem, but rather for the collection of data that will be used for the CL and the establishment of hypotheses on the presence of systemic contradictions. Figure 30 illustrates a prototype of the spatial organization of the CL (Virkkunen & Newham, 2013). As previously noted, Sutter (2011) identifies to the need to distinguish between two types of activity within developmental interventions: the activity that is the target of transformation, and the joint activity of participants and researchers seeking to transform the target activity. In this context, the CL can be apprehended as a collective activity on a collective activity (Engeström, Sannino, & Virkkunen, 2014).

The CL device is comprised of three sets of three surfaces, each set representing a different area of focus. Vertically, these spaces are organized according to temporality, with the past, present, and future represented. The spaces are also organized horizontally according to different degrees of abstraction and generalization.

The first surface, located on the right side of Figure 30, represents mirror data. The mirror data presented in these scenarios are typically professional situations captured on video, which the participants are required to address. The objective is to provide participants with an understanding of the challenges faced by practitioners and the innovative solutions they have developed to address these challenges. In addition to video images, it is also possible to present excerpts from interviews or discussions, statistics, comments from customers or schoolchildren, and so on. The objective is to encourage reflexivity through the controversies that may arise from the dialogue between CL participants.

The left-hand side of the surface is reserved for theoretical and conceptual instruments. Here, participants are invited to engage with the activity system model as a psychological instrument, enabling them to construct their past and present activity system, to become aware of and analyze the systemic contradictions underlying the recurring problems experienced by participants, and to reconstruct the activity system in order to overcome these contradictions. This is a focus on reflection from a systemic perspective. However, this is not the only tool that will be employed.

The third surface (Ideas, Tools) is reserved for intermediate ideas that may emerge during the discussion. The CL typically commences by comparing mirror data to identify recurring issues (Mirror, Present). The second step is to identify the historical genesis of these problems (Mirror, Past) and collectively construct the past (Model, Past) and present (Model, Present) activity system. At this stage, participants analyze the contradictions present in the activity system that lead to the current recurring problems. The subsequent stage involves the theoretical construction of a prospective activity system, accompanied by the delineation of the local solutions and instruments to be implemented. This stage is characterized by an expansion of the object of activity (Engeström et al., 2003; Murphy, Manzanares, Murphy, & RodriguezManzanares, 2014a, 2014b).

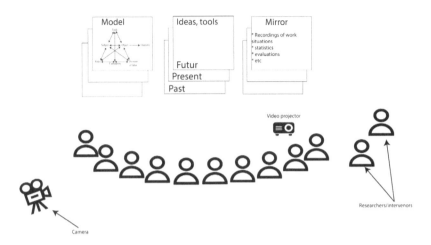

Figure 30: Prototypical model of a Change Laboratory according to Virkkunen and Newham (2013).

As observed by Vilela et al. (2020), the CL method is more akin to a toolkit that can be adapted to suit the specific characteristics of the activity or activity network in question. A few variations can be identified, without fundamentally altering the method or its objectives. For instance, in '*Boundary-Crossing Laboratories*', the unit of analysis encompasses two or more activity systems, whereas the traditional form of CL is conducted within a single activity system. Similarly, if CLs are conducted principally in the workplace, adaptations linked to the COVID-19 pandemic have necessitated an online organization of the method. Some researchers had already utilized this online organization. For instance, in the CL she conducts remotely in the context of higher education, Englund (2018) notes that this form of online organization of the laboratory of change presents no particular limitations in the CL she conducts remotely in the context of higher education.

In the wake of the outbreak of the COVID-19 pandemic, a working group was established to consider the adaptations needed to conduct CL online. This group was led by Brett Blight[24] of Lancaster University and Maria Spante of the Center for Activity Theory at West University in

---

[24] Brett Blight is also the initiator of a website presenting a wealth of resources for conducting a Change Laboratory. https://bureaudechangelab.pubpub.org

Sweden (Spante et al., 2023). CL has also inspired other forms of intervention that claim a filiation. For instance, the Learning Lab initiative spearheaded by Aydin Bal in his decolonial interventionist research (Bal, 2016; Bal et al., 2018; Bal, Kozleski, Schrader, Rodriguez, & Pelton, 2014) is a case in point.

Finally, to support the idea that CL remains an open intervention method, it should be noted that certain adaptations can be implemented that allow participants to be even more involved in the collection of mirror data. For example, participants may be asked to form groups to collect this data, thus replacing the researcher's initial ethnographic work prior to the CL sessions.

Methodological Principles of a Change Laboratory

CL is not solely defined by a material context. It is underpinned by three methodological principles that distinguish it from other approaches and strongly support the way it is conducted by the person or persons involved. To overlook one of these principles is to negate CL's potential to transform one or more activity systems.

The three principles are as follows (Engeström & Sannino, 2014):

• The principle of ascension from the abstract to the concrete.
• The principle of double stimulation.
• The principle of transformative agency.

The following sections will present these three principles in turn, demonstrating their utility in the design and implementation of a CL.

The Principle of Ascending from the Abstract to the Concrete

The first fundamental principle is known as the '*principle of the ascent from the abstract to the concrete*.' The somewhat obscure-sounding name actually refers to the dialectical method itself. This principle is challenging to grasp, yet without it, the CL risks becoming a mere juxtaposition of isolated ideas and problems, analyzed on the basis of disparate data. The CL learning process is expansive and supports the reconceptualization of an entire activity system. This involves redefining and expanding the object of activity.

The dialectical method is centered on conceptualizing the core essence of the object of activity. This framework establishes the ascent from the abstract to the concrete as the core and architecture of expansive learning. Consequently, to achieve mastery of expansive learning, it is essential to master and apply the dialectical method. The principle of ascending from the abstract to the concrete can be presented at first glance as the core of the dialectical method used by Marx in writing '*The Capital*' to investigate a concrete historical object: the capitalist mode of production. For him, this is the most effective method for achieving this goal, whereby abstract determinations lead to a reproduction of the concrete through thought.

The method's ability to study a concrete object in its developmental process made it a valuable tool for activity theorists. Vygotsky, for instance, asserts that psychology must identify its own '*capital*' (Vygotsky, 1997c). Dafermos (2018) notes that in the 1920s, the investigation of the method utilized by Marx was still in its infancy. The debate on dialectics reached its peak in the 1960s, after a period of limited and complex study between the 1930s and 1950s. In the 1950s and 1960s, a new generation of researchers emerged, including Ilyenkov, who demonstrated that thought develops through the ascent from the abstract to the concrete.

In other words, the method of ascending from the abstract to the concrete is a method of conceptualizing a concrete object as an organic whole. The core of the method is the theoretical pursuit of the essence of a phenomenon (for example, in Marx's framework, the capitalist mode of production) through the logical development of its internal contradictions.

This process will be presented into three steps. First, it is important to differentiate this principle from traditional scientific approaches and the use of variables, factors, or determinants. Secondly, we present the dialectical dance between the present, past, and future, and demonstrate how this dialectical dance unfolds in the expansive learning cycle. This will enable us to comprehend how the dialectic undergirds the unfolding of a CL. In a third step, we present the notions of abstraction and concreteness in greater detail to introduce the concept of the '*germ cell*.'

Indifference to the Variables of the Dialectical Method

To introduce the principle of the method of ascending from the abstract to the concrete, it is necessary to distinguish the dialectical method from the traditional methods used in empirical research to produce new knowledge. We will do so with an example provided by Tolman (1999).

Let's suppose that we observe differences in mathematical results distributed by class. It is possible that the actions and attitudes of teachers may be contributing factors in the observed distribution of student performance. Teachers are divided into two groups, as follows. The independent variable in this case is *'lenient'* and *'strict'*. This is the variable whose variations influence the value of the dependent variables. In this example, the dependent variable is mathematical achievement, as measured by standardized tests. The results indicate a statistically significant correlation that explains 60 % of the variance. Having arrived at this result, the researcher believes he has established a truth, i.e. a link between teachers' attitudes and students' mathematical results. However rigorous this procedure may be, it is unable to provide any concrete evidence for the main authors of CHAT. Furthermore, the procedure is unable to provide insight into the dynamic process behind students' mathematical performance. Instead, the researcher began with one abstraction (student mathematical performance) and linked it to another abstraction (teacher attitudes) using statistical methods. To gain a deeper understanding of the underlying dynamics, it is essential to adopt a *'genetic method'*.

To demonstrate this, let's take a second example. A researcher measures the heart rate of a lumberjack. The variation in heart rate is plotted against time, and the diagram indicates the type of task performed by the woodcutter. Three tasks are performed by the logger: felling the tree, delimbing, and piling. The results show statistically significant differences in heart rates according to the type of task performed. The task is significantly more intense for heaping. However, the analysis does not provide insight into the process (of activity) that leads to such a temporal variation in heart rate. For instance, it is unclear why and how the woodcutter alternates between tasks, why he performs the least costly task after the most costly, and what the basis is for his decision to change tasks.

The method of ascending from the abstract aims to account for the concrete processes behind abstractions. The method of ascending from the abstract to the concrete requires a genetic reconstruction that elucidates the dynamics of a process in its concrete form. This reconstruction must identify the connections between abstractions and the real world. Tolman (1999) provides an example of this method in an account of Leontiev's research.

> In a report of research on the development of the learning motive in children, Leontiev gave a very detailed account of how the play motive is transformed into the learning motive during the preschool and early school years. The work depended on (1) a general understanding of the societal structure of activity and its motivation, and of the senses and meanings that goals and motives have for individual children; (2) a clear specification of what was involved in children's learning in school; and (3) information gained from casual conversations with the children, as well as from observing their participation in organized games and their reactions to irregularities in school routine. In some instances, dependent and independent variables are identifiable after the fact, but it is clear that Leont'ev was not thinking in those terms. Large samples and measurement played a role in the studies, but there is no indication that statistical analyses were ever used or needed (Tolman, 1999, p. 78).

The method of ascending from the abstract to the concrete as described by Tolman is notable for its complete indifference to variables, in contrast to traditional analysis procedures. Furthermore, authors of CHAT have developed a critical attitude towards research that employs the variable analysis scheme. In the field of psychology, Veresov (2014) asserts that statistical analyses cannot answer two key questions:

- Does the attribute that is supposed to be measured by a statistical test really exist?
- Do variations in the attribute produce causal variations in the results of the measurement procedure?

Veresov states that it is not possible to prove that one or more different mechanisms underlie the behavior coded as a variable, nor can a causal relationship be proven from the pattern of covariations between variables.

In another field, sociology, Blumer (1956) offered a critical analysis of the limitations of a variable-based approach in sociology. This approach tends to simplify the complexity of human groups by reducing them to variables and their relationships. He identifies several shortcomings, including:

- The absence of limits to what can be called a variable and to their selection by the researcher. Everything or almost everything can be considered a variable, and no rule is likely to establish a limit to the determination of variables.
- The absence of generic variables. Abstract categories are generally culture-specific and localized. Consequently, some variables appear to represent characteristics that may be considered generic (for example, the age variable), yet in reality, they fail to acknowledge the manner in which age can manifest differently in disparate societies and at varying historical periods.

One of the key limitations of a variable-based approach is the assumption that it provides an accurate explanation of processes. However, this fails to account for interpretation processes that are specific to social groups:

> The variables which designate the results or effects of the happenings which play upon the experience of people would be the outcome of the process of interpretation. Present-day variable analysis in our field is dealing predominantly with such kinds of variables. There can be no doubt that, when current variable analysis deals with matters or areas of human group life which involve the process of interpretation, it is markedly disposed to ignore the process. The conventional procedure is to identify something which is presumed to operate on group life and treat it as an independent variable, and then to select some form of group activity as the dependent variable. The independent variable is put at the beginning part of the process of interpretation and the dependent variable at the terminal part of the process. The intervening process is ignored or, what amounts to the same thing, taken for granted as something that need not be considered. [...] This idea that in such areas of group life the independent variable automatically exercises its influence on the dependent variable is, it seems to me, a basic fallacy. There is a process of definition intervening between the events of experience presupposed by the independent variable and the formed behavior represented by the dependent variable (Blumer, 1956, p. 686).

In this critical stance toward the variable-based analysis scheme, the method of ascending from the abstract to the concrete demonstrates the underlying objective: an analysis of concrete processes in their dynamic.

The Dance of Dialectics and Expansive Learning

The method of ascending from the abstract to the concrete is designed to highlight processes in their concrete deployment. However, this is not sufficient to provide an understanding of how the method of ascending from the abstract to the concrete provides the *'transformative'* potential of CLs.

In this second stage of the presentation, we address the idea that a historical approach is necessary to conceptualize an object conceived as a process. This historical approach is of particular importance for conceptualizing social change and envisioning future developments (Dafermos, 2018). It is the foundation of the dialectical method, insofar as dialectics is a way of examining the development of things in their interconnections. However, for CHAT theorists, development is not conceived as a gradual accumulation of qualitative changes, but as a qualitative bifurcation that results from contradictions (see Chapter 9). Consequently, the study of historical phenomena is not merely the examination of their *'stages of development'*. Rather, it entails investigating the process of transition from one stage to another. In other words, it necessitates an investigation of the historicity behind history, or the logic of historical development.

This historical orientation is central to the Vygotskian approach to studying the development of higher psychic functions.

> To study something historically means to study it in the process of change; that is the dialectical method's basic demand. To encompass in research the process of a given thing's development in all its phases and changes – from birth to death – fundamentally means to discover its nature, its essence, for 'It is only in movement that a body shows what it is'. Thus, the historical study of behavior is not an auxiliary aspect of theoretical study, but rather forms its very base (Vygotsky, 1978, pp. 64–65).

The historical method represents the fundamental tenet of CL methodology. In order to develop an activity system, it is essential to comprehend its underlying development logic. Tolman (1999) posits that while variable-based analysis procedures are readily comprehensible and implementable by an undergraduate student, the method of ascending from the abstract to the concrete is considerably more challenging to grasp, given that:

> The principles of the methodology (as distinct from methods and procedures) must be mastered. These cannot be translated into appropriate procedures without experience, intuition, and intelligence, coupled with a sound theoretical understanding of the phenomenon under study. In short, there

are no rules. The very idea of a fixed set of abstract rules violates the concrete conception of the problem (Tolman, 1999, p. 78).

However, we diverge from Tolman's pessimistic assertion that dialectics is a subtle '*art*' to be appropriated. While the method of ascending from the abstract to the concrete is not reduced to a set of rules and procedures, it makes progress through stages that can be described. It can thus be seen as a '*dance with time*', as Ollman (2008) puts it, with four stages that proceed from the present to the past to the future, and then back to the present.

The typical ideal cycle of expansive learning and the seven expansive learning actions represent this dance over time. In expansive learning theory, the reconceptualization of an activity takes place through seven learning actions.

- (1) Question, criticize or reject certain aspects of accepted practice.
- (2) Analyze the situation, through a historical and cultural analysis to explain current practice, but also through a current and systemic analysis to point out contradictions within activity systems.
- (3) Model new relationships within an activity system to overcome the contradictions identified in (2).
- (4) Examine the model, make it work, exploit it and experiment with it, in order to fully grasp its dynamics, potential and limits.
- (5) Implement the model through practical applications, enrichments and conceptual extensions.
- (6) Evaluate/reflect on the process.
- (7) Consolidate the results into a new, stable form of practice.

These expansive learning actions are modeled within a cycle shown in Figure below.

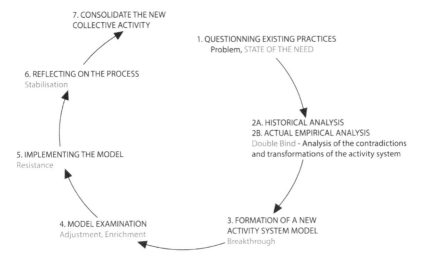

Figure 31: Expansive learning cycle according to Engeström (2015).

This dance with time can be observed in Virkkunen and Newham's (2013) presentation of the utilization of the CL's '*different spaces*' during CL sessions. The figure below provides a simplified representation of such navigation.

	MODELS / VISION	IDEAS / TOOLS	MIRROR
FUTUR	**7** Designing a future activity system ↔	**8** Planning new instruments Designing implementation ↔	**9** Tracking data and identifying needs for new developments
PRESENT	**6** Modeling the main contradictions in the current activity system ↔	**2** Identifying developmental challenges Ideas for future analysis ↔	**1** Example of a problem in participants' practice Video, interviews, etc.
PAST	**5** Analysis of transformations - identification of contradictions	**4** Identifying developmental periods ↔	**3** Data on historical changes in the activity system

Figure 32: Simplified representation of the journey through time using different spaces in a CL, after Virkkunen and Newham (2013, p. 18).

Thus, the realization of an expansive learning cycle within a CL begins in the present (steps 1 and 2), progresses to the past (steps 3, 4, and 5), returns to the present (step 6), then projects into the future (step 7), and searches in the present for the means to realize this future (step 8).

We have formulated the idea that, for Ollman, the dialectical method was a four-step process. The following table illustrates the relationship between Ollman's (2008) four stages and the expansive learning actions. It also indicates the objectives pursued by the analysis at each stage:

Table 12: Relating the stages of the dialectical method according to Ollman (2008) to expansive learning actions.

FOUR STAGES OF DIALECTICS ACCORDING TO OLLMAN (2008) AND TIME PERSPECTIVE	EXPANSIVE LEARNING ACTIONS	OBJECTIVE OF EACH STEP
STEP 1: IS TO ANALYZE THE CONNECTIONS IN THE PRESENT BETWEEN THE WHOLE AND THE PARTS PRESENT	Questioning existing practices	Relate experienced and recurring problems to identify 'developmental challenges' in which the group of participants will engage.
STEP 2: HISTORICIZING ANALYSIS PRESENT ⇒ PAST	Historical analysis	Search for preconditions in terms of contradictions in the past of the most important present connections found in step 1
	Current empirical analysis	Identify the main historically inherited contradictions linked to the problems identified in step 1.
STEP 3: SE PROJETER PRESENT ⇒ FUTURE	Forming a new model	Projecting the main contradictions from the past, through the present to their resolution and beyond into the future.
STEP 4: ORGANIZE FUTURE ⇒PRESENT	Examine the model	To organize, that is, to return to the present through the future,
	Implementing the model	and to look in the present at the preconditions for deploying such a future.

Table 12: Continued

FOUR STAGES OF DIALECTICS ACCORDING TO OLLMAN (2008) AND TIME PERSPECTIVE	EXPANSIVE LEARNING ACTIONS	OBJECTIVE OF EACH STEP
PAST (POST STAGE 4) ⇒ FUTURE	Reflecting on the process	Reflecting on new contradictions between old and new
PRESENT	Consolidating the new practice	Improving and optimizing the various areas of the activity system

The final two stages of this process have a somewhat unique status in that they extend beyond the stages identified in the dialectical method. These expansive learning actions occur in follow-up sessions several months after the conclusion of the analysis and planning period.

Abstract and Concrete in the Dialectical Method

The dialectical method, which involves moving from the abstract to the concrete, is a journey-based investigation that takes place over time. Its purpose is to collectively plan and realize a future that overcomes identified contradictions. However, this presentation does not provide an explanation of the rationale behind the method's name. What is meant by the term 'concrete'? What is meant by the term 'abstract'? Why refer to an ascent from the abstract to the concrete for a dialectical unity?

The first step in understanding this process is to consider the distinction that CHAT researchers make between phenomena and their essence. Time travel is simply a methodology for capturing and investigating the essence of a phenomenon, namely the internal connections of a developing entity. In this regard, Vygotsky, in line with Marx, placed significant importance on the differentiation between phenomenon and essence. This is because the essence of a phenomenon is inherently unobservable and not directly accessible. Against the empiricism that is characteristic of both objective and subjective methods, Vygotsky asserted that:

> If the essence of things and the form of their appearance directly coincided, says Marx [1890/1981 b, p. 825], all science would be superfluous. If in psychology appearance and being were the same, then everybody would be a scientist-psychologist and science would be impossible (Vygotsky, 1997c, p. 325).

This quotation is of great importance for its critical significance. In order to grasp it, it is necessary to immediately bring these categories of essence back to the question of activity and action in the context of CL. Only actions give rise to a concrete experience on which it is possible to make a reflexive return. However, by focusing on what professionals do in a work situation (their actions), we are left with the surface of phenomena, with what we can observe. It is not possible to gain an understanding of the historical essence of the phenomenon that explains the actions of the professionals being observed in the present moment.

In addition to missing the activity and its structure (not observable), it is also impossible to follow or understand the logic behind the development of this activity, which is apprehended at a given time. Even if we were able to observe these professionals over an extended period and attempt to account for changes in their approach, we would still be limited to a surface-level understanding of their behavior. We would be missing the essence of the phenomenon. Both objective and subjective methods used in work analysis prove inadequate for capturing the developmental logic of the phenomenon under study.

In order to observe this development and explain its logic, it is necessary to provoke it (for a similar critique, see Clot, 2000). By distinguishing phenomena from their essence, we have taken a step forward in defining dialectics and the method of ascending from the abstract to the concrete. This is not simply a journey through time; it is the highlighting of the essential relationships of a thing in development and the revelation of its historical origin and the perspectives of its evolution.

Let us now turn our attention to the essence of a phenomenon. Vygotsky introduced the concept of analyzing the essence of the development of higher psychic functions from a critique of the decomposition of a complex whole into separate parts. This critique highlighted the shortcomings of analyzing psychological phenomena into their separate parts, which are studied in isolation. Vygotsky's entire intellectual journey can be understood as the search for a 'germ cell' for psychology and his dissatisfaction with the results obtained (Yasnitsky, 2018). The core of the method of ascending from the abstract to the concrete consists in grasping the essence of a phenomenon by tracing and theoretically reproducing the logic of its development through the emergence and resolution of its internal contradictions. The essence of a concrete object in development is its essential relation.

Dialectics distinguishes two meanings for the notions of 'concrete' and *'abstract'*. In the first sense, the concrete can be understood as the sensory perception of the object, and the abstract as formal reasoning. This prevailing understanding of the categories of abstract and concrete was challenged by Ilyenkov in his 1960 work on the method of ascent from abstract to concrete in Marx's Capital (Ilyenkov, 1982/2008). In a second sense, and following the legacy of Hegel and Marx, he defines the abstract as an incomplete, one-sided reflection of an object in consciousness, as opposed to concrete knowledge as a unity of multiple definitions. Here, real concreteness is not immediate sensible knowledge, and is analyzed by disengaging abstract determinations to conceptually reproduce sensible reality, the starting point of analysis. The method of ascending from the abstract to the concrete begins with the *'real'* concrete and proceeds by means of abstraction (the intellectual activity that breaks the whole down into mental units) to produce a thought concrete (the reconstituted whole). This method allows for the grasping of the movement of things through thought.

Let us briefly explain why thinking dialectically means thinking the concreteness of things in their internal contradiction. The world as it appears to our consciousness is relationship and movement. For instance, when observing a candle burning, it is evident that the candle is not identical to itself over time; it undergoes a process of change and is consumed by the heat of the flame. However, in the process of understanding the world, the concepts that enable us to think about things present the movements between things and their relationship as external to things themselves. The wax of the candle remains wax even after it has been melted. Consequently, abstraction only allows us to represent the essence of a phenomenon as something stable and unchanging. This is the prevailing understanding of the notions of concrete and abstract: the concrete is movement, change, and the sensible; the abstract is the fixed, stable essence of the phenomenon and a phenomenon of the mind.

Dialectical thinking reverses the relationship between thing and relation. If we wish to access the essence of the real concrete, it is necessary to think of the relation as essential and constitutive of the thing itself:

> Everything is itself a relation, not externally, but within itself, not fortuitously in appearance, but necessarily in its essence. In other words, relation is not simply an external relationship between things, it is difference within identity, duality within unity, internal contradiction. And this is the starting point for the conception of concrete reality (Sève, 1980, p. 69).

This definition is of great importance, as Ilyenkov's (1982/2008) concrete refers to the theoretical representation of a developing object. In contrast, the abstract is something partial, removed from its concrete relationships and its concrete whole. For instance, in the study of home care conducted by Engeström, Nummijoki, and Sannino (2012), the abstraction of elderly people's physical mobility was concretized in a movement consisting of getting up from the chair without support. This movement represents a resolution of the contradiction between safety (the risk of falling when the elderly person remains physically active) and autonomy (the need to remain physically active in order to remain autonomous). We will revisit this example with the concept of *'germ cell'* later in the discussion. As Sève (1980) notes, dialectical thinking entails not limiting oneself to the representation of abstract entities with their properties considered fixed. Dialectical thinking entails considering the constitutive relationships of each entity within its logic of development.

> The substitution of an analysis of contradictory relationships for a simple abstraction of things in all contexts represents a claim to knowledge that purports to be scientific in the dialectical sense of the term [...] In this manner, the concrete, the unity of diversity, can be genuinely attained, and the fundamental notion that the world must not be regarded as a complex of completed entities but as a complex of processes can be implemented (Sève, 1980, pp. 70–71).

Ilyenkov's ideas exerted a profound influence on the activity theorists of his era (Bakhurst, 2019). These included Leontiev, of course, but also Davydov, who advanced the concept of the ascent from the abstract to the concrete in the domains of psychology and pedagogy[25]. Among Davydov's important contributions is the distinction between empirical thinking and theoretical generalization (Davydov, 1990b). This distinction is based on a critique of empiricism in the field of traditional education.

In his essay on the principles of generalization and conceptualization, Davydov seeks to account for the conceptualization processes involved in designing training curricula (Davydov, 1990b). Building upon Ilyenkov's work, the ascent from the abstract to the concrete refers to the

---

[25] Davydov began his research under the guidance of Galperine. In collaboration with Elkonin, he devised an educational research program in the 1960s, which

method of forming concepts or '*thought concreteness*'. It is important to clarify what Davydov (and Ilyenkov) means by a concept.

A concept is not a general notion whose definition can be considered satisfactory. The content of a concept is not, and cannot be, a definition that characterizes the fixed properties of a thing (sense 2 of the abstract). Instead, it is the exposition of the thing's relationships and contradictions (sense 2 of the concrete). A concept has the capacity to generate novel ideas, rather than being reduced to a simplistic definition (in Ilyenkov's sense). In this sense, a concept captures the genesis or essence of a phenomenon in the internal relationships that set the phenomenon in motion. Vygotski (2014) illustrates such a process with the steam engine.

> The fundamental process of the steam engine, as conceived in the drawings of its inventor, differs significantly from the processes observed in particular steam engines. The system of steam power utilization is therefore based on the discovery of a very simple relationship, which was then understood and modeled into different variations. However, analysis has shown that in the steam engine, the fundamental process does not appear in a pure state, but is masked by all kinds of secondary processes. When the circumstances ancillary to the main process were eliminated and an ideal steam engine was constructed, the researcher encountered the mechanical equivalent of heat. This illustrates the power of abstraction, which presents the process to be examined in its pure, independent, and uncovered state (Vygotski, 2014, p. 189).

Forming a concept therefore involves identifying the germ cell that contains the principal contradiction from which it will develop. In this sense, a concept is generative only when it is understood as a process that takes us from the contradictory, abstract germ cell to its concrete manifestations. For Ilyenkov (1982/2008):

> Every concept (if it is really a well-developed concept and not merely a verbally fixed general notion) is therefore a concrete abstraction, however contradictory that may sound from the standpoint of old logic (Ilyenkov, 1982/2008, p. 60).

The concept of pesticides (Levins & Lewontin, 1985) can be employed as a second example of a concept to illustrate the idea of the '*germ cell*' as a

---

challenged the prevailing model of empirical knowledge transmission in traditional schools.

concrete form of a concept. Pesticides are both a chemical substance that travels through the environment and poisons living things (especially pests), and a commodity produced and sold for profit. This contradictory dimension inherent in the pesticide concept explains the development of production. For instance, a pesticide must:

- Constitute a poison at recommended dosages.
- Be soluble so that it can be sprayed on fields.
- Not to be too persistent, to avoid complaints and increase profit levels. In this sense, it is in the interest of manufacturers to develop more toxic but less persistent products.

The process of concept formation is not solely the domain of thought or scientific work. Concepts are formed and embedded in everyday life, particularly in productive work. In other words, everyone constructs concepts on a daily basis (Engeström, 2020b). However, following Davydov, it is necessary to distinguish between empirical and theoretical thinking. Empirical thinking is pre-theoretical in that it differentiates and classifies phenomena but does not penetrate the essence of phenomena by uncovering the concrete form in germ-cell form. Categories are employed to transform a problem into a closed phenomenon that can be registered, calculated, and postponed rather than transformed. In contrast, theoretical thinking is about organizing the chaos of reality into a well-defined framework, that of a category that is already known, stabilized, decontextualized, and abstract (Engeström, 2007a). Unlike empirical thinking, theoretical thinking, as defined by Davydov, is fundamental to solving practical problems:

> In Davydov's theory of the formation of theoretical concepts, the initial problem situation or task represents a diffuse sensory concreteness. It is manipulated and transformed – experimented with – to find its basic explanatory relationship or germ cell, which will be represented with the help of a model. These actions of transformation and modeling involve tracing the origin and genesis of the problem. The model itself is examined and used to generate and solve further problems. This enrichment and diversification of the abstract model leads to the ascending to the concrete, that is, to a conceptually mastered systemic concreteness that opens up possibilities for development and innovation (Engeström, 2020a, p. 35).

In the context of a CL, the method of ascending from the abstract to the concrete enables professionals to grasp the essence of an object (and therefore of a activity system, insofar as it is the object that defines the activity system) by tracing and theoretically reproducing the logic of its historical development through the resolution of its internal contradictions. A new idea or theoretical concept is initially produced in the form of a simple, explanatory relationship: a germ cell.

During the expansive learning cycle, the initial abstract relationship is transformed into a complex object, a new form of practice. Thus, within a CL, theoretical generalization requires experimentation and analysis of problematic situations (mirror, present) in order to identify the germ cell behind them. In this context, CL participants seek to identify the mechanisms that generate the problematic phenomena they encounter in their day-to-day work, i.e. the contradictions. The discovery of this generative principle then enables them to identify new possibilities for overcoming them, by redesigning a new activity system around a larger object.

The seven actions of the expansive learning cycle within CL structure the principle of conceptualizing the real concrete. Moreover, this cycle of ascent from the abstract to the concrete bears resemblance to the epistemic actions proposed by Davydov in his work. However, there are notable differences. For Davydov, conceptualization primarily serves to acquire well-defined cultural content. In contrast, for Engeström, conceptualization is primarily employed to construct new cultural practices:

> The actions of an expansive cycle bear a close resemblance to the six learning actions put forward by Davydov (2008). Davydov's theory is, however, oriented at learning activity within the confines of a classroom where the curricular contents are determined ahead of time by more knowledgeable adults. This probably explains why it does not contain the first action of critical questioning and rejection, and why the fifth and seventh actions, implementing and consolidating, are replaced by 'constructing a system of particular tasks' and 'evaluating' – actions that do not imply the construction of actual culturally novel practices (Engeström, 2020a, p. 37).

The Identification of a Germ Cell as a Product of the Ascent from the Abstract to the Concrete

As previously stated, identifying the germ cell represents the initial step in the generation of a new concept for a new activity. The defining characteristics of a germ cell, as outlined by Engeström (2020a), are as follows:

- The germ cell is the most basic unit that encapsulates the characteristics of the entire system. This concept is also supported by

Vygotski (1987), who posits that the meaning of a word is a unit that contains the properties of verbal thought and reflects the unity of thought and speech in its simplest form. For Vygotsky, this basic unit, which is a living and indivisible part of the whole, is the meaning of the word.

- In order to represent the general properties of the complex totality in the simplest form, the germ cell must contain a fundamental contradiction. This is what gives the concept its dynamic dimension, i.e. it can be thought of as a process rather than a fixed thing (as is the case with Davydov's empirical thinking).

- The germ cell is generally little investigated, as it often goes unnoticed in practice. The fact that it remains unnoticed refers to the fact that access to this germ cell implies a theoretical examination, insofar as the germ cell is hidden by the appearance of things.

- The germ cell opens up prospects for multiple applications, extensions, and future developments. Rather than a definition that locks the object into a fixed categorization, the germ cell opens up new possibilities by conceiving the concrete object in motion, its very development.

The germ cell is not an entity in itself, but rather a concept that enables us to account for the generative character of the concept. It is not merely a concept that exists in words and representations; it is embedded in practices. The following three examples of the germ cell are based on research and/or various interventions.

The first example is an analysis of expansive learning within an ecological agricultural cooperative on the outskirts of Helsinki. The cooperative, established in 2011, leases fields in the Helsinki suburbs and employs salaried farmers to cultivate organic fruit and vegetables, which are subsequently sold and distributed to members. Despite its growing popularity, the cooperative's financial stability is uncertain, necessitating the recruitment of new members to ensure financial sustainability. However, this necessity for growth is a source of significant concern for the management committee, as it consistently generates considerable stress when it comes to securing the future. Over the course of 27 meetings, the members of the management committee developed a new concept based on the identification of a contradiction between two key elements: (1) the need to recruit ever more members to ensure the cooperative's financial sustainability, and (2) the cooperative concept and the original idea, which simply involved producing healthy food without stress. This contradiction between financial sustainability and the original cooperative concept generates a motive conflict between recruiting more and more members on the one hand and leaving the competition on the other. This conflict of motives was resolved within the management committee by the decision to limit the number of members to 200 and by the development of a concept: expansive degrowth. This concept refers to the desire to limit the growth of the cooperative, while at the same time taking action to expand, promote, and enable the establishment of new cooperatives based on the same model.

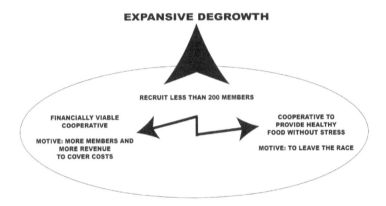

Figure 33: The germ cell in an agricultural cooperative and the formation of the concept of expansive degrowth.

In the formative intervention conducted by Engeström, Nummijoki, and Sannino (2012) with home care assistants in the Helsinki municipality, a concept emerges in the CL aimed at developing the idea of patient mobility that the home care assistants wish to integrate into their practice. This germ cell represents a contradiction between two motives: safety and autonomy. In the lives of the elderly, this contradiction is illustrated in the actions of getting out of one's chair. On the one hand, the fear of falling and the desire for safety prompt them to utilize furniture as a readily available aid. While this solution offers the advantage of making their actions easier, it also has the disadvantage of making them dependent on help. Conversely, the desire to maintain a certain degree of autonomy may result in the elderly refraining from using the furniture.

This situation presents a more challenging and higher-risk scenario, but it offers the advantage of enabling the elderly to maintain a certain degree of autonomy by integrating physical exercise into their normal routine.

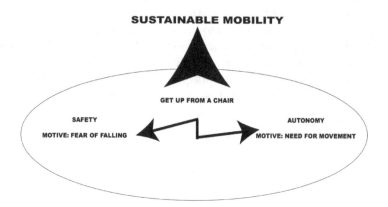

Figure 34: The germ cell of the concept of sustainable mobility in the elderly according to (Engeström, Nummijoki, & Sannino, 2012).

The ascent from the abstract to the concrete is the discovery of the mechanism that generates the movement of concrete reality. Engeström, Nummijoki, and Sannino (2012, p. 292), the most demanding criterion of a germ cell is that it must carry in itself the foundational contradiction of the complex whole.

The Principle of Double Stimulation

If the principle of ascending from the abstract to the concrete is the *structuring principle* of a change laboratory, then the principle of double stimulation is its *energetic principle*, so to speak.

The design of the tasks proposed by the facilitator at each stage in the process of moving from the abstract to the concrete can be considered an *application* of the double-stimulation method derived from the work of Vygotsky (Engeström, 2007b). While Hopwood and Gottschalk (2017) distinguish between three distinct applications of the principle of double stimulation (i.e. a common practice for controlling one's behavior in everyday life; an experimental method; and a central principle in formative approaches, including CL), it can be seen as a key explanatory principle of voluntary action. Sannino and Engeström (2016, p. 60), argue that '*If we ignore the conflict of motives and the voluntarist aspect, double stimulation is easily reduced to just another term referring to the general notion of mediation*'. This warning is of great importance if we are to understand the method and not reduce it to collective reflection guided by the use of artifacts designed by an intervenor.

In essence, the principle of double stimulation encapsulates the mechanism by which humans can emerge from a meaningless situation by transforming it. It refers to the process by which an individual mobilizes an artifact to control their own behavior. Double stimulation commences with a conflict of motives and is resolved by voluntary action (Thorne, 2015). The principle itself thus refers to the mechanism by which human beings can intentionally get out of a conflictual situation by transforming their situation or solving difficult problems. One example of double stimulation is counting to three to resolve the conflict between the desire to sleep and the desire to wake up. In this example, there is a conflict between two motives: (a) The subject must get up. (b) The subject does not want to get up. The subject controls the situation through the use of an auxiliary stimulus (counting to three) to give rise to the voluntary action (getting up).

Vygotsky's Instrumental Method or Double Stimulation

The principle of double stimulation is the foundation of the Vygotskian method. This method is sometimes referred to as the instrumental method or the genetic method (Stetsenko, 2016b) notes that the term '*double stimulation*' is outdated due to its behaviorist associations. Nevertheless, the designation is currently employed by researchers engaged in this process (Donatelli, Vilela, Querol, & Gemma, 2020; Engeström, 2007b; Engeström et al., 2015; Hopwood & Gottschalk, 2017; Junior et al., 2023; Moffitt & Bligh, 2021; Morselli & Sannino, 2021; Nuttall, 2022; Ritella & Hakkarainen, 2012; Sannino, 2015a, 2015b, 2016; Sannino & Laitinen, 2015; Vänninen et al., 2021; Virkkunen & Ristimaki, 2012), we have chosen to retain this designation.

In Sève (2014, p. 31), the double-stimulation method is described as '*the pinnacle of the experimental philosophy*' of Vygotsky and his colleagues. The method involves presenting a first series of stimuli, which are then followed by a second series. This second series makes it difficult for the child to make a choice, thereby breaking down the moments of the voluntary act and revealing its internal structure.

What, then, is the originality of the experimental approach developed by Vygotsky and his colleagues? Vygotski (2014) defines all higher psychic functions as mediated psychic phenomena in that they mobilize psychological instruments. In contrast to behaviorism or reflexology, the unit of analysis cannot be the link between a stimulus (A) and a behavioral response (B). Instead, it is the triadic relationship between a stimulus (A), a psychological instrument (I), and a behavioral response.

This framework guides the development of an experimental method that introduces a second series of stimuli into the experiment to study the genesis of higher psychic functions. Vygotsky provides an illustrative example of this procedure in his analysis of the mediated processes of attention (2014, pp. 372–373), citing an experiment attributed to Leontiev. In this experiment, the experimenter engages in a question-and-answer game with the child, employing a series of pledges and prohibitions, such as *'neither yes nor no; do not name white or black'*. The experimenter poses questions that imply the type of response that is prohibited. In this context, it is possible to provide an answer, but this requires significant focus and self-control on the part of the child. It is not feasible for an 8- to 9-year-old to complete this task without error. However, the introduction by the experimenter of a second stimulus in the form of a card significantly alters the experiment. *'The child is suddenly provided with external auxiliary means to solve the internal task – that is, concentrating and stretching his attention – and passes from immediate to mediated attention'* (p. 373).

Vygotsky (1978) describes the general structure and function of the double-stimulation method as follows:

> Our approach to the study of these processes is to use what we call the functional method of double stimulation. The task facing the child in the experimental context is, as a rule, beyond his present capabilities and cannot be solved by existing skills. In such cases a neutral object is placed near the child, and frequently we are able to observe how the neutral stimulus is drawn into the situation and takes on the function of a sign. Thus, the child actively incorporates these neutral objects into the task of problem solving. We might say that when difficulties arise, neutral stimuli take on the function of a sign and from that point on the operation's structure assumes an essentially different character. By using this, approach, we do not limit ourselves to the usual method of offering the subject simple stimuli to which

we expect a direct response. Rather, we simultaneously offer a second series of stimuli that have a special function. In this way, we are able to study the process of accomplishing a task by the aid of specific auxiliary means; thus we are also able to discover the inner structure and development of the higher psychological processes (Vygotsky, 1978, p. 64).

Vygotsky posits that a second stimulus may serve as a sign, thereby mediating higher psychological functions. In this capacity, they become means, psychological instruments aimed at controlling internal behavior. Vygotski (2014, p. 572) notes that *'this is why every tool is immediately a stimulus: if it were not a stimulus, if in other words it did not possess the capacity to influence behavior, it could not be a tool either'*. It is not always the case that the experimenter provides these tools; in some instances, the subject is responsible for actively constructing them. Ultimately, any *'sign'* can become a means of controlling higher psychic processes, and it proves to be *'less predetermined'* than the working tool.

Engeström (2007b) provides an illustrative example of the construction of a second stimulus through academic cheating. In preparation for an examination, students must devise methods for formulating responses to examination questions (Stimulus 1). This is achieved through the creation of a cheat sheet (Stimulus 2), which must possess two essential characteristics: it must be sufficiently compact to evade detection by the examination proctor, and its content must be meticulously selected to represent the most crucial and essential elements for answering the examination questions. Once the cheat sheet has been constructed effectively, the final phase is relatively straightforward: a simple word allows students to picture a complex concept. At the same time, constructing the cheat sheet represents an act of agency that goes beyond the limits of what the system allows. In light of this, it is evident that Vygotsky's methodological approach is distinguished by the integration of participants' agency into the experimental protocol.

How Double Stimulation Engages Volition: The Waiting Experiment

The initial importance of double stimulation lies not, contrary to the most common interpretation, in the development of skills or the improvement of the problem-solving process. Rather it lies in the formation of willpower (Sannino & Engeström, 2023). This dimension is particularly highlighted in the experience of waiting, which Vygotsky considers the paradigmatic example of his method. This waiting experiment is attributed to Lewin by Vygotsky, but was actually carried out by Lewin's student Dumbo, under conditions quite different from those described by Lewin and Vygotsky. A recent article by Sannino and Engeström (2023) gives a detailed account of the discrepancies between Vygotsky, Lewin and Dumbo's experiment.

In the waiting experiment described by Vygotsky, an experimenter brings a subject into an empty room and then leaves them to wait. In a state of confusion, the subject enters a state of indecision. A conflict emerges between the subjects' desire to wait for the experimenter's return and their need to leave. Vygotsky observed that virtually all subjects sought external cues to help them regulate their behavior. For instance, a subject might utilize their watch to determine an appropriate time to leave, based on the position of the hands. This example is paradigmatic in that it enables Vygotsky to account for the emergence of willpower.

> The person, using the power of things or stimuli, controls his own behavior through them, grouping them, putting them together, sorting them. In other words, the great uniqueness of the will consists of man having no power over his own behavior other than the power that things have over his behavior. But man, subjects to himself the power of things over behavior, makes them serve his own purposes and controls that power as he wants. He changes the environment with the external activity and in this way affects his own behavior, subjecting it to his own authority (Vygotsky, 1997c, p. 212).

In other words, investigations that employ the principle of double stimulation always rely on the subject's willingness and agency, with the aim of facilitating and making visible the subject's volitional action (Sannino & Engeström, 2023). It should be noted that Vygotsky never conducted this experiment, and Lewin's student Dumbo did so under slightly different conditions and with different aims. Dumbo sought to capture the emotions and anger of the participants. Furthermore, in her experiment, she remained in the room and observed the subject's reactions, maintaining visual contact with the subject while refraining from responding to him.

In any case, the key aspect of the double stimulation process is the underlying motive conflict in the use of an artifact to control one's own behavior. Building on the insights of Vygotskian theory, Sannino (2015b) has developed a model to account for the various stages of the process. This model comprises two stages, designated T1 and T2. The first stage, T1, encompasses four phases and corresponds to the moment of decision formation. The four phases are as follows:

- 1. Stimulus conflict
- 2. Motive conflict
- 3. Conversion of a stimulus into an auxiliary pattern
- 4. Closure

In the waiting experiment, phase 1 corresponds to a conflict between two stimuli: on the one hand, being asked to wait; on the other, finding oneself in an empty room. In phase 2, the stimulus conflict is converted into a motive conflict, for example, '*wait*' or '*leave the room.*' It is important to note that phase 3 is of particular importance in this first phase. This is the conversion of a stimulus into an auxiliary pattern. For instance, the hands of a watch can be converted into the motif of leaving the room from a specific position of the hands. In the case of the waiting experiment, phase 4a commences when the hands reach the position specified by the subject. This is the phase during which the stimulus and the auxiliary pattern are in direct opposition. Phase 4b represents the termination of the connection between the stimulus and the auxiliary pattern. Finally, stage 2 corresponds to the quasi-automatic implementation of the conditioned response.

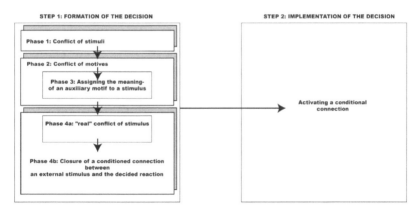

Figure 35: Double stimulation model after Sannino and Laitinen (2015).

Sannino and Laitinen (2015) sought to replicate this experiment with 25 individuals (Experiment 1) and then Sannino (2016) conducted it with collectives (Experiment 2). In Experiment 1, participants were escorted to a room with a one-way mirror and informed that the experiment was about to commence. While awaiting further instructions, the subjects were observed by the experimenters through the one-way mirror and recorded on video. The experiment was terminated after 30 minutes, unless the participant chose to leave the room before then. The waiting period was followed by an interview that combined stimulated recall and a semi-directed interview to allow the subject to externalize their thoughts. In their experiment, 56 % of participants (14 cases) demonstrated full compliance with the model developed by Sannino (2015b). The nine cases that did not present all the phases were due to the participants' decision to remain in the room for a duration exceeding the experiment itself, which was more than 30 minutes. In accordance with Vygotsky's example, the participants set a time limit. It is noteworthy that in five instances, the second stimulus utilized by the participants was introduced by them and was not part of the experimental setup. For instance, one participant had brought a cup of coffee and decided to finish it before leaving. Another participant consulted his diary and commenced reading an article. He informed himself that he would complete the article and then depart. Another participant was writing a list of items to purchase.

The model proposed by Sannino (2015b) builds upon Vygotsky's model. While the latter focused solely on data from the experimental setting, the results demonstrate that activities to be performed outside the experimental setting are involved in the movement and transitions between the different phases. Consequently, the transitions between the different phases of the model must be considered in the context of the broader environment that subjects bring to the experimental situation. For instance, the act of remaining stationary is not necessarily indicative of compliance with the experiment. Rather, it is a method of allowing participants to complete a task that they had previously planned to perform.

In Experiment B, Sannino (2016) attempted to replicate the experiment with collectives, thereby attempting to go beyond the individual orientation. The experiment was conducted with seven collectives of three or four participants, none of whom were acquainted with one another prior to the experiment. The results indicate that the model validated with individuals (Experiment A) is less effective with collectives. Despite the presence of phases 1 (stimulus collision) and 2 (motive conflict), the adoption and pursuit of second stimuli (phase 3 and subsequent phases of the model) were infrequent. The collective configuration impeded individual efforts to overcome motive conflicts and pursue second stimuli.

These results may initially appear to present challenges to the implementation of the double-stimulus method in a collective learning (CL) setting with collectives. However, this is not the case. The double-stimulation method provides the necessary experimental structure to identify the history of higher psychic functions. In this type of experiment, subjects are always exposed to stimuli that the experimenter cannot control externally. It may seem paradoxical, but the experimental situation can trigger, but never produce, the subject's psychological phenomena. In this context, the key aspect of a CL process is the manner in which participants challenge the framework initially set by the facilitator.

Transformative Agency

As previously stated, the waiting experiment is significantly distinct from conventional experimental studies of human behavior. In this experiment, the locus of control is largely shifted from the researchers to the participants. This experiment enables us to observe how participants initiate and progress through their actions. The experiment also tests the foundations of Vygotsky's theoretical and methodological ideas regarding the emergence of volitional action through the use of double stimulation.

The principle of double stimulation demonstrates how an individual can gain the power to mobilize external resources to determine their own behavior. This principle is presented as a key factor in enabling humans to transform both the world around them and themselves (Sannino, 2015b). Furthermore, it is the central epistemological principle of an activity approach, in that humans create or utilize instruments to determine their own activities. In this context, the key term refers to agency, which is defined as breaking with a given frame of action and taking the initiative to transform it. This notion of agency is central to the experiences of expectation that we have described.

When this notion of agency is applied to collectives seeking to transform their activity, we refer to it as transformative agency. In the context of a collective learning (CL) initiative, it refers to the initiative necessary for a collective to take the initiative in transforming its activity system. The double stimulation method supports transformative agency, which signals the quality of expansive learning within a CL (Sannino et al., 2016). In this context, differences in the intervenor's initiatives or suggestions are not a negative factor. In fact, they are productive deviations that indicate the presence of transformative agency. Therefore, any initiative taken by the participants in relation to the framework proposed by the facilitator should be encouraged and supported.

The Change Laboratory Versus Some Intervention Principles

The objective of this section is not to critique alternative approaches to intervention; rather, it aims to highlight three key principles in the design of a CL. These three principles can be summarized as follows:

The following principles should be considered when designing a CL:

- Putting a reflexive and a systemic vision into tension, and not just reflexively analyzing their practice.
- Enabling participants to reconceptualize the object of their activity, and not just highlighting and responding to problems.
- Fostering heterogeneity of viewpoints, rather than relying on a principle of subsidiarity.

Reflexivity Versus Ascent from Abstract to Concrete

CL is based on methods that distance it from a straightforward discussion of work-related issues and mobilize reflexivity. In this respect, it cannot be confused with '*work-related discussion space*' for a number of reasons (for a presentation see for example Rocha, Mollo, & Daniellou, 2017). First, in reflective practice, professionals are led to discuss their actions on the basis of methods that solicit their reflexivity. A number of methods have made it possible to use the reflexive nature of intentional action to examine the work done in work situations. We're thinking in particular of the methods of elicitation interview (Vermersch,

2000) and self-confrontation (Mollo & Falzon, 2004; Theureau, 2010) which are explicitly based on an empirical phenomenological approach (Poizat, Flandin, & Theureau, 2022; Vermersch, 1999). The aim of these methods is to provide an account of the action performed by describing the phenomena of consciousness and experience, relying on techniques designed to put past experience into words. Unlike CL, the unit of analysis remains the situation for the actor, who analyzes his own action on the basis of his traces, and not the activity system, which is the historical and cultural context of the situation described reflexively.

The use of reflexive methods is not only a way of analyzing the knowledge and know-how of actors, but also a tool used by professionals to learn from their practice. However, the concept of reflexivity is one that focuses on the present of action. It involves the use of techniques to bring a past moment to life in order to describe in detail the course of a completed action. In this way, the concept of reflexivity temporally embraces issues of learning in the present from the past.

Paraphrasing Vianna and Stetsenko (2014, p. 576), we could say that CL differs from reflexive methods in that its goal is to intervene in the status quo by providing access to cultural tools that enable participants to create their future in a society that must itself be created, rather than simply reproduced or adapted. Reflexive methods tend to lock learning and development into the situation, and their premise that development and learning are rooted in experiential presence in the world is thus not free of connotations of adaptation to the status quo. In this sense, the notions of reflexivity, situated action, or community of practice *'require further critical elaboration to more resolutely break away from the idea that individuals need to adapt to what is "given" in the present in order to develop and learn'* (Vianna & Stetsenko, 2014, p. 579). In the context of research, notions of learning within a community of practice do not entirely eliminate the idea of adaptation to the status quo. Nor does it seem adequate to account for learning in a world of constant change and transformation. The main premise of a CL is that development and learning occur through the collective contribution to the transformation of communities of practice (Hefetz & Ben-Zvi, 2020).

When learning and development are linked to the transformation of community practices, they are radically future-oriented. However, the notion of reflexivity has the disadvantage of being directed towards the present of a situation (admittedly past) but relived. The notion of reflexivity, and its grounding in experience and the work situation, does not allow us to really address the historical causes underlying present actions. Nor does it allow us to develop a forward-looking vision on the basis of the historical contradictions highlighted. Nor do they allow us to re-elaborate the present on the basis of a projected world (or activity system).

While it may seem that reflexive methods and the change laboratory are at odds, this is not the case. CL relies on reflexive methods and confrontation with the traces of actions in work situations as a first stage in the discussion of practices. However, if we stop at this stage, we run the risk of slipping into a problem solving or continuous improvement method, without any real change or transformation of an activity system.

It is this vision of a form of adaptation (of work situations) to man, or vice versa, of adaptation of man to the situation that needs to be overcome within a CL. Based on the methodological principles of ascending from the abstract to the concrete and of double stimulation, learning and development can be seen as creative and collaborative processes of participants acting together to transform their activity system with the help of invented cultural supports and mediators. Let's emphasize again the articulation between experiential and systemic points of view that the tools make possible in this process of moving from the abstract to the concrete.

CL can thus be understood as a collective journey through the zone of proximal development. This zone of proximal development, an important concept in Vygotsky, has been redefined by Engeström (2015, p. 138) as '*the distance between the current everyday actions of individuals and the historically new form of social activity that can be collectively generated as a solution to the double constraint potentially embedded in everyday actions*'. The Figure below shows this zone of development and the historically evolved form of societal activity that is the goal of a CL.

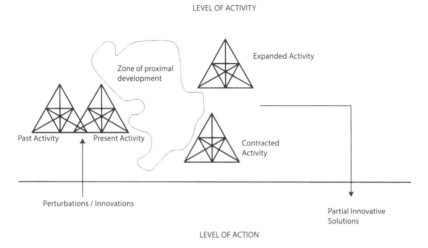

Figure 36: Establishing a zone of proximal development in intervention from Engeström (2001).

In other words, and to use an analogy in the form of a condensed slogan, where certain intervention approaches that focus on issues of participation, reflexivity and learning from situations suggest *'that it is possible to improve the world'*, CL and formative interventions could be based on the slogan *'that another collectively constructed world is possible'*. CL is about actually building the future of one or more activity systems. CL opposes a reformist vision, or in Gramsci's words, a transformist perspective as opposed to a transformative perspective (Avis, 2009).

Improving Versus Transforming an Activity System

The development of activity systems generated by this expansive learning cannot be anticipated. In this respect, CL represents an intervention approach that departs from a standard linear conception in which goals are determined in advance by those involved. In this respect, CL is the antithesis of *'change management'* approaches to transforming organizations through top-down approaches (Virkkunen, 2007).

In Figure below, adapted from Virkkunen (2007), four forms of intervention are distinguished: vertically, interventions aimed at improving the activity without transforming the object, and interventions aimed at qualitatively transforming the very object of the activity; horizontally, interventions carried out by experts in charge of diagnosing and leading change are distinguished from interventions carried out on the basis of an open transformation process based on the very learning process carried out by the participants. CL is located in the upper right quadrant.

Based on the concept of reflexivity and taking the work situation as the unit of analysis, some intervention approaches can only focus on local problems, confusing symptoms with historically inherited systemic causes, i.e. contradictions. They cannot imagine a process of reconceptualization of the object of activity and the subsequent redefinition of an activity system.

Finally, CL is a departure from intervention approaches in which the process is guided by experts. Instead, the process is primarily led by participants, making transformative agency the main criterion of intervention quality (Sannino et al. 2016).

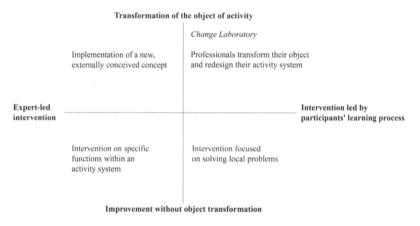

Figure 37: Different forms of intervention, according to Virkkunen (2007).

The Principle of Subsidiarity Versus Polyphony of the Object of Activity

Based on the premise that a work organization that allows for individual and collective regulation through work-related discussion space is likely to limit psychosocial risks, a number of studies have suggested that the principle of subsidiarity is fundamental to the implementation of an intervention. This principle suggests not doing at a given hierarchical level what can be done more effectively at a lower level.

There is then a risk of amplifying psychosocial risks, as indirectly illustrated by Launis and Pihlaja's (2007a, 2007b) intervention on stress. Using CHAT and CL (Launis & Pihlaja, 2007a, 2007b) show that it's not only the increase in workload that generates stress, but also regular changes in work organization and synchronicities in change processes that generate malaise and stress at work by creating local disturbances and recurring problems. These asynchronisms are defined as differences in the development of objects that guide collective activity at each hierarchical level of the company. In their intervention, the professionals worked with the health and safety departments and researchers to develop a new production system based on partnership. However, the entire division of labor was not represented. In a way, the intervention followed the principle of subsidiarity. The model developed by the CL participants therefore had to be accepted by managers before it could be implemented. The authors note that:

> In order to be implemented, this model first had to be accepted by managers, but in 2003 it was in line with management policy. In 2004, however, the center's management decided to reorganize services into three independent production lines: catering, building maintenance, and cleaning. This line organization represented a return to a classic mass service organization and caused frustration among team members: 'It's better if we just do our daily work. I knew from the beginning of the project that they didn't want to implement the workers' ideas' (team member, 2003) (Launis & Pihlaja, 2007a, p. 96).

Most of the asynchronies identified by the authors are vertical asynchronies, due to the fact that each level of the work organization operates with partially different concepts or objects. In this context, and the example illustrates this well, the principle of subsidiarity adopted in certain interventions needs to be discussed for at least two reasons:

- It is likely to generate vertical asynchronies and forms of frustration when solutions generated at one level are not accepted at another.
- It is a particularly conservative principle in that it does not allow for collective discussion of the vertical division of labor.

In this context, the composition of CL participants must take into account the diversity of viewpoints in the vertical division of labor. This observation opens up new challenges for the consideration of power and authority relations within these CLs (Lémonie et al., 2021). Thus, within the CLs, and against this principle of subsidiarity, it is necessary to build a heterogeneous collective that reflects the division of labor, in order to put into work the plural and heterogeneous dimension of the relationship with the object of the activity system.

Key Tasks and Artifacts in a Change Laboratory

In CL, the process of moving from the abstract to the concrete is instrumented by artifacts. It is possible to distinguish seven key artifacts commonly used within a CL. Thus, while the activity system is usually presented as '*a cognitive instrument*' (Yvon, 2015) mobilized within CL to enable the analysis of an activity, it is ultimately far from being the only artifact used. The seven artifacts classically used are:

- Mirror data.
- Historical wall.
- The model of an expansive learning cycle.
- Activity system model.
- The model of the zone of proximal development.
- The emerging model of a new activity in the form of a germ cell.
- Planning sheets in the form of Gantt charts, for example.

These various artifacts are summarized in the following table (Table 12), together with their functions in the expansive learning process.

Table 13: Different artifacts used in a Change Laboratory and their function in the expansive learning process.

ARTIFACT	REPRESENTATION	USE IN THE EXPANSIVE LEARNING CYCLE	FUNCTION IN THE PROCESS
MIRROR DATA	[26]	QUESTIONING PRACTICES	Document the symptoms of contradictions. Serve as a first stimulus.
HISTORIC WALL		HISTORICAL ANALYSIS	Identify the developmental periods of the activity system. Explore the contradictions involved in moving from one period to another.
EXPANSIVE LEARNING CYCLE MODEL			Identify past and current actions in the collective transformation of an activity system. Deepen historical analysis. Identify actions to be taken.
ACTIVITY SYSTEM MODEL		HISTORICAL ANALYSIS ACTUAL EMPIRICAL ANALYSIS	Move from experiential reflection to a conceptual representation of a past or present activity system. Identify systemic contradictions.

(continued)

---

[26] We've used a logo to represent an audio-video recording of work situations. Mirror data can also be statistical data, interview extracts, or extracts from previous CL sessions.

Table 13: Continued

ARTIFACT	REPRESENTATION	USE IN THE EXPANSIVE LEARNING CYCLE	FUNCTION IN THE PROCESS
REPRESEN-TATION OF THE PROXIMAL DEVELOP-MENT ZONE		MODELING	Define future directions for the activity system. Define ways of expanding and reconceptualizing the object of the activity.
EMERGING MODEL OF THE NEW ACTIVITY		MODELING	Represent the germ cell of the object of the future activity.
PARTIAL PROJECTS		IMPLEMEN-TATION	Move the activity system into the zone of proximal development.

It is not uncommon for the artifacts provided by the interventionist to be used in ways that differ from the original plan prior to the intervention. The artifacts are thus transformed, modified, and their uses redirected to enable them to control behavior and support volition. In the context of the instrumental genesis approach (Rabardel, 1995), we can say that these artifacts are instrumentalized to enable them to become instruments of behavioral control and volitional support (Engeström & Sannino, Forthcoming; Lémonie & Bationo-Tillon, Forthcoming).

For instance, in a recent intervention with the management committee of an Institut National Supérieur du Professorat et de l'Éducation (INSPÉ), we first confronted the management committee (CODIR) with a professional situation concerning the student recruitment committee by asking the head of the schooling department, who heads this committee, to give a detailed account of how it works (presentation of a student's file, allocation statistics for each of the five INSPÉ sites, allocation criteria, percentage of wishes granted, etc.). Following the presentation of the Student Recruitment Committee by the Head of School, the other members of the Steering Committee were invited to comment on the information presented. The initial discussion focused on the selection criteria and assignments that have budgetary implications for each component. It also focused on the attractiveness of each site. The second stimulus mobilized was a diagram that was discussed, revised during the CL session, and used as a basis for analysis (Figure 38). This second stimulus was the basis for the group's idea of a historical overview and a discussion of the future of each of the sites in the light of the current conditions of distance learning related to the pandemic. The idea of pooling certain teaching resources was raised and should be discussed again in the light of a historical analysis.

When the researchers proposed this matrix in the second session, it was initially intended to serve as mirror data, allowing participants to recall the main points of discussion that had emerged in session 1. However, as we returned to this matrix, it gradually came to be seen as a possible steering tool for identifying the direction of the activity system. At the same time, the idea of building and looking at the historical trajectory became a necessity for the participants. This historical analysis was carried out in session 3, starting with the biographical trajectory of each of the participants and then, based on these traces, identifying the development periods of the institution and the contradictions that lie behind them.

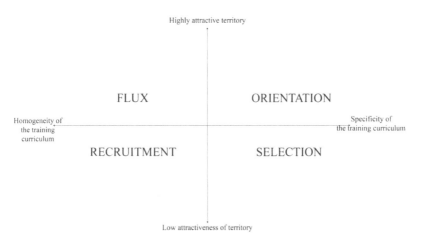

Figure 38: Example of a second stimulus used in a CL at a University Teacher Training Institute.

The following table summarizes the task design and use of the various artifacts over the course of a CL. It is, of course, only a typical, ideal example that must be adapted to the specific needs of the customer.

Table 14: Example of Task Design for Expansive Learning cycle Based on the Double Stimulation Method.

EXPANSIVE LEARNING ACTIONS	MIRROR DATA	FIRST STIMULUS	SECOND STIMULUS	SPEAKER'S ACTION
QUESTION EXISTING PRACTICES	Situation videos – narrative report	Identify practice problems and innovations. Identify elements that contribute to problems encountered.	Concepts as disturbances, prescribed/actual discrepancies.	Encourage participants to talk about their actions and the problems they have encountered.
			Activity system model	Encourage a shift from a situated to a systemic viewpoint.
HISTORICAL ANALYSIS	Timeline based on interviews or developed during the session, historical documents.	Model activity system changes over time	Chart to identify changes in the main elements of the activity system. Concept of 'developmental period'.	Encourage the identification of developmental periods
	Table of developmental periods	Identify the principles of change from one period to another	Concept of contradiction. Activity system model.	Investigate how previous contradictions led to the current activity system
CURRENT EMPIRICAL ANALYSIS	Current activity system	Identify the differences between intention and results; between positive results and side effects	Statistics, activity system model	Develop hypotheses about current contradictions

MODELING	Activity system developed earlier. Audio-video recording of other practices.	Identify the fundamental contradiction in the object of the activity. Develop an extended alternative vision of the object. Identify who needs to be involved.	Activity system with different forms of contradiction (primary, secondary, etc.). Transformation matrix. Activity system embedded in its network.	Better understand the contradictions at work. Support the possibilities of change and transformation of the object.
EXAMINATION	Videos and documents representing test cases.	Identify how current and future activity systems differ in each case.	Model developed by participants.	Identify the consequences of activity system development on participants' actions.
IMPLEMENTATION	Video recording of previous sessions	Project, plan the introduction of the future activity system: what needs to be changed now to implement the new activity system? Implement certain aspects of the new model in practice. Note the consequences, the problems.	Project sheet	Identify the prerequisites for implementing new activity systems.
REFLECTION ON THE PROCESS	Video recording of previous sessions	Identify the elements that support or restrict expansive learning. Identify how participants have changed their view of the new activity.	Expansive learning cycle. Models developed by participants.	Pay close attention to the quaternary contradictions generated by the implementation of the new model.
CONSOLIDATION	Interviews with participants	Clarifying certain concepts	Models developed by participants	Consider how the process continues without the intervener's presence

The Phase Before Change Laboratory

To the best of our knowledge, there are few studies that focus on the pre-laboratory phase of change. CLs are demanding forms of intervention for both researchers and participants. It would be beneficial to have a diagnostic tool to assess whether expansive learning efforts need to be accompanied or whether a less demanding intervention can be implemented. Such an assessment tool would also assist in determining the focus of the intervention.

In this regard, Dinh and Sannino (2024) developed a tool as part of their support for a school education reform in Vietnam. This diagnostic tool is based on the key concepts of CHAT: the object of activity, the activity system and its contradictions, expansive learning and transformative agency, and the collective zone of proximal development.

Data were collected through semi-structured interviews based on three main themes:

- (1) Teachers' experiences of global education reform.
- (2) Teachers' experiences of implementing a competency-based curriculum.
- (3) teachers' views on the future of the school and their work.

The interviews were analyzed using the CHAT concepts outlined above. Four questions emerged to interrogate and analyze the interviews:

- (1) How do participants talk about students (the object of the activity) in relation to the new curriculum?
- (2) What might be the indications of the main contradictions that the school faces with the new curriculum and how are they located in the activity?
- (3) In what phase of a possible expansive learning process is this school, in terms of the agentive actions undertaken in relation to the new curriculum?
- (4) What could be the main indicators of the dimensions of the zone of proximal development envisaged in the school?

This research is invaluable in that it allows us to envisage a pre-intervention diagnostic work based on semi-directed interviews, in addition to any other methods (observation, study of official documents, etc.). Once more, it is crucial to have a solid grasp of the fundamental concepts and theoretical frameworks.

Some Examples of Change Laboratories

The following table is not an exhaustive analysis of a CL. Instead, it summarizes a few examples of change labs in different fields. These few examples do not, of course, exhaust all the fields in which CL have been used as a method of intervention and research.

Table 15: Examples of Change Laboratory interventions.

DOMAIN, PUBLICA-TION AND COUNTRY	PARTICIPANTS INSTITUTION	PURPOSE OF INTERVEN-TION – DEMAND	CL DESCRIP-TION	EXAMPLES OF MIRROR DATA USED
AGRICUL-TURE (MUKUTE, 2015) LESOTHO	Farmers	Use land more efficiently and sustainably to produce more food and ecological services.	Not described (too short according to the researcher to implement the entire expansive learning cycle)	Extracts from interviews with farmers, agricultural extension workers and an agronomy researcher
NETWORK AGAINST CHILD LABOR (DONATELLI ET AL., 2020) BRAZIL	Representatives of public institutions for education, health, social development, labor and income, employers and employees in the jewelry industry, and social control organizations.	Designing the new COMETIL network structure	7 sessions of 2 hours spread over one year	Accident report of a 5-year-old child who swallowed acid. Interview extracts.
HELSINKI CITY UNIVERSITY LIBRARY (ENGESTRÖM ET AL., 2012) FINLAND	Library staff, researchers representing research teams	Creating a new service model for university libraries in response to the digital crisis	8 weekly sessions	Interviews with customers and employees about their problems and needs

(continued)

Table 15: Continued

DOMAIN, PUBLICA-TION AND COUNTRY	PARTICIPANTS INSTITUTION	PURPOSE OF INTERVEN-TION – DEMAND	CL DESCRIP-TION	EXAMPLES OF MIRROR DATA USED
HÔPITAL (CUVELIER ET AL., 2023) FRANCE	Intensive care unit team	Implementation of work-related discussion space	7 sessions of 2 hours	Narratives of a patient's care pathway based on interviews conducted
PRIORITY EDUCATION NETWORK (REP) (LÉMONIE, GROSS-TEPHAN, & TOMÁS, 2019) FRANCE	Members of steering committees for priority education networks	Development of REP management activities. Support for public policy.	5 sessions Combination of local and academic sessions	Map of priority education networks. Extract from a verbatim interview with a REP steering committee.

Chapter 11

Formative Interventions in Relation to Other Interventionist Approaches

In the final analysis, it can be said that ergonomists have worked hard to achieve emancipation through work, which requires a global reversal of the productive and societal paradigms at work (Guérin et al., 2021, p. 375).

This chapter builds upon the preceding discussion by examining the characteristics of formative interventions in a comparative approach. It should be noted that formative interventions are not, of course, the only research approach that proposes to produce results based on interventions.

In order to conduct this comparison, it is first necessary to develop an analytical framework for comparing different interventionist approaches. This reading and analysis grid will be based on two characteristics: the first refers to the consideration of agency, the second to the level of transformation of the intervention.

As previously stated, the CL methodology, which is based on the double stimulation method, explicitly incorporates agency as a key component of the intervention methodology. Additionally, it serves as an indicator of the quality of learning. Furthermore, it is necessary to determine whether the anticipated transformations occur at the level of an activity system and whether they involve expansive learning.

The distinctive feature of CL is that it is also founded upon a robust theoretical framework (Nicolini, 2012). In a discussion of the links between formative interventions and action research at a symposium of the International Society for Cultural Activity Research (ISCAR) held in San Diego in 2008, Engeström argued that 'action research' was not a coherent method, nor a substitute for a viable methodology built on the cultural-historical tradition of activity (Somekh & Nissen, 2011, p. 93). One of the primary justifications for the distinctive nature of formative interventions is that they are informed by a theoretical framework that facilitates the development of coherent methodological principles. Nevertheless, we will refrain from making a direct comparison in this regard, although the underlying theoretical dimensions are alluded to in the subsequent developments.

This chapter will examine three distinct research approaches. The first is action research (AR), which was initially developed by Kurt Lewin, a German psychologist and professor at the University of Berlin until the rise of the Nazi regime. Lewin was also a close associate of Vygotsky (Yasnitsky, 2015). In particular, Lewin's work inspired the double-stimulation method through the waiting experiment, which was conducted by his student Dumbo (see previous chapter).

The second of these approaches is the Design-Based Research method, initiated by the work of Brown (1992) and Collins (1992). This method aims to produce knowledge about learning by designing and implementing learning environments on the basis of hypotheses.

The third of these approaches is also rooted in CHAT and stems from the Nordic tradition of participatory approaches. One of the most prominent figures in this approach is Bødker from Aahrus University in Denmark, who, simultaneously with Engeström, built his research on Leontiev's work. The UTOPIA project aimed to enable workers to design technologies with an openly democratic political orientation.

There are five primary reasons for selecting these three approaches.

The first reason is the attempt to align them with the framework of formative interventions. For instance, Action Research approaches were the subject of an issue in the journal Mind, Culture and Activity (2011). Design Based Research approaches were also the subject of a special issue in the Journal of The Learning Sciences (2016), which subsequently was published in book form (Cole, Penuel, & O'Neill, 2018). Finally, the Participatory Design approach has been the subject of several texts discussing its contributions in relation to the Change Laboratory, while also calling for possible rapprochement (Bødker, 2009).

The second reason is their interventionist nature. Each of these approaches, like CL, is based on the epistemological principle of creating new knowledge by means of intervention. In their own ways, they seek to overcome the dichotomy between theory and practice, and to make practice the arbiter of theory.

The third reason is that each approach places the ideas of learning, development, and design at the heart of intervention. For example, the DBR approach can be described as emblematic within the learning sciences (Penuel et al., 2016). The Participatory Design approach is often described as a Nordic tradition in the field of Human-Computer Interaction, and more broadly in the field of design. However, it is unclear whether these approaches address the same type of learning. Do they emphasize creative and developmental learning?

The fourth reason is that each of these approaches claims to be a participatory methodology. Sometimes in their name (Participatory Design). Or sometimes in the way they are presented. However, this adjective seems to obscure rather than illuminate these methodologies. The fifth reason for the popularity of these approaches is their international circulation, which allows us to gain insight into the debates within and between approaches. This is likely to provide some keys for comparison with the CL.

However, it is important to note that the limits of this chapter require us to present the generic characteristics of each approach. A more comprehensive study would undoubtedly present a more nuanced picture than the one proposed here. The subject under discussion is methodology, that is, the set of principles that organize and give meaning to the methods used. As will be demonstrated throughout this chapter, the same methods can be used in radically opposed directions. Consequently, the focus of this chapter is on questioning the methodology, and the relationships between the aims pursued, the methods used and the theoretical underpinnings. In this manner, we will be deconstructing the sometimes-convenient labels of 'participatory method', which largely conceal the actual processes implemented in research interventions.

In Search of an Analytical Framework for Comparing Approaches

The term *'participative approaches'* encompasses a multitude of forms of worker involvement. Some interventions merely involve operators as *'informants'*, while others genuinely increase workers' power to act as designers of their work. In some instances, workers or participants in the participatory approach are involved only in certain phases (e.g. implementation or evaluation of a system), while in others, operators are involved throughout the entire intervention process (from initial analysis to implementation and evaluation of the system).

The notion that workers can be the designers of their own work is of significant importance in the context of CHAT and formative interventions. In CL, participants aim to learn extensively how to develop their activity system. In this way, they are not reduced to the simple role of informants for a survey and diagnosis carried out by a researcher or facilitator. Similarly, the perspectives for transformation are the result of a design by the participants on the basis of a survey carried out by the CL participants. A brazilian group has experienced the shortcomings and dissatisfaction of an intervention approach that carries out a diagnosis on the basis of an analysis carried out by a facilitator and proposes axes of transformation involving expansive learning that is difficult to carry out.

> We only acquire full knowledge of reality when we identify resistance to its transformation. Explanations before an intervention provide hypotheses, i.e. provisional explanations of the origin of disturbances which interfere with an activity. Who should have agency in the process of analysis, formulation of solutions, testing, and implementation of changes? Which should be the role of interventionists and the internal actors of organizations (Virkkunen & Newnham, 2013) when one of the goals is to promote learning and agency by means of transformation? Therefore, in spite of the recommended care with validation, self-confrontation, and feedback provision, local actors might not expand their learning to a higher level, namely, the transformative learning needed to change the activity model which first gave rise to work-related disturbances. They might remain as mere spectators, actors who perform narrow-scoped actions, and sources for consultation, while they do not see themselves as owners of the process of transformation (Vilela et al., 2020, p. 7).

In light of the inherent contradictions inherent in their intervention, they have integrated CL as an interventionist methodology. Workers have undergone a transformation, moving from the role of '*simple informants*', enabling researchers to make a diagnosis, to that of '*agents of transformation*'. The researchers' role has also evolved, moving from 'researcher and diagnostician' to '*facilitators and mediator of expansive learning*'. The figure below illustrates the expansive learning outcome of this group of Brazilian researchers and practitioners.

Figure 39: Development of an intervention model. From a model centered on diagnosis to a model mobilizing a formative intervention approach (From Vilela et al., 2020).

As previously stated, one of the defining characteristics of CLs is their capacity to facilitate transformative agency. This refers to the ability of participants to challenge the status quo and take the initiative to transform it (Virkkunen, 2006, p. 49).

The notion of transformative agency considers the initiative of participants within the formative intervention approach to transform the activity system at the center of the analysis. It therefore refers to actions taken in the direction of transforming an activity system. Transformative agency is thus not reduced to an individual acceptance of agency; rather, it describes the search and efforts of participants in the quest for transformations. The notion of transformative agency is rooted in the concept of action. It ultimately underscores the crucial importance of expansive transitions from individual initiatives to collective actions to accomplish the systemic change necessary for the development of an activity system. At this point, we can identify a first continuum ranging from research and interventions whose process is led by the researcher with simple validation by the workers to interventions that place the concept of transformative agency centrally in a process that is led by the workers with the support of one or more researchers.

The second implication of the concept of transformative agency is that it enables us to break with a given framework of action. The concept's centrality in the process implies a clear departure from local problem-solving interventions. As previously stated, CL is not about solving local problems; rather, it is about redesigning an activity system based on the identification of historically accumulated contradictions within an activity system. Problems, as well as dilemmas, conflicts, are only seen as symptoms. Consequently, there are two distinct movements within the context of CL: the initial transition from actions to the analysis of the activity system, and the subsequent shift from the current form of the activity system to a novel form.

A second axis distinguishes CL from other forms of methodology. On the one hand, there are approaches that remain centered on action, emphasizing the role of reflexivity and the focus on transforming situations. On the other hand, there are approaches that seek to look beyond problems, dilemmas, and conflicts in situated action to the historically inherited systemic causes at the root of these problems, in order to transform an activity system.

The two axes identified permit the construction of a matrix for the purpose of comparing CL with the three approaches mentioned. This matrix is presented in Figure 40 below.

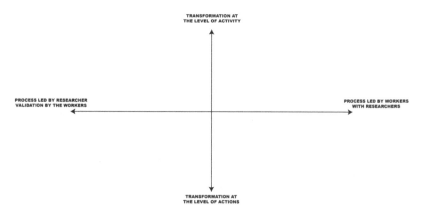

Figure 40: Matrix used to compare different forms of intervention-research.

Design Based Research

Definition of Design Based Research

Design-Based Research (DBR) is a methodology that seeks to study learning in environments that have been designed with the dual aim of enhancing learning and developing theory (Sanchez & Monod-Ansaldi, 2015). Design-based research (DBR) can be defined as a process that integrates design and '*scientific methods*' to enable researchers to pursue the dual goals of designing useful products for educational intervention and developing effective theory to solve individual and collective problems in education (Easterday, Lewis, & Gerber, 2014).

Although the primary motivation for DBR is to enhance the relevance of learning research to classroom teaching, there is no logical reason why this type of research and intervention cannot be applied outside the school setting (Reimann, 2011).

The literature in the learning sciences has witnessed a notable increase in research that defines itself in relation to this methodology. The term first appeared in 2002 (Hoadley, 2002) and was explicitly formulated to replace the term '*design experiment*', which was initially proposed by Brown (1992) and Collins (1992). In Brown's (1992) terms, the objective was to move experimentation from the laboratory to the classroom.

> An effective intervention should be able to migrate from our experimental classroom to average classrooms operated by and for average students and teachers, supported by realistic technological and personal support (Brown, 1992, p. 143).

However, this change of experimental location must not detract from the laboratory's experimental '*rigor*' in the selection and implementation of variables. Therefore, while DBR study learning in a '*situated context*', it remains understood in terms of dependent and independent variables. The methodological task for the researcher is therefore to identify the variables to be implemented in the design of the learning environment.

The design of the learning environment is thus directly linked to an underlying theory that can be subjected to an intervention test. In this sense, the theory is '*responsible for the design activity*' (Cobb, Confrey, diSessa, Lehrer, & Schauble, 2003, p. 2010). This is an intermediate theory insofar as '*grand theories*' such as constructivism '*often do not provide detailed guidance on the organization of instruction*' (Cobb et al., 2003, p. 10). Consequently, it is necessary for the researcher to draw on a 'relatively modest' theory specific to identified learning content when designing a learning environment. This is the approach proposed by Tiberghien, Vince, and Gaidioz (2009). They illustrate the transition from '*grand theories*' to '*a more modest theory*' in the context of physics education, demonstrating how to design a physics teaching sequence.

The testing of the learning environment, its revision, and the iterative process that results play a role similar to that of the variation of independent variables in laboratory experimentation. In order to achieve this, the researcher conducting a DBR must identify, within the complexity of teaching-learning situations, the variables that will be the focus of the study and the '*accessory*' variables.

DBR is research in the sense that it aims to develop a theory which, at the source of the design, is then tested and revised in successive iterations, enabling a systematic analysis to be carried out:

> Design experiments are conducted to develop theories, not merely to empirically tune '*what works*'. These theories are relatively humble in that they target domain-specific learning processes (Cobb et al., 2003, p. 9).

Although they do not deviate from the experimental paradigm from which they draw their inspiration, DBR have a highly pragmatic interventionist aim. Since intervention is the basis for the production of an effective theory of educational phenomena, DBR can be described as interventionist research (Hoadley & Campos, 2022) aimed at systematically controlling changes in a learning environment in order to study the effects of these changes on learning. As Barab and Squire (2004, p. 5) observe, the project is designed not only to meet local needs but also to advance a theoretical agenda, to discover, explore, and confirm theoretical relationships.

One way of representing this dual orientation of DBR is to situate them in the '*Pasteur quadrant*' (Greeno, 2016). This model, formulated by Stokes (2011), has been proposed to characterize scientific research. In the classical tradition, research is presented in the form of a continuum organized around a classic opposition between basic and applied research. This presentation gives rise, on the one hand, to a form of opposition between rigor and relevance (Schön, 1996), on the other hand, a direction of research that goes from basic science to applied science (the latter finding its origin in the former) and finally a form of a division of labor where the practitioner is responsible for translating and implementing in their practice the knowledge derived from research. A critique of this posture in the field of physical and sports education research can be found in Lémonie, Gal-Petitfaux, and Wallian (2012).

Stokes (2011) proposes a quadratic model of scientific research structured by two questions relating to fundamental understanding and consideration for use. DBR are situated in the top-right quadrant, i.e. concerned both with advancing fundamental knowledge about learning and with considerations for the utility and uses of the knowledge produced (Barab, 2014).

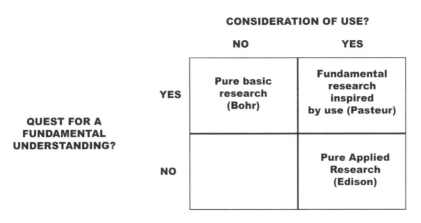

Figure 41: Quadratic model of scientific research according to Stokes (2011).

CHAT also falls into this quadrant insofar as it aims to enable the advancement of fundamental knowledge about human activity, expansive learning and development while promoting profound societal change (Greeno, 2016). However, although in the same quadrant, CHAT and DBR formative intervention methodologies diverge quite radically on their conception of causality and empirical validation processes.

DBR involves studying learning in environments designed, modified and systematically controlled by a researcher. DBR approaches combine empirical educational research and the design of learning environments on theoretical grounds, with the objective of explaining and understanding the circumstances under which, how, and why a technological innovation functions (Collective, 2003). In this context, the validation process is based on the linking, a classic approach in empirical research, which enables the search for regularities between two sets of data: the characteristics of the designed learning environment, on the one hand, and learning outcomes on the other (Greeno, 2016). The objective is to arrive at a form of conjecture in the form: '*If [design feature] then [learning]*'. In this validation process, randomized trials can be conducted to provide statistical support for the data. However, this approach to causality is both reductive and philosophically problematic (Maxwell, 2004, p. 3). It views causality as the regularity between two sets of variables and uses the term cause primarily for the systematic relationship between variables, rather than for causal processes (Maxwell, 2004). In contrast, rather than viewing causality as a relationship between two sets of data, CHAT *'believes that causation can actually be observed and reconstructed as a real sequence of events. It uses historical methods and narrative evidence, as well as close observation and recording of unfolding chains of events'* (Engeström, 2011, p. 610). The principle of ascending from the abstract to the concrete, as described in the previous chapter, provides an illustrative example of this conception of causal processes as opposed to approaches in terms of variables, factors, or determinants.

The Methodological Process of Design-Based Research

The DBR methodological process comprises a series of iterative phases of research that integrate design and scientific method. This enables the pursuit of two distinct agendas: the production of useful knowledge and the development of a theory relating to a domain of knowledge. Easterday et al. (2014) present a six-phase process.

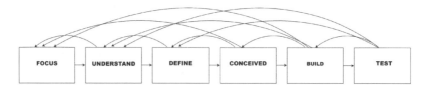

Figure 42: The Process of Design Based Research, from Easterday, Lewis, and Gerber (2014, p. 319).

In the initial orientation phase, the researchers delineate the target audience, the overarching theme, and the specific scope of the project. The second phase, designated as the comprehension phase, is predicated upon an assessment by the researcher of the learners' existing level of knowledge, the field of knowledge, the challenges encountered, and the solutions that have been implemented or that already exist. This preliminary design phase entails an understanding of the nature of the problem and the underlying reasons for it, as well as the cultural context and the distinctive characteristics of the learning environment.

The third phase, the definition phase, defines the objectives, research questions, and evaluation procedures. This phase transforms an 'indeterminate problem with no solution' into a determinate problem that can be solved.

In the fourth phase, the design phase, designers (or researchers) draw up a plan to develop a solution to the problem identified in the previous phase. The aim is to 'identify' and anticipate *'whether it will work'*.

The fifth phase is the implementation phase, which commences with the implementation of the device designed by the researcher(s). The sixth and final phase is a testing phase, which involves formative evaluations and iterative trials to test the effectiveness of the design and the soundness of the theoretical hypotheses. Although presented sequentially, the DBR phases are not linear. Figure 42 illustrates the possibility of backtracking at each stage, with each phase re-examining the preceding phases.

DBR do not fundamentally diverge from the rigor and causality model of classical experimental methods. While the objective is to illustrate the distinctions between laboratory and ecological settings in the classroom (Barab, 2014; Collins, Joseph, & Bielaczyc, 2004), the approach entails utilizing design as a means of adapting experimental methods, their rigor, and assumed objectivity to the complex and partly indeterminate environment of the classroom. The delimitation of the problem, control over design and implementation, and variation in the tests carried out enable this translation of the experimental method into the classroom. This position is exemplified by the way in which a classroom is apprehended as a set of dependent and independent variables. Thus, Collins et al. (2004) contrast psychological approaches in the laboratory with those carried out in the DBR:

> Psychological experiments use a methodology of controlling variables, where the goal is to identify a few independent and dependent variables and hold all the other variables in the situation constant. In design experiments, there is no attempt to hold variables constant, but instead the goal is to identify all the variables, or characteristics of the situation, that affect any dependent variables of interest (Collins et al., 2004, p. 20).

The classroom is thus apprehended as a closed world analyzable in terms of dependent and independent variables without breaking or discussing with the epistemological presuppositions and the notion of mechanical causality behind laboratory experiments. The DBR can thus be presented as participating in the Evidence-Based Education movement.

In this context, DBR involves context engineering to enhance learning and generate evidence-based claims (Barab & Squire, 2004).

The Classroom as Laboratory and Unit of Analysis In Design Based Research

It is therefore unsurprising that Cole and Packer (2016) can observe wryly that while, with DBR, the learning sciences have moved out of the laboratory, *'they haven't escaped very far'*. Indeed, the majority of DBR are rooted in the classroom, presented outside of any institutional framework, which appears to be a considerable distance from the goal of conducting research *'in the real world'*. Packer and Maddox (2016, p. 17) describe the successive shifts in the naming of the unit of analysis in Collins et al.'s (2004) article: real-world situations (p. 16), learning environments (p. 18) educational frameworks (p. 21), and finally, classrooms.

Two principal criticisms can be leveled at this unit of analysis, which is frequently formulated in terms of *'learning environment'*. The first pertains to the vague definition of this unit of analysis (context or learning environment), which is often accompanied by a positive attribute:

> The notion of learning environment is usually presented with an attribute. We have dynamic learning environments (e.g. Barab & Kirshner, 2001), innovative learning environments (e.g. Kirschner, 2005), powerful learning environments (e.g. De Corte, Verschaffel, Entwistle, & van Merriënboer, 2003), collaborative learning environments (e.g. Beers, Boshuizen, Kirschner, & Gijselaers, 2005), networked learning environments (e.g. Wasson, Ludvigsen, & Hoppe, 2013), smart learning environments (e.g. Dodds & Fletcher, 2004), real-life learning environments (e.g. Järvelä & Volet, 2004), authentic learning environments (e.g. Herrington & Oliver, 2000), and many, many more (Engeström, 2009a, p. 18).

The notion of a learning environment or context is of central importance, yet it is poorly defined and conceptualized. When it is defined, it is represented in a static, concentric form. This representation is the opposite of the way the notion of context is conceived in CHAT: dynamic, hierarchical and *'woven together'* (see Chapter 4). Moreover, in the CHAT framework, the notion of context or environment is clearly defined in its structure: context is the activity system (Cole & Engeström, 1993). In light of this criticism, some researchers have mobilized the activity system in the results analysis phase, without making CHAT central to the design process (Eames & Aguayo, 2020). This non-conceptualization of context allows DBR to present themselves as a toolbox (Barab, 2014), but it limits the possibilities for theoretical elaboration.

A second criticism is that the focus on the classroom indicates a lack of attention to the institutional structures in which the projects are embedded. These structures are nonetheless important for the implementation of the intervention. In the majority of DBR, the design focuses on creating a learning environment focused on a well-specified domain and integrating digital technologies. In doing so, the researchers (or designers) construct a well-defined, relatively closed environment that presents a challenge when implemented. Engeström (2009a) succinctly summarizes the issue as follows:

> However, the researchers expect that the bubble they have constructed is somehow so powerful that it will have significant effects of the quality of learning and motivation. When this does not happen, or the results are less impressive than expected, the typical conclusion is: We need improvements in the learning environment and more studies based on the same basic design (Engeström, 2009a, p. 19).

In the process, test iteration aims not only to validate theoretical hypotheses, but also to complete a design process. The metaphor of solving computer '*bugs*' is particularly illuminating here: '*The design is constantly revised based on experience, until all the bugs are worked out*' (Collins et al., 2004, p. 18).

This concern for control is achieved by closing down the notion of the learning environment. The logical question that inevitably arises is whether the types of innovations that researchers have studied using DBR are small-scale, incremental, and sustainable, or whether they are capable of bringing about truly disruptive change. In their literature review, Anderson and Shattuck (2012) note the almost exclusive focus of DBR on relatively limited incremental improvement processes within a given institution:

> The interventions developed in these studies could be characterized as small improvements to the design, introduction, and testing of sustaining technologies and practices in classroom or distance education contexts (Anderson and Shattuck, 2012, p. 24).

In any case, the majority of DBR, by seeking to integrate design as a means of closing off and controlling experimentation, do not seek to truly transform educational practices by identifying the main contradictions running through activity systems. Instead, they aim to improve processes by anchoring design in the resolution of local and limited problems.

Participants' Roles in Design-Based Research

A significant criticism of DBR pertains to the linearity of the intervention process, which fails to consider the agency of the actors – teachers and students alike. In numerous articles on DBR, the distinctions between participants, designers, and researchers are not clearly delineated (Bannan-Ritland, 2003). In most cases, the researcher assumes the role of designer (some articles alternatively refer to the researcher as both a participant and a designer for the same individual). The role of practitioner participants is defined in terms of the scope and limits of the project. However, when these participants are designated, it is often the researcher's or research team's involvement in practice that is emphasized, rather than the practitioners' involvement in the research and design process (Cobb et al., 2003). Consequently, if the implementation of DBR involves learning, it is the learning of researchers and/ or designers that is emphasized: *'Researchers manage the design process, cultivate the relationship with practitioners, and, above all, develop their understanding of the research context'* (Wang & Hannafin, 2005, p. 9). The desire to include participants (teachers and students) remains vague and without any methodological or theoretical justification ever being put forward. In design experiments, efforts are made to involve different participants in the design process in order to bring their diverse expertise to bear on the production and analysis of the design. But this expertise is only called upon to adapt and optimize the design locally: *'Consequently, the design may be better optimized given the constraints of the local setting and addressing participant concerns'* (Wang and Hannafin, 2005, p. 9).

Within this framework, DBR approaches are similar to user-centered design approaches. *'Even when they are taken into consideration, teachers are not empowered. [...]. A practitioner's role is to be a usability tester and adopt a designed artifact'* (Juuti & Lavonen, 2006, p. 56).

In sum, within the DBR literature, it appears that researchers are assumed to design the project (potentially by inquiring into participants' needs or conducting an ethnographic survey), teachers are assumed to implement it, and researchers are assumed to analyze the *'effects'* on student learning using procedures akin to the classical experimental method. For Engeström (2011, p. 602): *'Much of the literature on design experiments seems to take for granted the traditional designer-led model of innovation and ignore the recent turn toward user-led or 'democratic' innovations (Von Hippel, 2005)'.*

Similarities and Differences Between Change Laboratory and Design Based Research

Design-based research (DBR) shares with formative interventions an orientation towards the investigation of learning. In the case of DBR, the aim is to study learning in a context designed by one or more researchers. However, the learning studied by DBR is reduced to its academic form of acquiring predefined content that guides the design choices, mobilization, and evaluation of a theory. No mention is made of the learning required by practitioner participants to implement the devices. The learning required by researchers to carry out projects is mentioned, but these are not analyzed. The division of labor resulting from DBR's linear methodology means that teachers or participants are largely confined to the role of informants during the investigation phase, testing usability and implementing the device designed by the researcher(s).

In contrast to CL, participants do not initiate the design. The absence of a break with the concept of causality in experimental approaches leads DBR to close off the learning environment and use design as a means of controlling variables. Variation in iterative testing is used to identify the role and impact of independent variables on selected dependent variables. By seeking to identify and rigorously control all variables, the '*innovations*' of DBR approaches are often limited to improvements or local responses to local problems. Inherited systemic contradictions within activity systems are never acknowledged, as the institutional context is not considered. In conclusion, the DBR space can be summarized as shown in the figure below.

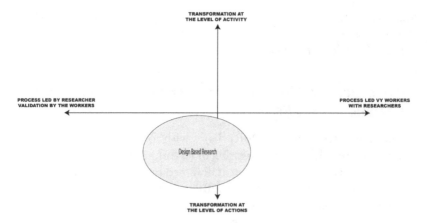

Figure 43: Design Based Research in comparative matrix.

Participatory Design

Definition of Participatory Design

The origins of participatory design (PD) research can be traced back to Scandinavia in the late 1970s and 1980s. At this time, information technologies were beginning to penetrate the workplace. Workers' unions, lacking experience with these technologies, were faced with a conflict of motives: either to accept these new technologies, which represented a break with traditional working methods, exerted ever-tighter control over their work, and automated a large proportion of the tasks to be carried out; or to reject these technologies outright.

Researchers assisted in implementing a third approach: enabling workers to be the designers of technologies, thus allowing them to retain control over their work. The UTOPIA project (1981–1985) exemplifies this research orientation and represents a pioneering project that was subsequently generalized. This approach has led to the recognition of the value of involving users in the design process as a means of improving the final product. This can be described as a Nordic design tradition. While the UTOPIA project is emblematic of this approach, it builds upon earlier projects carried out in Scandinavia in the 1970s, in which researchers supported and analyzed trade unions' attempts to influence the use of technology in the workplace.

The UTOPIA project was initiated in 1981 by the typographers' union with the objective of developing tools to enhance the skills of workers in the graphic arts industry in light of the advent of graphic workstations. Four main activities were carried out throughout the project (Bødker et al., 2000):

- Mutual learning between project participants, including graphics workers and computer and social science researchers.
- Specifying the requirements of a system for the layout and processing of newspaper images.
- Studying the pilot implementation of an image system in real production.
- Disseminating results to the community of researchers and graphics workers.

A significant outcome of UTOPIA was the methodology established to involve workers and designers on an equal footing. At the core of participatory design (PD) approaches is the recognition of individuals' right to participate in shaping the environments in which they operate (Ehn, 2009). The fact that the UTOPIA project was initiated by the Nordic trade unions is a notable aspect of this. The fundamental idea behind the project is that those who will be affected by the changes resulting from the implementation of information and communication technologies should have the opportunity to influence the design of these technologies and the practices that involve their use. The result of this political orientation is the need to reverse traditional approaches and find ways of involving workers in design, rather than involving designers in the world of workers. This is not simply a question of quality, although this obviously remains central, but of the values carried by these methodologies. In this context, Suchman (2009) introduces a collective work on PD and makes the following observation:

> Some readers may be surprised to find the voice of organized labor represented here as well. Such representation is critical in a discussion dominated to date by managerial and engineering perspectives. Until we become familiar with and take seriously each other's concerns, there will be little hope for a mutually satisfactory future in the development of work and technology (Suchman, 2009, p. viii).

PD research is not limited to improving information systems or technologies; it also aims to empower workers to the extent that they are involved in and can shape the design of information systems (Clement & Besselaar, 1993). Since the *'paradigmatic'* example of the UTOPIA project, Participatory Design practices have evolved significantly to better engage workers in the participatory design process. These developments have taken place along two complementary dimensions.

A significant transformation has occurred in the techniques employed, accompanied by a shift away from techniques that are solely rational in nature. Games are increasingly being utilized in place of models, while imagination and fantasy are gradually replacing the traditional cycle of analysis and goal setting. Furthermore, there has been a notable shift towards involving a diverse range of workers, rather than focusing on a single category of worker, as was the case with the typographers in the UTOPIA project. This is exemplified by the following description of a project (Bødker, Grønbaek, & Kyng, 2009):

> The design process, as any process taking place in an organization, is a political one and leads to conflict. Managers who order an application see things differently from the workers who will use it. Different groups of users will need different things from the application, and system designers often pursue their own interests. Conflicts are inherent in the process. If they are ignored, the solution may be less useful and continue to create problems (Bødker et al., 2009, p. 158).

The Participatory Design process

The PD co-design process comprises four phases (see Figure 44)

- A phase of familiarization of the researchers with the work, through interviews and demonstrations carried out by the operators.
- A phase in which existing problems and new ideas for work organization and IT tools are compiled by means of critiques and imagining the future.
- An organizational game phase to study current roles, new technological possibilities, modified roles and the implementation of an action plan.
- The phase of embodying ideas through mock-up design, cooperative prototyping and testing of the modified organization.

It is important to note that in this process, it is not merely a question of designing a new artifact; rather, it is a question of designing a new organization to make the artifact acceptable. The outcome of this orientation is an expansion of the notion of acceptability typically employed in research. For an artifact to become acceptable, it must not only facilitate the development of quality work and the skills of workers, but it must also be made acceptable through profound changes to the organization of work (and therefore the activity system) in which it is embedded. In this approach, the design of the artifact is not the sole focus; rather, the entire activity system, including the artifact, is considered (Adelé, Cippelletti, Dionisio, Lémonie, & Bobilier-Chaumon, 2024).

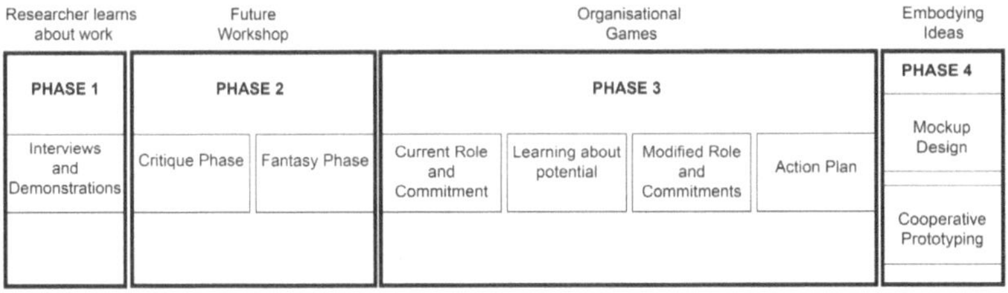

Figure 44: Participatory Design process according to Bødker et al. (2009, p. 163).

Phase 1 is an ethnographic phase that precedes the actual intervention process. In this phase, the researcher's goal is to learn about the materials, tasks, tools, and cooperation between people in the workplace. The researcher uses interviews and focus, following Engeström (1987) *'not only on the normal state of affairs, but also on exceptions and problems'* (Bødker et al., 2009, p. 164).

Phase 2 brings together techniques known as *'Future Workshop'*, originally developed by Jungk and Müllert (1987) for groups of resource-constrained citizens wishing to have a say in public decision-making processes. The objective of this phase is to *'highlight a common problem situation, generate visions of the future, and discuss how these visions can be realized'* (Bødker et al., 2009, p. 164). The objective of the critical phase is to enable a large group to identify and articulate current problems. If this understanding had previously been initiated in the interview work by the researchers, the idea was to share the understanding of the workers' point of view. This phase enabled the researchers to group together themes (four), some of which served as support for the organizational games.

In phase 3, the design process is played out like a theatrical stage, with the script co-written by researchers, designers, and workers. The current roles and commitments are enacted in scenarios that reflect the problem situations identified in stages 1 and 2.

As can be observed, there are some notable differences with CL. Firstly, the critical and imaginative phase is not linked to a confrontation with *'mirror materials'*, but rather to a form of *'brainstorming'* (p. 165) that enables an inventory of difficulties to be made. Secondly, the historical dimension of the origin of problems is minimized. In this framework, the process is essentially forward-looking. The organizational game (phase 3) moves from the current situation to an imagined future and back to the present (Bødker et al., 2009, p. 167), while phase 2 moves from expressed difficulties to an imaginative, future-oriented phase. Although not present in the intervention presented above, Bødker deems a historical analysis necessary and borrows Engeström's concept of contradiction to understand and analyze images of artifact use:

> To learn something about the present shape and use of an artifact, a historical analysis of the artifacts as well of practice is needed (Engeström, 1987). That artifacts are historical devices also means that artifacts in use are under less or more continuous reconstruction (Bødker, 1996, p. 150).

The process of redesigning or evolving the use of an artifact involves resituating it within an activity system riddled with historical contradictions. In this sense, the redesign of an artifact system also implies the redesign of an activity system:

> To design an artifact means not only to design the object which can be used by human beings as artifacts in a specific kind of activity. As the use of artifacts is part of social activity, we design new conditions for collective activity, e.g. new division of labor, and other new ways of coordination, control and communication (Bødker, 1991, p. 46).

However, it should be noted that this process is not explicitly supported by a collaborative process of reconceptualization of the object of activity. This is not to suggest that such a process does not occur in real processes. Finally, while design processes are supported by a set of artifacts introduced by the researcher into the CL as in PD, their uses are not supported by the double stimulation method in PD research. In contrast, PD seeks to enhance workers' engagement in the process by making the artifacts and tasks more engaging.

The theorization of the UTOPIA project was supported by CHAT. This resulted in a highly influential work, which, like Engeström's book, helped disseminate CHAT to the design of human-machine interfaces. As Bertelsen and Bødker (2003) note, prior to the mid-1980s, CHAT was not a central theoretical framework for all the experiments conducted in Scandinavia during the 1970s. In his thesis, Bødker (1991) draws upon the second generation of CHAT and the work of Leontiev to theorize the collaborative design process. Similarly, she aligns with Engeström (1987) in her view of design as a collective learning activity:

> Design is a process of learning, both when viewed as a collective process and as an individual process for the participants. The different groups involved learn about practice of the other participating groups. For the computer experts, this involves learning about the work and prerequisites of the application domain. For the users who participate, learning about computers is involved together with learning about design of computer applications. For all groups the confrontation with practices of other groups contributes to learning about their own practice. This, at the same time, brings to design an innovative character: the confrontation with different practices, and thus, with one's own, is opening possibilities for new ways of doing things, and transcending the traditional practice of the users (Bødker, 1991, p. 45).

Bødker's use of CHAT is characterized by three main points. Firstly, she adopts Leontiev's three-level structuring (Activity, Actions, Operations) to describe collective activities. Secondly, she draws on the idea of crystallization inherited from Leontiev: human instruments crystallize human operations. In this sense, the historical development of activity can to some extent be analyzed in terms of the development of artifacts mediating human actions. In Bødker's work, instruments are not only inherited but also the object of a collective activity of conception and redefinition. Finally, Spinuzzi (2020b) notes that Bødker, without using the term *'constellations of interconnected activities'* (p. 6), mobilizes this idea in the sense that the object of one activity is likely, in particular, to become the instrument of a second activity. As Bertelsen and Bødker (2003) observe:

> In actual use, artifacts most often mediate several work activities, and the contradictions and conflicts arising from this multitude of use activities are essential for activity-theoretical artifact analysis and design (Bertelsen & Bødker, 2003, p. 295).

Is Participatory Design only 'Participatory' in Scandinavia?

The fact that PD were structured on the basis of experiences in Scandinavian countries in the 1970s and 1980s raises the question of the trajectory of this research in its internationalization phase. The UTOPIA experience has been at the heart of several international congresses of the HCI community, contributing to the internationalization not only of the approach, but also of CHAT within this community.

The adoption of this orientation in other contexts has significantly transformed the original approach and its underlying philosophy, while simultaneously giving rise to a multitude of approaches. PD have also become autonomous and, as a form of '*label*', now encompass a vast range of approaches. In an article tracing this internationalization of PD, Spinuzzi (2005a) demonstrates the shifts and differences by contrasting the emblematic example of the UTOPIA project with a book on '*contextual design*' (Holtzblatt & Beyer, 1997). In the first case, as previously stated, design is truly participatory, involving workers on an 'equal footing' with social science and computer science researchers. Moreover, the project's values are underpinned by the demand for democracy within the company. In the work by Holtzblatt and Beyer (1997), the design project is structured by a well-regulated division of labor. Designers learn about work, develop new models of work, and design software based on these models. Workers, although considered '*co-designers*', are in charge of informing the designers. They do not actually do any design work. '*It is their responsibility to fulfill their designated roles, not to engage in system design*' (Holtzblatt & Beyer, 1997, p. 371).

It is of particular importance to our purposes that Spinuzzi (2005a) notes that Holzblatt and Beyer employ the same technique as the researchers of the UTOPIA project, citing it as if the prototyping method used were a continuation of the UTOPIA project, whereas it is in fact an ideological about-face. As Spinuzzi (2005a) points out:

> The two instances of prototyping seem diametrically opposed. UTOPIAn mock-ups were based on Marxist theory; contextual design was capitalist through and through. In the UTOPIA project, academics partnered with a union and were financed with governmental grant money; InContext sold its services to corporations. UTOPIAn mock-ups were meant to turn workers into genuine, involved designers, not just to test, ratify, or tweak the work of external designers; contextual design's prototyping component was designed to minimally disrupt work, relieving workers of the additional

work of design, so it encouraged them to make minor changes and suggestions–but explicitly not to become designers themselves (Spinuzzi, 2005a, p. 412).

The same words, the same references to mask radically different projects[27]. Methods lose their meaning if they are not linked to a serious methodological discussion. Very often, PD methods and approaches are treated as a research field or orientation, not as a methodology.

> The distinction may be important in principle, but in practice, it has become an escape hatch that allows practitioners to label their work 'participatory design' without being accountable to established, grounded precedent (Spinuzzi, 2005b, p. 163).

As we have pointed out, the majority of the methods used in the UTOPIA project (Ehn, 2009), as well as subsequent developments (Bødker et al., 2009) of these methods, were aimed at fostering worker involvement in the design process. The reception and subsequent development of PD in the U.S. significantly altered the initial paradigm.

> In the United States, because of relatively weak labor unions and a focus on functionality rather than workplace democracy, participatory design has tended to be implemented through nonintrusive methods: workplace microethnographies rather than walkthroughs and workshops, small-scale card-matching exercises rather than large-scale organizational games, and one-on-one prototyping sessions that focus on confirming developed ideas rather than group prototyping sessions that emphasize exploration (Spinuzzi, 2005b, p. 165).

From the point of view of worker involvement and participation, the distinction made by Blomberg, Suchman, and Trigg (1997) between *functional empowerment* and *democratic empowerment* seems useful:

> Functional empowerment holds work groups accountable for the results of tasks, and in return gives them a degree of power over how to execute the tasks. Democratic empowerment ideally gives workers a decision-making role in operational planning as well as organizational and technological change (Blomberg et al., 1997, p. 281).

---

[27] This situation is not specific to Participatory Design. Often, the use of fashionable vocabulary conceals a profound lack of involvement and rigor in the use of these concepts and their insertion into a project. The result is a stagnation of scientific debate due to the real impossibility of debating.

The concept of democratic empowerment is closely aligned with the notion of transformative agency, which has been identified as a key principle of learning quality within CLs (Sannino, 2015b, 2023; Virkkunen, 2006). The UTOPIA project, through its co-design process and pursuit of an ideal of democracy within the company, can be seen to have aimed at a principle of democratic empowerment (Ehn, 2009). This enabled workers to have a say in defining both the tools used and the organization of work. In contrast, projects in the United States have clearly shifted towards functional empowerment. In the project led by Holtzblatt and Beyer (1997), co-design takes on a completely different meaning: it is about teaching workers to critically examine their work practices, explore their tacit knowledge, and determine how to integrate technology into them.

The examples provided by Spinuzzi (2005a, 2005b) illustrate the shift in PD research when it was adopted in the USA. Spinuzzi employs the concept of translation in reference to the work of Callon (1984) to analyze 4 PD research projects and demonstrates the successive shift in the meaning of the original Scandinavian approach. While he playfully invokes the term '*betrayal*', he immediately underscores that any form of translation is a form of '*betrayal*', thereby attempting to weaken the term. However, the idea he defends is that the methods and techniques employed are adapted to the American context.

On the contrary, I would argue that this is a betrayal in the sense that, by adapting to this context, PD methods have lost the objective of truly transforming the status quo. Instead, they have merely become tools for efficiency, effectiveness, and productivity, without providing workers with the power to challenge the existing order.

Participatory Design That Matters? Expanding the Initial Participatory Design Project

The shift in initial approaches to PD has also been noted by the main initiators of the approach. In a recent article, Bødker and King (2018) provide a critical analysis of the international literature in this regard from the perspective that PD need to be '*reinvigorated*' to meet current and future challenges vis-à-vis technologies that penetrate our lives beyond work. In this context, it is evident that PD must assume a more prominent role in addressing significant issues. This entails enabling individuals and communities to assume control and participate in the development and delivery of technological solutions, usage processes, and future developments that matter to them and their peers (p. 4.1). This approach can be perceived as a continuation of the original PD approach and a form of extension akin to the emergence of a fourth generation of CHAT work.

Conversely, Bødker and King (2018) observe that, as PD have become increasingly internationalized, they have concentrated on addressing 'small questions' pertaining to the everyday challenges of use:

> However, the focus of most present-day PD is on how to facilitate direct collaboration between users and designers in codesign processes to engage with everyday issues of use, through technology or otherwise. This role has been adapted by HCI at large, leading to what we see as a focus on small issues (in contrast to big and important ones) such as products and techno-logical solutions that the users like, rather than on solutions that profoundly change their activities as well as the goals they are supported in pursuing (Bødker & King, 2018, p. 4:2).

Bødker and King (2018) propose a revitalization of PD to ensure that it becomes what it originally was: a tool for people to influence issues important to their lives. They address four major criticisms of current PD research literature.

(1) Reduction to the here and now: Many projects focus on design processes to the detriment of project scope. Projects tend to pri-oritize local learning without adequately considering the broader implications of this learning. This often results in a lack of tangible outcomes that could inform future actions. Consequently, there is a lack of commitment from PD research projects, which prioritize participation over project ambition.

(2) Limited technological ambition: The majority of contemporary PD projects focus on products that are often disconnected from IT and the development of new technological solutions. They do not adequately challenge existing technological solutions. With a few exceptions, *'Projects rarely question the tools available and there seems to be no real concern for the long-term learning of users regarding digital thinking and digital/software possibilities in a democratic perspective with a few exceptions such as'* (Bødker & King, 2018, p. 4:7). New digital platforms designed to appeal to a select few through the involvement of a large number of people are not subject to critical analysis in PD research. Questions about the

historical development and future prospects of new technologies are not addressed.

(3) Benevolence: The majority of current projects downplay the conflictual dimension of participatory design processes through a 'positive' discourse (such as the term co-construction). Antagonisms are rarely acknowledged. It is evident that the reduction of projects to the functionality of artifacts and the reduction of projects to uses inevitably leads to the neglect of conflictual dimensions and power relations expressed in PD research projects.

(4) The reduction of politics to ethics: For Bødker and King (2018), it is problematic that politics has been reduced to how researchers should behave and act fairly when involving users in projects. In many contemporary PD projects, there is a dearth of attention paid to the underlying contradictions that give rise to differences in viewpoints, or to the consequences of designers and researchers taking sides with one or other of the parties involved. '*This means that the methodological focus on e.g. working with prototypes for the sake of giving (direct) users a voice has increased, but the user's voice is not placed in a context of potential conflict*' (p. 4.9).

Formative Interventions and Participatory Design

Formative interventions and PD research are both grounded in CHAT (Bødker & Klokmose, 2011). They also share the idea that these forms of intervention are not fields or directions of research, but methodologies for generating action-based knowledge about how people affect their everyday activities and how these activities can be proactively shaped. Finally, they share a '*codesign*' approach in the sense understood by Spinuzzi (2020b, p. 2).

> By codesign, I do not mean the stepwise, linear design experiments that Engeström has recently contrasted with formative interventions (Engeström, 2011). Rather, I mean the interventionist research approach in which researchers and participants deliberate about current, unsatisfactory conditions, then collaborate to develop intentional solutions that address those conditions by transforming the activity.

In contrast to DBR approaches, PD approaches place greater emphasis on the transformative agency of actors and the idea that it is not possible to design an artifact without also redesigning the collective activity in which this artifact will be embedded. However, it is important to note that the original Scandinavian approach has been imported into the United States, which may influence the interpretation of the approach in this context. The recent critique by Bødker and King (2018), two pioneers of PD research, alerts us to the risk of a shift from a research approach that, by overlooking the political implications underlying the original approach, may inadvertently evolve towards a design approach in which workers become mere informants and evaluators of an intervention approach led from start to finish by researchers. This shift is associated with a loss of ambition in the design approach, where the artifacts designed are anchored closely to the performance of a task. In so doing, the anchoring of PDs in CHAT is reduced by focusing only on the action level.

In light of the above, it is possible to draw up the space of PD research on the following matrix. The matrix (Figure 45) illustrates that PD research does not constitute a unified field, but rather a multiplicity of approaches. Some of these approaches appear to be at odds with the aspirations of CL.

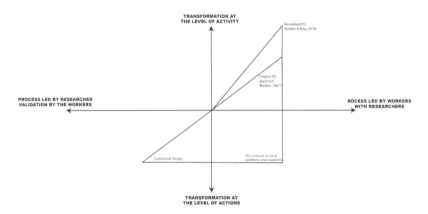

Figure 45: Participatory Design in comparative matrix.

Participatory Action Research

Definition of Participatory Action Research

Although difficult to define, Participatory Action Research (PAR) can be described as a collaborative process of research, education and action explicitly oriented towards social transformation (Kindon, Pain, & Kesby, 2007). PAR are therefore a participatory and democratic process aimed at developing practical knowledge in pursuit of worthwhile human objectives (Reason & Bradbury, 2001). They seek to unite or overcome the dichotomies between theory and practice, action and reflection, in the search for answers to practical problems of importance to a community.

Although widely used in education, action research has been mobilized as a research method in other fields: information systems (e.g. Davison, Martinsons, & Malaurent, 2021), health (e.g. Meyer, 2000), agriculture (e.g. Song & Vernooy, 2010), to name a few.

This research has its roots in the work of Kurt Lewin (Chaiklin, 2011). He is often referred to as the '*inventor*' of the term '*action research*'. Since its inception, action research has been a critical, alternative family of research within the social sciences. Lewin's vision was for social science research to solve concrete social problems and create lasting change. To achieve this, six principles structured research as Lewin envisioned it:

- A cyclical process of planning, action, and evaluation of results.
- Collaboration between researchers and practitioners throughout the research process.
- Collective decision making guided by the principles of collective decision making.
- Consideration of the value systems and power structures of the parties involved in the research.
- Dissemination of research to all stakeholders.
- The dual agenda of research aimed at solving practical problems and producing new knowledge.

It is not easy, and perhaps not very realistic, to define an AR model given the great diversity of approaches (Cassell & Johnson, 2006). This diversity, which is present in DBR and PD approaches, is probably even greater in AR approaches. For example, Chandler and Torbert (2003) identify 27 types of action research based on a model constructed from three categories on three different dimensions (time – past, present, future; research path – subjective, multiple, generalized; practice – 1st, 2nd, 3rd person). Cassell and Johnson (2006) identify five main types of action research based on different philosophical positions underlying the research process. These five main types of action research are:

- Experimental action research practices, mainly derived from the early work of Lewin.
- Inductive action research practices.
- Participatory action research (PAR).
- Participatory action research practices.
- Deconstructive action research practices.

In addition to the underlying philosophical positions, the types or varieties of action research are distinguished by the types of problems and questions they generally address, the types of contexts in which they take place (e.g. classrooms for classroom action research), and the types of people involved.

It should also be noted that, despite these classifications, the boundaries between different types of action research are sometimes blurred. Their names are indicative of this, and the use of labels makes it difficult to examine the differences between approaches. For example, in PAR, some authors singularize their approach by the audience involved, such as Youth Participatory Action Research (Mirra, Garcia, & Morrell, 2015), while others do so by the critical dimension: Critical Participatory Action Research (Kemmis, McTaggart, & Nixon, 2014). Sometimes authors alternate between using action research, then participatory action research, then critical participatory action research. The title of Kemmis et al.'s (2014) book is symptomatic of these shifts: it includes both Action Research in the title and Critical Participatory Action Research in the subtitle.

Theoretically, PAR is part of a pragmatist perspective on research (Kemmis, 2009). References to Dewey are therefore classic in the work, especially in the field of education. However, the question of the relationship or compatibility between PAR and CHAT is an important point of discussion in the literature (Somekh & Nissen, 2011). A special issue of the journal Mind, Culture & Activity was dedicated to this dialog. More specifically, both Langemeyer (2011) and Chaiklin (2011) place the Vygotskian methodological legacy and the approach developed by Lewin in tension and dialogue.

For Chaiklin (2011), both CHAT and AR propose research practices that transcend conventional oppositions (science/non-science; observation/intervention; etc.). He materializes these proposals through a series of enumerated claims, three of which are explicitly central to both Vygotsky and Lewin. These three statements are:

- The improvement or transformation of social practices is an immediate consideration and an important guiding principle in the formulation of research questions.
- The necessity to intervene in social practices to acquire basic knowledge, making it impossible to maintain a distinction between research and action.
- The meaningless epistemological assumptions about the relationship between scientific knowledge and social practices that make the distinction between 'basic' and 'applied' research is not tenable.

Some research that is part of PAR relies on CHAT (e.g. Aas, 2014), insofar as PAR are broadly compatible with CHAT (Wells, 2011). For example, Edwards (2000) argues that at the macro level there are strong similarities between PAR and CHAT in that both focus on collective agency and capacity building for informed change. In particular, CHAT could undoubtedly better inform and guide the PAR process (Edwards, 2000). For other authors, the similarities between CHAT and PAR are such that CHAT-derived methods, such as formative interventions, can be defined as a form of PAR:

> It is interesting to note the overlap between action research and post-Vygotskian activity theory, which sees human activity as mediated by cultural tools and social contexts, particularly as they are regulated by rules governing behavior and divisions of labor according to organizational roles (Somekh, 2008, p. 5).

The Process of Participatory Action Research

In general, action research follows a cyclical process. The first phase is an observation to determine what's happening in the field. The second phase is one of reflection, leading to planning for change (phase 3). The action research process can be modeled as follows (Figure 46).

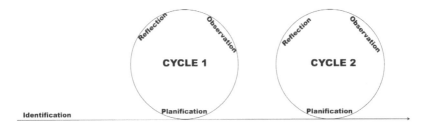

Figure 46: The cyclical process of Action Research.

This type of modeling is common, but also very generic. The PAR process itself appears to be more complex than this schematization suggests. It certainly doesn't follow the usual stages of conventional scientific research design, which seems to begin with formulating a research question, formulating a hypothesis, setting up experimental or observational conditions to test the hypothesis, collecting '*data*', analyzing the results, and developing an interpretation that links the new findings to the research literature. Nor does it always follow the steps of planning, acting, observing, reflecting, then re-planning, acting again, observing again, reflecting again, and so on that Kurt Lewin (1951) described as being at the heart of action research. In the context of PAR, Kemmis et al. (2014) note that:

> Action research is rarely as neat as this spiral of self-contained cycles of planning, acting and observing, and reflecting suggests. The stages overlap, and initial plans quickly become obsolete in the light of learning from experience (Kemmis et al., 2014, p. 18).

Interestingly, the authors point out that self-analysis aimed at significant change must be based on a dialectical vision of the relationship between the individual and the collective. In this framework, the practice to be studied and remedied is seen as historically and socially constructed and reconstructed through the human agency and actions of the participants. This dialectical analysis of practice by the group is based on a historical analysis: practice is conceived as historically evolving, and the authors' idea is to document historical changes in practice from what they call '*top sight*'. Here we see how close we are to the CL approach to analysis. This aerial perspective is described by Spinuzzi as a '*top sight* (Spinuzzi, 2018b) or by Engeström (1990b) as a system view.

However, unlike the historical analysis carried out in CL, PAR are not based on a theory of change in social practices. In the work of Kemmis et al. (2014), the concepts of contradiction and dialectic appear only four times. For CHAT and formative interventions, the concept of contradiction is central because it is the explanatory concept for changes in activity systems. It allows studying the historicity of the activity system beyond the history of the activity system. It also makes it possible to delineate a proximal zone of development.

Furthermore, although the practice itself is defined in their work, Kemmis et al. (2014) do not propose an architecture for this unit of analysis. Practice is reconstructed and analyzed from 5 perspectives:

- Individual-objective (behavior).
- Individual-subjective (action).
- Social objective.
- Social subjective.
- Reflexive-dialectical.

But there's nothing to help us understand what really unites the different perspectives represented in their work.

Actors' Agency: A Concern for Participatory Action Research

PAR share with popular education the pedagogical dimension that allows people to acquire knowledge about the causes of social injustices that negatively affect their living conditions (Mirra et al., 2015). However, unlike popular education movements, '*pedagogy*' is mainly achieved through research, which ranges from identifying key questions, collecting and analyzing data, and deciding what actions to take as a result of the research findings. It can thus be said that the research process is not carried out with the participants (and even less on the participants!), but that all participants in a RAP are researchers working within a negotiated framework and with collectively constructed tools. All participants are also stakeholders in a particular institution, organization, or community. Thus, PAR aims to respond to problems that affect that organization, institution, or community by engaging participants in a process of social change, of which research is a means. There is thus a double valence to the notion of participation in PAR: participants are both participants in the research and participants in their community or organization (McTaggart, Nixon, & Kemmis, 2017).

The idea that social change is underpinned by the participation and engagement of participants in the research process is central to the critical orientation of PAR. This focus on stakeholder participation throughout the research process is justified by the ineffectiveness of externally driven change. In the field of education, for example, Elliott (1993) points out that:

> Attempts to change the pedagogical practices of teachers by changing schools and social systems through hierarchically Initiated and controlled reforms tend to be resisted and are likely to fail (Elliott, 1993, p. 173).

The same observation is made by Virkkunen (2006)[28] to justify the need for the change laboratory methodology.

> Research findings concerning the high failure rate in top-down change programs (Beer, Eisenstatt, & Spector, 1990; Ciborra, 2002) indicate that this kind of sharp vertical division of labor is becoming increasingly problematic in the current conditions of rapid technological development. Its proponents tend to underestimate the need for the knowledge and creative contribution of grass-roots level practitioners in the transformation of an activity system. Practitioners' knowledge and experience is needed not only for developing the way in which they perform their specific tasks, but also in renewing the whole activity system in which they are involved. Methods of developmental intervention do not traditionally support the active, collaborative involvement of practitioners in the transformation of activity systems, however (Virkkunen, 2006, pp. 44–45).

Thus, despite the apparent diversity of objectives and methods mobilized in the literature (Kemmis et al., 2014), there are two strong ideas behind the idea of participation in PAR.

- Recognition of the capacity of people living and working in particular contexts to actively participate in all aspects of the research process.

---

[28] In this article, Virkkunen notes (p.44) that: *"Even the Scandinavian approach of designing new computer systems in a participatory way (Ehn & Kyng, 1991) and participatory action research (Whyte, 1991) emphasize participation at the level of individual tasks rather than at the level of the activity system as a whole"*. We offer a more nuanced perspective than Virkkunen on this point.

- Participant-driven research is aimed at improving or transforming practices and their contexts by the participants themselves.

CL and formative interventions share these two ideas with PAR. The process of inquiry in CL is carried out by participants with the help of researchers who provide tools for analyzing historicity. However, unlike some forms of PAR, the process in formative interventions is structured by an expansive learning theory.

The Level of Transformation in Participatory Action Research

The extent of the problems encountered depends on the type of action research being conducted. We mentioned earlier that some forms of action research focus on teachers' classroom practices. In doing so, they rely almost exclusively on reflexivity and remain at the level of action, since they do not propose to question the institutional structures behind teachers' pedagogical actions.

Thus, one criticism of classroom-based action research is that it is naive in failing to consider the system that structures classroom action. By focusing on classroom actions, this type of action research neglects the structural causes of teachers' actions. For Elliott (1993):

> From a normative-functionalist perspective, the classroom action research movement neglects the ways in which the system structures the activities of teachers in classrooms to limit and constrain their freedom to innovate. It is naive to assume that individual teachers can significantly transform their practices by reflecting on data they collect about their interactions with students in those physical spaces called classrooms. According to such critics, school-based action research projects fall within the misconceptions of a naive hermeneutic which views action as originating in the intentional activities of free agents and grounded in their subjective interpretations of the situations and events they experience. The subjective interpretations of teachers are mere shadows, masking structural constraints on human action (Elliott, 1993, p. 178).

Aware of the need to extend the unit of analysis to the school, some action research projects have focused on working with managers. However, attempts to change teachers' pedagogical practices by changing schools and social systems through reforms initiated and controlled by the hierarchy tend to meet with resistance and are likely to fail. Drawing on structuration theory, Elliott (1993) points to the need to involve the wider school community in transforming school practices:

> The school as an organization embraces a complex system of roles and relationships which includes a variety of subsystems. These subsystems may be so interlocking that it will be difficult to initiate change in one without corresponding changes in the others occurring. Discourse grounded in data about classroom practices needs to include school administrators, parents and employers, and teachers who have special responsibilities for curriculum planning and the assessment of pupils' progress. Moreover, the focus of school-based action research needs to be broadened to cover the range of practices represented in this wider group. Only in this way can the different cultures that shape practices within the different subsystems develop on a basis of mutual understanding (Elliott, 1993, p. 185).

In response to this expansion, Edwards notes that CHAT is precisely a prime theoretical candidate for exploring an extended level of analysis to the school in PAR that seek to transform teachers' professional culture:

> If action research, as Elliott signals, is also concerned with system change, it arguably needs an analytic tool at the systems level, which is compatible with its attention to agency and informed action. It would seem that an exploration of the systemic analyses […] direct attention to how the histories of systems impinge in complex ways on current and future actions (Edwards, 2000, p. 201).

As we can see, the level of action within PAR oscillates between the level of classroom action and that of a system of action that represents a school and involves the entire school community in action research.

Formatives Interventions and Participatory Action Research

As we have just seen, the PAR is located on the right side of our matrix (Figure 47). From an agentic perspective, the professionals involved in research are true researchers, engaged throughout the research process. Where in DBR, or in some versions of PD, there was a clear division of labor between researchers and participants, in PAR the boundaries tend to blur.

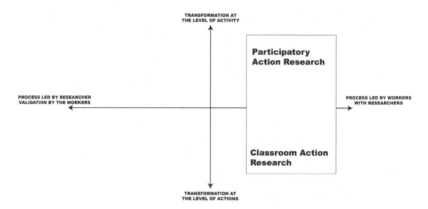

Figure 47: Participatory Action Research and Classroom Action Research in the comparative matrix.

From the point of view of the level of transformation sought, it oscillates between the level of action (especially in classroom-centered action research) and the level of activity when PAR seek to challenge the frame of actions. In this case, CHAT seems to be a relevant framework for responding to this level of targeted transformation (Edwards, 2000) and/ or dialectical thinking (and thus moving from the abstract to the concrete) for considering the historicity of this level (Kemmis et al., 2014).

From this, we might conclude that formative interventions are a form of participatory action research whose specificity is to be strongly guided by CHAT and expansive learning theory.

Towards Forms of Hybridization?

To facilitate a comprehensive comparison, we have employed three distinct research methodologies. It is important to note that there is no reason to conclude that one approach is superior to another.

Having reached this stage, we may now consider whether there is potential for combining the different approaches, and under what circumstances such a combination would be feasible. Indeed, in a recent article Karanasios et al. (2021) note that, to their knowledge, there are no CL focused on the design of instruments or new technologies.

This approach [Formative Intervention] has hitherto been largely unexplored for using, designing, and acting with technology or its role in addressing such challenges. Rather, disciplines concerned with technology have essentially developed along separate paths (Karanasios et al., 2021, p. 5).

We have seen in this chapter how the disciplines concerned with technology design have relied on CHAT to build a framework for intervention and research, PD, with a relative proximity to CL (in its original version or in the version revived by Bødker & King, 2018). Bødker (2009) highlights the close relationship between CHAT and formative interventions, as well as the potential for these two approaches to complement, or even articulate, each other:

I hope that DWR is ready to join forces with participatory design in finding new ways of dealing with our changing everyday lived lives, beyond the take-it-or-leave-it voting with the feet that underpins the above-described consumerism and beyond the equally individualistic expansion of cognitivism (Norman, 2002) that seems to inspire many technology development projects. After all, with its roots in sociocultural psychology, DWR is well suited to this (Bødker, 2009, p. 285).

At the same time, new technologies present significant challenges to activity theory, prompting the possible need to rethink the traditional categories of activity systems. For instance, when engaging with social media platforms like Facebook, it becomes difficult to determine whether the user is engaging with the community or the platform itself. When we work with collaborative robots (cobots), should they be considered an instrument or a division of labor?

Whatever the case may be in terms of future developments, the process of hybridizing and articulating different approaches requires a lot of theoretical and methodological work. In our view, it is not a matter of bricolage, but of a serious and unbiased analysis of the various contradictions inherent in each approach.

The desire to articulate approaches does not only exist between PD and CL (Penuel, 2014). Recently, there have been discussions between DBR approach and formative interventions. Engeström's strong critique of such approaches (2009a, 2011) seems to have been a catalyst for such discussions, allowing researchers enrolled in DBR to move towards a coherent methodology, rather than an articulation of methods stemming from the translation of classical experimental methodology to the classroom:

In this respect, design-based research is not a coherent theory or methodology for intervention, nor have many learning scientists believed it should be. Even so, some within the learning sciences argue that the time has come to develop design-based research as a methodology (Penuel, 2014, pp. 99–100).

In this context, the question arises under which conditions it is possible to contribute to the development of formative interventions without *'the very idea of formative intervention research running the risk of losing its rigor and becoming blurred'* (Engeström & Sannino, 2014, p. 118). Given the specificity of formative interventions, we believe that such hybridization must respect five principles.

The first of these principles is to explicitly distinguish between action and activity in CHAT, and to rely on the activity system as the unit of analysis and as the main object of the development goal. This avoids resorting to ill-defined units of analysis (such as the concepts of environments or contexts) or sticking to transformation goals centered on work situations. In other words, it breaks with an approach that seeks to improve work within an existing framework, rather than transforming the work environment through approaches that involve the actors.

The second principle relates to the structuring of the intervention with the principle of moving from the abstract to the concrete. The method of allowing the participants to reconceptualize the object of their activity by analyzing its historicity and highlighting the contradictions within the activity systems is essential for identifying and projecting themselves into the future. This makes it possible to define a proximal zone of development and to anchor the real utopia in the concrete, i.e. in the conceptualization of the movement of an activity system. However, this principle is demanding in terms of understanding and implementation.

The third principle is to support the efforts of the participants through double stimulation. CL is not a co-design methodology that removes conflictuality from the analysis. The principle of double stimulation places the conflictuality of motives at the center of supporting participants' will.

The fourth principle refers to transformative agency. Everything possible must be done to place participants in the role of agents of transformation of their activity system. Intervention cannot be satisfied with organizational solutions devised by others.

The fifth principle refers to the necessary heterogeneity of participants in terms of their function. The transformation of the work environment cannot be satisfied with respect for the managerial principle of subsidiarity, which prevents the conflictuality inherent in the object of the activity system from being put to work.

Taken together, these five principles form a kind of minimal grammar for intervention that allows for thoughtful hybridization without resorting to potentially dangerous or ethically questionable bricolage (Nuttall, 2022).

At this point, the reader might think that hybridization is no longer an option. But this is not the case. To illustrate this process, in a CL we seek to integrate elements of research-creation (Bationo-Tillon, Cozzolino, Krier, & Nova, 2024; Gosselin & Le Coguiec, 2006) with the idea that the hybridizations of artistic and scientific practices as they occur in research-creation could be an engine for expansive learning. We worked in the direction of finding new tertiary artifacts and tasks that would enable participants to find or identify a desirable future.

There are other possibilities for hybridization, perhaps by articulating sequences or mini cycles of expansive learning within the intervention. For example, the participants' redefinition of a new activity system could lead to a participatory design of the new technologies to be introduced later. This is undoubtedly a way of involving the PD and CHAT communities in joint efforts.

Far from limiting the possibilities, these five principles together define a space of possibility, a space for the development of formative interventions.

Conclusion of Part 3

Formative interventions are *'involving'* in that they seek to support actors' expansive learning and transformative agency. They aim for a level of transformation that goes beyond the task at hand. They aim to create something new by extricating themselves from immediate experience and reflexivity, from actions and tasks, to enable participants to break away from a framework of action often thought of as unchanging or beyond the reach of actors.

Dialectical thinking lies at the heart of training interventions. Enabling participants to become agents of change means giving them the dialectical tools to analyze their own activity. We cannot conclude this section without recalling the lessons of Vygotsky in *'The Historical Meaning of Crisis in Psychology'*:

- It is necessary to analyze processes, not objects, and it is therefore necessary to grasp developments. In formative interventions, activity is viewed in its movement, and it is in this movement of activity that participants can identify inherited historical contradictions. Grasping the historicity of activity is therefore not a superfluous process, but the very condition enabling participants to project a future and realize it by transforming their activity.

- We need to explain, not describe. We need to move on from describing external manifestations to highlighting the essence of a phenomenon: its fundamental contradictions. Without this, all science would be superfluous, to paraphrase Marx. However, such an explanation is only possible by relying on external manifestations. This link between manifestation and the essence of phenomena is achieved by ascending from the abstract to the concrete, and from a first-person or experiential perspective to a third person or system perspective.

Formative interventions incorporating these principles are methodologies geared towards human emancipation and the mastery of a desirable future. Anchoring on the notion of activity system is fundamental here insofar as the activity system is not only what gives meaning to actions, but it possesses the characteristics of the whole as a whole. As Levant (2018, p. 106) points out: *'Local activity systems appear as not only possessing the basic characteristics of the whole, but also as the entry point into interpreting and changing it'*.

Conclusion: The Urgency of Expansive Learning in the 21st Century

This book presents a history of CHAT, the main concepts, and the underlying materialist and dialectical philosophy. The project has evolved, as have the concepts, but the anchoring in materiality, in a historical and materialist vision, as well as the anchoring in practice, has endured. Similarly, the political orientation and underlying values have remained consistent.

In accordance with Nicolini (2012), we posit that CHAT is a robust theory. It transcends numerous dichotomies, including those between the individual and society, the local and the global, the cultural and the natural, and the internal and the external. Nevertheless, its history remains incomplete. The current emergence of a fourth generation of CHAT is indicative of the ongoing evolution of this theoretical framework.

Rather than being a *'ready-to-use'* label, the adaptation of CHAT to meet the challenges of the 21st century necessitates in-depth work on concepts as well as methods, on the division of labor as well as on communities. It necessitates working on the contradictions that run through our own research and intervention activities. And it certainly involves scientific and professional controversy. In this respect, CHAT is not only a *'strong theory'*, but also a *'demanding theory'*.

This requirement is evident in a recent work that revisits the concept of agency to extricate it from idealistic acceptance or simply linking it to actions without taking into account the activity in which they are embedded and which they carry out. In light of the contemporary challenges that we face, it is necessary to rethink and reconceptualize the notion of agency. This will demonstrate the limitations of competing or older conceptualizations:

> Understandings of agency as an inherent quality residing within the individual, or as an outcome of a vaguely defined interplay between individuals and their social contexts, are ontologically and epistemologically fallacious,

morally wanting and insufficient to respond to today's pressing societal needs (Hopwood & Sannino, 2023, p. 1).

In addition to the conceptual aspects, the methodologies employed also require attention. This necessitates an expansion of the temporal and spatial scope of interventions. In the context of the phenomenon of '*runaway objects*,' a crucial question for contemporary society is how ordinary people can conceptualize and act on complex phenomena whose implications and consequences can be dramatic. It is necessary to determine how to articulate situational scales of analysis with scales that relate to the planet as a whole. How can local actions have a global impact? How can we engage people in the face of resignation and pessimism? How can we engage workers in the profound transformation of our modes of production that global warming implies? How can we educate our children so that, as adults, they have a comprehensive understanding of a world that is accelerating? How can individuals be empowered to assume control of their collective destiny in an accelerating world?

The necessity of expansive learning to meet the challenges of our times is such that it must be incorporated into research activities, universities, and more broadly into education and training (Loorbach & Wittmayer, 2023). Furthermore, it is crucial to ensure that the legacy of CHAT is not overlooked and that its potential for growth and advancement is seized in the face of these new challenges.

Consequently, as Levant (2018) posits, transformations in our productive practices necessitate more than a mere change of perspective or reflection on the role of humans in the world. Rather, they necessitate the implementation of theoretical frameworks and intervention strategies that prioritize human activity as a central factor, given that it has become the primary geological force on the planet.

It is our firm conviction that CHAT has the capacity and the requisite qualities to meet the challenges of the 21st century.

Postface
The where-to of 4th generation cultural-historical activity theory

– By Annalisa Sannino –

Yannick Lémonie's book addresses key classic and contemporary themes of cultural-historical activity theory. The volume appears when this field of scholarship is attempting to come to terms with the new historical and geological epoch we are living. After the relatively stable period of the Holocene, the consequences of destructive impact of human activity on the planet's ecosystems are becoming blatantly visible. Ongoing discussions among activity theorists and beyond, within and across academic circles and domains of practice increasingly revolve around the *where-to* of this research paradigm.

In these specific circumstances, more than merely an introduction, this book is an invitation to what is technically referred to in CHAT scholarship as expansive learning. It is an invitation to a journey toward a destination which we do not yet know, which we nevertheless start to realize to be necessary. For this reason, I particularly like the apt metaphor of the journey that the author utilized as the figurative common thread of the volume.

For me this is an opportunity to take on the key themes the book proposes as if they were kedge anchors for exploring the where-to of the fourth generation of CHAT. Hopefully others will join in, after reading this book to foster a much-needed warping in the turbulent waters of contemporary academic work. The perspective I am adopting here is primarily one of a CHAT scholar reflecting on the disorienting circumstances in which this tradition is moving step by step toward its fourth generation of theorizing and formative interventions.

Major institutional shifts in academic work have been witnessed and discussed for decades, and the expression *The University in Ruins* used by Bill Readings (1996) is still valid. We know today that the structural diagnosis performed by Readings of the deep institutional transformations in the function of the university was correct. His warning '*The social role of the university as an institution is now up for grabs*' (Readings, 1996, p. 2) sharply resonates in the neoliberal university. Today, nearly thirty years later, university researchers and teachers may experience the contradiction between the market model and the solidarity/responsibility model (LaCapra, 1998) in more suffocating and disorienting ways than before. This is because the epochal challenges faced by humanity and life on the planet are such that the institution of the university cannot any longer afford waiting to significantly reinvent itself. To paraphrase Readings (1996): It is now even more unclear than before what role the university can play within society and what the exact nature of this society is to begin with, and the changing institutional form of the university is something that intellectuals must creatively engage with.

More than a century of development in CHAT, also outlined in Yannick Lémonie's book, offers solid grounds for reimagining and at the same time enacting roles academic research on human activity can play in society. Tentative steps are being undertaken, for instance, by 4th generation CHAT researchers to join the civil society in shaping object-oriented policies. This is how CHAT scholarly activism is reshaping itself today. The theoretical and methodological implications of this are complex and entail refocusing CHAT conceptual lenses in line with the demands that current historical circumstances set for addressing acute societal challenges.

The proposition of historicity is particularly central in the steps awaiting CHAT to develop in its 4th generation. The very task of consolidation of a unit of analysis for the 4th generation requires investing in the historical development of activities in ways that have not been pursued before. The widely distributed nature of 4th generation foci carries with it demands on how to address processes of learning and transformation of activities spanning over multiple years, as well as over multiples sectors and hierarchical levels. 4th generation research agendas may endorse and engage with the historicity proposition by establishing strong links with the civil society in the making of alternatives to capitalism.

The pursuit of enacted utopias is part of this attempt at reconnecting university research with collective endeavors which struggle to maintain momentum despite being essential to support life and its flourishing on our planet. For university research, such an undertaking entails not only digging into the history of these enacted utopias, but also to connect with those who have devoted their lives to them. The conceptual and methodological tools CHAT has developed over a century can serve as powerful instruments to support the enactment of these utopias while at the same time reinventing the roles of the institution of the university in society.

Engaging with the proposition of historicity in this sense means to fulfill the Freirean commitment to critical conscientization in the pedagogy of the oppressed (Freire, 1970a, 1970b) by performing object-oriented participatory analyses of activities within the civil society. As Lémonie clearly reminds us in this volume, these analyses go beyond immediate experience of contradictions. They instead attempt to grasp the dialectics of their becoming, encompassing specific activity systems or even networks of activity systems to identify and contribute to coalescing cycles of expansive learning. May this be a call that the institution of university, which we academics represent, will not miss this time?

References

Aas, M. (2014). Towards a reflection repertoire: Using a thinking tool to understand tensions in an action research project. *Educational Action Research, 22*(3), 441–454. doi:10.1080/09650792.2013.872572

Adamides, E. D. (2020). Activity-based analysis of sociotechnical change. *Systems Research and Behavioral Science, 37*(2), 223–234. doi:10.1002/sres.2616

Adelé, S., Cippelletti, E., Dionisio, C., Lémonie, Y., & Bobilier-Chaumon, M.-E. (2024). Prospecting cooperative intelligent transport systems acceptance by road management teams through activity theory – A qualitative study. *Behaviour & Information Technology*, 1–18. doi:10.1080/0144929X.2024.2301960

Ageyev, V. S. (2003). Vygotsky in the mirror of cultural interprétations. In A. Kozulin, B. Gindis, V. S. Ageyev, & M. Miller (Eds.), *Vygotsky's educational theory in cultural context* (pp. 432–449). Cambridge: Cambridge University press.

Allen, D., Karanasios, S., & Slavova, M. (2011). Working with activity theory: Context, technology, and information behavior. *Journal of the American Society for Information Science and Technology, 62*, 776–788. doi:10.1002/asi.21441

Anderson, T., & Shattuck, J. (2012). Design-based research: A decade of progress in education research? *Educational Researcher, 41*(1), 16–25. doi:10.3102/0013189x11428813

Argyris, C., & Schön, D. A. (2001). Renverser la relation chercheur/praticien. In C. Argyris & D. Schön (Eds.), *Apprentissage organisationnel* (pp. 55–80). Louvain-la-Neuve: De Boeck Supérieur.

Arievitch, I. M. (2017). *Beyond the brain. An agentive activity perspective on mind, development, and learning.* Rotterdam: Sense Publisher.

Arnseth, H. S. (2008). Activity theory and situated learning: Contrasting views of educational practice. *Pedagogy, Culture and Society, 16*(3), 289–302. doi:10.1080/14681360802346663

Augustsson, D. (2021). Expansive learning in a Change Laboratory intervention for teachers. *Journal of Educational Change, 22*(4), 475–499. doi:10.1007/s10833-020-09404-0

Avis, J. (2007). Engeström's version of activity theory: A conservative praxis? *Journal of Education and Work, 20*(3), 161–177. doi:10.1080/13639080701464459

Avis, J. (2009). Transformation or transformism: Engeström's version of activity theory? *Educational Review, 61*(2), 151–165. doi:10.1080/00131910902844754

Bakhurst, D. (2009). Reflections on activity theory. *Educational Review, 61*(2), 197–210. doi:10.1080/00131910902846916

Bakhurst, D. (2019). Punks versus Zombies: Evald Ilienkov and the battle for soviet philosophy. In V. A. Lektorski & M. F. Bykova (Eds.), *Philosophical thought in Russia in the second half of the 20th century* (pp. 53–78). London: Bloomsbury academic.

Bakhurst, D. (2023). *The heart of the matter: Ilyenkov, Vygotsky and the courage of thought*. Leiden: Brill.

Bal, A. (2016). From deficit to expansive learning: Policies, outcomes, and possibilities for multicultural education and systemic transformation in the United States. In J. LoBianco & A. Bal (Eds.), *Learning from difference: Comparative accounts of multicultural education* (Vol. 16, pp. 171–190). Dordrecht: Springer.

Bal, A., Afacan, K., & Cakir, H. I. (2018). Culturally responsive school discipline: Implementing Learning Lab at a high school for systemic transformation. *American Educational Research Journal, 55*(5), 1007–1050. doi:10.3102/0002831218768796

Bal, A., Kozleski, E. B., Schrader, E. M., Rodriguez, E. M., & Pelton, S. (2014). Systemic transformation from the ground-up: Using Learning Lab to design culturally responsive schoolwide positive behavioral supports. *Remedial and Special Education, 35*(6), 327–339. doi:10.1177/0741932514536995

Bal, A., Waitoller, F. R., Mawene, D., & Gorham, A. (2020). Culture, context, and disability: A systematic literature review of cultural-historical activity theory-based studies on the teaching and learning of students with disabilities. *Review of Education, Pedagogy, and Cultural Studies*, 1–45. doi:10.1080/107144 13.2020.1829312

Bannan-Ritland, B. (2003). The role of design in research: The integrative learning design framework. *Educational Researcher, 32*(1), 21–24. doi:10.3102/00131 89X032001021

Barab, S. (2014). Design-based research: A methodological toolkit for engineering change. In J. E. Sawyer (Ed.), *The cambridge handbook of the learning sciences* (2nd ed., pp. 151–170). Cambridge: Cambridge University Press.

Barab, S., & Kirshner, D. (2001). Guest editors' introduction: Rethinking methodology in the learning sciences. *The Journal of the Learning Sciences, 10*(1–2), 5–15. doi:10.1207/S15327809JLS10-1-2_2

Barab, S., & Squire, K. (2004). Design-based research: Putting a stake in the ground. *Journal of the Learning Sciences, 13*(1), 1–14. doi:10.1207/s15327809jls1301_1

Barabanchtchikov, V. A. (2007). La question de l'activité dans la psychologie russe. In V. Nosulenko & P. Rabardel (Eds.), *Rubistein aujourd'hui: nouvelles figures de l'activité humaine* (pp. 63–81). Toulouse: Octarès.

Barends, E., Janssen, B., ten Have, W., & ten Have, S. (2014). Effects of change interventions: What kind of evidence do we really have? *Journal of Applied Behavioral Science, 50*(1), 5–27. doi:10.1177/0021886312473152

Bateson, G. (1980). Vers une écologie de l'esprit, tome 2 Paris. *Éditions du Seuil.*

Bationo-Tillon, A., Cozzolino, F., Krier, S., & Nova, N. (2024). *En quête d'images. Écritures sensibles en recherche-création.* Paris: Presses du Réel.

Beer, M., Eisenstatt, R. A., & Spector, B. (1990). *The critical path to corporate renewal.* Cambridge: Harvard Business School Press.

Beers, P. J., Boshuizen, H. P. E., Kirschner, P. A., & Gijselaers, W. H. (2005). Computer support for knowledge construction in collaborative learning environments. *Computers in Human Behavior, 21*(4), 623–643. doi:10.1016/j.chb. 2004.10.036

Bernstein, N. (1996). *Dexterity and its development.* New York, London: Psychology Press.

Bertelsen, O. W., & Bødker, S. (2003). Activity theory. In J. M. Caroll (Ed.), *HCI models, theories, and frameworks: Toward a multidisciplinary science* (pp. 291–324). San Francisco: Morgan Kaufmann Publishers.

Biesta, G. J. J. (2010). Why 'What Works' still won't work: From evidence-based education to value-based education. *Studies in Philosophy and Education, 29*(5), 491–503. doi:10.1007/s11217-010-9191-x

Blackler, F. (2011). Power, politics, and intervention theory: Lessons from organization studies. *Theory & Psychology, 21*(5), 724–734. doi:10.1177/0959354311418146

Blackler, F., Crump, N., & McDonald, S. (2000). Organizing processes in complex activity networks. *Organization, 7*(2), 277–300. doi:10.1177/135050840072005

Blackler, F., & McDonald, S. (2000). Power, mastery and organizational learning. *Journal of Management Studies, 37*(6), 833–852. doi:10.1111/1467-6486.00206

Bligh, B., & Flood, M. (2015). The Change Laboratory in higher education: Research-intervention using Activity theory. In J. Huisman & M. Tight (Eds.), *Theory and methods in higher education research.* Bingley: Emerald.

Bligh, B., & Flood, M. (2017). Activity theory in empirical higher education research: Choices, uses and values. *Tertiary Education and Management, 23*(2), 125–152. doi:10.1080/13583883.2017.1284258

Bloch, M. (1949/2023). *Apologie pour l'histoire ou métier d'historien.* Paris: SHS Éditions.

Blomberg, J., Suchman, L., & Trigg, R. (1997). Back to work: Renewing old agendas for cooperative design. In M. King & L. Mathiassen (Eds.), *Computers and design in context* (pp. 267–288): MIT Press.

Blumer, H. (1956). Sociological analysis and the 'variable'. *American Sociological Review, 21*(6), 683–690. doi:10.2307/2088418

Blunden, A. (2010). *An interdisciplinary theory of activity.* Leiden – Boston: Brill.

Blunden, A. (2016a). Perezhivanie: From the dictionary of psychology. *Mind Culture and Activity, 23*(4), 272–273. doi:10.1080/10749039.2016.1225310

Blunden, A. (2016b). Translating Perezhivanie into English. *Mind Culture and Activity, 23*(4), 274–283. doi:10.1080/10749039.2016.1186193

Blunden, A. (2019). *Hegel for social movements*: Brill.

Blunden, A. (2023). *Activity theory. A critical overview.* Leiden, Boston: Brill.

Bødker, S. (1991). *Through the interface: A human activity approach to user interface design.* Hillsdale, NJ: Erlbaum.

Bødker, S. (1996). Applying activity theory to video analysis: How to make sense of video data. In B. Nardi (Ed.), *Human-computer interaction. Context and consciousness-Activity Theory and human-computer interface* (pp. 147–174): MIT Press.

Bødker, S. (2009). Past experiences and recent challenges in participatory design research. In A. Sannino, H. Daniels, & K. D. Gutiérrez (Eds.), *Learning and expanding with activity theory.* (pp. 274–285). New York, NY: Cambridge University Press.

Bødker, S., Ehn, P., Sjögren, D., & Sundblad, Y. (2000). *Co-operative design – Perspectives on 20 years with 'the Scandinavian IT Design Model'.* Paper presented at the Proceedings of NordiCHI.

Bødker, S., Grønbaek, K., & Kyng, M. (2009). Cooperative design: Techniques and experiences from the scandinavian scene. In D. Schuler & A. Namioka (Eds.), *Participatory design: Principles and practices* (pp. 157–176). Boca Raton: CRC Press.

Bødker, S., & King, M. (2018). Participatory design that matters – Facing the big issues. *ACM Transactions on Computer-Human Interaction, 25*(1), Article 4. doi:10.1145/3152421

Bødker, S., & Klokmose, C. N. (2011). The human–artifact model: An activity theoretical approach to artifact ecologies. *Human–Computer Interaction, 26*(4), 315–371. doi:10.1080/07370024.2011.626709

Bonneau, C. (2013). *Contradictions and their concrete manifestations: An activity-theoretical analysis of the intra-organizational co-configuration of open source software.* Paper presented at the 29th EGOS Colloquium. http://www.egosnet.org/jart/prj3/egos/resources/dbcon_def/uploads/a4Uzt_EGOS2013_full-paper_ST-50_CBonneau-final2.pdf

Borer, V., Yvon, F., & Durand, M. (2015). Analyser le travail pour former les professionnels de l'éducation? In V. Borer, M. Durand, & F. Yvon (Eds.), *Analyse du travail et formation dans les métiers de l'éducation* (Vol. 7–29). Bruxelles: De Boeck.

Bøttcher, L., & Dammeyer, J. (2012). Disability as a dialectical concept: Building on Vygotsky's defectology. *European Journal of Special Needs Education, 27*(4), 433–446. doi:10.1080/08856257.2012.711958

Boudra, L., Lémonie, Y., Grosstephan, V., & Nascimento, A. (2023). The cultural-historical development of occupational accidents and diseases prevention in France: A scoping review. *Safety Science, 159*, 106016. doi:10.1016/j.ssci.2022.106016

Bound, H. (2022). Flipping the lens from educator to learner. In H. Bound, J. Pei Ling Tan, & R. Lim Wei Ying (Eds.), Pedagogies for future-oriented adult learners. Flipping the lens from teaching to learning (pp. 3–16). Cham: Springer.

Bourgeois, E., & Mornata, C. (2012). Apprendre et transmettre dans le travail. In E. Bourgeois & M. Durand (Eds.), *Apprendre du travail* (pp. 53–67). Paris: PUF.

Bratus, B. S. (2022). The 'Word' and 'Deed': Toward a history of the academic relationship between Aleksei Leont'ev and Lev Vygotskii. *Journal of Russian & East European Psychology, 59*(1–3), 29–42. doi:10.1080/10610405.2022.2115784

Bronckart, J.-P. (2013). Qu'est-ce que le développement humain? Interrogations, impasses et perspectives de clarification. In J. Friedrich, R. Hofstetter, & B. Schneuwly (Eds.), *Une science du développement est-elle possible? Controverses du début du XXe siècle* (pp. 207–226). Rennes: PUR.

Bronfenbrenner, U. (1977). Toward an experimental ecology of human development. *American Psychologist*, 513–531. doi:10.1037/0003-066X.32.7.513

Brossard, M. (2013). Enseignement-apprentissage scolaire et d.veloppement: analyse d'un exemple. In J.-P. Berni. & M. Brossard (Eds.), Vygotski et l' école. Apports et limites d'un modèle théorique pour penser l' éducation et la formation (pp. 21–34). Bordeaux: Presses Universitaires de Bordeaux.

Brown, A. L. (1992). Design experiments: Theoretical and methodological challenges in creating complex interventions in classroom settings. *Journal of the Learning Sciences, 2*(2), 141–178. doi:10.1207/s15327809jls0202_2

Brown, J. S., Collins, A., & Duguid, P. (1989). Situated cognition and the culture of learning. *Educational Researcher, 18*(1), 32–42. doi:10.3102/0013189X018001032

Bryk, A. S. (2015). 2014 AERA distinguished lecture:Accelerating how we learn to improve. *Educational Researcher, 44*(9), 467–477. doi:10.3102/0013189x15621543

Bryk, A. S. (2017). Accélérer la manière dont nous apprenons à améliorer. *Éducation et didactique, 11*(11–2), 11–29. doi:10.4000/educationdidactique.2796

Bullinger, A. (2017). *Le développement sensori-moteur de l'enfant et ses avatars. Tome 2.* Paris: Eres.

Caldwell, H., Krinsky, J., Brunila, M., & Ranta, K. (2019). Learning to common, commoning as learning: The politics and potentials of community land trusts in New York City. *ACME: An International Journal for Critical Geographies, 18*(6), 1207–1233.

Callon, M. (1984). Some elements of a sociology of translation: Domestication of the scallops and the fishermen of St Brieuc Bay. *The Sociological Review, 32*(1_suppl), 196–233. doi:10.1111/j.1467-954X.1984.tb00113.x

Canolle, F., & Vinot, D. (2021). What is your PhD worth? The value of a PhD for finding employment outside of academia. *European Management Review, 18*(2), 157–171. doi:10.1111/emre.12445

Cassell, C., & Johnson, P. (2006). Action research: Explaining the diversity. *Human Relations, 59*(6), 783–814. doi:10.1177/0018726706067080

Cesarino, L. (2020). What the Brazilian 2018 elections tell us about post-truth in the neoliberal-digital era. *Cultural Anthropology Field Sites.*

Chaiklin, S. (2011). Social scientific research and societal practice: Action research and cultural-historical research in methodological light from Kurt Lewin and Lev S. Vygotsky. *Mind, Culture, and Activity, 18*(2), 129–147. doi:10.1080/1074 9039.2010.513752

Chaiklin, S. (2019). The meaning and origin of the activity concept in Soviet psychology with primary focus on A. N. Leontiev's approach. *Theory & Psychology, 29*(1), 3–26. doi:10.1177/0959354319828208

Chandler, D., & Torbert, B. (2003). Transforming inquiry and action: Interweaving 27 flavors of action research. *Action Research, 1*(2), 133–152. doi:10.1177/14767503030012002

Chantre, É., Le Bail, M., & Cerf, M. (2014). Une diversité de configurations d'apprentissage en situation de travail pour réduire l'usage des engrais et pesticides agricoles. *Activites, 11*(2). doi:10.4000/activites.1061

Choudry, S. (2023). Power relations within division of labor – The key to empowering learners from marginalized backgrounds in mathematics classrooms. *Mind, Culture, and Activity,* 1–17. doi:10.1080/10749039.2023.2287448

Ciborra, C. (2002). *The Labyrinths of information. Challenging the wisdom of systems.* Oxford: Oxford University Press.

Clement, A., & Besselaar, P. V. d. (1993). A retrospective look at PD projects. *Communications of the ACM, 36*(6), 29–37. doi:10.1145/153571.163264

Clemmensen, T., Kaptelinin, V., & Nardi, B. (2016). Making HCI theory work: An analysis of the use of activity theory in HCI research. *Behaviour & Information Technology, 35*(8), 608–627. doi:10.1080/0144929X.2016.1175507

Clot, Y. (2000). La formation par l'analyse du travail: pour une troisième voie. In B. Maggi (Ed.), Manières de penser, manières d'agir en éducation et en formation (pp. 133–156). Paris: PUF.

Clot, Y. (2001). Clinique du travail et action sur soi. In J. Friedrich (Ed.), *Théories de l'action et éducation* (pp. 255–277): De Boeck Supérieur.

Clot, Y. (2006). *La fonction psychologique du travail*. Paris: PUF.

Clot, Y. (2008). *Travail et pouvoir d'agir*. Paris: PUF.

Clot, Y. (2009). Clinics of activitity: The dialogue as instrument. In A. Sannino, H. Daniels, & K. D. Gutierez (Eds.), *Learning and expanding with activity theory* (pp. 286–302). Cambridge: Cambridge University Press.

Clot, Y. (2010). Au-delà de l'hygiénisme: l'activité délibérée. *Nouvelle revue de psychosociologie, 10*(2), 41–50. doi:10.3917/nrp. 010.0041

Clot, Y. (2015). Vygotski avec Spinoza, au-delà de Freud. *Revue philosophique de la France et de l'étranger, 140*(2), 205–224. doi:10.3917/rphi.152.0205

Clot, Y. (2017). L'intervention: entre terrain et laboratoire. In A. L. Ulman, A. Weill-Fassina, & T. H. Benchekroun (Eds.), *Intervenir. Histoires, recherches, pratiques* (pp. 185–190). Toulouse: Octares.

Clot, Y., & Béguin, P. (2004). L'action située dans le développement de l'activité. *Activites, 01*(2). doi:10.4000/activites.1237

Clot, Y., Faïta, D., Fernandez, G., & Scheller, L. (2002). Entretiens en autoconfrontation croisée: une méthode en clinique de l'activité. *Education Permanente, 146*, 17–27.

Clot, Y., & Stimec, A. (2013). « Le dialogue a une vertu mutative », les apports de la clinique de l'activité. *Négociations, 19*(1), 113–125. doi:10.3917/neg.019.0113

Cobb, P., Confrey, J., diSessa, A., Lehrer, R., & Schauble, L. (2003). Design experiments in educational research. *Educational Researcher, 32*(1), 9–13. doi:10.3102/0013189x032001009

Cole, M. (1996). *Cultural psychology: A once and future discipline*. Cambridge: Harvard University Press.

Cole, M. (1999). Cultural psychology: Some general principles and a concrete example. In Y. Engeström, R. Miettinen, & R.-L. Punamaki (Eds.), *Perspectives on activity theory* (pp. 87–106). Cambridge: Cambridge University Press.

Cole, M. (2009). The Perils of translation: A first step in reconsidering Vygotsky's Theory of Development in relation to formal education. *Mind Culture and Activity, 16*(4), 291–295. doi:10.1080/10749030902795568

Cole, M. (2019). Re-covering the idea of a tertiary artifact. In A. Edwards, M. Fleer, & L. Bøttcher (Eds.), *Cultural-historical approaches to studying learning and development. Societal, Institutional and personal perspectives* (pp. 303–321). Singapour: Springer.

Cole, M., & Engeström, Y. (1993). A cultural-historical approach to distributed cognition. *Distributed cognitions: Psychological and educational considerations*, 1–46.

Cole, M., & Engeström, Y. (2007). Cultural-historical approaches to designing for development. In J. Valsiner & A. Rosa (Eds.), *The Cambridge handbook of sociocultural psychology* (pp. 484–507). Cambridge: Cambridge University Press.

Cole, M., Levitin, K., & Luria, A. (2006). *The autobiography of Alexander Luria. A dialogue with the making of mind.* Mahwah: Lawrence Erlbaum Associates.

Cole, M., & Packer, M. (2016). A bio-cultural-historical approach to the study of development. *Advances in Culture and Psychology*.

Cole, M., Penuel, W. R., & O'Neill, D. K. (2018). *Cultural-historical activity theory approaches to design-based research.* London and New York: Routledge.

Collective, D.-B. R. (2003). Design-Based Research: An emerging paradigm for educational inquiry. *Educational Researcher, 32*(1), 5–8. doi:10.3102/0013189x032001005

Collins, A. (1992). *Toward a design science of education.* Berlin, Heidelberg.

Collins, A., Joseph, D., & Bielaczyc, K. (2004). Design research: Theoretical and methodological issues. *Journal of the Learning Sciences, 13*(1), 15–42. doi:10.1207/s15327809jls1301_2

Cosseron, M., & Treguier-Rosario, S. (2021). *Expérimentation d'un Laboratoire du Changement au sein d'une Maison d'Accueil Spécialisée: pour une approche systémique des causes de l'absentéisme.* (Master). Conservatoire National des Arts et Métiers,

Costa, S. V., Macaia, A. A. S., Maeda, S. T., Querol, M. A. P., Seppanen, L. E., & Vilela, R. A. G. (2018). Change laboratory: A method for understating the crisis between public university and society. *Saude E Sociedade, 27*(3), 769–782. doi:10.1590/s0104-12902018170845

Cuvelier, L. (2023). Constructive activity and expansion of the object: Cross-fertilization between activity theories. *Mind, Culture, and Activity*, 1–18. doi:10.1080/10749039.2023.2211804

Cuvelier, L., Boudra, L., Boursaly, P., Flessel, N., Grosstephan, V., Poujol, L., . . . Nascimento, A. (2023). Apprendre à perdre du temps: l'exemple d'espaces de discussion sur l'activité de travail. *Soins cadres, 32*(141), 10.1016/j.scad.2023.1001.1003

Dafermos, M. (2014). Vygotsky's analysis of the crisis in psychology: Diagnosis, treatment, and relevance. *Theory & Psychology, 24*(2), 147–165. doi:10.1177/0959354314523694

Dafermos, M. (2015). Activity theory: Theory and practice. In I. Parker (Ed.), *Handbook of critical psychology* (pp. 261–270). London: Routledge.

Dafermos, M. (2016). Critical reflection on the reception of Vygotsky's theory in the international academic communities. *Cultural-Historical Psychology, 12*(3), 27–46. doi:10.17759/chp. 2016120303

Dafermos, M. (2018). *Rethinking cultural-historical theory: A dialectical perspective to Vygotsky.* Singapore: Springer.

Dafermos, M. (2019). Developing a dialectical understanding of generalization: An unfinalized dialogue between Vygotsky and Davydov. In *Subjectivity and Knowledge* (pp. 61–77): Springer.

Dafermos, M. (2020). Reconstructing the fundamental ideas of Vygotsky's theory in the contemporary social and scientific context. In A. Tanzi Neto, F. Liberali, & M. Dafermos (Eds.), *Revisiting Vygotsky for social change: Bringing together theory and practice* (pp. 13–30). Berne: Peter Lang.

Dafermos, M., Chronaki, A., & Kontopodis, M. (2020). Cultural-historical activity theory travels to Greece: Actors, contexts and politics of reception and interpretation. *Cultural-Historical Psychology, 16*(2), 33–41. doi:10.17759/chp. 202016020

Daniellou, F., & Rabardel, P. (2005). Activity-oriented approaches to ergonomics: Some traditions and communities. *Theoretical Issues in Ergonomics Science, 6*(5), 353–357.

Daniels, H. (2001). *Vygotsky and pedagogy.* London, New York: Routledge.

Daniels, H. (2006). Rethinking Intervention: Changing the cultures of schooling. *Emotional and Behavioural Difficulties, 11*(2), 105–120. doi:10.1080/13632750600619273

Daniels, H., Cole, M., & Wertsch, J. V. (2007). *The Cambridge companion to Vygotsky.* Cambridge: Cambridge University Press.

Davids, K., Glazier, P., Araújo, D., & Bartlett, R. (2003). Movement systems as dynamical systems: The functional role of variability and its implications for sports medicine. *Sports medicine, 33*, 245–260. doi:10.2165/00007256- 200333040-00001

Davies, P. (1999). What is evidence-based education? *British Journal of Educational Studies, 47*(2), 108–121. doi:10.1111/1467-8527.00106

Davison, R. M., Martinsons, M. G., & Malaurent, J. (2021). Research perspectives: Improving action research by integrating methods. *Journal of the Association for Information Systems, 22*(3), 1. doi:10.17705/1jais.00682

Davydov, V. V. (1990a). Problems of activity as a mode of human existence and the principle of monism. In V. P. Lektorski (Ed.), *Activity: The theory, methodology and problems* (pp. 127–132). Orlando, Helsinki, Moscou: Paul M. Deutsch Press.

Davydov, V. V. (1990b). *Type of generalization in instruction: Logical and psychological problems in the structuring of school curricula.* Reston, VA: National Council of Teachers of Mathematics.

Davydov, V. V. (1999). The content and unsolved problems of activity theory. In R.-L. Punamäki, R. Miettinen, & Y. Engeström (Eds.), *Perspectives on activity theory* (pp. 39–52). Cambridge: Cambridge University Press.

Davydov, V. V. (2008). *Problems of developmental instruction: A theoretical and experimental psychological study* (Vol. Nova). New York.

De Corte, E., Verschaffel, L., Entwistle, N., & van Merriënboer, J. (2003). *Powerful learning environments: Unravelling basic components and dimensions.* Amsterdam: Pergamon.

De la Torre, J. (2022). *Learning together in the face of the contamination of a river basins in Mexico: University establishing a social bond with a local community.* Paper presented at the Communication au séminaire RESET-CRADLE, Online.

de La Ville, V.-I., Leca, B., & Magakian, J.-L. (2011). Vygotski aujourd'hui en management. *Management & Avenir, 42*(2), 78–88. doi:10.3917/mav.042.0078

De Landsheere, V. (1992). *L'éducation et la formation.* Paris: PUF.

Detchessahar, M., Gentil, S., Grevin, A., & Stimec, A. (2015). Quels modes d'intervention pour soutenir la discussion sur le travail dans les organisations ?Réflexions méthodologiques à partir de l'intervention dans une clinique. *@GRH, 16*(3), 63–89. doi:10.3917/grh.153.0063

Dinh, H., & Sannino, A. (2024). Toward a diagnostic toolkit for intervention in teachers' agency during curriculum reform: Groundwork for a Change Laboratory in Vietnam. *Teaching and Teacher Education, 140,* 104494. doi:10.1016/j.tate.2024.104494

Dodds, P., & Fletcher, J. (2004). Opportunities for new 'smart' learning environments enabled by next-generation web capabilities. *Journal of Educational Multimedia and Hypermedia, 13*(4), 391–404.

Donatelli, S., Vilela, R. A. G., Querol, M. A. P., & Gemma, S. F. B. (2020). Collective development of a flow of care for children and teenagers exposed to work: Using the double stimulation method. *Interface-Comunicação, Saúde, Educação, 24.*

Dubet, F. (2019). Educational inequalities: Structures, processes, and models of justice. The debate in France over the last fifty years. *Revue Europeenne Des Sciences Sociales, 57*(2), 111–136. doi:10.4000/ress.5736

Durand, M. (1993). Apprentissage, strtégies de recherches et optimisation de la performance. In J.-P. Famose (Ed.), *Cognition et Performance* (pp. 61–78). Paris: INSEP Éditions.

Durand, M. (2008). Un programme de recherche technologique en formation des adultes. Une approche enactive de l'activité humaine et l'accompagnement de son apprentissage/développement. *Éducation & didactique, 2*(3), 97–121. doi:10.4000/educationdidactique.373

Durand, M., & Barbier, J.-M. (2003). L'activité: un objet intégrateur pour les sciences sociales. *Recherche et formation, 42,* 99–117. doi:10.3406/refor.2003.1831

Eames, C., & Aguayo, C. (2020). *Designing mobile learning with education outside the classroom to enhance marine ecological literacy.* Retrieved from

Easterday, M. W., Lewis, D. R., & Gerber, E. M. (2014). *Design-based research process: Problems, phases, and applications.* Boulder, CO: International Society of the Learning Sciences.

Edwards, A. (2000). Looking at action research through the lenses of sociocultural psychology and activity theory. *Educational Action Research, 8*(1), 195–204. doi:10.1080/09650790000200104

Ehn, P. (2009). Sandinavian design: On participation and skill. In D. Schuler & A. Namioka (Eds.), *Participatory design* (pp. 41–77). Boca Raton: CRC PRESS.

Ehn, P., & Kyng, M. (1991). Cardboard Computers. In J. Grennbaum & M. Kyng (Eds.), *Design at work: Cooperative design of computer systems* (pp. 169–196). Hillsdale, NJ: Lawrence Erlbaum Associates.

Elhammouni, M. (2015). Marxist psychology and dialectical method. In I. Parker (Ed.), *Handbook of critical psychology* (pp. 271–279). London: Routledge.

Elliott, J. (1993). What have we learned from action research in school-based evaluation? *Educational Action Research, 1*(1), 175–186. doi:10.1080/0965079930010110

Eloi, S. (2022). *Approche socio-instrumentale de l'activité humaine. Développement dialectique dans le champ des Pratiques Physiques Sportives et Artistiques.* (Diplôme d'Habilitation à Diriger les Recherches). Paris Est Créteil, Retrieved from https://hal.science/hal-04333092v1.

Engeness, I., & Lund, A. (2020). Learning for the future: Insights arising from the contributions of Piotr Galperin to the cultural-historical theory. *Learning, Culture and Social Interaction, 25,* 100257. doi:10.1016/j.lcsi.2018.11.004

Engeström, Y. (1970). *Koulutus luokkayhteiskunnassa-johdatus kapitalistisen yhteiskunnan koulutusongelmiin*: Gummerus.

Engeström, Y. (1987). *Learning by expanding: An activity-theorical approach to developmental research.* Helsinki: Orienta-Konsultit.

Engeström, Y. (1990a). *Learning, working and imagining: Twelve studies in activity theory.* Helsinki: Orienta-Konsultit.

Engeström, Y. (1990b). When is a tool? Multiple meanings of artifacts in human activity. In Y. Engeström (Ed.), *Learning, working and imagining: Twelve studies in activity theory* (pp. 171–195). Helsinki: Orienta-Konsultit.

Engeström, Y. (1993). Developmental studies of work as a testbench of activity theory: The case of primary care medical practice. In S. Chaiklin & J. Lave (Eds.), *Understanding practice: Perspectives on activity and context* (pp. 64–103). Cambridge: Cambridge University Press.

Engeström, Y. (1995). Objects, contradictions and collaboration in medical cognition: An activity-theoretical perspective. *Artificial Intelligence in Medecine, 7,* 395–412. doi:10.1016/0933-3657(95)00012-U

Engeström, Y. (1996a). Development as breacking away and opening up: A challenge to vygotsky and piaget. *Swiss Journal of Psychology, 55,* 126–132.

Engeström, Y. (1996b). Developmental work research as educational research: Looking ten years back and into the zone of proximal development. *Nordisk Pedagogik, 16,* 131–143.

Engeström, Y. (1996c). Interobjectivity, ideality, and dialectics. *Mind, Culture, and Activity, 3*(4), 259–265. doi:10.1207/s15327884mca0304_5

Engeström, Y. (1999a). Activity theory and individual and social transformation. In Y. Engeström, R. Miettinen, & R.-L. Punamäki (Eds.), *Perspectives on activity theory* (pp. 19–38). Cambridge: Cambridge University Press.

Engeström, Y. (1999b). Innovative learning in work teams: Analyzing cycles of knowledge creation in practice. In Y. Engeström, R. Miettinen, & R.-L. Punamaki (Eds.), *Perspectives on activity theory* (pp. 377–406). Cambridge: Cambridge University Press.

Engeström, Y. (2000a). Activity theory as a framework for analysing and redesigning work. *Ergonomics, 43*(7), 960–974. doi:10.1080/001401300409143

Engeström, Y. (2000b). Can people learn to master their future? *Journal of the Learning Sciences, 9*(4), 525–534. doi:10.1207/s15327809jls0904_8

Engeström, Y. (2000c). From individual action to collective activity and back: Developmental work research as an interventionist methodology. In P. Luff, J. Hindmarsch, & C. Heath (Eds.), *Workplace studies: Work practice and informing system design* (pp. 150–166). Cambridge: Cambridge University Press.

Engeström, Y. (2001). Expansive learning at work: Toward an activity theoretical reconceptualization. *Journal of Education and Work, 14*(1), 133–156. doi:10.1080/13639080020028747

Engeström, Y. (2005). *Developmental work research: Expanding activity theory in practice.* Berlin: Lehmanns Media.

Engeström, Y. (2006). From well-bounded ethnographies to intervening in Mycorrhizae activities. *Organization Studies, 27*(12), 1783–1793. doi:10.1177/0170840606071898

Engeström, Y. (2007a). From stabilization knowledge to possibility knowledge in organizational learning. *Management Learning, 38*(3), 271–275. doi:10.1177/1350507607079026

Engeström, Y. (2007b). Putting Vygotsky to work. The Change Laboratory as an application of double stimulation. In H. Daniels, M. Cole, & J. V. Wertsch (Eds.),

The Cambridge companion to Vygotsky (pp. 363–382). Cambridge: Cambridge University Press.

Engeström, Y. (2008). *From teams to knots. Activity-theoretical studies of collaboration and learning at work.* Cambridge: Cambridge University Press.

Engeström, Y. (2009a). From learning environments and implementation to activity systems and expansive learning. *Actio: An International Journal of Human Activity Theory, 2,* 17–33.

Engeström, Y. (2009b). The future of activity theory: A rough draft. In A. Sannino, H. Daniels, & K. D. Gutierez (Eds.), *Learning and expanding with activity theory.* New York: Cambridge University Press.

Engeström, Y. (2011). From design experiments to formative interventions. *Theory & Psychology, 21*(5), 598–628. doi:10.1177/0959354311419252

Engeström, Y. (2015). *Learning by expanding (2nd edition): an activity-theoretical approach to developmental research.* Cambridge: Cambridge University Press.

Engeström, Y. (2016). *Studies in expansive learning.* Cambridge: Cambridge University Press.

Engeström, Y. (2017). Improvement versus transformation. *Éducation & didactique, 11*(2), 31–34. doi:10.4000/educationdidactique.2718

Engeström, Y. (2018). *Expertise in transition expansive learning in medical work preface.* Cambridge: Cambridge University Press.

Engeström, Y. (2020a). Ascending from the abstract to the concrete as a principle of expansive learning. *Psychological Science and Education, 25*(5), 31–43. doi:10.17759/pse.2020250503

Engeström, Y. (2020b). Concept formation in the wild: Towards a research agenda. *Éducation & didactique, 14*(2), 99–113. doi:10.4000/educationdidactique.6816

Engeström, Y., Engeström, R., & Suntio, A. (2002). Can a school community learn to master its own future? An activity-theoretical study of expansive learning among middle school teachers. In G. Wells & G. Claxton (Eds.), *Learning for life in the 21st century: Sociocultural perspectives on the future of education.* (pp. 211–224). Malden: Blackwell Publishing.

Engeström, Y., & Escalante, V. (1996). Mundane tool or object of affection? The rise and fall of the Postal Buddy. In B. Nardi (Ed.), *Context and consciousness: Activity theory and human-computer interaction.* Cambridge: The MIT Press.

Engeström, Y., Kaatrakoski, H., Kaiponen, P., Lahikainen, J., Laitinen, A., Myllis, H., … Sinikara, K. (2012). Knotworking in academic libraries: Two case studies from the university of Helsinki. *Liber Quaterly, 21*(3/4), 387–405. doi:10.18352/lq.8032

Engeström, Y., Kajamaa, A., & Nummijoki, J. (2015). Double stimulation in everyday work: Critical encounters between home care workers and their elderly clients. *Learning, Culture and Social Interaction*, *4*(1), 48–61. doi:10.1016/j. lcsi.2014.07.005

Engeström, Y., & Keruoso, H. (2007). From workplace learning to inter-organizational learning and back: The contribution of activity theory. *Journal of Workplace Learning*, *19*(6), 336–342. doi:10.1108/13665620710777084

Engeström, Y., Nummijoki, J., & Sannino, A. (2012). Embodied Germ Cell at work: Building an expansive concept of physical mobility in home care. *Mind, Culture and Activity*, *19*(3), 287–309. doi:10.1080/10749039.2012.688177

Engeström, Y., Puonti, A., & Seppänen, L. (2003). Spatial and temporal expansion of the object as a challenge for reorganizing work. In D. Nicolini, S. Gherardi, & D. Yanow (Eds.), *Knowing in organizations: A practice-based approach* (pp. 151–186). Armonk: Sharpe.

Engeström, Y., Rantavuori, J., & Kerosuo, H. (2013). Expansive learning in a library: Actions, cycles and deviations from instructional intentions. *Vocations and Learning*, *6*(1), 81–106. doi:10.1007/s12186-012-9089-6

Engeström, Y., Rantavuori, P., Ruutu, P., & Tapola-Haapala, M. (2022). The hybridisation of adolescents' worlds as a source of developmental tensions: A study of discursive manifestations of contradictions. *Educational Review*, 1–22. doi:10.1080/00131911.2022.2033704

Engeström, Y., Rantavuori, P., Ruutu, P., & Tapola-Haapala, M. (2023a). Finding life beyond the classroom walls: A Change Laboratory supporting expansive de-encapsulation of school. *Éducation & didactique*, *18*(2), 125–141.

Engeström, Y., Rantavuori, P., Ruutu, P., & Tapola-Haapala, M. (2023b). From future orientation to future making. Towards adolescents transformative agency. In N. Hopwood & A. Sannino (Eds.), *Agency and transformation* (pp. 107–138). Cambridge: Cambridge University Press.

Engeström, Y., & Sannino, A. (2010). Studies of expansive learning: Foundations, findings and future challenges. *Educational Research Review*, *5*(1), 1–24. doi:10.1016/j.edurev.2009.12.002

Engeström, Y., & Sannino, A. (2011). Discursive manifestations of con-tradictions in organizational change efforts: A methodological frame-work. *Journal of Organizational Change Management*, *24*(3), 368–387. doi:10.1108/09534811111132758

Engeström, Y., & Sannino, A. (2012). What happened to process theories of learning. *Learning, Culture and Social Interaction*, *1*, 45–56. doi:10.1016/j. lcsi.2012.03.002

Engeström, Y., & Sannino, A. (2014). On the methodological demands of forma-tive interventions. *Mind, Culture and Activity*, *21*(2), 118–128. doi:10.1080/107 49039.2014.891868

Engeström, Y., & Sannino, A. (2020). From mediated actions to heterogenous coalitions: Four generations of activity-theoretical studies of work and learning. *Mind Culture and Activity*, 20. doi:10.1080/10749039.2020.1806328

Engeström, Y., & Sannino, A. (Forthcoming). Genèse instrumentale et double stimulation: regards vygotskiens complémentaires sur l'apprentissage et le développement humain. In A. Bationo-Tillon, F. Decortis, G. Bourmaud, & V. Folcher (Eds.), *Approche instrumentale. Expansion et devenirs*. Toulouse: Octares.

Engeström, Y., Sannino, A., & Virkkunen, J. (2014). On the methodological demands of formative interventions. *Mind, Culture, and Activity*. doi:10.1080/10749039.2014.891868

Englund, C. (2018). Exploring interdisciplinary academic development: The Change Laboratory as an approach to team-based practice. *Higher Education Research & Development, 37*(4), 698–714. doi:10.1080/07294360.2018.1441809

Eyme, J. (2017). Engeström ou la troisième génération de la « théorie de l'activité ». In J.-M. Barbier & M. Durand (Eds.), *Encyclopédie d'anlyse des activités* (pp. 495–506). Paris: PUF.

Farnea, V., & Jeanpierre, L. (2013). Des utopies possibles aux utopies réelles. Entretien avec Erik Olin Wright. *Tracés. Revue de Sciences humaines, 24*, 231–243. doi:10.4000/traces.5672

Feigenberg, J. M. (2014). *Nikolai Bernstein. From reflex to the model of the future*. Zürich, Berlin: LIT Verlag.

Fenwick, T., Edwards, R., & Sawchuk, P. (2015). *Emerging approaches to educational research: Tracing the socio-material*. London: Routledge.

Ferreira, B. E., Vilela, R. A. G., Nascimento, A., Almeida, I. M., Lopes, M. G. F., Braatz, D., & Mininel, V. A. (2023). Occupational risks prevention in hospitals based on the cultural-historical activity theory. *Ciença Saude Coletiva*.

Foot, K. A. (2001). Cultural-historical activity theory as practical theory: Illuminating the development of a conflict monitoring network. *Communication Theory, 11*(1), 56–83. doi:10.1111/j.1468-2885.2001.tb00233.x

Foot, K. A. (2002). Pursuing an evolving object: A case study in object formation and identification. *Mind, Culture, and Activity, 9*(2), 132–149. doi:10.1207/S15327884MCA0902_04

Frambach, J. M., Driessen, E. W., & vander Vleuten, C. P. M. (2014). Using activity theory to study cultural complexity in medical education. *Perspectives in Medical Education, 3*, 190–203. doi: 10.1007/s40037-014-0114-3

Fraser, J., & Yasnitsky, A. (2015). Deconstructing Vygotsky's victimization narrative: A re-examination of the 'Stalinist suppression' of Vygotskian theory. *History of the Human Sciences, 28*(2), 128–153. doi:10.1177/0952695114560200

Freire, P. (1970a). Cultural action and conscientization. *Harvard Educational Review, 40*, 452–457. doi:10.17763/haer.40.3.h76250x720j43175

Freire, P. (1970b). *Pedagogy of the oppresed.* New York: Continuum.

Freire, P. (1975). *Educação Política e Conscientização.* Lisboa: Sá da Costa.

Freire, P. (1991). *L'Éducation dans la ville.* Paris: Éditions Païdeia.

Friedrich, J. (2010). *Lev Vygotski: médiation, apprentissage et développement. Une lecture philosophique et épistémologique.* Genève: Université de Genève.

Gal'perin, P. (1984). Memories of A. N. Leont'ev. *Soviet Psychology, 23*(1), 57–62. doi:10.2753/RPO1061-0405230157

Galperine, P., Engeness, I., & Thomas, G. (2023). *Psychological significance between tools use by humans and animals. P. Y. Galperin's dissertation.* Cham: Springer.

Garrido, C. L. (2022). *Marxism and the materialism worldview.* Dubuque, Carbondale: Midwestern Marx Publishing Press.

Gibson, J. J. (1979/2014). *Approche écologique de la perception visuelle.* Putois, Bellevaux: Éditions Dehors.

Giddens, A. (2003). *Runaway world. How globalization is reshaping our lives.* New York: Routledge.

Giest, H. (2018). Vygotsky's defectology: A misleading term for a great conception. *Educação, 41*(3), 334–346. doi:10.15448/1981-2582.2018.3.31725

Gillespie, A., & Zittoun, T. (2010). Using resources: Conceptualizing the mediation and reflective use of tools and signs. *Culture & Psychology, 16*(1), 37–62. doi:10.1177/1354067x09344888

Gindis, B. (1995). The social/cultural implication of disability: Vygotsky's paradigm for special education. *Educational Psychologist, 30*(2), 77–81. doi:10.1207/s15326985ep3002_4

Goertzen, J. R. (2008). On the possibility of unification: The reality and nature of the crisis in psychology. *Theory & Psychology, 18*(6), 829–852. doi:10.1177/0959354308097260

González Rey, F. (2020). Can the concept of activity be considered as a theoretical device for critical psychologies? In M. Fleer, F. González Rey, & P. E. Jones (Eds.), *Cultural-historical and critical psychology: Common ground, divergences and future pathways* (pp. 79–97). Singapore: Springer Singapore.

Gosselin, P., & Le Coguiec, É. (2006). *Recherche création: Pour une compréhension de la recherche en pratique artistique*: PUQ.

Gramsci, A. (1971). Selection from Prison Notebooks. Eds. *Quintin Hoare & Geoffrey Smith. New York: International.*

Greeno, J. G. (2016). Cultural-historical activity theory/design-based research in Pasteur's Quadrant. *Journal of the Learning Sciences, 25*(4), 634–639. doi:10.108 0/10508406.2016.1221718

Gramsci, A. (1971). Selection from Prison Notebooks. Eds. *Quintin Hoare & Geoffrey Smith. New York: International.*

Greeno, J. G., & Engeström, Y. (2014). Learning in activity. In R. K. Sawyer (Ed.), *The Cambridge handbook of the learning sciences* (2 ed., pp. 128–148). Cambridge: Cambridge University Press.

Gregor, S. (2006). The nature of theory in information systems. *MIS Quarterly,* 611–642.

Guérin, F., Pueyo, V., Béguin, P., Garrigou, A., Hubault, F., Maline, J., & Morlet, T. (2021). *Concevoir le travail, le défi de l'ergonomie.* Toulouse: Octarès.

Haapasaari, A., Engeström, Y., & Keruoso, H. (2016). The emergence of learners' transformative agency in a Change Laboratory intervention. *Journal of Education and Work, 29*(2), 232–262. doi:10.1080/13639080.2014.900168

Haapasaari, A., & Kerosuo, H. (2015). Transformative agency: The challenges of sustainability in a long chain of double stimulation. *Learning Culture and Social Interaction, 4,* 37–47. doi:10.1016/j.lcsi.2014.07.006

Hackel, M., & Klebl, M. (2014). The double path of expansive learning in complex socio-technical change processes. *Outlines: Critical Practice Studies, 15*(1), 4–27. doi:10.7146/ocps.v15i1.15829

Hardman, J. (2008). Researching pedagogy: An activity theory approach. *Journal of Education, 45*(1), 65–95.

Hasse, C. (2024). Activity theory, socratic ignorance and posthumanism. In A. Levant, K. Murakami, & M. McSweeney (Eds.), *Activity theory. An introduction* (pp. 219–242): Ibidem.

Hatch, M.J. (1997). Irony and the social construction of contradiction in the humor of a management team. Organization Science, 8(3), 275–88. doi: 10.1287/ orsc.8.3.275

Hausdorff, J. M., Purdon, P. L., Peng, C.-K., Ladin, Z., Wei, J. Y., & Goldberger, A. L. (1996). Fractal dynamics of human gait: stability of long-range correlations in stride interval fluctuations. *Journal of Applied Physiology, 80*(5), 1448–1457. doi:10.1152/jappl.1996.80.5.1448

Hefetz, G., & Ben-Zvi, D. (2020). How do communities of practice transform their practices? *Learning, Culture and Social Interaction, 26,* 100410. doi:10.1016/j. lcsi.2020.100410

Heron, J., & Reason, P. (1997). A participatory inquiry paradigm. *Qualitative Inquiry, 3*(3), 274–294. doi:10.1177/107780049700300302

Herrington, J., & Oliver, R. (2000). An instructional design framework for authentic learning environments. *Educational Technology Research and Development*, 23–48.

Ho, J. P. Y., Victor Chen, D.-T., & Ng, D. (2016). Distributed leadership through the lens of activity theory. *Educational Management Administration & Leadership*, *44*(5), 814–836. doi:10.1177/1741143215570302

Hoadley, C. (2002). *Creating context: Design-based research in creating and understanding CSCL*. Paper presented at the CSCL.

Hoadley, C., & Campos, F. C. (2022). Design-based research: What it is and why it matters to studying online learning. *Educational Psychologist, 57*(3), 207–220. doi:10.1080/00461520.2022.2079128

Holtzblatt, K., & Beyer, H. (1997). *Contextual design: Defining customer-centered systems*: Elsevier.

Holzman, L. (2006). What kind of theory is activity theory?: Introduction. *Theory & Psychology, 16*(1), 5–11. doi:10.1177/0959354306060105

Hopwood, N., & Gottschalk, B. (2017). Double stimulation 'in the wild': Services for families with children at-risk. *Learning Culture and Social Interaction, 13*, 23–37. doi:10.1016/j.lcsi.2017.01.003

Hopwood, N., & Sannino, A. (2023). Motives, mediation and motion: Towards an inherently learning and development orientated perspective on agency. In N. Hopwood & A. Sannino (Eds.), *Agency and transformation* (pp. 1–34). Cambridge: Cambridge University Press.

Houssaye, J. (2011). Pédagogie, le constat: le changement ne se fait pas. *Carrefours de l'éducation* (4), 109–121.

Huotari, R. (2008). Development of collaboration in multiproblem cases some possibilities and challenges. *Journal of Social Work, 8*(1), 83–98. doi:10.1177/1468017307084741

Hurtado, S. L. B., Vilela, R. A. G., Almeida, I. M., Filho, J. M. J., Querol, M. A. P., Rocha, R., … Costa, S. V. (2020). Contributions from the Change Laboratory to the analysis and prevention of accidents' model. In R. A. D. Vilela, M. A. P. Querol, S. L. B. Hurtado, G. C. O. Cerveny, & M. G. R. Lopes (Eds.), *Collaborative development for the drevention of occupational accidents and diseases. Change Laboratory in worker's health* (pp. 207–223). Cham, Switzerland: Spinger.

Hutchins, E. (1995). *Cognition in the wild*. Cambridge, London: MIT Press.

Iaroshevskii, M. G. (1995). Bez istorii pusta metodologiia. *Voprosy Psikhologii, 4*, 141–146.

Ilyenkov, E. (2002). Shkola dolzhna uchit myslit [Schools must teach thinking]. Moscow/Voronezh: Moskovskii Psikhologo-Sotsialnyi Institut.

Ilyenkov, E. V. (1982/2008). *The dialectics of the abstract and the concrete in Marx's Capital*: Aakar Books.

Ivaldi, S., Sannino, A., & Scaratti, G. (2022). Is 'co' in coworking a short for contradictions? *Qualitative Research in Organizations and Management: An International Journal, 17*(5), 38–63. doi:10.1108/QROM-06-2020-1970

Järvelä, S., & Volet, S. (2004). Motivation in real-life, dynamic, and interactive learning environments: Stretching constructs and methodologies. *9*(4), 193–197. doi:10.1027/1016-9040.9.4.193

Jornet, A., & Roth, W. M. (2016). Perezhivanie: A monist concept for a monist theory. *Mind Culture and Activity, 23*(4), 353–355. doi:10.1080/10749039.2016.1199703

Jungk, R., & Müllert, N. (1987). *Future workshops: How to create desirable futures*. London: Inst. for Social Inventions.

Junior, O. A. F., Lesama, M. F., & Querol, M. A. P. (2023). Transformative agency by double stimulation in an ecological agroforestry association from Brazil. Reflections from a Change Laboratory intervention. In N. Hopwood & A. Sannino (Eds.), *Agency and transformation* (pp. 289–310). Cambridge: Cambridge University Press.

Juuti, K., & Lavonen, J. (2006). Design-based research in science education: One step towards methodology. *Nordic studies in science education, 2*(2), 54–68.

Kant, V. (2016). Extending the Repertoire of activity theory in HCI: N. A. Bernstein and the role of the body. *Interacting with Computers, 28*(4), 479–500. doi:10.1093/iwc/iwv019

Kaptelinin, V. (2003). Learning with artefacts: Integrating technologies into activities. *Interacting with Computers, 15*(6), 831–836. doi:10.1016/j.intcom.2003.09.006

Kaptelinin, V. (2005). The object of activity: Making sense of the sense-maker. *Mind, Culture, and Activity, 12*(1), 4–18. doi:10.1207/s15327884mca1201_2

Kaptelinin, V., & Nardi, B. (2006). *Acting with technology. Activity theory and interaction design*. London: MIT Press.

Kaptelinin, V., & Nardi, B. (2018). Activity theory as a framework for human-technology interaction research. *Mind Culture and Activity, 25*(1), 3–5. doi:10.1080/10749039.2017.1393089

Karanasios, S., Nardi, B., Spinuzzi, C., & Malaurent, J. (2021). Moving forward with activity theory in a digital world. *Mind, Culture, and Activity, 28*(3), 234–253. doi:10.1080/10749039.2021.1914662

Kaup, C., & Brooks, E. (2022). Cultural-historical perspective on how double stimulation triggers expansive learning. *Designs for Learning, 14*(1), 151–164. doi:10.16993/dfl.206

Kelso, J. A. S. (1995). *Dynamic patterns: The self-organization of brain and behavior.* Cambridge, MA: MIT Press.

Kemmis, S. (2009). Action research as a practice-based practice. *Educational Action Research, 17*(3), 463–474. doi:10.1080/09650790903093284

Kemmis, S., McTaggart, R., & Nixon, R. (2014). *The action research planner: Doing critical participatory action research.* Cham: Springer.

Keruoso, H., & Jokinen, E. (2023). Transformative agency and the cultivation of innovations in frontline homelessness work. In N. Hopwood & A. Sannino (Eds.), *Agency and transformation* (pp. 311–335). Cambridge: Cambridge University Press.

Kindon, S., Pain, R., & Kesby, M. (2007). *Participatory action research approaches and methods: Connecting people, participation and place.* New York: Routledge.

Kirschner, P. A. (2005). Learning in innovative learning environments. *Computers in Human Behavior, 21*, 547–554. doi:10.1016/j.chb.2004.10.022

Kloetzer, L., & Clot, Y. (2016). Modèles de l'activité. In *Psychologie du Travail et des Organisations* (pp. 302–307). Paris: Dunod.

Kloetzer, L., Clot, Y., & Quillerou-Grivot, E. (2015). Stimulating dialogue at work: The activity clinic approach to learning and development. In L. Filiettaz & S. Billett (Eds.), *Francophone perspectives on learning through work* (pp. 49–70). Dordrecht: Springer.

Komar, J., Seifert, L., & Thouvarecq, R. (2015). What variability tells us about motor expertise: Measurements and perspectives from a complex system approach. *Movement & Sport Sciences-Science & Motricité* (89), 65–77. doi:10.1051/sm/2015020

Kozulin, A. (1984). *Psychology in Utopia. Toward a social history of soviet psychology.* Cambridge, London: MIT Press.

LaCapra, D. (1998). The university in ruins? *Critical Inquiry, 25*, 32–55.

Lahoual, D. (2017). *Conceptualiser les activités constructives et le développement du sujet capable. Le cas de la médiation à l'art orientée jeune public dans un musée d'art moderne et contemporain.* (Thèse de doctorat). Université Paris 8 – Saint-Denis,

Langemeyer, I. (2006). Contradictions in Expansive Learning: Towards a critical analysis of self-dependent forms of learning in relation to contemporary socio-technological change. *FQS. Forum: Qualitative Social Research, 7*(1). doi:10.17169/fqs-7.1.76

Langemeyer, I. (2011). Science and social practice: Action research and activity theory as socio-critical approaches. *Mind, Culture, and Activity, 18*(2), 148–160. doi:10.1080/10749039.2010.497983

Langemeyer, I., & Roth, W. M. (2006). Is cultural-historical activity theory threatened to fall short of its own principles and possibilities as a dialectical social science. *Outlines: Critical Practice Studies*(2), 20–42. doi:10.7146/ocps.v8i2.2090

Larsen, D. P., Nimmon, L., & Varpio, L. (2019). Cultural historical activity theory: The role of tools and tensions in medical education. *Academic Medicine, 94*(8), 1255–1255. doi:10.1097/acm.0000000000002736

Latour, B. (2005). *Reassembling the social. An introduction to actor network theory.* Oxford: Oxford University Press.

Latour, B. (2006). *Changer la société. Refaire de la sociologie.* Paris: La découverte.

Latour, B. (2010). *Cogitamus. Six lettres sur les humanités scientifiques.* Paris: La découverte.

Latour, B. (2019). L'apocalypse c'est enthousiasmant. Interview to the newspaper "Le Monde", 31th May.

Launis, K., & Pihlaja, J. (2007a). Changes in production concepts emphasize problems in work-related well-being. *Safety Science, 45*(5), 603–619. doi:10.1016/j.ssci.2007.01.006

Launis, K., & Pihlaja, J. (2007b). Les asynchronismes et les perturbations comme outil d'analyse des problèmes liés au bien-être au travail. *Activites, 04*(2). doi:10.4000/activites.1705

Lave, J. (1988). *Cognition in practice: Mind, mathematics and culture in everyday life.* Cambridge: Cambridge University Press.

Lave, J., & Wenger, E. (1991). *Situated learning. Legitimate peripheral participation.* Cambridge: Cambridge University Press.

Lektorski, V. P. (1990). *Activity: The theory, methodology and problems.* Orlando, Helsinki, Moscou: Paul M. Deutsch Press.

Lektorski, V. P. (1999). Activity theory in a new era. In Y. Engeström, R. Miettinen, & R.-L. Punamäki (Eds.), *Perspectives on activity theory* (pp. 65–69). Cambridge: Cambridge University Press.

Lektorsky, V. P. (2009). Mediation as a means of collective activity. In A. Sannino, H. Daniels, & K. D. Gutierez (Eds.), *Learning and expanding with activity theory* (pp. 75–87). Cambridge: Cambridge University Press.

Lémonie, Y. (2019). Des marges de manœuvre à la diversité et à la variabilité motrice dans la prévention des TMS. *Le travail humain, 82*(1), 67–97. doi:10.3917/th.821.0067

Lémonie, Y. (2020). Formation des enseignants et temporalités: une mise en perspective sous le prisme de la théorie historico-culturelle de l'activité. In C. Borges, B. Lenzen, & D. Loizon (Eds.), *Entre l'université et l'école. La temporalité dans l'alternance en formation professionnelle en enseignement d'éducation physique* (pp. 229-). Laval: Presses Universitaires de Laval.

Lémonie, Y. (2022). *Penser la crise et au-delà: résilience, apprentissage expansif et développement des systèmes d'activité.* Paper presented at the La fabrique de l'ergonomie, Paris.

Lémonie, Y. (2023). O que é esta atividade, especificamente humana, à qual chamamos trabalho?: O exemplo de Leontiev sobre a caça primitiva. *Laboreal, 19*(3). doi:10.4000/laboreal.21373

Lémonie, Y., & Bationo-Tillon, A. (Forthcoming). Les processus d'Instrumentation/Instrumentalisation comme indicateurs de l'agentivité transformatrice dans les interventions développementales. In A. Bationo-Tillon, G. Bourmaud, V. Folcher, & F. Decortis (Eds.), *Approche instrumentale: Expansion et devenir.* Toulouse: Octares.

Lémonie, Y., Gal-Petitfaux, N., & Wallian, N. (2012). Sciences de l'intervention et Éducation Physique et Sportive. *Cahiers du CEDREPS, 12*, 177–189.

Lémonie, Y., & Grosstephan, V. (2021). Le laboratoire du changement: une méthodologie d'intervention au service de la transformation du travail. *Revue d'anthropologie des connaissances, 15*(2). doi:10.4000/rac.21846

Lémonie, Y., & Grosstephan, V. (2022). Looking out of the box and beyond boundaries: How cultural-historical activity theory can inform and support the development of inclusive educational practices? In Veber, Gollu, Skade, & Greiten (Eds.), *Umgang mit Heterogenität. Chancen und Herausforderungen für schulpraktische Professionalisierung.* Klinkhardt.

Lémonie, Y., Grosstephan, V., & Tomás, J.-L. (2019). *Supporting a policy of success for disadvantaged schools: Identification of contradictions around hierarchical power issues between activity systems.* Paper presented at the 35ème EGOS conférence. Enlightening the future: The challenge for organizations, Edinburgh, UK.

Lémonie, Y., Grosstephan, V., & Tomás, J.-L. (2021). From a sociological given context to changing practice: Transforming problematic power relations in educational organizations to overcome social inequalities. *Frontiers in Psychology, 11*(3640). doi:10.3389/fpsyg.2020.608502

Leontiev, A. (1959/1976). *Le développement du psychisme.* Paris: Éditions sociales.

Leontiev, A. (1974). The problem of activity in psychology. *Soviet Psychology, 13*(2), 4–33. doi:10.2753/RPO1061-040513024

Leontiev, A. (1975/2021). *Activité, Conscience, Personnalité.* Paris: Éditions Delga.

Leontiev, A. (1978). *Activity consciousness and personality.* Prentice-Hall.

Leontiev, A. (1981). *Problems of the development of the mind* (Vol. Progress Publishers): Moscow.

Leontiev, A. (1995). Ecce Homo. *Journal of Russian & East European Psychology, 33*(4), 35–46. doi:10.2753/RPO1061-0405330435

Leontiev, A. (2009). *The development of mind*: Marxist Internet Archive.

Leontiev, A.N., & Luria, A.R. (1956). Les conceptions psychologiques de L.S. Vygotsky. In Vygotsky L.S. Recherches choisies en psychologie (p. 4-36). Moscou.

Levant, A. (2018). Two, three, many strands of activity theory! *Educational Review, 70*(1), 100–108. doi:10.1080/00131911.2018.1388619

Levins, R., & Lewontin, R. (1985). *The dialectical Biologist.* Cambridge: Harbard Universirty Press.

Lewin, K. (1951). *Field theory in social science: Selected theoretical papers (Edited by Dorwin Cartwright.).* New York: Harper.

Liaw, S.-S., Huang, H.-M., & Chen, G.-D. (2007). An activity-theoretical approach to investigate learners' factors toward e-learning systems. *Computers in Human Behavior, 23*(4), 1906–1920.

Lompscher, J. (2006). The cultural-historical activity theory. In P. H. Sawchuk, N. Duarte, & M. Elhammouni (Eds.), *Critical perspectives on Activity. Exploration across education, work and evryday life* (pp. 35–51). Cambridge: Cambridge University Press.

Loorbach, D. A., & Wittmayer, J. (2023). Transforming universities. *Sustainability Science.* doi:10.1007/s11625-023-01335-y

Lopes, M. G. R., Vilela, R. A. G., Querol, M. A. P., & de Almeida, I. M. (2020). Challenges to Change Laboratory learning in a dynamic and complex civil construction project. *Collaborative Development for the Prevention of Occupational Accidents and Diseases: Change Laboratory in Workers' Health*, 131–144.

Lorino, P. (2017). L'activité, processus collectif de signification et d'organisation. In J.-M. Barbier & M. Durand (Eds.), *Encyclopédie d'analyse des activités* (pp. 921–943). Paris: PUF.

Lorino, P. (2019). Herbert Simon : pour un bilan raisonné du cognitivisme. [Herbert Simon: For a reasoned assessment of cognitivism]. *Projectics / Proyéctica / Projectique, 24*(3), 79–92. doi:10.3917/proj.024.0079

Lotz-Sisitka, H., Mukute, M., Chikunda, C., Baloi, A., & Pesanayi, T. (2017). Transgressing the norm: Transformative agency in community-based learning for sustainability in southern African contexts. *International Review of Education, 63*(6), 897–914. doi:10.1007/s11159-017-9689-3

MacDougall. (2009). *Born to run.* Chamonix: Éditions Guérin.

Maidansky, A. (2021). Anton Yasnitsky and René van der Veer (eds.): Revisionist revolution in Vygotsky studies.

Malm, A. (2019). Against hybridism: Why we need to distinguish between nature and society, now more than ever. *Historical Materialism, 27*(2), 156–187. doi:10.1163/1569206X-00001610

Marquetti, A., Schonerwald da Silva, C. E., & Campbell, A. (2012). Participatory economic democracy in action: Participatory budgeting in Porto Alegre, 1989–2004. *Review of Radical Political Economics, 44*(1), 62–81.

Martins, J. B. (2013). Notes on the relationship between Vygotsky and Leontiev: The 'troika', did it ever exist. *Dubna Psychological Journal, 1*, 84–94.

Marx, K. (1844/1972). *Manuscrits de 1844.* Paris: Éditions sociales.

Marx, K. (1963/2017). *Le capital.* Paris: Gallimard.

Marx, K. (1968). *Misère de la philosophie.* Paris: Éditions sociales.

Marx, K., & Engels, F. (2012). *L'idéologie allemande.* Paris: Éditions sociales.

Maturana, H., & Varela, F. (1994). *L'arbre de la connaissance.* Paris: Addison-Westley.

Maxwell, J. A. (2004). Causal explanation, qualitative research, and scientific inquiry in education. *Educational Researcher, 33*(2), 3–11. doi:10.3102/0013189X033002003

McTaggart, R., Nixon, R., & Kemmis, S. (2017). Critical participatory action research. In L. L. Rowell, C. D. Bruce, J. M. Shosh, & M. M. Riel (Eds.), *The Palgrave International handbook of action research* (pp. 21–35). New York: Palgrave Macmillan US.

Meijer, O. G., & Bruijn, S. M. (2007). The loyal dissident: N.A. Bernstein and the double-edged sword of Stalinism. *J Hist Neurosci, 16*(1–2), 206–224. doi:10.1080/09647040600720979

Meshcheryakov, A. (2009). *Awakening to life. On the education of deaf-blind children in the Soviet Union*: Marxists Internet Archive.

Mestdagh, L. (2021). Du matériel au ségrégatif: l'objet comme outil de régulation de l'espace public. *Transversales*(19), https://ube.hal.science/hal-03286867/document.

Meyer, J. (2000). Using qualitative methods in health related action research. *BMJ, 320*(7228), 178–181.

Meyers, E. M. (2007). From activity to learning: Using cultural historical activity theory to model school library programmes and practices. *Information Research-an International Electronic Journal, 12*(3), 16. Retrieved from <Go to ISI>://WOS:000246384600007

Miettinen, R. (1998). Object construction and networks in research work: The case of research on cellulose-degrading enzymes. *Social Studies of Science, 28*(3), 423–463. doi:10.1177/030631298028003003

Miettinen, R. (1999). The riddle of things: Activity theory and actor-network theory as approaches to studying innovations. *Mind Culture and Activity, 6*(3), 170–195.

Miettinen, R. (2009). Contradictions of high-technology capitalism and the emergence of new forms of work. In A. Sannino, H. Daniels, & K. D. Gutierez (Eds.),

Learning and expanding with activity theory (pp. 160–175). Cambridge: Cambridge University Press.

Minick, N. (2005). The development of Vygotsky's thought. An introduction to thinking and speech. In H. Daniels (Ed.), *An introduction to Vygotsky* (pp. 32–56). New York: Routledge.

Mironenko, I. A. (2013). Concerning interpretations of activity theory. *Integrative Psychological and Behavioral Science, 47*(3), 376–393. doi:10.1007/s12124-013-9231-5

Mirra, N., Garcia, A., & Morrell, E. (2015). *Doing youth participatory action research: Transforming inquiry with researchers, educators, and students.* London, New York: Routledge.

Moffitt, P., & Bligh, B. (2021). Online tasks and students' transformative agency: Double-stimulation as a design principle for synchronous online workshops. *Journal of Vocational Education & Training*, 1–24. doi:10.1080/13636820.2021.1998792

Mollo, V., & Falzon, P. (2004). Auto- and allo-confrontation as tools for reflective activities. *Applied Ergonomics, 35*(6), 531–540.

Morozov, E. (2013). *To save everything, click here: The folly of technological solutionism*: PublicAffairs.

Morris, D. (1992). The Mondragon System: Cooperation at work. *Institute for Local Self-Reliance and Infinity, 202*, 898–1610.

Morselli, D., & Sannino, A. (2021). Testing the model of double stimulation in a Change Laboratory. *Teaching and Teacher Education, 97*, 103224. doi:10.1016/j.tate.2020.103224

Mukute, M. (2015). *Developmental work research. A tool for enabling collective agricultural innovation.* Wageningen: Wageningen Academic Publishers.

Mukute, M., & Lotz-Sisitka, H. (2012). Working with cultural-historical activity theory and critical realism to investigate and expand farmer learning in Southern Africa. *Mind Culture and Activity, 19*(4), 342–367. doi:10.1080/10749039.2012.656173

Mukute, M., Mudokwani, K., McAllister, G., & Nyikahadzoi, K. (2018). Exploring the potential of developmental work research and Change Laboratory to support sustainability transformations: A case study of organic agriculture in Zimbabwe. *Mind Culture and Activity, 25*(3), 229–246. doi:10.1080/10749039.2018.1451542

Munn, Z., Peters, M. D. J., Stern, C., Tufanaru, C., McArthur, A., & Aromataris, E. (2018). Systematic review or scoping review? Guidance for authors when choosing between a systematic or scoping review approach. *BMC Medical Research Methodology, 18*(1), 143. doi:10.1186/s12874-018-0611-x

Murphy, E., Manzanares, M. A. R., Murphy, E., & RodriguezManzanares, M. A. (2014a). *Contradictions and Expansive Transformation in the Activity Systems of Higher Education International Students in Online Learning.* Hersey: Igi Global.

Murphy, E., Manzanares, M. A. R., Murphy, E., & RodriguezManzanares, M. A. (2014b). *From Contradictions to Expansive Transformations in Technology-Mediated Higher Education.* Hersey: Igi Global.

Nechaev, N. N. (2022). Toward the problem of reconciling Lev Vygotskii's cultural historical psychology with Aleksei Leont'ev's Activity Theory. *Journal of Russian & East European Psychology, 59*(1–3), 43–63. doi:10.1080/10610405.2022.2115 787

Newell, K. M. (1986). Constraints on the development of coordination. In M. G. Wade & H. T. A. Whiting (Eds.), *Motor development on children: Aspects of coordination and control* (pp. 341–360). Boston: Martinus Nijhoff.

Nicolini, D. (2012). *Practice, theory, work, and organization.* Oxford: Oxford University Press.

Noë, A. (2009). *Out of our heads: Why you are not your brain, and other lessons from the biology of consciousness.* New York: Hill & Wang.

Norman, D. A. (1982). Learning and memory. San Francisco: Freeman.

Norman, D. A. (2002). Emotion and design: Attractive things work better. Interactions Magazine, 9(4), 36–42. doi: 10.1145/543434.543435

Nosulenko, V., & Rabardel, P. (2007). *Rubinstein aujourd'hui.* Toulouse: Octares.

Nummijoki, J., Engeström, Y., & Sannino, A. (2018). Defensive and expansive cycles of learning: A study of home care encounters. *Journal of the Learning Sciences, 27*(2), 224–264. doi:10.1080/10508406.2017.1412970

Nussbaumer, D. (2012). An overview of cultural historical activity theory (CHAT) use in classroom research 2000 to 2009. *Educational Review, 64*(1), 37–55. doi:1 0.1080/00131911.2011.553947

Nuttall, J. (2022). Formative interventions and the ethics of double stimulation for transformative agency in professional practice. *Pedagogy, Culture & Society, 30*(1), 111–128.

O'Keefe, M., Wade, V., McAllister, S., Stupans, I., Miller, J., Burgess, T., … Starr, L. (2014). Rethinking attitudes to student clinical supervision and patient care: A change management success story. *BMC Medical Education, 14*, 8. doi:10.1186/1472-6920-14-182

Oliveira, S. S., Brito, J., & Lacomblez, M. (2012). Agir en compétence dans les centres d'appels : dilemmes entre emploi, travail et santé. *Perspectives interdisciplinaires sur le travail et la santé* (14–2). doi:10.4000/pistes.2593

Ollman, B. (2005). *La dialectique mise en oeuvre. Le processus d'abstraction dans la méthode de Marx.* Paris: Syllepse.

Ollman, B. (2008). Why dialectics? Why now? In B. Ollman & T. Smith (Eds.), *Dialectics for the new century* (pp. 8–25): Pallgrave Macmillan.

Ollman, B., & Smith, T. (2008). *Dialectics for the new century.* New York: Palgrave MacMillan.

Paavola, S., Lipponen, L., & Hakkarainen, K. (2004). Models of innovative knowledge communities and three metaphors of learning. *Review of Educational Research, 74*(4), 557–576. doi:10.3102/00346543074004557

Packer, M., & Maddox, C. (2016). Mapping the territory of the learning sciences. In M. A. Evans, M. J. Packer, & R. K. Sawyer (Eds.), *Reflections on the learning sciences* (pp. 126–154). New York: Cambridge University Press.

Parker, I. (1999). Against relativism in psychology, on balance. *History of the Human Sciences, 12*(1), 61–78. doi:10.1177/09526959922120496

Pastré, P. (2002). L'analyse du travail en didactique professionnelle. *Revue Française de Pédagogie*(138), 9–17.

Pastré, P. (2007). Analyse du travail et formation. *Recherches en Éducation, 4*, 23–28.

Pastré, P., & Vergnaud, G. (2006). La didactique professionnelle. *Revue Française de Pédagogie, 154*(1), 12–12.

Penuel, W. R. (2014). Emerging forms of formative intervention research in education. *Mind, Culture and Activity, 21*(2), 97–117. doi:10.1080/10749039.2014.884137

Penuel, W. R., Cole, M., & O'Neill, D. K. (2016). Introduction to the special issue. *Journal of the Learning Sciences, 25*(4), 487–496. doi:10.1080/10508406.2016.1215753

Pham, M. T., Rajić, A., Greig, J. D., Sargeant, J. M., Papadopoulos, A., & McEwen, S. A. (2014). A scoping review of scoping reviews: Advancing the approach and enhancing the consistency. *Res Synth Methods, 5*(4), 371–385. doi:10.1002/jrsm.1123

Pihlaja, J. (2005). *Learning in and for production. An activity theoretical study of the historical development of distributed systems of generalizing.* Helsinki: Helsinki University Press.

Ploettner, J., & Tresseras, E. (2016). An interview with Yrjö Engeström and Annalisa Sannino on activity theory. *Bellaterra Journal of Teaching & Learning Language & Literature, 9*(4), 87–98. doi:10.2436/20.3008.01.147

Poizat, G., Durand, M., & Theureau, J. (2016). The challenge of activity analysis for training objectives. *Le travail humain, 79*(3), 233–258. doi:10.3917/th.793.0233

Poizat, G., Flandin, S., & Theureau, J. (2022). A micro-phenomenological and semiotic approach to cognition in practice: A path toward an integrative approach to studying cognition-in-the-world and from within. *Adaptive Behavior,* 10597123211072352. doi:10.1177/10597123211072352

Postholm, M. B. (2012). Teachers' professional development: A theoretical review. *Educational Research, 54*(4), 405–429. doi:10.1080/00131881.2012.734725

Poulain, E. (2017). *Mémoire de master professionnel en ergonomie.* Cnam, Paris.

Prenkert, F. (2010). Tracing the roots of activity systems theory: An analysis of the concept of mediation. *Theory & Psychology, 20*(5), 641–665. doi:10.1177/0959354310375329

Prost, A. (1968). *Histoire de l'enseignement en France.* Paris: Presses Universitaires de France.

Prot, B., & Schneuwly, B. (2013). Développement chez l'enfant – développement chez l'adulte. Formation générale – Formation professionelle des adultes. Introduction et clarification du thème. In J.-P. Bernié & M. Brossard (Eds.), *Vygotsi et l'école. Apports et limites d'un modèle théorique pour penser l'éducation et la formatoion* (pp. 218–222). Bordeaux: Presses Universitaires de Bordeaux.

Querol, M. A. P. (2011). *Learning challenges in biogas production for sustainability. An activity theoretical study of a network from a swine industry chain.* (PhD). Helsinky University, Helsinki.

Quiniou, Y. (2006). Pour une actualisation du concept d'aliénation. [For a Rethinking of the Concept of Alienation]. *Actuel Marx, 39*(1), 71–88. doi:10.3917/amx.039.0071

Rabardel, P. (1995). *Des hommes et les technologies. Approche cognitive des instruments contemporains.* Paris: Armand Colin.

Rantavuori, J., Engeström, Y., & Lipponen, L. (2016). Learning actions, objects and types of interaction: A methodological analysis of expansive learning among pre-service teachers. *Frontline Learning Research, 4*(3), 1–27. doi:10.14786/flr.v4i3.174

Ratner, C., & Silva, D. N. H. (2017). *Vygotsky and Marx: Toward a marxist psychology*: Taylor & Francis.

Readings, B. (1996). *The university in ruins.* Harvard: Harvard University Press.

Reason, P., & Bradbury, H. (2001). *Handbook of action research. Participative inquiry and practice.* London, Thousand Oaks, New Delhi: Sage Publications.

Reimann, P. (2011). Design-based research. In L. Markauskaite, P. Freebody, & J. Irwin (Eds.), *Methodological choice and design: Scholarship, policy and practice in social and educational research* (pp. 37–50). Dordrecht: Springer Netherlands.

Ria, L., Saury, J., Sève, C., & Durand, M. (2001). Les dilemmes des enseignants débutants: Études lors des premières expériences de classe en Education Physique. *Science et Motricité, 42*, 47–58.

Ricard, J., & Medeiros, J. (2020). Using misinformation as a political weapon: COVID-19 and Bolsonaro in Brazil. *Harvard Kennedy School Misinformation Review, 1*(3).

Ritella, G., & Hakkarainen, K. (2012). Instrumental genesis in technology-mediated learning: From double stimulation to expansive knowledge practices. *International Journal of Computer-Supported Collaborative Learning, 7*(2), 239–258. doi:10.1007/s11412-012-9144-1

Robichaud, D., & Turmel, P. (2014). Quelle juste part? Normativité, remplaçabilité et portée. *Philosophiques, 41*(1), 177–193. doi:10.7202/1025731ar

Rocha, R., Mollo, V., & Daniellou, F. (2017). Le débat sur le travail fondé sur la subsidiarité: un outil pour développer un environnement capacitant. *Activites, 14*(2), 1–26. doi:10.4000/activites.2999

Rogoff, B., & Lave, J. (1984). *Everyday cognition: Development in social context.* Cambridge: Harvard University Press.

Roth, W. M. (2001). Publish or stay behind and perhaps perish: Stability of publication practices in (Some) social sciences. *Soziale Systeme, 11*(1), 129–150. doi:10.1515/sosys-2005-0108

Roth, W. M. (2007). On mediation:Toward a cultural-historical understanding. *Theory & Psychology, 17*(5), 655–680. doi:10.1177/0959354307081622

Roth, W. M. (2008). On theorizing and clarifying. *Mind, Culture and Activity, 15*(3), 177–184. doi:10.1080/10749030802186579

Roth, W. M. (2014). Activity Theory. In T. Teo (Ed.), *Encyclopedia of Critical Psychology* (pp. 25–31). Springer New York.

Roth, W. M. (2017). Neoformation: A dialectical approach to developmental change. *Mind, Culture, and Activity, 24*(4), 368–380. doi:10.1080/10749039.2016.1179327

Roth, W. M., & Jornet, A. (2016). Perezhivanie in the light of the later Vygotsky's Spinozist turn. *Mind Culture and Activity, 23*(4), 315–324. doi:10.1080/10749039.2016.1186197

Roth, W. M., Lee, Y.-J., & Hsu, P. L. (2009). A tool for changing the world: Possibilities of cultural-historical activity theory to reinvigorate science education. *Studies in Science Education, 45*(2), 131–167. doi:10.1080/03057260903142269

Rückiem, G. (2009). Digital technology and mediation: A challenge to activity theory. In A. Sannino, H. Daniels, & K. D. Gutierez (Eds.), *Learning and expanding with activity theory* (pp. 88–111). Cambridge: Cambridge University Press.

Sanchez, É., & Monod-Ansaldi, R. (2015). Recherche collaborative orientée par la conception. Un paradigme méthodologique pour prendre en compte la complexité des situations d'enseignement-apprentissage. *Éducation et didactique*(9–2), 73–94. doi:10.4000/educationdidactique.2288

Sannino, A. (2008). From talk to action: Experiencing interlocution in developmental interventions. *Mind, Culture, and Activity, 15*(2), 234–257. doi:10.1080/10749030802186769

Sannino, A. (2011). Activity theory as an activist and interventionist theory. *Theory & Psychology, 21*(5), 571–597. doi:10.1177/0959354311417485

Sannino, A. (2015a). The emergence of transformative agency and double stimulation: Activity-based studies in the Vygotskian tradition. *Learning Culture and Social Interaction, 4,* 1–3. doi:10.1016/j.lcsi.2014.07.001

Sannino, A. (2015b). The principle of double stimulation: A path to volitional action. *Learning Culture and Social Interaction, 6,* 1–15. doi:10.1016/j.lcsi.2015.01.001

Sannino, A. (2016). Double stimulation in the waiting experiment with collectives: Testing a Vygotskian model of the emergence of volitional action. *Integrative Psychological and Behavioral Science, 50*(1), 142–173. doi:10.1007/s12124-015-9324-4

Sannino, A. (2020). Enacting the utopia of eradicating homelessness: Toward a new generation of activity-theoretical studies of learning. *Studies in Continuing Education,* 1–17. doi:10.1080/0158037X.2020.1725459

Sannino, A. (2023a). Problem identification in Change Laboratories: Workplace learning to eradicate homelessness. In H. Bound, A. Edwards, K. Evans, & A. Chia (Eds.), *Workplace learning for changing social and economic circumstances* (pp. 201–218). London: Routledge.

Sannino, A. (2023b). Toward a power-sensitive conceptualization of transformative agency. In N. Hopwood & A. Sannino (Eds.), *Agency and transformation* (pp. 35–55). Cambridge: Cambridge University Press.

Sannino, A. (2024). Foundations of educational studies of agency: An activity-theoretical critique. In A. Levant, K. Murakami, & M. McSweeney (Eds.), *Activity theory: An introduction* (pp. 295–326). Stuttgart: Ibidem-Verlag.

Sannino, A., Daniels, H., & Gutierrez, K. D. (2009a). Activity theory between historical engagement and future-making practice. In A. Sannino, H. Daniels, & K. D. Gutierrez (Eds.), *Learning and expanding with activity theory* (pp. 1–15). Cambridge: Cambridge University Press.

Sannino, A., Daniels, H., & Gutierrez, K. D. (2009b). *Learning and expanding with activity theory.* Cambridge: Cambridge University Press.

Sannino, A., & Engeström, Y. (2016). Relational agency, double stimulation and the object of activity: An intervention study in a primary school. In A. Edwards (Ed.), *Working relationally in and across practices: Cultural-historical approaches to collaboration* (pp. 58–77): Cambridge University Press.

Sannino, A., & Engeström, Y. (2018). Valuable innovations out of nonsense? Expansive Organizational Learning and Transformative Agency in the Mann Gulch Disaster and in the Finnish Homelessness Strategy. *Teoria E Pratica Em Administracao-Tpa, 8*(2), 60–79. doi:10.21714/2238-104X2018v8i2S-40728

Sannino, A., & Engeström, Y. (2023). In search of an experiment: From Vygotsky to Lewin and Dembo and back to the future. In G. Marsico & L. Tateo (Eds.),

Humanity in Psychology: The Intellectual Legacy of Pina Boggi Cavallo (pp. 159–177). Cham: Springer International Publishing.

Sannino, A., Engeström, Y., & Lemos, M. (2016). Formative interventions for expansive learning and transformative agency. *Journal of the Learning Sciences, 25*(4), 599–633. doi:10.1080/10508406.2016.1204547

Sannino, A., & Laitinen, A. (2015). Double stimulation in the waiting experiment: Testing a Vygotskian model of the emergence of volitional action. *Learning Culture and Social Interaction, 4*, 4–18. doi:10.1016/j.lcsi.2014.07.002

Sannino, A., & Sutter, B. (2011). Cultural-historical activity theory and interventionist methodology: Classical legacy and contemporary developments. *Theory & Psychology, 21*(5), 557–570. doi:10.1177/0959354311414969

Savoyant, A. (1984/2010). Définition et voies d'analyse de l'activité collective des équipes de travail. *Travail et Apprentissage, 4*, 108/118.

Sawchuk, P. (2006). Activity and power: Everyday life and development of working-class groups. In P. Sawchuk, N. Duarte, & M. Elhammouni (Eds.), *Critical perspectives on activity; explorations across education, work and everyday life* (pp. 238–268). Cambridge: Cambridge University Press.

Schmidt, R. A. (2003). Motor schema theory after 27 years: Reflections and implications for a new theory. *Research Quaterly for Exercice and Sport, 74*(4), 366–375. doi:10.1080/02701367.2003.10609106

Schneuwly, B. (2013). La notion de développement revisitée dans la perspective d'enseignement (scolaire) et de formation (des adultes). In J.-P. Bernié & M. Brossard (Eds.), *Vygotski et l'école. Apports et limites d'un modèle théorique pour penser l'éducation et la formation* (pp. 309–325). Pessac: Presses Universitaires de Bordeaux.

Schön, D. (1996). À la recherche d'une nouvelle épistémologie de la pratique et ce qu'elle implique pour l'éducation des adultes. In J.-M. Barbier (Ed.), *Savoirs théoriques et savoirs d'action* (pp. 201–222). Paris: PUF.

Schwartz, Y. (2007). Un bref aperçu de l'histoire culturelle du concept d'activité. *Activites, 04*(2). doi:10.4000/activites.1728

Schwartz, Y. (2015). Vygotski/Spinoza. *Revue philosophique de la France et de l'étranger, 140*(4), 561–566. doi:10.3917/rphi.154.0561

Scribner, S. (1985). Vygotsky's uses of history. In J. V. Wersch (Ed.), *Culture communication and cognition. Vygotskian perspectives* (pp. 119–145). New York: Cambridge University Press.

Sève, L. (1980). *Une introduction à la philosophie marxiste (3ème édition)*. Paris: Éditions Sociales.

Sève, L. (1998). Sciences et dialectiques de la nature. Paris: La dispute.

Sève, L. (2008). *Penser avec Marx aujourd'hui. Tome II. L'homme?* Paris: La dispute.

Sève, L. (2014). *Penser avec Marx aujourd'hui. Tome III. La philosophie?* Paris: La dispute.

Sève, L., & Guespin-Michel, J. (2005). *Émergence, complexité et dialectique: sur les systèmes dynamiques non-linéaires.* Paris: Odile Jacob.

Shvarts, A., & Bakker, A. (2019). The early history of the scaffolding metaphor: Bernstein, Luria, Vygotsky, and before. Mind, Culture, and Activity, 26(1), 4-23. doi:10.1080/10749039.2019.1574306

Simeonova, B., Kelly, P. R., Karanasios, S., & Galliers, R. (2024). Power as present-in-actions in mundane information systems work. *Journal of the Association of Information Systems.*

Somekh, B. (2008). Action research. In L. M. Given (Ed.), *The Sage encyclopedia of qualitative research methods* (pp. 4–7). London: Sage.

Somekh, B., & Nissen, M. (2011). Cultural-historical activity theory and action research. *Mind, Culture, and Activity, 18*(2), 93–97. doi:10.1080/10749039.201 0.523102

Song, Y., & Vernooy, R. (2010). Seeds of empowerment: Action research in the context of the feminization of agriculture in southwest China. *Gender, technology and development, 14*(1), 25–44. doi:10.1177/097185241001400102

Spante, M., Moffitt, P., Bligh, B., Lémonie, Y., Matsamoto, R., Munday, D., … Fiona, R. (2023). Why do an online Change Laboratory? *Bureau de Change Laboratory.* doi:10.21428/3033cbff.17652647

Spante, M., Varga, A., & Carlsson, L. (2021). Triggering sustainable professional agency: Using Change Laboratory to tackle unequal access to educational success collectively. *Journal of Workplace Learning, ahead-of-print*(ahead-of-print). doi:10.1108/JWL-02-2021-0019

Spencer, R. W. (2012). Open innovation in the eighteenth century. *Research-Technology Management, 55*(4), 39–43. doi:10.5437/08956308X5504074

Spinuzzi, C. (2005a). Lost in the translation: Shifting claims in the migration of a research technique. *Technical Communication Quarterly, 14*(4), 411–446. doi:10.1207/s15427625tcq1404_3

Spinuzzi, C. (2005b). The methodology of participatory design. *Technical communication, 52*(2), 163–174.

Spinuzzi, C. (2011). Losing by expanding: Corralling the Runaway Object. *Journal of Business and Technical Communication Theory, 25*(4), 449–486. doi:10.1177/1050651911411040

Spinuzzi, C. (2018a). From superhumans to supermediators: Locating the extraordinary in CHAT. In A. Yasnitsky (Ed.), *Questioning Vygotsky's legacy: Scientific psychology or heroic cult* (pp. 137–166). New York: Routledge.

Spinuzzi, C. (2018b). *Topsight 2.0. A guide to studying, diagnosing, and fixing information flow in organizations.* Austin: Urso Press.

Spinuzzi, C. (2020a). Scaling change labs: A response to 'From Mediated Actions To Heterogenous Coalitions: Four Generations of Activity-theoretical Studies of Work and Learning'. *Mind, Culture, and Activity,* 1–8. doi:10.1080/10749039.2020.1840594

Spinuzzi, C. (2020b). Trying to predict the future: third-generation activity theory's codesign orientation. *Mind Culture and Activity, 27*(1), 4–18. doi:10.1080/10749039.2019.1660790

Star, S. L., & Griesemer, J. R. (1989). Institutional ecology, translations' and boundary objects: Amateurs and professionals in Berkeley's Museum of Vertebrate Zoology. *Social Studies of Science, 19*(3), 387–420. doi:10.1177/030631289019003001

Steiner, P. (2005). Introduction cognitivisme. *Labyrinthe, 20*(1), 13–39.

Stengers, I. (1987). *D'une science à l'autre. des concepts nomades.* Paris: Seuil.

Stergiou, N., & Decker, L. M. (2011). Human movement variability, nonlinear dynamics, and pathology: Is there a connection? *Human Movement Science, 30*(5), 869–888. doi:10.1016/j.humov.2011.06.002

Stetsenko, A. (1995). The role of the principle of object-relatedness in the Theory of Activity. *Journal of Russian & East European Psychology, 33*(6), 54–69. doi:10.2753/RPO1061-0405330654

Stetsenko, A. (2005). Activity as object-related: Resolving the dichotomy of individual and collective planes of activity. *Mind Culture and Activity, 12*(1), 70–88. doi:10.1207/s15327884mca1201_6

Stetsenko, A. (2015). Theory for and as social practice of realizing the future. In J. Martin, J. Sugarman, & K. Slaney (Eds.), *The Wiley handbook of theoretical and philosophical psychology* (pp. 102–116): Wiley Online Library.

Stetsenko, A. (2016a). Moving beyond the relational worldview: Exploring the next steps premised on agency and a commitment to social change. *Human Development, 59*(5), 283–289. doi:10.1159/000452720

Stetsenko, A. (2016b). Vygotsky's theory of method and philosophy of practice: Implications for trans/formative methodology. *Educação,* s32-s41. doi:10.15448/1981-2582.2016.s.24385

Stetsenko, A. (2017). *The transformative mind: Expanding Vygotsky's approach to development and education.* Cambridge: Calmbridge University Press.

Stetsenko, A. (2019). *Radical-transformative agency: Continuities and contrasts with relational agency and implications for education.* Paper presented at the Frontiers in Education.

Stetsenko, A. (2020). Hope, political imagination, and agency in Marxism and beyond: Explicating the transformative worldview and ethico-ontoepistemology.

Educational Philosophy and Theory, 52(7), 726–737. doi:10.1080/00131857.2019.1654373

Stetsenko, A. (2021). Scholarship in the context of a historic socioeconomic and political turmoil: Reassessing and taking stock of CHAT. Commentary on Y. Engeström and A. Sannino 'from mediated actions to heterogenous coalitions: Four generations of activity-theoretical studies of work and learning'. *Mind, Culture, and Activity, 28*(1), 32–43. doi:10.1080/10749039.2021.1874419

Stetsenko, A. (2022). Radicalizing theory and Vygotsky: Addressing crisis through activist-transformative methodology. *Human Arenas.* doi:10.1007/s42087-022-00299-2

Stetsenko, A. (2023). The task of reality and the reality as the task. Connecting Cultural-Historical Activity Theory with the radical scholarship of resistance. In N. Hopwood & A. Sannino (Eds.), *Agency and Transformation* (pp. 56–83). Cambridge: Cambridge University Press.

Stetsenko, A., & Arievitch, I. M. (1997). Constructing and deconstructing the self: Comparing post-Vygotskian and discourse-based versions of social constructivism. *Mind Culture and Activity, 4*, 160–173. doi:10.1207/s15327884mca0403_3

Stetsenko, A., & Arievitch, I. M. (2004). The Self in Cultural-Historical Activity Theory: Reclaiming the Unity of Social and Individual Dimensions of Human Development. *Theory & Psychology, 14*(4), 475-503. doi: 10.1177/0959354304044921

Stetsenko, A., & Arievitch, I. (2014). Vygotskian collaborative project of social transformation: History, politics, and practice in knowledge construction. In A. Blunden (Ed.), *Collaborative projects: An interdisciplinary study* (pp. 217–238). London: Haymarket Books.

Stokes, D. E. (2011). *Pasteur's quadrant: Basic science and technological innovation*: Brookings Institution Press.

Suchman, L. (1987). *Plans and situated action. The problem of human-machine communication.* Cambridge: Cambridge University Press.

Suchman, L. (2009). Forewords. In D. Schuler & A. Namioka (Eds.), *Participatory design: Principles and practices.* Boca Raton: CRC Press.

Sutter, B. (2011). How to analyze and promote developmental activity research? *Theory & Psychology, 21*(5), 697–714. doi:10.1177/0959354311419704

Świergiel, W., Pereira Querol, M., Rämert, B., Tasin, M., & Vänninen, I. (2018). Productivist or multifunctional: An activity theory approach to the development of organic farming concepts in Sweden. *Agroecology and Sustainable Food Systems, 42*(2), 210–239. doi:10.1080/21683565.2017.1394414

Tanzi Neto, A., Liberali, F., & Dafermos, M. (2020). *Revisiting Vygotsky for social change: Bringing together theory and practice.* New York: Peter Lang.

Temprado, J.-J. (1991). Les apprentissages décisionnels en EPS. In J.-P. Famose, P. Fleurance, & Y. Touchard (Eds.), *Apprentissage moteur: rôle des représentations* (pp. 131–156). Parus: Éditions revue EPS.

Thelen, E. (2000). Motor development as foundation and future of developmental psychology. *International Journal of Behavioral Development, 24*(4), 385–397. doi:10.1080/016502500750037937

Thelen, E., & Smith, L. B. (1996). *A dynamic system approach to the development of cognition and action.* Boston: MIT Press.

Theureau, J. (2004a). L'hypothèse de la cognition (ou action) située et la tradition d'analyse du travail de l'ergonomie de langue française. *Activites, 1*(2), 11–25. doi:10.4000/activites.1219

Theureau, J. (2004b). *Le cours d'action: méthode élèmentaire.* Toulouse: Octarès.

Theureau, J. (2005a). Le programme de recherche « cours d'action » et l'étude de l'activité, des connaissances et de l'organisation. In P. Lorino (Ed.), *Entre connaissance et organisation: l'activité collective* (pp. 115–132). Paris: La Découverte.

Theureau, J. (2005b). Les méthodes de construction de données du programme de recherche sur les cours d'action et leur articulation collective, et…la didactique des activités physiques et sportives? *Impulsions, 4*, 281–301.

Theureau, J. (2010). Les entretiens d'autoconfrontation et de remise en situation par les traces matérielles et le programme de recherche « cours d'action ». *Revue d'anthropologie des connaissances, Vol 4, 2*(2), 287–322. doi:10.3917/rac.010.0287

Theureau, J. (2019). *Le cours d'action. Économie et activités suivi de Note sur l'éthique.* Toulouse: Octares.

Thomazet, S., & Mérini, C. (2015). L'école inclusive comme objet frontière. *La nouvelle revue de l'adaptation et de la scolarisation*(2), 137–148. doi:10.3917/nras.070.0137

Thorne, S. L. (2015). Mediated life activity, double stimulation, and the question of agency. *Learning, Culture and Social Interaction, 4*, 62–66. doi:10.1016/j.lcsi.2014.10.002

Tiberghien, A., Vince, J., & Gaidioz, P. (2009). Design-based research: Case of a teaching sequence on mechanics. *International Journal of Science Education, 31*(17), 2275–2314. doi:10.1080/09500690902874894

Tikhomirov, O. K. (1999). The theory of activity changed by information technology. In Y. Engeström, R. Miettinen, & R.-L. Punamahi (Eds.), *Perspectives on activity theory* (pp. 347–359). Cambridge: Cambridge University Press.

Tkachenko, O., & Ardichvili, A. (2017). Cultural-historical activity theory's relevance to HRD: A review and application. *Human Resource Development Review, 16*(2), 135–157. doi:10.1177/1534484317696717

Toiviainen, H., & Vetoshkina, L. P. (2018). Learning for the complex object of work in a digital printing network. *Studia paedagogica, 23*(2), 25–42. doi:10.5817/SP2018-2-3

Tolman, C. W. (1999). Society versus context in individual development: Does theory make a difference? In Y. Engeström, R. Miettinen, & R.-L. Punamäki (Eds.), *Perspectives on activity theory* (pp. 70–86). Cambridge: Cambridge University Press.

Toomela, A. (2000). Activity theory is a dead end for cultural-historical psychology. *Culture & Psychology, 6*(3), 353–364. doi:10.1177/1354067X0063005

Toomela, A. (2008). Commentary: Activity theory is a dead end for methodological thinking in cultural psychology too. *Culture & Psychology, 14*(3), 289–303. doi:10.1177/1354067x08088558

Tosey, P., Visser, M., & Saunders, M. N. (2012). The origins and conceptualizations of 'triple-loop' learning: A critical review. *Management Learning, 43*(3), 291–307. doi:10.1177/1350507611426239

van der Riet, M. (2017). Developmental work research: A tool for enabling collective agricultural innovation. *Mind Culture and Activity, 24*(1), 85–88. doi:10.1080/10749039.2016.1232410

Van der Veer, R., & Valsiner, J. (1991). *Understanding Vygotsky: A quest for synthesis.* Oxford, UK: Blackwell Publishing.

Van der Veer, R., & Yasnitsky, A. (2016a). Translating Vygotsky. Some problems of transnational Vygotskyan science. In A. Yasnitsky & R. Van der Veer (Eds.), *Revisionnist revolution in Vygotsky studies* (pp. 143–174). London and New York: Routeldge.

Van der Veer, R., & Yasnitsky, A. (2016b). Vygotsky the published. Who wrote Vygotsky and what Vygotsky actually wrote. In A. Yasnitsky & R. Van der Veer (Eds.), *Revisionist revolution in Vygotsky studies* (pp. 73–93). London and New York: Routeldge.

van der Veer, R., & Zavershneva, E. (2011). To Moscow with love: Partial reconstruction of Vygotsky's trip to London. *Integr Psychol Behav Sci, 45*(4), 458–474. doi:10.1007/s12124-011-9173-8

Vänninen, I., Querol, M. A. P., & Engeström, Y. (2015). Generating transformative agency among horticultural producers: An activity-theoretical approach to transforming Integrated Pest Management. *Agricultural Systems, 139*, 38–49. doi:10.1016/j.agsy.2015.06.003

Vänninen, I., Querol, M. A. P., & Engeström, Y. (2021). Double stimulation for collaborative transformation of agricultural systems: The role of models for building agency. *Learning, Culture and Social Interaction, 30*, 100541. doi:10.1016/j.lcsi.2021.100541

Varela, F., Thompson, E., & Rosch, E. (1991). *The embodied Mind: Cognitive Science and Human Experience*. Cambridge: MIT Press.

Vasilyuk, F. (1991). *The psychology of experiencing*: Harvester Wheatsheaf.

Vaysse, C., Laurent, C., Ysebaert, L., Chantalat, E., & Chaput, B. (2019). France: The first country to ban a type of breast implant linked to anaplastic large cell lymphoma. *Aesthetic Surgery Journal, 39*(8), NP352-NP353. doi:10.1093/asj/sjz142

Veresov, N. (1999). *Undiscovered Vygotsky*. Frankfurt am Main: Peter Lang.

Veresov, N. (2005). Marxist and non-Marxist aspects of the cultural-historical psychology of L.S. Vygotsky Studies. *Outlines: Critical Practice Studies, 1*, 73–93. doi:10.7146/ocps.v7i1.2110

Veresov, N. (2014). *Method, methodology and methodological thinking. In M. Fleer & A. Ridgway (Eds.), Visual methodologies and digital tools for researching with young children* (pp. 215–228). Berne: Springer.

Veresov, N., & Fleer, M. (2016). Perezhivanie as a theoretical concept for researching young children's development. *Mind Culture and Activity, 23*(4), 325–335. doi:10.1080/10749039.2016.1186198

Vermersch, P. (1999). Pour une psychologie phénoménologique. *Psychologie Française, 44*(1), 7–18.

Vermersch, P. (2000). *L'entretien d'explicitation*. Paris: ESF Éditeurs.

Vetoshkina, L. P. (2018). *Anchoring craft: The object as an intercultural and intertemporal unifying factor*. University of Helsinki., Helsinki.

Vetoshkina, L. P., & Paavola, S. (2021). From the abstract to the concrete and beyond: The winding road of constructing a conceptual framework. *Outlines: Critical Practice Studies, 22*(1). doi:10.7146/ocps.v22i1.126225

Vianna, E., & Stetsenko, A. (2014). Research with a transformative activist agenda: Creating the future through education for social change. In J. Vadeboncoeur (Ed.), *Learning in and across contexts: Reimagining education* (pp. 575–602). National Society for the Studies of Education Yearbook.

Vilela, R. A. G., Jackson, J. M., Querol, M. A. P., Gemma, S. F. B., Takahashi, M. A. C., Gomes, M. H. P., … de Almeida, I. M. (2018). Expansion of the object of surveillance for occupational accidents: History and challenges underwent by a reference center aiming at prevention. *Ciencia & Saude Coletiva, 23*(9), 3055–3066. doi:10.1590/1413-81232018239.21952016

Vilela, R. A. G., Querol, M. A. P., Almeida, I. M., & Filho, J. M. J. (2020). Worker's health: From diagnosis to formative intervention. In R. A. D. Vilela, M. A. P. Querol, S. L. B. Hurtado, G. C. O. Cerveny, & M. G. R. Lopes (Eds.), *Collaborative dévelopment for the prevention of occupational accidents and diseases* (pp. 3–12). Cham, Switzerland: Springer.

Vilela, R. A. G., Querol, M. A. P., Hurtado, S. L. B., & Lopes, M. G. R. (2020). *Collaborative development for the prevention of occupational accidents and diseases. Change Laboratory in workers' health.* Cham: Springer.

Vilela, R. A. G., Querol, M. A. P., Lopes, M. G. R., & Virkkunen, J. (2014). The Change Laboratory as a tool for collaborative transforming work activities: An interview with Jaakko Virkkunen. *Saude E Sociedade, 23*(1), 182–189. doi:10.1590/s0104-12902014000100027

Virkkunen, J. (2006). Dilemmas in building shared transformative agency. *Activites, 3*(3–1). doi:10.4000/activites.1850

Virkkunen, J. (2007). Le développement collaboratif d'un nouveau concept pour une activité. *Activites, 04*(2). doi:10.4000/activites.1758

Virkkunen, J., & Ahonen, H. (2011). Supporting expansive learning through theoretical-genetic reflection in the Change Laboratory. *Journal of Organizational Change Management, 24*(2), 229–243. doi:10.1108/09534811111119780

Virkkunen, J., & Newham, D. S. (2013). *The Change Laboratory. A tool for collaborative development of work and education.* Rotterdam: Sense Publishers.

Virkkunen, J., & Ristimaki, P. (2012). Double stimulation in strategic concept formation: An activity-theoretical analysis of business planning in a small technology firm. *Mind Culture and Activity, 19*(3), 273–286. doi:10.1080/10749039.2012.688234

Virkkunen, J., & Schaupp, L. (2008). From change to development: Expanding the concept of intervention. *Theory & Psychology, 21*(5), 629–655. doi:10.1177/0959354311417486

Von Hippel, E. (2005). *Democratizing innovation.* Cambridge, MA: MIT Press.

Vygodskaya, G. L. (1999). Vygotsky and problems of special education. *Remedial and Special Education, 20*(6), 330–332. doi:10.1177/074193259902000605

Vygotski, L. S. (1927/1999). *La signification historique de la crise en psychologie.* Lausanne, Paris: Delachaux et Niestlé.

Vygotski, L. S. (1987). *Pensée et langage.* Paris: La dispute.

Vygotski, L. S. (1994). *Defectologie et deficience mentale.* Neuchâtel: Delachaux et Niestlé.

Vygotski, L. S. (2002). Le problème de la conscience. In Y. Clot (Ed.), *Avec Vygotski.* Paris: La Dispute.

Vygotski, L. S. (2014). *Histoire du développement des fonctions psychiques supérieures.* Paris: La Dispute.

Vygotski, L. S. (2018). *Cours de pédologie.*

Vygotsky, L. S. (1929). II. The problem of the cultural development of the child. *The Pedagogical Seminary and Journal of Genetic Psychology, 36*(3), 415–434. doi:10.1080/08856559.1919.10532201

Vygotsky, L. S. (1978). *Mind in Society: The development of higher psychological processes*. Cambridge: Harvard University Press.

Vygotsky, L. S. (1981). The genesis of higher mental functions. In J. V. Wertsch (Ed.), *The concept of activity in soviet psychology* (pp. 144–188). Sharpe Publisher.

Vygotsky, L. S. (1987a). *The collected works of LS Vygotsky, vol. 2: Problems of general psychology, including the volume thinking and speech*: Springer.

Vygotsky, L. S. (1987b). *The collected works of LS Vygotsky, vol. 3: Problems of the theory and history of psychology*: Springer Science & Business Media.

Vygotsky, L. S. (1989). Concrete human psychology. *Soviet Psychology, 27*(2), 53–77. doi:10.2753/RPO1061-0405270253

Vygotsky, L. S. (1993a). *The collected works of L. S. Vygotsky, vol.2: The fundamentals of defectology (abnormal psychology and learning disabilities)*. New York, NY, US: Plenum Press.

Vygotsky, L. S. (1993b). *The collected works of L. S. Vygotsky. Volume 2: The fundamentals of defectology (abnormal psychology and learning disabilities)*. New York: Plenum.

Vygotsky, L. S. (1997a). *The collected works of L. S. Vygotsky, Vol. 4: The history of the development of higher mental functions*. New York, NY, US: Plenum Press.

Vygotsky, L. S. (1997b). *Educationnal psychology*. Boca Raton: St. Lucie Press.

Vygotsky, L. S. (1997c). The historical meaning of the crisis in psychology: A methodological investigation. In L. S. Vygotsky (Ed.), *The collected works of L.S. Vygotsky: Vol. 3, Problems of the theory and history of psychology*. New York: Plenum Press.

Vygotsky, L. S. (1998). *The collected works of LS Vygotsky, vol. 5: Child psychology*. New York: Plenum.

Vygotsky, L. S. (2012). *The collected works of LS Vygotsky, vol. 6: Scientific legacy*: Springer Science & Business Media.

Vygotsky, L. S. (2019). *LS Vygotsky's pedological works: Volume 1. Foundations of pedology*: Springer.

Vygotsky, L. S., & Luria, A. (1992). *Studies of the history of behavior. Ape, Primitive. Child*. Lawrence Erlbaum Associates.

Wang, F., & Hannafin, M. J. (2005). Design-based research and technology-enhanced learning environments. *Educational technology research and development, 53*(4), 5–23. doi:10.1007/BF02504682

Warmington, P. (2008). From 'activity' to 'labour': Commodification, labourpower and contradiction in Engeström's activity theory. *Critical Social Studies, 2*, 4–19. doi:10.7146/ocps.v10i2.1972

Wartofsky, M. (1979). *Models: Representation and scientific understanding*. Dordrecht: Reidel.

Wasson, B., Ludvigsen, S., & Hoppe, U. (2013). *Designing for change in networked learning environments* (Vol. 2). Springer Science & Business Media.

Weber, M. (1992). *Essai sur la théorie de la science*. Paris: Pocket.

Wells, G. (2011). Integrating CHAT and Action Research. *Mind, Culture, and Activity, 18*(2), 161–180. doi:10.1080/10749039.2010.493594

Wertsch, J. (Ed.). (1981). *The concept of activity in Soviet psychology*. Armonk, NY: M. E. Sharpe.

Wertsch, J. (1985). *Vygotsky and the social formation of mind*. Cambridge: Harvard University Press.

Wertsch, J. (1994). The primacy of mediated action in sociocultural studies. *Mind, Culture, and Activity, 1*(4), 202–208. doi:10.1080/10749039409524672

Whyte, W. F. (1991). *Participatory action research*. Newbury Park: Sage Publications.

Wisner, A. (1995). Situated cognition and action: Implication for Ergonomic Work analysis and anthropotechnology. *Ergonomics, 38*(8), 1542–1558. doi:10.1080/00140139508925209

Witte, S. P., & Haas, C. (2005). Research in activity: An analysis of speed bumps as mediational means. *Written Communication, 22*(2), 127–165. doi:10.1177/0741088305274781

Wittezaele, J.-J. (2008). Chapitre 1. La double contrainte : un concept fondateur. In *La double contrainte* (pp. 11–30). Louvain-la-Neuve: De Boeck Supérieur.

Wright, E. O. (2010). *Envisionning real Utopias*. London: Verso.

Yamagata-Lynch, L. C. (2010). *Activity systems analysis methods. Understanding complex learning environments*. Dordrecht: Springer.

Yamazumi, K. (2007). Human Agency and educational research: A new problem in activity theory. *Actio: An International Journal of Human Activity Theory* (1), 19–39.

Yamazumi, K. (2008). A hybrid activity system as educational innovation. *Journal of Educational Change, 9*(4), 365–373.

Yamazumi, K. (2021). *Activity theory and collaborative intervention in education. Expanding learning in japanese schools and communities*. London: Routledge.

Yanchar, S. C. (2011). Using numerical data in explicitly interpretive, contextual inquiry: A 'practical discourse' framework and examples from Engeström's research on activity systems. *Theory & Psychology, 21*(2), 179–199. doi:10.1177/0959354310393777

Yasnitsky, A. (2011). Vygotsky circle as a personal network of scholars: Restoring connections between people and ideas. *Integrative Psychological and Behavioral Science, 45*(4), 422. doi:10.1007/s12124-011-9168-5

Yasnitsky, A. (2015). A transnational history of 'the beginning of a beautiful friendship': The birth of the cultural-historical Gestalt psychology of Alexander Luria, Kurt Lewin, Lev Vygotsky, and others. In A. Yasnitsky (Ed.), *Revisionist revolution in Vygotsky studies* (pp. 201–226). London, New York: Routledge.

Yasnitsky, A. (2018). *Vygotsky. An intellectual biography.* London, New York: Routledge.

Yasnitsky, A. (2019). *Questioning Vygotsky's legacy*: New York: Routledge.

Yasnitsky, A., & Ferrari, M. (2008). Rethinking the early history of post-Vygotskian psychology: The case of the Kharkov School. *History of Psychology, 11*(2), 101–121. doi:10.1037/1093-4510.11.2.101

Yvon, F. (2015). Analyse de l'activité et formation des cadres scolaires. In V. Borer, M. Durand, & F. Yvon (Eds.), *Analyse du travail et formation dans les métiers de l'éducation* (pp. 49–67). Bruxelles: De Boeck.

Zaporozhets, A. V., Gal'perin, P. I., & El'konin, D. B. (1995). Problems in the psychology of activity. *Journal of Russian & East European Psychology, 33*(4), 12–34. doi:10.2753/RPO1061-0405330412

Zavershneva, E., & Van der Veer, R. (2018). *Vygotsky's notebooks. A selection.* Singapour: Springer.

Zlobin, N. S. (1990). Activity – Labor – Culture. In V. P. Lektorski (Ed.), *Activity: The theory, methodology and problems* (pp. 57–66). Orlando, Helsinki, Moscou: PMD Press.

Zouinar, M., & Cahour, B. (2013). Activité et expérience vécue: quels liens. In C. Van de Leemput, C. Chauvin, & C. Hellemans (Eds.), *Activités humaines, technologie et bien être* (pp. 69–74). Bruxelles: Presses Universitaires de Bruxelles.

Table of Illustrations

Table of Tables

Acknowledgements

As I compose these brief lines of gratitude, I am compelled to recall the counsel imparted by a professor during my defense of my master dissertation in didactics. In essence, his advice was as follows: to be 'objective' and to 'truly' engage in research, one must eschew amicable relations with colleagues. Fortunately, I have never followed this advice. I believe that commitment to research requires solid friendships, both because it provides the necessary energy and because controversy, which is both inevitable and fundamental, takes place without ulterior motives.

I would like to express my gratitude to the individuals who provided me with encouragement, support, and guidance throughout the writing process. They offered me their insights and expertise, and they provided me with a sense of community and belonging. They invited me into their homes in Nordic and snow-covered lands, in the sun of Provence, and on the shores of a Swiss lake. They shared moments of exchange, discussion, and productive disagreement until late at night or early in the morning.

The willingness of the contributors to engage in collective work across disciplinary boundaries, to overcome territorial battles and historical contradictions, was essential for the completion of this book. Consequently, this book is a collective object, the result of friendships and encounters as much as of a long journey within, but sometimes at the frontier or margin (as the case may be) of different activity systems, different histories, different institutions, different cultures and different scientific disciplines. The author's solitude is thus an illusion, the surface of a deeply collective process involving numerous individuals to whom I am indebted.

First and foremost, I would like to express my gratitude to Yrjö Engeström and Annalisa Sannino for kindly agreeing to read the book and write its preface and afterword. With their two contributions, the text is well 'framed'. Their significant contribution to the development of CHAT makes me particularly proud that they accepted this mission. I am indebted to them and fortunate to have had the opportunity to learn from them, initially through reading their work and subsequently through discussions in Paris, Helsinki, Geneva. These discussions always had the distinct flavor of their friendship, optimism, and intellectual power.

My efforts in pursuing this work are greatly indebted to the advice and encouragement of Anne Bationo-Tillon and Vincent Grosstephan. Without their guidance, I would not have possessed the necessary motivation for this project. Moreover, it is a noteworthy account of a friendship that has endured for over two decades, as well as numerous discussions that gave rise to the genesis of this book and some of the ideas that were developed in it. The project was initiated and sustained by repeated encouragement and late-night discussions over a bottle of Mercurey in a partly confined world and France. It is my hope that our collaboration will continue to be constructive, productive, and useful, as well as a source of pleasure for all three of us.

A number of other individuals agreed to review selected portions of this work and provided me with invaluable advice and encouragement. I would like to acknowledge the contributions of Lionel Roche, Pauliina Rantavuori, Lucie Cuvelier, and Jean-Luc Tomás. Each in their own way, they provided valuable insights that helped me to think more critically.

Furthermore, I would like to express my gratitude to Yohann Metay, a renowned French comedian, for reading Chapter 4 and providing a live analysis of his latest show, which took place around Mont Blanc (the renowned 512). In this analysis, he delineated the roles of the stage manager, the producer, and the actor. This analysis demonstrated that this book was not only accessible to academic readers but could also serve as a tool for professionals. His humor and friendship, as well as our discussions about the writing process and 'dealing with critics,' helped me to avoid, I hope, making 'un sublime sabotage' (another of the artist's must-see shows). I am also indebted to Céline Monsauret for making her artistic production available to me. Her compositions have provided musical accompaniment on numerous occasions when I have been engaged in computer-based activities.

This book also benefits greatly from the empirical research and intervention work. I would like to express my gratitude to Patrick Picard, Marie Gibely, and Aurelia Truong Quang of the Alain Savary Center at the Institut Français de l'Éducation for including us in their research-intervention group on Priority Education networks in France and for repeatedly inviting us to Lyon with Vincent. I would also like to pay tribute to Alain Pothet, whose untimely death represents both a shock and a significant loss for Priority Education. His defense of the idea – which has unfortunately become subversive – of 'equality of intelligences' (a reference to Jacques Rancière), his insistence on 'being useful' in the fight against social injustice, his courage of action in the face of renunciation or indifference, his authenticity, his smile and his sparkling eye will certainly be sorely missed. This book is dedicated to him because, in my view, he exemplifies the kind of individual who, along with the other members of the Centre Alain Savary, is committed to the fight for human emancipation and social justice on a daily basis.

I would like to thank three other people who are important to me in this project. Firstly, I would like to thank Bernard Schneuwly, who accepted the manuscript for the 'Vygotskij' series published by Peter Lang. Secondly, I would like to thank Yves Clot and Germain Poizat. In this book, I discuss the 'course of action' and 'clinic of activity' approaches in an episodic manner, not so much to situate their controversies with CHAT, but to finally characterize in an instrumental way a conception of activity or intervention following the work of Yrjö Engeström and his colleagues. I believe that this discussion is essential and should be pursued, as, in my opinion, controversy nourish scientific work. It is not intended to reach consensus, but rather to strengthen all parties involved and identify new avenues for the advancement of their respective projects. In this regard, Yves and Germain are exemplary interlocutors, with whom I have enjoyed fruitful exchanges and learning.

Finally, this book was funded by a grant from the Agence Nationale de la Recherche as part of the ANR PRCI ITAPAR project (ANR-19-CE-26–0021). The Franco-Brazilian project has the objective of enabling the development of real utopias in the prevention of occupational accidents and diseases. I would like to express my gratitude to the French team of the project for allowing me to carry out this writing project.

Exploration

Ouvrages parus

Education: histoire et pensée

- Cristian Bota: *Pensée verbale et raisonnement. Les fondements langagiers des configurations épistémiques.* 260 p., 2018.
- Catherine Bouve: *L'utopie des crèches françaises au XIXe siècle. Un pari sur l'enfant pauvre. Essai socio-historique.* 308 p., 2010.
- Pierre Caspard: *La famille, l'école, l'État. Un modèle helvétique, XVIIᵉ-XIXᵉ siècles.* 236 p., 2021.
- Loïc Chalmel: *La petite école dans l'école – Origine piétiste-morave de l'école maternelle française.* Préface de J. Houssaye. 375 p., 1996, 2000, 2005.
- Loïc Chalmel: *Jean Georges Stuber (1722–1797) – Pédagogie pastorale.* Préface de D. Hameline, XXII, 187 p., 2001.
- Loïc Chalmel: *Réseaux philanthropinistes et pédagogie au 18e siècle.* XXVI, 270 p., 2004.
- Nanine Charbonnel: *Pour une critique de la raison éducative.* 189 p., 1988.
- Marie-Madeleine Compère: *L'histoire de l'éducation en Europe. Essai comparatif sur la façon dont elle s'écrit.* (En coédition avec INRP, Paris). 302 p., 1995.
- Jean-François Condette, *Jules Payot (1859–1940). Education de la volonté, morale laïque et soli- darité. Itinéraire intellectuel et combats pédagogiques au coeur de la IIIe République.* 316 p., 2012.

- Lucien Criblez, Rita Hofstetter (Ed./Hg.), Danièle Périsset Bagnoud (avec la collaboration de/unter Mitarbeit von): *La formation des enseignant(e)s primaires. Histoire et réformes actuelles / Die Ausbildung von PrimarlehrerInnen. Geschichte und aktuelle Reformen.* VIII, 595 p., 2000.

- Daniel Denis, Pierre Kahn (Ed.): *L'Ecole de la Troisième République en questions. Débats et controverses dans le* Dictionnaire de pédagogie *de Ferdinand Buisson.* VII, 283 p., 2006.

- Marcelle Denis: *Comenius. Une pédagogie à l'échelle de l'Europe.* 288 p., 1992.

- Joëlle Droux & Rita Hofstetter (Éd.): *Internationalismes éducatifs entre débats et combats (fin du 19e – premier 20e siècle).* 304 p., 2020.

- Patrick Dubois: *Le Dictionnaire de Ferdinand Buisson. Aux fondations de l'école républicaine (1878–1911).* VIII, 243 p., 2002.

- Marguerite Figeac-Monthus: *Les enfants de l'*Émile? *L'effervescence éducative de la France au tournant des XVIIIe et XIXe siècles.* XVII, 326 p., 2015.

- Nadine Fink: *Paroles de témoins, paroles d'élèves. La mémoire et l'histoire de la Seconde Guerre mondiale de l'espace public au monde scolaire.* XI, 266 p., 2014.

- Philippe Foray: *La laïcité scolaire. Autonomie individuelle et apprentissage du monde commun.* X, 229 p., 2008.

- Jacqueline Gautherin: *Une discipline pour la République. La science de l'éducation en France (1882–1914).* Préface de Viviane Isambert-Jamati. XX, 357 p., 2003.

- Daniel Hameline, Jürgen Helmchen, Jürgen Oelkers (Ed.): *L'éducation nouvelle et les enjeux de son histoire.* Actes du colloque international des archives Institut Jean-Jacques Rousseau. VI, 250 p., 1995.

- Béatrice Haenggeli-Jenni: *L'Éducation nouvelle: entre science et militance. Débats et combats au prisme de la revue* Pour l'Ère Nouvelle *(1920–1940).* VIII, 361 p., 2017.

- Rita Hofstetter: *Les lumières de la démocratie. Histoire de l'école primaire publique à Genève au XIXe siècle.* VII, 378 p., 1998.

- Rita Hofstetter, Charles Magnin, Lucien Criblez, Carlo Jenzer (†) (Ed.): *Une école pour la démocratie. Naissance et développement de l'école primaire publique en Suisse au 19e siècle.* XIV, 376 p., 1999.

- Rita Hofstetter, Bernard Schneuwly (Ed./Hg.): *Science(s) de l'éducation (19e-20e siècles) – Erziehungswissenschaft(en) (19.–20. Jahrhundert). Entre champs professionnels et champs disciplinaires Zwischen Profession und Disziplin.* 512 p., 2002.

- Rita Hofstetter, Bernard Schneuwly (Ed.): *Passion, Fusion, Tension. New Education and Educational Sciences – Education nouvelle et Sciences de l'éducation. End 19th – middle 20th century Fin du 19e – milieu du 20e siècle.* VII, 397 p., 2006.

- Rita Hofstetter, Bernard Schneuwly (Ed.), avec la collaboration de Valérie Lussi, Marco Cicchini, Lucien Criblez et Martina Späni: *Emergence des sciences de l'éducation en Suisse à la croisée de traditions académiques contrastées. Fin du 19e – première moitié du 20e siècle.* XIX, 539 p., 2007.

- Rita Hofstetter & Érhise (Éd.): *Le Bureau international d'éducation, matrice de l'internationalisme éducatif. (premier 20e siècle) Pour une charte des aspirations mondiales en matière éducative.* 650 p., 2022.

- Jean Houssaye: *Théorie et pratiques de l'éducation scolaire* (1): *Le triangle pédagogique*. Préface de D. Hameline. 267 p., 1988, 1992, 2000.
- Jean Houssaye: *Théorie et pratiques de l'éducation scolaire* (2): *Pratique pédagogique*. 295 p., 1988.
- Alain Kerlan: *La science n'éduquera pas. Comte, Durkheim, le modèle introuvable.* Préface de N. Charbonnel. 326 p., 1998.
- Francesca Matasci: *L'inimitable et l'exemplaire: Maria Boschetti Alberti. Histoire et figures de l'Ecole sereine.* Préface de Daniel Hameline. 232 p., 1987.
- Pierre Ognier: *L'Ecole républicaine française et ses miroirs.* Préface de D. Hameline. 297 p., 1988.
- Annick Ohayon, Dominique Ottavi & Antoine Savoye (Ed.): *L'Education nouvelle, histoire, présence et devenir.* VI, 336 p., 2004, 2007.
- Johann Heinrich Pestalozzi: *Ecrits sur l'expérience du Neuhof.* Suivi de quatre études de P.- Ph. Bugnard, D. Tröhler, M. Soëtard et L. Chalmel. Traduit de l'allemand par P.-G. Martin. X, 160 p., 2001.
- Johann Heinrich Pestalozzi: *Sur la législation et l'infanticide. Vérités, recherches et visions.* Suivi de quatre études de M. Porret, M.-F. Vouilloz Burnier, C. A. Muller et M. Soëtard. Traduit de l'allemand par P.-G. Matin. VI, 264 p., 2003.
- Viviane Rouiller: *«Apprendre la langue de la majorité des Confédérés». La discipline scolaire de l'allemand, entre enjeux pédagogiques, politiques, pratiques et culturels (1830– 1990).* XII, 390 p., 2020.
- Martine Ruchat: *Inventer les arriérés pour créer l'intelligence. L'arriéré scolaire et la classe spé- ciale. Histoire d'un concept et d'une innovation psychopédagogique 1874–1914.* Préface de Daniel Hameline. XX, 239 p., 2003.
- Jean-François Saffange: *Libres regards sur Summerhill. L'oeuvre pédagogique de A.-S. Neill.* Préface de D. Hameline. 216 p., 1985.
- Michel Soëtard, Christian Jamet (Ed.): *Le pédagogue et la modernité. A l'occasion du 250e anniv ersaire de la naissance de Johann Heinrich Pestalozzi (1746–1827).* Actes du colloque d'Angers (9–11 juillet 1996). IX, 238 p., 1998.
- Alain Vergnioux: *Pédagogie et théorie de la connaissance. Platon contre Piaget?* 198 p., 1991.
- Alain Vergnioux (éd.): *Grandes controverses en éducation.* VI, 290 p., 2012.
- Yves Verneuil: *Une question « chaude ». Histoire de l'éducation sexuelle à l'école (France, XXe– XXIe siècle),* 536 p., 2023.
- L.S. Vygotskij: *La science du développement de l'enfant. Textes pédologiques 1931–1934 de L.S. Vygotskij. Traduits par Irina Leopoldoff Martin. Édités et introduits par Irina Leopoldoff Martin et Bernard Schneuwly.* 432 p. 2018.
- Marie-Thérèse Weber: *La pédagogie fribourgeoise, du concile de Trente à Vatican II. Continuité ou discontinuité?* Préface de G. Avanzini. 223 p., 1997.

Recherches en sciences de l'éducation

- Sandrine Aeby Daghé: *Candide, La fée carabine et les autres. Vers un modèle didactique de la lecture littéraire.* IX, 303 p., 2014.

- Linda Allal, Jean Cardinet, Phillipe Perrenoud (Ed.): *L'évaluation formative dans un enseignement différencié*. Actes du Colloque à l'Université de Genève, mars 1978. 264 p., 1979, 1981, 1983, 1985, 1989, 1991, 1995.

- Claudine Amstutz, Dorothée Baumgartner, Michel Croisier, Michelle Impériali, Claude Piquilloud: *L'investissement intellectuel des adolescents*. *Recherche clinique*. XVII, 510 p., 1994.

- Bernard André: *S'investir dans son travail: les enjeux de l'activité enseignante*. XII, 289 p., 2013

- Guy Avanzini (Ed.): *Sciences de l'éducation: regards multiples*. 212 p., 1994.

- Daniel Bart: *Évaluation et didactique. Un dialogue critique*. 286 p., 2023.

- Daniel Bain: *Orientation scolaire et fonctionnement de l'école*. Préface de J. B. Dupont et F. Gen- dre. VI, 617 p., 1979.

- Jean-Michel Baudouin: *De l'épreuve autobiographique. Contribution des histoires de vie à la problématique des genres de texte et de l'herméneutique de l'action*. XII, 532 p., 2010.

- Alain Baudrit: *L'investigation collaborative: de la pratique d'enquête à la collaboration à distance*. 156 p., 2022.

- Véronique Bedin & Laurent Talbot (éd.): *Les points aveugles dans l'évaluation des dispositifs d'éducation ou de formation*. VIII, 211 p., 2013.

- Ana Benavente, António Firmino da Costa, Fernando Luis Machado, Manuela Castro Neves: *De l'autre côté de l'école*. 165 p., 1993.

- Jean-Louis Berger: *Apprendre: la rencontre entre motivation et métacognition*. Autorégulation dans l'apprentissage des mathématiques en formation professionnelle. XI, 221 p., 2015

- Bertrand Bergier: *Retours gagnants. De la sortie sans diplôme au retour diplômant*. 234 p., 2022.

- Denis Berthiaume & Nicole Rege Colet (Ed.): *La pédagogie de l'enseignement supérieur: repères théoriques et applications pratiques*. Tome 1: Enseigner au supérieur. 345 p., 2013.

- Anne-Claude Berthoud, Bernard Py: *Des linguistes et des enseignants. Maîtrise et acquisition des langues secondes*. 124 p., 1993.

- Anne-Claire Blanc, Vincent Capt (Ed.): *La tête et le texte. Formation initiale des enseignants primaires en didactique de la lecture et de l'écriture*. 242 p., 2020.

- Pier Carlo Bocchi: *Gestes d'enseignement*. L'agir didactique dans les premières pratiques d'écrit . 378 p., 2015.

- Cecilia Brassier-Rodrigues & Pascal Brassier (Ed.): *Internationalisation at Home. A collection of pedagogical approaches to develop students' intercultural competences*. 240 p., 2021

- Dominique Bucheton: *Ecritures-réécritures – Récits d'adolescents*. 320 p., 1995.

- Melanie Buser: *Two-Way Immersion in Biel/Bienne, Switzerland: Multilingual Education in the Public Primary School Filière Bilingue (FiBi). A Longitudinal Study of Oral Proficiency Develop- ment of K-4 Learners in Their Languages of Schooling (French and (Swiss) German)*. 302 p., 2020.

- Sandra Canelas-Trevisi: *La grammaire enseignée en classe. Le sens des objets et des manipulations*. 261 p., 2009.

- Vincent Capt, Mathieu Depeursinge et Sonya Florey (Dir.): *L'enseignement du français et le défi du numérique*. VI, 134 p., 2020.

- Jean Cardinet, Yvan Tourneur (†): *Assurer la mesure. Guide pour les études de généralisabi lité.* 381 p., 1985.

- Felice Carugati, Francesca Emiliani, Augusto Palmonari: *Tenter le possible. Une expérience de socialisation d'adolescents en milieu communautaire.* Traduit de l'italien par Claude Béguin. Préface de R. Zazzo. 216 p., 1981.

- Evelyne Cauzinille-Marmèche, Jacques Mathieu, Annick Weil-Barais: *Les savants en herbe.* Pré face de J.-F. Richard. XVI, 210 p., 1983, 1985.

- Vittoria Cesari Lusso: *Quand le défi est appelé intégration. Parcours de socialisation et de personnalisation de jeunes issus de la migration.* XVIII, 328 p., 2001.

- Nanine Charbonnel (Ed.): *Le Don de la Parole. Mélanges offerts à Daniel Hameline pour son soixante-cinquième anniversaire.* VIII, 161 p., 1997.

- Gisèle Chatelanat, Christiane Moro, Madelon Saada-Robert (Ed.): *Unité et pluralité des sciences de l'éducation. Sondages au coeur de la recherche.* VI, 267 p., 2004.

- Florent Chenu: *L'évaluation des compétences professionnelles. Une mise à l'épreuve expérimentale des notions et présupposés théoriques sous-jacents.* 347 p., 2015.

- Christian Daudel: *Les fondements de la recherche en didactique de la géographie.* 246 p., 1990.

- Bertrand Daunay: *La paraphrase dans l'enseignement du français.* XIV, 262 p., 2002. Jean-Marie De Ketele: *Observer pour éduquer.* (Epuisé)

- Mikaël De Clercq, Nathalie Roland, Florence Dangoisse, Mariane Frenay (dir.): *La transition vers l'enseignement supérieur. Comprendre pour mieux agir sur l'adaptation des étudiants en première année.* 230 p., 2023.

- Jean-Louis Derouet, Marie-Claude Derouet-Besson (Ed.): *Repenser la justice dans le domaine de l'éducation et de la formation.* VIII, 385 p., 2009.

- Ana Dias-Chiaruttini: *Le débat interprétatif dans l'enseignement du français.* IX, 261 p., 2015.

- Joaquim Dolz, Jean-Claude Meyer (Ed.): *Activités métalangagières et enseigne ment du français. Actes des journées d'étude en didactique du français (Cartigny, 28 février – 1 mars 1997).* XIII, 283 p., 1998.

- Pierre Dominicé: *La formation, enjeu de l'évaluation.* Préface de B. Schwartz. (Epuisé)

- Pierre Dominicé, Michel Rousson: *L'éducation des adultes et ses effets. Problématique et étude de cas.* (Epuisé)

- Pierre-André Doudin, Daniel Martin, Ottavia Albanese (Ed.): *Métacognition et éducation.* XIV, 392 p., 1999, 2001.

- Andrée Dumas Carré, Annick Weil-Barais (Ed.): *Tutelle et médiation dans l'éducation scientifique.* VIII, 360 p., 1998.

- Jean-Blaise Dupont, Claire Jobin, Roland Capel: *Choix professionnels adolescents. Etude longitudinale à la fin de la scolarité secondaire.* 2 vol., 419 p., 1992.

- Vincent Dupriez, Jean-François Orianne, Marie Verhoeven (Ed.): De l'école au marché du travail, l'égalité des chances en question. X, 411 p., 2008.

- Raymond Duval: *Sémiosis et pensée humaine – Registres sémiotiques et apprentissages intellec- tuels.* 412 p., 1995. Eric Espéret: *Langage et origine sociale des élèves.* (Epuisé)

- Jean-Marc Fabre: *Jugement et certitude. Recherche sur l'évaluation des connaissances.* Préface de G. Noizet. (Epuisé)

- Georges Felouzis et Gaële Goastellec (Éd.): *Les inégalités scolaires en Suisse. École, société et politiques éducatives.* VI, 273 p., 2015.
- Barbara Fouquet-Chauprade & Anne Soussi (Ed.): *Pratiques pédagogiques et éducation prioritaire.* VIII, 218 p., 2018.
- Monique Frumholz: *Ecriture et orthophonie.* 272 p., 1997.
- Pierre Furter: *Les systèmes de formation dans leurs contextes.* (Epuisé)
- Monica Gather Thurler, Isabelle Kolly-Ottiger, Philippe Losego et Olivier Maulini, *Les directeurs au travail. Une enquête au coeur des établissements scolaires et socio-sanitaires.* VI, 318 p., 2017.
- André Gauthier (Ed.): *Explorations en linguistique anglaise. Aperçus didac tiques.* Avec Jean-Claude Souesme, Viviane Arigne, Ruth Huart-Friedlander. 243 p., 1989.
- Marcelo Giglio & Francesco Arcidiacono (Ed.): *Les interactions sociales en classe: réflexions et perspectives.* VI, 250 p., 2017.
- Marcelo Giglio / Francesco Arcidiacono (eds.): *Social Interactions in the Classroom: Thoughts and Perspectives.* 230 p., 2024.
- Patricia Gilliéron Giroud & Ladislas Ntamakiliro (Ed.): *Réformer l'évaluation scolaire: mission impossible.* 264 p. 2010.
- Michel Gilly, Arlette Brucher, Patricia Broadfoot, Marylin Osborn: *Instituteurs anglais insti- tuteurs francais. Pratiques et conceptions du rôle.* XIV, 202 p., 1993.
- André Giordan: *L'élève et/ou les connaissances scientifiques. Approche didactique de la construc- tion des concepts scientifiques par les élèves.* 3e édition, revue et corrigée. 180 p., 1994.
- André Giordan, Yves Girault, Pierre Clément (Ed.): *Conceptions et connaissances.* 319 p., 1994.
- André Giordan (Ed.): *Psychologie génétique et didactique des sciences.* Avec Androula Henriques et Vinh Bang. (Epuisé)
- Corinne Gomila: *Parler des mots, apprendre à lire. La circulation du métalangage dans les activ- ités de lecture.* X, 263 p. 2011.
- Armin Gretler, Ruth Gurny, Anne-Nelly Perret-Clermont, Edo Poglia (Ed.): *Etre migrant. Approches des problèmes socio-culturels et linguistiques des enfants migrants en Suisse.* 383 p., 1981, 1989.
- Francis Grossmann: *Enfances de la lecture. Manières de faire, manières de lire à l'école maternelle.*
- Préface de Michel Dabène. 260 p., 1996, 2000.
- Michael Huberman, Monica Gather Thurler: *De la recherche à la pratique. Eléments de base et mode d'emploi.* 2 vol., 335 p., 1991.
- Jean-Marc Huguenin et Georges Solaux: *Évaluation partenariale des politiques publiques d'éd- ucation. L'expérience d'un dispositif d'évaluation du fonctionnement de l'enseignement primaire.* 139 p., 2017.
- Institut romand de recherches et de documentation pédagogiques (Neuchâtel): Connaissances mathématiques à l'école primaire: J.-F. Perret: *Présentation et synthèse d'une évaluation romande;* F. Jaquet, J. Cardinet: *Bilan des acquisitions en fin de première année;* F. Jaquet, E. George, J.-F. Perret: *Bilan des acquisitions en fin de deuxième année;* J.-F. Perret: *Bilan des acquisitions en fin de troisième année;* R. Hutin, L.-O. Pochon, J.-F. Perret: *Bilan des acquisitions en fin de quatrième année;* L.-O. Pochon: *Bilan des acquisitions en fin de cinquième et sixième année.* 1988–1991.

– Daniel Jacobi: *Textes et images de la vulgarisation scientifique*. Préface de J. B. Grize. (Epuisé)

– Marianne Jacquin, Germain Simons, Daniel Delbrassine (Ed.): *Les genres textuels en langues étrangères: entre théorie et pratique*. 372 p, 2019

– René Jeanneret (Ed.): *Universités du troisième âge en Suisse*. Préface de P. Vellas. 215 p., 1985.

– Samuel Johsua, Jean-Jacques Dupin: *Représentations et modélisations: le «débat scientifique» dans la classe et l'apprentissage de la physique*. 220 p., 1989.

– Constance Kamii: *Les jeunes enfants réinventent l'arithmétique*. Préface de B. Inhelder. 171 p., 1990, 1994.

– Albina Khasanzyanova & Eric Mutabazi (Eds.): *School, family and community against early school leaving. International perspectives*. 236 p., 2023.

– Helga Kilcher-Hagedorn, Christine Othenin-Girard, Geneviève de Weck: *Le savoir grammatical des élèves. Recherches et réflexions critiques*. Préface de J.-P. Bronckart. 241 p., 1986.

– Vanessa Lentillon-Kaestner et Valérian Cece (dir.): *Les différences entre élèves en éducation physique: un regard à 360 degrés!* 184 p., 2024.

– Georges Leresche (†): *Calcul des probabilités*. (Epuisé)

– Francia Leutenegger: *Le temps d'instruire. Approche clinique et expérimentale du didactique ordinaire en mathématique*. XVIII, 431 p., 2009.

– Olivia Lewi et Blandine Longhi (dir.): *Connecter et segmenter à l'écrit. Ponctuation et opérateurs linguistiques: deux défis pour l'enseignement*. 208p., 2022.

– Even Loarer, Daniel Chartier, Michel Huteau, Jacques Lautrey: *Peut-on éduquer l'intel li gence? L'évaluation d'une méthode d'éducation cognitive*. 232 p., 1995.

– Brigitte Louichon, Marie-France Bishop, Christophe Ronveaux (Ed.): *Les fables à l'école. Un genre patrimonial européen?* VII, 279 p., 2017.

– Georges Lüdi, Bernard Py: *Etre bilingue*. 4e édition. XII, 223 p., 2013.

– Valérie Lussi Borer: *Histoire des formations à l'enseignement en Suisse romande*. X, 238 p., 2017.

– Pierre Marc: *Autour de la notion pédagogique d'attente*. 235 p., 1983, 1991, 1995.

– Jean-Louis Martinand: *Connaître et transformer la matière*. Préface de G. Delacôte. (Epuisé)

– Jonas Masdonati: *La transition entre école et monde du travail. Préparer les jeunes à l'entrée en formation professionnelle*. 300 p., 2007.

– Marinette Matthey: *Apprentissage d'une langue et interaction verbale*. XII, 247 p., 1996, 2003.

– Paul Mengal: *Statistique descriptive appliquée aux sciences humaines*. VII, 107 p., 1979, 1984, 1991, 1994, 1999 (5e + 6e), 2004.

– Isabelle Mili: *L'oeuvre musicale, entre orchestre et écoles*. Une approche didactique de pratiques d'écoute musicale. X, 228 p., 2014.

– Henri Moniot (Ed.): *Enseigner l'histoire. Des manuels à la mémoire*. (Epuisé)

– Cléopâtre Montandon, Philippe Perrenoud: *Entre parents et enseignants: un dialogue impos- sible?* Nouvelle édition, revue et augmentée. 216 p., 1994.

– Christiane Moro, Bernard Schneuwly, Michel Brossard (Ed.): *Outils et signes. Perspectives actuelles de la théorie de Vygotski*. 221 p., 1997.

– Christiane Moro & Cintia Rodríguez: *L'objet et la construction de son usage chez le bébé. Une approche sémiotique du développement préverbal*. X, 446 p., 2005.

- Lucie Mottier Lopez: *Apprentissage situé. La microculture de classe en mathématiques.* XXI, 311 p., 2008.

- Lucie Mottier Lopez & Walther Tessaro (éd.): *Le jugement professionnel, au coeur de l'évaluation et de la régulation des apprentissages.* VII, 357 p., 2016.

- Gabriel Mugny (Ed.): *Psychologie sociale du développement cognitif.* Préface de M. Gilly. (Epuisé)

- Maurice Niwese (Éd.): *L'écriture du primaire au secondaire: du déjà-là aux possibles: Résultats de recherche du projet ECRICOL,* 276 p., 2022.

- Romuald Normand: *Gouverner la réussite scolaire. Une arithmétique politique des inégalités.* XI, 260 p., 2011.

- Sara Pain: *Les difficultés d'apprentissage. Diagnostic et traitement.* 125 p., 1981, 1985, 1992.

- Sara Pain: *La fonction de l'ignorance.* (Epuisé)

- Christiane Perregaux: *Les enfants à deux voix. Des effets du bilinguisme successif sur l'apprentissage de la lecture.* 399 p., 1994.

- Jean-François Perret: *Comprendre l'écriture des nombres.* 293 p., 1985.

- Anne-Nelly Perret-Clermont: *La construction de l'intelligence dans l'interaction sociale.* Edition revue et augmentée avec la collaboration de Michèle Grossen, Michel Nicolet et Maria-Luisa Schubauer-Leoni. 305 p., 1979, 1981, 1986, 1996, 2000.

- Edo Poglia, Anne-Nelly Perret-Clermont, Armin Gretler, Pierre Dasen (Ed.): *Pluralité culturelle et éducation en Suisse. Etre migrant.* 476 p., 1995.

- Jean Portugais: *Didactique des mathématiques et formation des enseignants.* 340 p., 1995.

- Laetitia Progin: *Devenir chef d'établissement. Le désir de leadership à l'épreuve de la réalité.* 210 p., 2017.

- Nicole Rege Colet & Denis Berthiaume (Ed.): *La pédagogie de l'enseignement supérieur: repères théoriques et applications pratiques. Tome 2. Se développer au titre d'enseignant.* VI, 261 p., 2015

- Yves Reuter (Ed.): *Les interactions lecture-écriture.* Actes du colloque organisé par THÉODILE-CREL (Lille III, 1993). XII, 404 p., 1994, 1998.

- Philippe R. Richard: *Raisonnement et stratégies de preuve dans l'enseignement des mathématiques.* XII, 324 p., 2004.

- Marielle Rispail et Christophe Ronveaux (Ed.): *Gros plan sur la classe de français. Motifs et variations.* X, 258 p., 2010.

- Yviane Rouiller et Katia Lehraus (Ed.): *Vers des apprentissages en coopération: rencontres et perspectives.* XII, 237 p., 2008.

- Guy Rumelhard: *La génétique et ses représentations dans l'enseignement.* Préface de A. Jacquard. 169 p., 1986.

- El Hadi Saada: *Les langues et l'école. Bilinguisme inégal dans l'école algérienne.* Préface de J.-P. Bronckart. 257 p., 1983.
- Jean-Pascal Simon, Francis Grossmann (Ed.): *Lecture à l'Université. Langue maternelle, seconde et étrangère.* VII, 289 p., 2004.
- Muriel Surdez: *Diplômes et nation. La constitution d'un espace suisse des professions avocate et artisanales (1880–1930).* X, 308 p., 2005.
- Marc Surian: *Didactique du français et accueil des élèves migrants. Objets d'enseignement, obsta- cles et régulation des apprentissages.* 242 p., 2018.
- Valérie Tartas: *La construction du temps social par l'enfant. Préfaces de Jérôme Bruner et Michel Brossard* XXI, 252 p., 2008.
- Joris Thievenaz, Jean-Marie Barbier et Frédéric Saussez (Dir.): *Comprendre/Transformer.* 292 p., 2020.
- Sabine Vanhulle: *Des savoirs en jeu aux savoirs en «je». Cheminements réflexifs et subjectivation des savoirs chez de jeunes enseignants en formation.* 288 p., 2009.
- Gérard Vergnaud: *L'enfant, la mathématique et la réalité. Problèmes de l'enseignement des mathématiques à l'école élémentaire.* V, 218 p., 1981, 1983, 1985, 1991, 1994.
- Ingrid Verscheure & Isabelle Collet (dir.): *Genre: didactique(s) et pratiques d'enseignement. Perspectives francophones.* 230 p., 2023.
- Joëlle Vlassis: *Sens et symboles en mathématiques. Etude de l'utilisation du signe «moins» dans les réductions polynomiales et la résolution d'équations du premier degré à inconnue.* XII, 437 p., 2010.
- Sylvain Wagnon: *Le manuel scolaire, objet d'étude et de recherche: enjeux et perspectives.* X, 310 p., 2019.
- Sylvain Wagnon (Éd.): *Normes, disciplines et manuels scolaires.* 232 p., 2022.
- Nathanaël Wallenhorst: *L'école en France et en Allemagne. Regard de lycéens, comparaison d'expériences scolaires.* IX, 211 p., 2013.
- Jacques Weiss (Ed.): *A la recherche d'une pédagogie de la lecture.* (Epuisé)
- Martine Wirthner: *Outils d'enseignement: au-delà de la baguette magique. Outils transforma- teurs, outils transformés dans des séquences d'enseignement en production écrite.* XI, 259 p., 2017.
- Richard Wittorski, Olivier Maulini & Maryvonne Sorel (Ed.). Les professionnels et leurs formations. Entre développement des sujets et projets des institutions. VI, 237 p., 2015.
- Tania Zittoun: *Insertions. A quinze ans, entre échec et apprentissage.* XVI, 192 p., 2006.
- Marianne Zogmal: *«Savoir voir et faire voir». Les processus d'observation et de catégorisation dans l'éducation de l'enfance.* 258 p., 2020.

Vygotskij – oeuvres et études

- David Auclair: *Moralité, autorité, normalité. Critique des courants organicistes du développement de l'enfant.* 283 p., 2022.
- Soraya De Simone: *Des médiations au cœur de la transmission du métier enseignant. Préface de Rita Hofstetter et Bernard Schneuwly.* 360 p., 2023.
- Yannick Lémonie: *Transformer & Comprendre. Une Introduction à la Théorie Historico-Culturelle de l'Activité.* 480 p., 2025.
- Yannick Lémonie: *Transforming & Understanding. An Introduction to Cultural-Historical Activity Theory.* 460 p., 2025.
- Bruno Védrines: *L'expérience de la subjectivité dans l'enseignement littéraire.* 388 p., 2023.
- L. S. Vygotskij: *Imagination. Textes choisis. Avec des commentaires et des essais sur l'imagination dans l'oeuvre de Vygotskij.* Édité par Bernard Schneuwly, Irina Leopoldoff Martin, Daniele Nunes Henrique Silva. 604 p., 2022.

www.peterlang.com

Printed by
CPI books GmbH, Leck